PARALEGAL CAREER GUIDE

Third Edition

Chere B. Estrin

Prentice
Hall

Upper Saddle River, New Jersey 07458

Library of Congress Cataloging-in-Publication Data
Estrin, Chere B.
    Paralegal career guide / Chere B. Estrin.—3rd ed.
      p. cm.
    Includes bibliographical references and index.
    ISBN 0-13-090864-9 (alk. paper)
    1. Legal assistants—Vocational guidance—United States. I. Title.

KF320.L4 E77 2001
340'.023'73—dc21
2001032168

Publisher: *Steve Helba*
Executive Editor: *Elizabeth Sugg*
Director of Production and Manufacturing: *Bruce Johnson*
Managing Editor: *Mary Carnis*
Manufacturing Buyer: *Cathleen Petersen*
Production Liaison: *Brian Hyland*
Design Director: *Cheryl Asherman*
Senior Design Coordinator: *Miguel Ortiz*
Cover Design: *Anthony Inciong*
Full Service Production/Formatting: *BookMasters, Inc.*
Editorial Assistant: *Anita Rhodes*
Printing and Binding: *Phoenix Book Tech.*

This publication is designed to provide accurate and authoritative information in regard to the subject matter covered. It is sold with the understanding that the publisher is not engaged in rendering legal, accounting, or other professional services. If legal advice or other expert assistance is required, the services of a competent professional person should be sought.

Pearson Education LTD.
Pearson Education Australia PTY, Limited
Pearson Education Singapore, Pte. Ltd.
Pearson Education North Asia Ltd.
Pearson Education Canada, Ltd.
Pearson Educación de Mexico, S.A. de C.V.
Pearson Education-Japan
Pearson Education Malaysia, Pte. Ltd.
Pearson Education, Upper Saddle River, New Jersey

10 9 8 7 6 5 4 3 2 1
ISBN 0-13-090864-9

To my nieces and nephews, Teresa, Cristina, Lindsey, Justin, Raul, Joy, Amy, and Aaron, without whom my life would be simply less loving and oh, so boring.

And—
To Allen Brody who lovingly and patiently taught me that dreams, can indeed, come true.

Contents

Foreword

Twenty years ago, not even the most perceptive and forward-thinking prognosticator could have imagined the paralegal profession of today. It is indeed a profession: large, diverse, respected, and a core part of the provision of legal services in the United States. Paralegal education, both basic and advanced, is part of the curricula of 2- and 4-year institutions of higher education throughout the country. And by all accounts, the paralegals of the coming decade will be better educated, more highly paid, and will perform more sophisticated work than any of their predecessors.

But where do you as a professional paralegal turn for guidance? Who tells the new graduate or the experienced professional how to deal with the day-to-day issues of a paralegal career? What is the shape of the market today? Where is it going? How do you find the job you want? What impresses? What depresses? What defines success for you as a paralegal, and how do you find it?

The range of opportunities presents challenges unknown in the early days of paralegalism. What issues do you face, what challenges do you have to overcome to achieve success and happiness in your career as a paralegal? How do these challenges change if you are working in a large law firm . . . for the government . . . for a small law firm . . . as an independent paralegal . . . for a nonprofit organization . . . or for a corporate legal department? How do you balance the plusses and minuses of these disparate environments?

Where do you find out the ins and outs of client service and career advancement? How do you know whether you're being paid fairly for your services? What do you do to make sure that your boss knows what good work you do? And what do you do if you feel as though you've reached a career dead-end?

As the director of one of the country's largest and most successful ABA-approved paralegal education programs, I face these kinds of questions every day. One of the best answers I can give is, "Have you read the new edition of Chere Estrin's *Paralegal Career Guide?*" Everyone in the legal community, not just paralegals, but law firm managers, attorneys, and others who work with paralegals, will find the newest edition of this classic work a gold mine of interesting, valuable, and practical information.

As the paralegal profession continues to grow, and reliance on paralegals as critical members of the legal service team becomes even more widespread, the kind of information Chere Estrin provides so ably becomes more and more valuable. Congratulations on coming to the right source for just what you need to know to start or grow your paralegal career!

Richard S. Shaffran, Esq.
Director
UCLA Extension Attorney Assistant Training Program

Preface

Since the first publication of this book in 1992 (and the second edition in 1996), my greatest satisfaction has come from readers who report, "I followed your instructions and my career zoomed." I have also been gratified by the many paralegals and paralegal educators who recommend my book to their students, colleagues, and bosses.

When I considered what needed revision for a new edition, a logical question arose. If it isn't broken, why fix it? Certainly, the basic information in the first and second editions remains as reliable today as it was in 1992 and again in 1996. However, our ever-changing world, as well as the rapidly changing paralegal field, calls for some changes.

In this third edition:

- I've reported on the cutting edge of technology which is vital to your career now and in the future. Certainly, the Internet has changed the way we deliver legal services.
- I've interviewed 20+ paralegals, managers, technology professionals, and litigation support managers. Their stories are not only interesting, but they also provide ideas for your own career.
- I've explored the latest in practice specialties including the controversial MDP's which, despite the outcome, offer more opportunities for paralegals.
- Stacey Hunt has been, once again, a real hero in writing a couple of dynamic chapters for litigation paralegals, the bulk of the profession. Her step-by-step guides are invaluable.
- I've added numerous resources found on the Internet. A handy guide is always useful.
- I've introduced new competitive strategies for moving your career along based upon what the workforce is like in the new millennium.
- I've added some information about the 26 states that now have a definition for paralegals, along with the controversial California decision for mandatory hiring requirements.

In the paralegal field, we are just beginning to see how the apparent impersonal dot-com world is cross-pollinating the field of law. Despite our culture's full entry into the electronic era, human beings, not Intel chips, continue to power the paralegal world. After all, the impact of one paralegal's job on a matter, case, or client is a highly personal experience. Word of mouth or the smile on an attorney's or client's face from a job well done by a paralegal beats out the Internet each and every time.

I trust that this third edition will guide you to transform your career into the vision you seek. I also wish you the reward of wonderful relationships with your bosses, coworkers, and peers. To report on your success, say hello, or ask questions, just send an e-mail to estrin@ estrin.com or write in care of my publisher, Elizabeth Sugg, Prentice Hall.

Chere B. Estrin, Ph.D.
Los Angeles, California

Acknowledgments

There are always those in the background who contribute to the success and wealth of information of any book. To those who have either knowingly or unknowingly played a part in the *Paralegal Career Guide, Third Edition*, I extend my sincere and always grateful appreciation:

My editor, Elizabeth Sugg, at Prentice Hall with whom I have had a relationship over the years that has proven to be wonderful and valuable over and over again;

Ric Shaffran, Director of the UCLA Attorney Assistant Training Program, who has encouraged me, written the foreword, and promises to find me a husband;

My partners and staff at The Estrin Organization: Andrew Spathis, Kevin Behan, Letty Marquez, Mike Decano, Mimi Belous, Bridgett Brooks, Gary Rote, and Bill MacMillen—without whom there would be no book;

George Mulqueen, my mentor, my friend;

Angela Collins, Placement Director at the UCLA Attorney Assistant Training Program who lets me teach the job search workshop so often;

Marilyn Haaker, a 20-year paralegal who keeps at this business in every way imaginable and who deserves an award for recently having twins;

Enika Pearson, Pearson Publications, who originated *Legal Assistant Today* magazine and got me into my writing career;

Eleanor Kendall who showed me there is no such thing as writer's block—only blocked wishes;

Stacey Hunt who wrote a couple of great chapters and continues to be a great writing partner;

My son, Joel Schneider, who makes my life go around;

And always, all the paralegals, administrators, lawyers, legal vendors, friends, and supporters who have given me incredible support throughout my entire career.

A special acknowledgment goes to the following reviewers:

Justine F. Miller, J.D.
Branford Career Institute

Grace A. Luppino, Esq.
Branford Career Institute

Linda Carbral Marrero, J.D.
Mercy College

About the Author

A well-known legal staffing trailblazer, Chere Estrin demonstrates a solid range of expertise: from CEO of The Estrin Organization, a Los Angeles-based legal and financial staffing organization; to senior executive in a $4 billion staffing conglomerate; to president of a legal staffing division in one of the country's top three international litigation support companies; to successful entrepreneur building one of the largest paralegal temporary staffing organizations in the country. Her history as an administrator in two Top Ten law firms allowed her access into this niche field.

Ms. Estrin founded C.B. Estrin and Associates in 1986, which quickly rose as one of the largest multioffice paralegal staffing organizations. The company was acquired by Interim, where Ms. Estrin held a senior management position as head of a $40 million division. She then joined The Quorum/Estrin Group as president of a division of an international litigation support company. She is now CEO of The Estrin Organization, a Los Angeles-based professional staffing organization. Ms. Estrin is a well-known national seminar leader and teaches at prestigious universities such as UCLA.

Recently featured in *Newsweek* magazine and *The Los Angeles Times* Business Section as head of a fast-tracking staffing company, her achievements and awards include winner of the Century City (Los Angeles) Chamber of Commerce prestigious "Woman of the Year 2000 Achievement Award"; finalist for *Inc.* magazine's "Entrepreneur of the Year Award"; and winner of *California Lawyer Magazine's* LAMMIE award. She was featured on the cover of *Legal Assistant Today* magazine as the legal field's "Career Guru." Ms. Estrin is the author of eight career books including *10 Unbeatable Steps to Phenomenal Career Success, The Successful Paralegal's Job Search Guide* (West), and *The Attorney Career Guide* (West, 2002).

In addition to her column in *Legal Assistant Today*, Ms. Estrin has been featured in *Newsweek* magazine, *The Los Angeles Times, The Chicago Tribune, New York Times, Working Woman, CNBC.com, BusinessWeek Online, Entrepreneur* magazine, *Frontier, The Daily Journal,* and *Entrepreneurial Edge* magazine.

Her experience as co-founding member of the Legal Assistant Management Association (LAMA); expertise; books; articles; quality reputation; and frequent guest speaking engagements has helped to firmly establish the Estrin name.

Introduction

On the last day of writing the first edition of the *Paralegal Career Guide,* I turned off my word processor, photocopied the only manuscript I had, and mailed it return-receipt requested off to my publisher. Five years later, on the last day of writing the second edition of the *Paralegal Career Guide,* I turned off my PC, after saving the manuscript to disk, printing an extra hard copy and electronically submitting it to my publisher. She painstakingly edited it, returning a hard copy via air courier. I took a red pen, manually made the edits and FedExed it back.

For the third edition of the *Paralegal Career Guide,* I sent off the manuscript electronically and never turned the PC off. My goal was to submit and edit this puppy online. I'm either aging rapidly, the business world is reeling from fast change, or both. Only four years later and we're living in a whole other world.

A friend of mine, upon hearing that I was to begin the third edition of this book, exclaimed, "Chere, how much *more* can you write about the career?" I felt I was right when I replied, "Plenty!" I am continually astounded at the changes and at the constant learning curve presented to today's workforce. Conversations no longer mean what they used to. Surfing is no longer just a beach activity; having a mouse in your house is no cause for alarm; and the lower case "e" allows you access into a strange new business world. No one under 30 can tell you what "cc" in a letter means (carbon copy); and not only has a "twenty-something" never heard of an IBM Selectric, the word does not even appear in Microsoft Word's dictionary. Geez, I had better slather on some wrinkle cream. I cut my teeth on one of those.

We can make the usual comments about how the paralegal career has changed over the years, but, frankly, I am stunned at how it has evolved. Just this year, California joined 26 other states which already have paralegal definitions in place either by statute, state supreme court rulings or guidelines promulgated by state bars. As of January 1, 2001, California paralegals must meet certain specified qualifications, and it will be unlawful for any person to claim the title of paralegal unless the qualifications are met. It is clear that while many of the duties remain the same over the years, the methodology for delivering legal services has changed dramatically.

Pundits have predicted that lawyers would upgrade the assignment level for paralegals. While that turned out to be true to some extent, the push behind that move was increased awareness of what paralegals can do combined with the rapid ascent of high technology and the Internet. No longer do paralegals sit with 3 x 5 cards, gluing exhibit tabs on by hand while dictating into a tape machine information later to be transcribed into a list that can be produced only alphabetically or chronologically.

Technology has changed the paralegal field by creating new positions, standards, and expectations. The new business world demands fast delivery, 24/7/365 service, expanded research capabilities, and low-cost legal services. Paralegals without technology skills are clearly left behind.

Another pronounced change to the field is the demand by clients for low-cost services. Gone are the days of bloated businesses blindly and faithfully paying any legal bill presented. The revolution to lower fees was clearly won by the client. Pressure for firms to find better ways to deliver low-cost legal services resulted in more serious legal assistant utilization. Clients are now aware that the word "paralegal" is not to be confused with "paraplegic." They know that paralegals do a good job at a less expensive rate and that their insistence that work is delegated to the lowest competent level has finally been heard. The fallout liberated paralegals and opened doors for far more career opportunities than were ever predicted a few short years ago. To that extent, in-house legal departments have beefed up so that it is no longer unusual for paralegals to move up to a corporate secretary or vice president role.

The third edition of the *Paralegal Career Guide* captures techniques to enhance your career and position you for success in the workforce of the new millennium. Because so much positive feedback was received about many of the career-enhancing techniques presented in the first and second editions, those sections that are still applicable and helpful today were kept. New sections, ideas, resources, and wonderful, interesting profiles about many of the paralegal heroes across the country have been added.

I have enjoyed a distinctly pleasurable learning experience over the past years. As CEO of my own legal staffing organization, president of a division of an international litigation support company, guest speaker, and author, I have listened to several thousand experienced and entry-level paralegals tell me their dreams, ambitions, and frustrations. What has always impressed me about paralegals is a never-ending quest for advancement and professionalism. It is not an easy challenge to blaze trails and pave roads in a profession that is quite new, given it is only about 35 years old in the 300-year-old law field.

That is why I have researched and gathered information and techniques designed to assist you with tactics and action plans to meet your long-term strategy career goals—maybe even to help you establish those goals. This career is changing swiftly, and in order to stay abreast of these changes, you must have knowledge of the recent changes in the workforce that affect you, along with an action plan to keep up with and surpass law firm expectations. This book can help you reach those goals.

Read it, digest it, and modify the techniques to fit your individual growth plan. Not all the techniques will work specifically for your plan. Take what will work, leave behind what won't, and think over the rest. Always bear in mind that **you** are the master of your destiny and keeper of your flame.

Keep going, keep learning, and, above all, keep advancing. I wish you outrageous success!

Chere Estrin
July 2001
Los Angeles, California

CHAPTER 1

After the Revolution: The Radically Changing Paralegal World

> Fear of success is one of the new fears I've heard about lately. And I think it's definitely a sign that we're running out of fears. A person suffering from fear of success is scraping the bottom of the fear barrel.
>
> Jerry Seinfeld, *SeinLanguage*, Bantam Books

Let's accept the fact that change has occurred in the legal field. Let's also accept the fact that these changes have affected the paralegal profession. Skills, attitudes, cultures, growth, financial objectives, lifestyles, and technology have transformed the way paralegals function within the career.

You can't blame law firms, really. They were only doing what they knew how to do. So the fees got a little excessive; billings got out of hand; pressure to achieve billable hours turned normally nice people into desperadoes. And, all right, maybe marble foyers, expensive art collections, private elevators, pistachio farms, and $10,000 original Biedermeyer lobby chairs *were* a tad exploitive. Divine decadence was the name of the game. Get with the program; use it or lose it.

Finally, clients had just about enough. Loading a one-shot, high-velocity bazooka pointed directly at legal fees, clients took aim, fired, and hit their target. Law firms, as we knew them, lay dead in their rooftop swimming pools. The revolution had started.

Winning the war was relatively easy. Clients used a new tactic, taking the enemy by surprise: they changed firms. In defense, law firms merged, purged, and downsized. They raced to buy technology—any technology. There was blood everywhere: Associates no longer were granted automatic partnership; technology took the place of typewriters and forced the firms to deliver services faster and with less rewriting; fees were lowered; nonproducing employees were shown the door. God, it was a mess.

The revolution had the greatest impact on the most unlikely choice in the legal field: the paralegal. Still hatching like a chick out of an egg, paralegals were eager to be useful and to show what they could do, roaming around in the educate-attorneys-and-clients training phase. There were no set standard hiring, educational, or certification requirements. Still undecided over a central name, they at least had it narrowed down to two: paralegal or legal assistant.

However, this little group had made its presence strongly felt. When the dust finally settled, the paralegal made out like a bandit. True, there was some embedded shrapnel left: Salaries had dipped somewhat and there were fewer jobs for seniors and managers, but conclusive evidence existed that this profession could literally save the industry. Paralegals were lower in cost than associates and were mostly well-educated, highly trained, revenue-generating angels from heaven. And their special feature was— they weren't ever going to ask for partnership.

Pressure to lower fees, fewer resources, less attorney time to spread around, and clients' acceptance and even insistence on using the field all contributed to this unlikely war hero. Who better to relieve attorneys of the dirty job of raising fees and to free clients from codependency on law firms? Why, the paralegal, of course.

Skills needed for today's job market are not what they used to be. Primary emphasis is on technology, oral and written communication, organization, efficiency, and interpersonal skills. Although the field once claimed that anyone who wanted to could be a paralegal, client insistence on lower costs and high-quality work product dictated otherwise. The market has changed dramatically. Paralegals must know how to adapt to those changes if for no other reason than to keep their jobs.

Paralegal jobs are found in more practice specialties, law firms, and corporations than ever before. Skills and knowledge of the field must be up-to-date if you expect to move up, over, or into another legal arena. Forward, substantive movement is essential for growth in any career. Because paralegals tend to follow horizontal career jumps rather than vertical, identifying and claiming new and improved growth areas can sometimes be complex.

The in-house legal departments of corporations have changed. Gone is the stigma—never entirely accurate—that a lawyer who worked in-house was probably not a good lawyer (translated: couldn't get into a major firm). Although paralegals never quite faced that stigma, in the past, fewer jobs existed with corporations, thereby limiting access to alternative career paths and vertical career climbs.

The paralegal role in the law firm changed as technology emerged and gave new definitions to jobs. By creating technology-related positions, the enlightenment added to, rather than subtracted from, paralegal job opportunities. Options for alternative growth were no longer limited to administrator, manager, or human resources director. Suddenly, there were new positions requiring paralegal skills.

The independent paralegal gave us quite a scare when paralegals allegedly involved in the unauthorized practice of law hit the news. But the trend toward consumer-direct paralegal services has increased, not decreased, and regulation of this arena seems imminent.

Billing rates have changed, not necessarily upwards so much as to the different possibilities presented to clients. Value billing, task-based, flat fees, and other arrangements (previously referred to as "exotic" billing) made life easier for clients while confusing law firms.

We are also witnessing the rise of the 24/7/365 worker. We now operate a working world that continues 24 hours a day, 7 days a week, 365 days per year. Futurists predict that some workers won't take any time off—that many law firms will function continuously with three and four shifts per day. Further, they say, workers will have such flexible schedules and portable tools that they can make themselves available to employers at any time.

To stay competitive in this global economy, firms will rely on employees who will be willing and able to work the flexible hours associated with an increasingly Internet-oriented, nonstop, global marketplace. These employees are very comfortable with the latest technology and skills, including navigating around the Internet. Relying heavily on portable tools, such as cell phones, laptops, handheld computers, and pagers, they include techno-savvy teens or graying baby boomers who have followed the development of the computer since its introduction as an ordinary tool into the workplace.

There is already evidence of this new worker. The Bureau of Labor Statistics conducted a survey of alternative work schedules in 1995 and concluded that 27 percent of the civilian labor force worked flexible schedules. That is the largest percentage since the BLS began tracking the data in 1985—and a huge increase from 1991, when only 15 percent of the labor force maintained flexible schedules.

According to John Challenger in *The Futurist* (October 2000), employees are becoming more and more isolated. Digitally mediated communications, such as e-mail and voice mail, increasingly replace face-to-face exchanges. The resulting decline in social skills may hinder team problem-solving and threaten productivity—vital components of the paralegal career.

Firms and corporations will address this problem through on-site counseling and special programs designed to bring employees together in social settings where they can finally meet one another.

Ironically, then, businesses that succeed in the future may be those that re-create workers' connections to society—which fierce economic competition in the early twenty-first century helped demolish.

These changes are not new to you. But refreshing your memory should remind you that observation without action will not move you along. There is growing evidence that stagnating paralegals are no longer given "sacred cow" status. Performance is what pays the bills, not loyalty or longevity with the firm.

In this third edition of the *Paralegal Career Guide,* we will explore options, career expansion, alternatives, and lateral moves along with suggestions and techniques for paving the road. Grab your laptops, charge your batteries, and let's pursue this riveting postrevolutionary age.

CHAPTER 2

Firing Up Commitment for Strategic Career Planning

Choose your changes.

Brian DeRoches, Ph.D., *Your Boss Is Not Your Mother*

Rx FOR A CHANGE-FATIGUED WORKFORCE

Jobs can be such a drag. Day in and day out, year after billable year. Routine and repetitious work. More and more pressure to bill more and more time. Same old, same old. One crisis after another. One more fire to put out and you'll qualify for the Extinguished Smokey the Bear Award.

Monotony creeps in. Enthusiasm disappears. Once vibrant souls physically perform but mentally snore. Drugged by lack of meaning and slowed by inhibitions, a paralegal can grind to a halt—never realizing the power within to create change.

Change requires commitment. A commitment is the pledging or binding of an individual to a course of action. Most people, when they agree to do something, will usually stick to that commitment. Not honoring a commitment has the same effect as being caught in a lie. Without a strong sense of purpose, commitment to your career or firm can rarely be fulfilled.

Put a cause on the table, however, and watch your career come alive. Paralegals who are fired up by a strong sense of purpose are full of passion and energized. They put their hearts and souls into their work. Here's a very simple fact: People don't really care about working for a firm or corporation. They want to work for a purposeful movement.

That's one of the prime reasons the paralegal career has gained as much momentum as it has in a relatively short period of time. You, as paralegals, have contributed to the movement. You have transcended the dullness of everyday career lives. There is an aspiration, a purpose that you can live by, identify with, and commit to.

Dry, commercial goals will not fire up commitment to your career. Law firm paralegals have a very hard time getting too emotionally involved with financial objectives such as 1,650 hour minimum billables, recruiting 25 new associates, or increasing partner profits. In-house paralegals rarely find that "getting to $100 million in five years" really fires them up.

In fact, these kinds of financial goals fail to take into consideration the growing backlash against business in America by working people. With many angry workers venting their rage by turning to extremist politicians, setting financial goals that do not benefit the worker can only hurt organizations. Do they think the public won't find out? Someone should tell top management that there's no such thing as an illiterate paralegal.

While employed by an international company involved in the legal field, I was president of one of the divisions but not a shareholder. The last 3 years represented a grueling fight and a tremendous struggle to shake loose enough financial and operational support to make our division grow.

During a long-term strategy meeting, we were told that one of the strategic goals was to put "profit in the shareholders' pockets." "BOING!" went bells and buzzers in my head. I had just lost a 5-month battle for my team and myself involving wrangling, substantiating, and clawing at the windows in a desperate attempt to get, after several dry years, a small 4 percent cost-of-living increase. Flashes of 3 solid years of staking my reputation and giving my well-known expertise, 180 percent commitment, and my weekends building this company from ground zero to a recognized force flashed before my eyes.

I stood up and said, "Sure. I'll be happy to 'put profit in the shareholders' pockets.' Here's how to go about it: you pay for MY Mercedes, give ME shares of stock, pay for MY membership in the country club, and level the playing field. Then, I may have one *very small* inkling why I should buy-in on this strategic goal." Well, I never was a shrinking violet.

Employees need a grand purpose, a mission with a larger meaning, a cause that means they are contributing something that has value. "Increased market share" or a "10 percent pretax profit" doesn't exactly inspire anyone. Law firms and organizations wonder why strategic goals, TQM, and reengineering don't live up to expectations. The organization asks more of everyone but fails to tie that request to the heartstrings of employees.

As master of your destiny, you need to identify what you want from this career and create a flexible plan to achieve those goals. Planning your career is no different from the strategic planning process used for organizational growth.

Career goals also need inspiration. "Becoming an expert on Concordance, Summation, and Access" isn't exactly going to bring tears to your eyes and put warmth in your heart. It's more likely to bring acid to your tummy. Neither is "becoming a paralegal administrator within a large firm." These kinds of lackluster goals curtail any sense of purpose.

I don't recall hearing the beloved Martin Luther King say, "I have a strategic plan." Instead, he shouted, "I have a dream!" and created a movement.

Start first strategically and follow up with objectives and action plans. Driving your plan are your dreams and purpose.

The secret to success in creating your strategic career plan is in commitment to change. That goal is attained through a chance to achieve; otherwise, organizations and professionals end up with hollow people. And people who don't believe in themselves can deliver little of their potential.

Paralegals want to know how they can make a difference. This gives meaning to the work, however mundane the accomplishment may seem. What counts is whether completing a task carries personal significance and recognition of achievement.

I attended an executive meeting where the chairman of the board announced that the corporation would undergo major changes over the course of the next year. To achieve that change and reach corporate financial goals, execs were instructed to "drive employees harder." Good people ended up leaving the company while divisions fell. The company was left at the starting gate. I think they're still blaming the troops.

The triumph someone feels in doing things right is a natural motivator and the best payoff. This feeling goes further than a tangible reward. A survey of video arcades showed that rewarding high scores with free games did little to increase playing. People plunk in their coins to see how well they can do.

Planning your career should take into account the need to achieve, feel important, gain recognition, and build momentum. Many paralegals end up in jobs they didn't actually think they were applying for, but now don't really know what they want. Whenever I am a guest speaker, I pose the question to attendees: "What do you want?" Inevitably, I get silence. The moment I ask, "What don't you want?" the room rocks and rolls.

The following analysis takes the "SWOT" approach and applies to your career. This approach has been used for years for strategic planning in organizations. It is a long process of thinking through what business you are in, assessing where you are, and where you want to be in what period of time. It includes an analysis of strengths, weaknesses, opportunities, and threats (to your career). From there, you can determine what purpose you seek and position you would prefer; it positions you to design a tactical and action plan to achieve your goals.

ENGINEERING YOUR CAREER

The SWOT (strengths, weaknesses, opportunities, and threats) analysis gained popularity in the early 1990s. It was designed to identify what accounts for success in a company. It was developed by the Massachusetts-based Boston Consulting Group in the early 1970s.

SWOT analysis was designed to match the strengths found in a company's internal environment with opportunities in the organization's external environment in a way that makes performance standards self-evident. When strengths, weaknesses, opportunities, and threats are identified, profiles should match goals. If there are inconsistencies, you need to take a closer look at what you are doing.

Taking a lot of liberties, and with apologies to the Boston Consulting Group in addition to every MBA program in the country, I found that while going through this exercise for corporate strategic planning, it provided a logical process to planning. The formula is transferable to other areas, such as your career. Rarely do we find such clear probing with matching results.

Using this analysis, we will seek to match your career (internal environment) with opportunities in the organization (external organization).

Before you can make a decision about reacting to an opportunity or threat, you must understand your own strengths and weaknesses. Then you know what you can best package and present to your current or future employer.

Once you know where you are going, you will be able to tell just how far you have to go. The SWOT analysis is a tool for looking internally at your professional career strengths and weaknesses, as well as externally for the opportunities and threats that come to you from outside.

Usually, this is a tool for group discussion and feedback from management. However, you can use the tool to enhance your self-understanding of where you are today and what you need to do to get to tomorrow (see Form 2–1).

Strengths: Your core competencies—those skills that you perform better than your peers or colleagues or that tie your skills to together. What are you especially proud of? This is your center for determining what you will do in the future. Always strive to build on your strengths.

Weaknesses: It's not easy to step up to the table and declare a weakness. The act of identifying weaknesses does not make you a bad paralegal. Some weaknesses you'll change; others you won't. Don't expect to be Super Para-

FORM 2–1
SWOT CAREER ANALYSIS

STRENGTHS:
Ex.: Excellent oral
       communication skills

_____

_____

_____

_____

WEAKNESSES:
Ex.: Fear of public
       speaking

_____

_____

_____

_____

OPPORTUNITIES:
Ex.: Workforce trend toward
       outsourcing

_____

_____

_____

_____

THREATS:
Ex.: Possible licensing

_____

_____

_____

_____

legal. You do need to decide those areas that can hold you back or fail to get you more sophisticated assignments. If given an opportunity to spend your money taking classes, where would you plop that dollar down?

Opportunities: The most difficult thing about opportunity is the ability to recognize it. What are the greatest challenges in this changing paralegal world? How does the information age help you? What will your clients and firms need in the future that you already hold the secret to? Where is there a need that you can fill in the firm? What need can you create? What global opportunities are there?

Threats: Some threats can be controlled, while others are out of your hands. What outside your control can weaken paralegal effectiveness? What can change the direction of the profession? How might technology hurt you? Does the Internet hurt you or help you? What happens when there is a glut of associates and paralegals on the market? What about government regulation? How does the economy play a part in job opportunities?

Here are a few questions you can ask yourself:

1. Do you love what you do?
2. Are you using all of your strengths, or are you working at a level below your capabilities?
3. Can you leverage your previous background by incorporating that knowledge into the paralegal career?
4. Why are you living with your weaknesses? Would improving these help you? Are they too costly or difficult to resolve?
5. What is holding you back?
6. Are your coworkers taking better advantage of the workplace than you?
7. What can you do to minimize potential threats to your career?
8. Are you prepared for the future workplace?

KEY FACTORS FOR SUCCESS

What is it you do exceptionally well? This exercise will help you focus. The process eventually leads to implementation.

Career counselors will always tell you to set goals and objectives. However, do you know if your goals are realistic? Do they fit your skills and abilities? If you know that, you can set objectives to help you reach your goals. You can't set down objectives to reaching your goals without first determining what has contributed to your career success (see Form 2–2).

Here are a few ideas for key success factors:

Compensation

1. Lead the trial team
2. Earn over $85,000 per year
3. Become the highest paid paralegal in my specialty

Marketing and Recognition

1. Am a noted author in my specialty
2. Am known in the field as the mergers and acquisition expert
3. Become wealthy as a paralegal entrepreneur

Professional Development

1. Am president of a national paralegal association
2. Can teach a writing class
3. Can get the CLA designation

Day-to-Day Job Duties

1. Am the first paralegal to work in the products liability department
2. Become the MIS director
3. Can get home every night before 6:30 P.M. (that is, live the lifestyle I choose)

FORM 2–2
KEY SUCCESS FACTORS

Think in terms of "If I _____ then I will be successful." There are four areas for career functions: compensation; marketing and recognition; professional development; and day-to-day job duties. Feel free to add more areas if necessary.

Compensation:
1. If I _____ then I will be successful.
2. If I _____ then I will be successful.
3. If I _____ then I will be successful.

Marketing and Recognition:
1. If I _____ then I will be successful.
2. If I _____ then I will be successful.
3. If I _____ then I will be successful.

Professional Development:
1. If I _____ then I will be successful.
2. If I _____ then I will be successful.
3. If I _____ then I will be successful.

Day-to-Day Job Duties:
1. If I _____ then I will be successful.
2. If I _____ then I will be successful.
3. If I _____ then I will be successful.

CREATING CAREER OBJECTIVES

Success factors generally define what we think we need to do in order to make our careers succeed. Career objectives turn the success factors into specific items to be accomplished. They should also include specific measurements to determine success (See Form 2–3).

THE ACTION PLAN

Listing your career objectives narrows your scope even further. Now, what do you have to do to get there? If, for example, you want to be president of a national paralegal association, and your objective is to get on the board and work your way up, what does that take?

FORM 2–3
CAREER OBJECTIVES

Compensation:
1. Lead the trial team: I must learn how to prepare summary judgments and answers to interrogatories. I can also take on fewer administrative duties.

Marketing and Recognition:
1. Am a noted author: I can contact paralegal publishers and submit an outline and proposal for a new book idea.

Professional Development:
1. Am president of a national organization: I need to campaign to be on the board and work my way up from there.

Day-to-Day Job Duties:
1. Be the first paralegal to work in the products liability department: I should take continuing education courses and see to it I am assigned to one of the products liability associates.

Once you decide what to do, you have to decide how you will get the work done. You must figure out when the task should be completed and how to measure success. For example:

1. Be president of a national paralegal association; get on the board and work my way up. My next step is: go to every monthly meeting and start meeting as many paralegals as I can.

2. The measurement of my success will be to (a) get known; (b) get nominated; and (c) win.

3. My deadline is September 19th.

4. Ask yourself if these action items work toward meeting the objectives.

LINKING SWOT ANALYSIS, OBJECTIVES, AND ACTION PLAN TO PURPOSE

Now, take a look at your objectives. How do they compare with your strengths? weaknesses? opportunities? threats? If, for example, one of your objectives is to become president of a national association but one of your weaknesses is fear of public speaking, you either need to join Toastmasters or find another objective.

How do opportunities compare? If there is an opportunity to run for local chapter president, better prepare far in advance.

How about threats? If standard educational requirements become mandatory, should you be thinking in terms of further education?

Now, let's tie this all back to *purpose*. If you concentrate on becoming president of a national association, ask yourself these questions: Why would I do this? What purpose does it serve? Where are the highs? Who benefits from my role and why?

You may find that the idea of pushing the profession forward, getting nationwide recognition, and taking the paralegal profession one more rung up the ladder is exciting to you. You can get behind the cause with personal involvement and a hands-on approach, ultimately furthering your profession.

Be defining your purpose or mission statement, you will build a dynamic sense of momentum in your career. Progress is compelling. Watch how others flock around when things start to come together for you. Everyone wants to be around a winner.

PARALEGAL INNER VIEW: HARRY HECK— FLYING ON THE CORPORATE JET

Name: Harry Heck
Corporation: Harrah's Entertainment, Inc., Las Vegas, Nevada
Title: Legal Assistant
Experience: 11 years
Education: A.A. degree in hotel management and a paralegal certificate
Professional achievements: Past present of the Clark County Legal Assistants Association, member of NALA, NALA liaison
Personal: 40 years old; enjoys eating out, cooking, reading, and traveling
Job duties: I work at the corporate legal department in the employment area rather than at a property. We oversee all EEOC and NLRB charges and all employment litigation. A typical day for me might be drafting a response to an EEOC charge, reviewing employment files, talking to the property HR people, and preparing a response which could be five to ten pages with 30 exhibits. I coordinate outside counsel requests. There's no litigation in-house. I talk with outside counsel around the country and assist in the matters of litigation. I've been at Harrah's 11 months. Harrah's used to be based in Memphis but they moved the law department out here. Prior to Harrah's, I was a freelance paralegal for 2 years doing construction

litigation and large document intensive cases. At that time, I was the only certified Summation trainer in Nevada.

Biggest challenge: Coordinating a lot of information in an expeditious manner.

Most gratifying experience: Dealing with the properties. There are 22 right now around the country and over 45,000 employees. I enjoy learning the HR area of law. I've never worked in this area before and I enjoy learning.

Harry, what's the best thing about this job?

The attorney I work for. He allows me a lot of freedom. He enjoys teaching. I don't have a lot to do with the properties but I do some traveling for investigations. I get to stay at the properties and fly on the corporate jet.

How did you get into the paralegal field?

I was laid off from a job and didn't work so I thought about going to paralegal school. I got my first job at a law firm reviewing documents for $5.00 an hour. I later got a 120 percent raise. I stayed with that firm for 4 years. I really enjoyed that. It was much more useful than school. The attorney taught me a lot. Every Friday, we had a group meeting about the cases. I would listen to the strategy ideas and learned more.

How does working in a corporation compare to a law firm?

There are pluses and minuses to both. There's a lot more bureaucracy in a corporation. The largest firm in Las Vegas is 25 attorneys, and I worked there. I'm used to more one-on-one. Here, I have to go through a different approval process. The benefits are the paralegal is more the manager in a corporation. We're managing rather than doing the litigation. A paralegal can excel in that area and there's room for advancement. In a firm, you're going to be a paralegal unless you go into management. In a corporation, there are other areas to journey into such as HR or risk management. The corporation has a very good bonus plan. There's also tuition reimbursement, full medical, dental, optical, and 18 days off.

How's the money?

Not nearly as good as it should be. Paralegals can earn in the low to mid-$40s. There are not a lot of temp agencies that are exclusively legal. Firms don't like to use temps.

What's the field like in Las Vegas?

The paralegal field is growing here. Ten years ago, there weren't nearly as many. It's helped with the influx of a lot of California firms coming into the market. There's more of a professional paralegal emerging. The city is growing at a rate of 5,000 people a month. It used to be you knew everyone on the case. It's not that way anymore, and no one takes a chance on verbal agreements anymore.

Where do you go from here?

I don't know. I'm really enjoying the employment area—wherever that may take me.

Any advice for your colleagues?

The best advice I can give is to get a job at a law firm even if you don't have the education. Be a runner. Be a file clerk. The best paralegals I've seen have an understanding of the firm. The firm notices people who are good with a good work ethic. It's better to advance that way.

What do you think is the future of the profession?

At some point, there's going to have to be some sort of set standard that people who call themselves paralegals need to reach. That's a problem that we know. The people who don't have the knowledge are given the title and that hurts everyone who does have the knowledge and experience.

CHAPTER 3

Educating Paralegals

> By A.D. 2000, one can retire with a comfortable income at the age of 50; and retirement will be compulsory at 60, except for those with skills in scant supply.
>
> R. G. Ruste, *American Heritage*, 1967

Congratulations to those of you who purchased this book because you are seeking to enter the paralegal profession and to those of you looking to continuously expand your education. This relatively new field (it's only about 35 years old) has shown itself to be a permanent fixture in an industry that is more than 200 years old. You may be asking yourself what it is that paralegals do. Usually, the answer is anything that lawyers do with the exception of: (1) practicing law, (2) negotiating fees, and (3)representing clients. The definition of a paralegal (or legal assistant) has been defined and redefined over the past years. Currently, the American Bar Association has issued this definition of a paralegal:

> A legal assistant or paralegal is a person, qualified by education, training, or work experience, who is employed or retained by a lawyer, law office, corporation, governmental agency, or other entity, and who performs specifically delegated substantive legal work for which a lawyer is responsible.

On January 1, 2000, California joined the ranks of 26 other states which already have paralegal definitions in place, either by statute, state supreme court ruling, or guidelines promulgated by state bars, which define paralegals/legal assistants as those who work under the supervision of an attorney. What makes California unique is that it has already added the definition of a legal document assistant (a person who prepares legal forms generally directly to the public) to its Business and Professions Code, Section 6400. Under this code, those who type legal forms directly for the public must meet certain education criteria, post a $25,000 bond, and register with the County Recorder's Office. California is the only state with two separate statutes that differentiate paralegals (those who work under the supervision of an attorney) from legal document assistants (those who provide services directly to the public).

Despite the efforts by consumers and certificated paralegals to provide guidelines and discipline themselves, many individuals take advantage of California's lax laws relating to the paralegal profession. So, as of January 2, 2001, a paralegal must meet certain specified qualifications, and it is unlawful for any person to identify herself as a paralegal unless the qualifications are met.

The educational requirements of a paralegal are very clear. A paralegal must meet at least one of the following educational requirements:

1. A certificate of completion of a paralegal program approved by the American Bar Association

2. A certificate of completion of a paralegal program at, or a degree from, a postsecondary institution that requires the successful completion of a minimum of 24 semester, or equivalent, units of law-related courses and that has been accredited by a national or regional accrediting organization or approved by the Bureau for Private Postsecondary and Vocational Education

3. A baccalaureate degree or an advanced degree in any subject, a minimum of 1 year of law-related experience under the supervision of an attorney who has been an active member of the State Bar Association for at least the preceding 3 years or who has practiced in the federal courts of the state for at least the preceding 3 years, and a written declaration from this attorney stating that the person is qualified to perform paralegal tasks

4. A high school diploma or general equivalency diploma, a minimum of 3 years of law-related experience under the supervision of an attorney who has been an active member of the State Bar of California for at least the preceding 3 years or who has practiced in the federal courts of this state for at least the preceding 3 years, and a written declaration from this attorney stating that the person is qualified to perform paralegal tasks; this experience and training shall be completed no later than December 31, 2003.

California is also unique in that it is the only state in which paralegals will be required to maintain MCLE credits and continuing education. This provision of the bill requires those utilizing the title of paralegal to certify with their supervising attorney 4 hours of continuing education in legal ethics every 3 years; and 4 hours of general law or the paralegal's specialized area every 4 years. Be sure to find out whether your state has changed education or hiring practices. You may not be aware that these changes have taken place.

The goal of any program is to prepare students to function as ethical, effective, and efficient professionals in law firms or in-house legal departments, businesses, and government, military, and nonprofit organizations. Always under the supervision of an attorney, you will need to gain instruction in legal theory, practical legal applications, and legal skills. You'll be exposed to a variety of legal professionals, including attorneys, paralegals, judges, support staff and clients.

Here are just a few of the courses you may take when enrolled in a school or paralegal program:

Civil litigation
Legal research and analysis
Introductory legal principles
Civil procedure
Contracts
Corporations: formation, maintenance and dissolution
Criminal law
Securities law
Employee compensation and benefit plans
Estate planning and probate
Entertainment law
Bankruptcy law
International law
Real property law
Torts
Intellectual property
Employment and labor law
Personal injury law
Family law
Environmental law
Computer training such as word processing, graphics, spreadsheets, and
    database management programs.

One of the specific skills you might learn through an educational institution is how to work with corporate certificates:

- Preparing and filing articles of incorporation and certificates of amendment
- Drafting bylaws
- Drafting proxy statements

- Composing notices, agendas, waivers, resolutions and minutes of meetings, and actions of boards of directors and shareholders
- Preparing notices of issuance
- Preparing stock certificates and transferring records
- Drafting request for consent to transfer
- Assisting in completing and filing reports to government agencies for qualified employee benefit plans
- Preparing disclosures for real estate transactions
- Assisting in drafting portions of SEC registration statements, forms, and reports

You might also learn the elements of litigation:

- Drafting complaints and answers
- Composing interrogatories and answers
- Summarizing and indexing depositions
- Preparing motions and answers
- Preparing motions for summary judgment
- Preparing motions to dismiss and demurrers
- Assisting in preparation of memoranda of points and authorities
- Outlining deposition questions
- Originating and controlling document and discovery information retrieval systems
- Preparing and organizing trial exhibits
- Preparing judgments
- Preparing fact statements from trial records for use in appellate briefs
- Researching and abstracting public records
- Performing simple research including Shepardizing and cite-checking
- Drafting bankruptcy petitions, schedules, and proofs of claim

While some paralegals enter the field in order to test the waters before entering law school, so do some secretaries before entering the paralegal field. Jumping from legal secretary to paralegal can be tough, however. It all depends on the attitudes of the firms in your region. Some smaller cities and towns are more apt to promote a legal secretary to paralegal than are larger, metropolitan cities. (See chapter 28 on legal secretaries.) Legal secretaries are increasingly hard to find. There is some question as to what the field will look like as more and more individual dependence is placed upon personal computers and the Internet. Perhaps the legal secretary of the future will be more of an administrative assistant.

If you want to take classes, here are just a few that may be available. Check with your local community colleges, vocational schools, or universities for their offerings.

Court structure and the legal system
Law office procedures
Civil litigation
Family law
Personal injury
Bankruptcy
Word processing for the law office
Law office terminology
Bookkeeping/accounting
Spreadsheets
Database Management
Business English/grammar
Dictation and transcription

Some states, such as California, offer a Certified Legal Secretary certificate. Check with the National Association for Legal Secretaries (NALS) to find out whether the certification is offered in your state.

The legal field has embraced professional development for paralegals. Right on the tail of the CLA and PACE certifications is the CLM^{SM} program designed by the Association of Legal Administrators (ALA). The CLM is a voluntary certification program for legal administrators which is centered around three basic components: prerequisites, including specific educational programs and years of experience; a written examination; and recertification requirements consisting of a minimum of 36 hours of relevant course work during each 3-year period following initial certification. To request an information and application packet for the Certified Legal Manager Program, call ALA Headquarters at 847-816-1212. The packet is also available from ALA's Fax-on-Demand service. Members dial 800-345-5141, press 8-ALA's access code, and enter their membership number.

ALA also offers the Essential Competencies of Legal Administrators (ECLA), a comprehensive, interactive more than 2-day course which was developed out of ALA's Knowledge, Skills and Abilities (KSA) study. In this study, legal administrators and managing partners identified the most important on-the-job skill set of successful principal administrators. The intensive course addresses many of the critical elements of law office administration through handouts, role-playing, case studies, group discussion, and more.

If you are a seasoned paralegal who is thinking about moving up to legal administrator or paralegal manager, or if you are a paralegal who has a dual role, this course may be for you. According to the ALA, the program benefits many types of legal managers including:

- Principal administrators in law firms with fewer than 30 attorneys
- Functional specialists in law firms with more than 30 attorneys, who are looking to build legal-management expertise outside of their specialty; this may be a good avenue for those of you seeking a paralegal administrator position
- Any legal administrator new to the profession
- Anyone who needs to be brought up-to-date in key areas of legal management.

The ECLA program is divided into five modules and is led by a group of nationally renowned educators. Module topics include financial systems management; office systems management; the administrator as leader; principles of law office management; and human resources management.

The cost of attending the program is $595 (at press time). To register or request more information, contact the Director of Professional Development at 847-816-1212 or check the ALA Web site at www.alanet.org.

ALA also offers teleseminars which are one of the hottest education vehicles in the legal management industry. You can learn about human resources and administration issues right in your office. You can invite many of your firm's members to listen in at the same time. Just a few of the topics include: staffing the law firm; mastering your life; and the annual technology conference. The site license fee for callers from the United States (at press time) is $149 ($159 for late registrants). Canadian callers pay US$159 (US$169 for late registrants). The tuition fee includes one set of materials (you may make copies for other participants in your firm) and one toll-free telephone connection to the seminar. For more information on the programs or to register call 800-775-7654 or fax 715-833-5216. The programs are also available on audio tapes.

If You Are Just Starting Out

Paralegal programs run the gamut: vocational schools, correspondence schools, community college 2-year degree programs, proprietary schools, extension courses, and 4-year degree programs. For some universities, graduate school entry tests are required. Programs are also available within the Army and Marine Corps for those seeking military careers.

Today's hiring requirements generally lean toward a B.A. degree; B.A./B.S. and graduate degree; or B.A. degree and paralegal certificate, many times from an ABA-approved school. Paralegals without legal background or 2-year or 4-year degrees may have a hard time in today's market.

Paralegals who have extensive work experience in the field and who started before certificates or B.A.s were routinely required may find experience can be substituted for the degree. Other paralegals who have postgraduate degrees and highly specialized backgrounds in areas such as biotechnology, trademark and patent, intellectual property, pharmaceutical, medicine, nursing, engineering, and other scientific training may not need a certificate.

Paralegal schools and programs come and go. Most of the time it's a result of economics and whether the community can support the school.

Master's Degree Programs

A little-known career-boosting opportunity is the paralegal master's program. This exciting occurrence is a tribute to the many changes within the legal profession. These advanced degree programs are aimed at both the career paralegal seeking to advance and pre-law majors who have changed law school plans but want to remain in the field.

According to Shelly Widoff, a well-known paralegal educator, entrepreneur, and director of the paralegal program at Boston University, the degree has opened up many new and innovative career options. In her article in *Legal Assistant Today* magazine (March 1996), Widoff cites Frank Kopecky, program director at the University of Illinois at Springfield, who says the mayor of Springfield is a graduate of the program. Further, Widoff states, Marymount University, located in Arlington, Virginia, has recently responded to its Washington, D.C., audience of legal professionals by offering an M.A. degree in legal administration. Marymount's program director, according to the *LAT* article, says 11 graduates were paralegals who found law office management a viable alternative to law school.

According to Widoff, six programs currently offer the master's program.

- University of Illinois at Springfield in Springfield, Illinois
- Marymount University in Arlington, Virginia
- Montclair State University in Upper Montclair, New Jersey
- Webster University in St. Louis, Missouri
- Duke University School of Law in Durham, North Carolina
- Auburn University at Montgomery, in Montgomery, Alabama

Programs include Masters of Arts in Legal Studies, Legal Administration, and Masters of Science in Justice and Public Safety. The programs have a healthy track record: one started in 1977, three in the 1980s, and one in 1995.

Curricula vary, offering public law emphasis; legal specialty training with additional graduate level courses within the School of Business Management; paralegal administration; law office management; dispute resolution; law office management and technology; and law office management for those interested in human resource management, labor relations, and applied organizational behavior. Options exist in law enforcement, corrections, and jurisprudence.

Admission to the program at Duke University is limited to those who have achieved distinction in other professional careers, such as medicine, and want to enhance their careers through a yearlong program. Admission in other programs requires a baccalaureate degree, and some also require a graduate entrance exam, such as the GMAT, GRE, or LSAT.

Ambitious students have found careers in government (with a focus on public law, administration, and advocacy); administrative positions within the health care field; the FBI; court system administration; teaching; and legal assistant management. The program assists those needing management, financial, and computer information expertise.

Education is a passkey for career survival and better job performance. Recessions, downsizing, push back of legal fees, and streamlined operations have removed continuing education as an employee benefit from most budgets. Use your money wisely; get the best education you can afford.

CERTIFICATION STANDARDS

Growth and development of the paralegal profession has created a standard of measurement of achievement through certification credentials. The purpose of the certification programs is to provide a demonstrable knowledge of core skills and abilities and of general and substantive law. State certification programs provide a credible way for paralegals to demonstrate their advanced knowledge of state law and procedure.

Two programs through the national paralegal associations are the CLA (Certified Legal Assistant) and PACE (Paralegal Advanced Competency Exams). CLA was established in 1976 as a professional self-regulatory program offering a nationwide credential. This is an ongoing, voluntary program to encourage the growth of the legal assistant program. It was originally designed by NALA (National Association of Legal Assistants, 1516 S. Boston #200, Tulsa, Oklahoma 74119 (918) 587-6828). Among some bar associations that offer associate membership to paralegals, the CLA has been mentioned as a qualification.

States vary as to their certification requirements. The Mississippi Bar Ethics Committee approved use of the CLA credential. In Louisiana, the State Paralegal Association approved development of the Louisiana Certified Paralegal (LCP) exam. Within 3 years of completion of the LCP exam, the paralegal must obtain the CLA. Florida Legal Assistants established their first program in the early 1980s. In California, CAPA (California Alliance of Paralegal Association) announced an agreement with NALA to develop and administer a California certification program. Both Florida and California adopt the CLA credential as part of the state certification process. The Legal Assistants Division of the State Bar of Texas also offers a certification program.

The Certified Legal Assistant examination is used as a basis for statewide certification programs in California, Florida, and Louisiana. Paralegals with the CLA credential in these states may prove advanced certification in state law and procedure in various areas. NALA has published survey data indicating that the CLA is a positive factor in salary and compensation levels as well as billing rates. A short course is offered through NALA. It is an intensive workshop covering areas such as the American legal system, judgment and analytical ability, contracts, administrative law, real estate, civil litigation, legal research, and business organizations. Participants surviving the 2½ day exam refer to it as the "mini-bar."

More than 10,000 legal assistants have achieved the CLA designation. Of these, more than 800 Certified Legal Assistants have achieved advanced certification in specialty areas of practice. NALA boasts that more than 20,000 legal assistants have participated in the program.

The National Federation of Paralegal Associations (NFPA) (P.O. Box 33108, Kansas City, Missouri 64114, telephone 816-941-4000) offers PACE—Paralegal Advanced Competency Exams. PACE exams are currently offered at more than 200 locations as a result of a contract with Sylvan Learning Centers.

The new NFPA examination requires the paralegal who takes the test to have completed a bachelor's degree and a paralegal program within an institutionally accredited paralegal program, which may be embodied within the bachelor degree, and a minimum of 2 years experience. To take the second tier, individuals are required to have 4 years of paralegal experience. To assist individuals who graduate from paralegal programs during the next few years to be prepared to take the exam, NFPA is recommending the levels of education be standardized and increased.

The differences setting the PACE exam apart from other tests have caused some controversy between paralegal associations. The PACE exam

- Is developed by a professional testing company
- Is supported by an independent committee comprised of attorneys, educators who are not attorneys, paralegals, and members of the general public
- Is administered by an independent entity, and

its proceeds are donated to a foundation exclusively utilized for the expansion of the paralegal profession. This exam became available only as recently at 1996. Upon successful completion of the exam, the paralegal will be able to use the credential Certified Paralegal. The exam is, at this writing, voluntary, and a trend to watch closely.

There is a grandparenting option to enable paralegals to substitute work experience for formal education. Within 1 year of when the exam is available, paralegals with 5 years' work experience are eligible to take the second-tier exam.

Each state varies in acceptance of certification by peers and hiring authorities. Presently, some paralegals fear mandatory regulation of the profession will set it back. Others feel that standardization should start with educational requirements; others feel education is not as important as passing a mini-bar exam. For information in your state, call NFPA or NALA and, by all means, check with your local paralegal association, schools, and potential employers to discover whether the certification designation has any bearing on compensation or advancement.

Action Items

If you are considering studying for a CLA or PACE certification and are unsure as to its value, then an informal telephone survey is helpful in making an individual decision whether to sit for the exam. If the paralegal associations in your state have supported either the CLA or PACE designation for all paralegals, chances are at some point in the future (if not now) the designation may be a hiring preference. Only time will tell.

1. Informally survey firms (or in-house departments) similar to yours. Find out
    a. Are they aware of what certification is? Some may be confused with receiving a certificate from a paralegal institution.
    b. If so, does the designation set you apart in any way from other paralegals?
    c. Does it weigh more, less, the same, or not at all with a paralegal certificate?
    d. Will the firm acknowledge the designation through monetary or other reward?
    e. Does it make a difference in hiring decisions?

2. Once you have completed your survey (do not survey fewer than 10

firms), analyze the responses. If most of the firms you spoke with did not know about the designation, it is probably best to resurvey them in about 6 months. If you decide not to sit for the exam based on survey results, be sure to resurvey these firms and other firms in about a year. Opinions, hiring trends, and available candidates are all decision-swaying factors.

CHAPTER 4

Talking the Talk: Admission Ticket to the New Business Realities

> Is this the audience participation part? I'll give you a topic: *The Prince of Tides* was neither about a prince nor the tides. Discuss, discuss.
>
> Barbra Streisand, to her audience, in *Barbra, The Concert* recorded live at Madison Square Garden, New York City

FUTURE PREDICTIONS

Welcome. You have just entered the magical kingdom of the New Business Realities. As you get on the bus, please check your inhibitions at the door. You will no longer need loyalty or long-term commitments.

Please fasten your seat belts and hang on for a bumpy ride. I'd like to take a moment to show you around. We're very proud of what we've done here. During our tour, I will be happy to translate New Business talk into English. However, if you have any questions, please do not ask me. We don't yet have a proven track record, so I will be unable to answer anything accurately.

Over on your left-hand side is our "happy place," one of our biggest transformations in the magical kingdom. Please put on your blinders so the bright light won't be too much of a distraction. Here, you will see the biggest job-reduction cuts in law firm history. This is called downsizing. Our "happy place" is moving so quickly that reassessing careers in midstream is a common occurrence.

Over there, past the ecosystems, please take notice of the field that was once proud of its employee-retention numbers. We now call that outsourcing.

Continuing deeper into the tour and just over that hill, you'll see the land of good and plenty. Please do not feed the lawyers. It will only upset them. The firms you will observe here are very eager to prove they have more bottom-line profits. Some people call this corporate anorexia, but we're proud of our brand new process and call it reorganization. We have achieved our stunning success through huge staff reductions, referred to as operating improvements.

Please take a moment of silence as we now pass our graveyard. Donations for the families of demised 386s, 486s, and IBM Selectrics are greatly appreciated.

And now, as we chug up the hill on the final leg of our journey, please bow your heads in honoring the thousands of law firm professionals who lost their jobs so we can enjoy this moment. Without their dedicated efforts, we could not have achieved success.

As we depart, we would like to thank you for joining us today. We do hope you have seen the light. Please watch your step carefully.

According to the World Future Society, jobs as we know them today are vanishing. This prediction for the future does not exclude legal assistants. The processes by which we deliver legal services continue to change. To stay in the forefront, you must learn how to manage and dispense up-to-date knowledge in order to subsist with Corporate America's new work plan.

Law firms have habitually held on to the belief that they were exempt from radical change. This arrogant thinking flipped 180 degrees when clients finally seized control over runaway fees. Workers in the legal field were no longer protected from workplace changes. Immunity had run out.

Futures with much more innovative assignments seem evident for paralegals. But in order to take advantage of them, you must have an enlightened and informed view of this changing marketplace. Get ready to say "buh-bye" to confining parameters surrounding conventional job descriptions. The workplace has changed, and hopefully you have been paying attention.

Quality, thoroughness, and initiative score workers precious points. Unfortunately, it's no longer enough. Whether seeking a new job or advancement in your present position, you'll have to talk the talk to get through the door. Once there, you'll be expected to demonstrate just how you walk the walk.

KEY CAREER-BUILDING STRATEGY

Develop the ability to convey in-depth knowledge of current trends, technology, and practices directly affecting job performance. Employers seek those who move with the current, not those who are stuck in the mud.

Staff and expense reductions have manifested themselves in the form of technology, infrastructure revisions, outsourcing, and downsizing. From this revolution, an entirely new business vocabulary has evolved. To skip over this communication tool is to signal to the business world or law firm that you have not evolved.

To make sure you change along with the workplace, develop new and innovative techniques for acquiring more professional development. Your approach to valuing and gaining continuing education must revolve around your desire to get ahead in your career. Whatever you do, the time has passed for reenactment of the battle-weary entitlement cry. You know the one: "We still have to teach attorneys how to utilize us." (Note to paralegals: Start making lemonade out of lemons. Teaching attorneys how to utilize you is, thankfully, a blessing in disguise. This never ending process just happens to be the best way for you to influence the development of your career.)

Only you can be responsible for pushing your profession forward. Accept responsibility for your career by:

1. Discovering what options are available
2. Understanding and interpreting the plethora of new technology and terminology
3. Developing a strategy plan for more innovative assignments
4. Communicating, executing, evaluating, and revising the plan
5. Continuing to learn the terminology.

LINGO FOR THE NEW BUSINESS REALITIES

Keeping up with rapid changes in our day-to-day business language is an indication of a person listening to change. Law firms are breaking from conventional business approaches to invent whole new business ecosystems. As a paralegal, you are expected to think outside the box of the traditional role. Interfacing with clients and knowledge of business practices are now part of employer expectations. As an employee, you're probably experiencing a new type of business atmosphere in the firm or corporation that no longer respects traditional infrastructures. By assuming the role of a watchperson of cultural change, you can actively participate in shaping your career. Otherwise, you can only watch from the sidelines.

Here are a few career-related key words and trends that can affect the paralegal career as they fade in and out throughout the next few years:

Survivor Syndrome: The mental and emotional state of those employees who escaped downsizing. Symptoms of the syndrome usually include an increase in sick days, loss of productivity or quality control, disinterest in firm or corporate functions, and little enthusiasm about new services, clients, products, or new hires.

Full-Time Employee: An employee who works a full work week, 35 to 40 hours, and is directly employed by the firm with full benefits, perks, and salary increase opportunities. This employee was previously referred to as a "permanent" employee.

Background Checking Services: Companies that conduct screenings through identity verification; employment and education; criminal and civil records; Department of Motor Vehicles; and SSN. A variety of other preemployment screening services are also provided to human resource managers.

Captives: A nonadmitted, nonrated insurance company, owned by its insureds, that provides coverage unavailable or unaffordable in the insurance marketplace.

Cyber-Recruiting: Recruiting in cyberspace; online recruiting.

Business Ecosystems: Businesses or firms spanning a variety of industries. A law firm can traverse at least four major industries, such as information, communications, personal computers, and consumer electronics. It may also include an extended web of suppliers and clients across market segments (coined by James Moore, *The Death of Competition: Leadership & Strategy in the Age of Business Ecosystems,* HarperCollins).

HRMS: Human Resource Management Services. Consulting folks.

Diversity Awareness: Awareness and sensitivity to ethnic backgrounds, gender, age, racial, religious, cultural, geographical, hierarchical, and any other differences among employees in the workplace. With diversity, possibilities for opportunities become limitless because assumptions about potential are not restricted.

Relocation Services: A company providing relocation cost management and consulting services, including policy counseling, home marketing assistance, home disposition services, closing services, and property management. Other services are destination services, transportation management, outsourcing, policy design/development, group move management, employee opinion surveys, and expense administration/processing.

Downshifters: A group of people who want to bring the whole rat race at work down to a slower speed, so they don't have to "get a life" because they already have one. They want to slow down to upshift in other areas of their lives. There are two camps: those who want to break out of the corporate mold—temporarily or permanently—and those who just want to work less.

Family-Friendly: A law firm or corporation that provides flextime, job-sharing, or customized hours to accommodate an employee's family responsibilities. Employees do not have brownie points subtracted for desiring to spend time with families.

Flex-Staff: Another term for temporary employees.

Baby Boomers: A nicely aging group of middle-aged people born right after World War II (around 1946) up until and including 1960. Currently, it is the second largest age group in the United States.

Gen-Xers: The children of Baby Boomers, young adults estimated at 44 million born from 1965 to 1976.

Echo-Boomers: Those born from 1977 to 1997, estimated at 80 million strong, the largest generation ever. (Baby Boomers are estimated at 77 million.) Aliases are Generation Y, Net (or Internet) Generation, Nexter, Millennials, Nintendo Generation.

Down-Aging: According to Faith Popcorn, in *Clicking* (HarperCollins) people are acting younger and younger, as in 80-year-old marathon runners.

Virtual Office: A technology-driven trend toward more nontraditional work sites: working from home or another set location via computer linkup, video conferencing, fax, modem, cell phone, beeper (see chapter 6).

Core Competencies: The nucleus of an organization's business that allows access to a wide variety of markets, makes a significant contribution to the business and its clients, and is difficult for competitors to imitate; what the company does best.

Legal Cost Control/Management Services: Outraged clients forced creation of a new business that services corporations: invoice auditing. Services include bill review and audit, legal cost management training, task-based billing implementation, billing guidelines, and legal bill processing. These companies effectuate substantial legal cost savings for clients.

Contingent Workforce: Workers who are contracted, temporary, project, or flex-staff.

Distributed Work: Another term for virtual office.

Alternative Work Sites: Another term for virtual office.

Mobile Work: Another term for virtual office.

Job-Sharing: One full-time position split between two or more employees.

Productivity Centers: Branch offices converted into temporary offices with an emphasis on what's more commonly known as the corporate mailroom. It's the nerve center for mobile workers. Employees check their mobile mail slots for hard-copy documents such as mail, faxes, and printed computer material they may have initiated from home or a client's office. Workers can have temporary work space such as a traditional desk or office, work pod, or team room.

Team Room: A work room for the team to convene. Conference rooms usually play this role.

New Work Options: In the first years of the new millennium, only slightly more than half (57 percent) of all work options will be derivatives of traditional work arrangements, according to *Upsizing the Individual in the Downsized Organization* by Robert Johansen and Rob Swigart (Addison-Wesley Publishing Co.).

PEO: Professional employer organizations provide outsourcing services for employee leasing; a growing trend is for companies and law firms to outsource payroll, benefits, and human resource affairs using PEOs. Presently, there are approximately 2,500 office nationwide. Certain states require licensing: Utah, Florida, South Carolina, New Mexico, Arizona, Texas, Oregon, Maine, Nevada, New Hampshire, Tennessee, Minnesota, and Rhode Island. If your firm is interested in this concept, or if you are looking for an alternative career, contact American Staffing Association in Alexandria, Virginia.

Employee Leasing: A growing trend wherein staffing organizations assume responsibility for all or part of the company's employees. The staffing organization takes over the associated costs and benefits and leases them back to the company. (See PEO.) The staffing organization relieves the company of benefits provision and administration, such as ERISA, workers' compensation, employee benefits, and dealing with the federal government on pension plans.

Prime Time: Employees typically with one-year longevity may qualify for this flex benefit. People can reduce their hours and still maintain full-benefit coverage. They can cut back to 32 hours or even down to 20 (a part-time job). Most use the option for 6 months to 2 years. Working mothers use it to ease back into the workplace after a maternity leave, and older employees use it to transition into retirement.

Sabbaticals: A designated time (such as 6 weeks) combined with vacation given with the understanding that time off is geared toward professional development.

Self-Directed Work Teams: A team approach to a project or department run without day-to-day management supervision. The team sets its own goals, objectives, deadlines, and tactical approach.

Skills Gap: The gap between skills employees have and the skills companies need. According to the research of Max Messmer, CEO of Robert Half International, deficits are most prevalent in three areas:

1. Basic analytical, communications, and organizational skills, necessary for entry-level, white-collar positions

2. Technological skills needed for a wide range of job classifications

3. Leadership skills that allow managers to pursue a strategic corporate vision for greater long-term competition

Sticky Floor: A term coined by Shelly Wallace (founder of the Law Registry, a national legal staffing company) referring to career women who hold themselves back. The antithesis to those on the sticky floor are those who hit the glass ceiling.

Confrontophobia: Fear of confronting people or situations. (This is definitely a sign that we've run out of neuroses.) Coined by Dr. Judith Brills, *Gender Traps.*

Technoliteracy: Really, really understanding information technology.

Technophobe: Really, really afraid of information technology.

Road Warrior: A professional who travels constantly as part of her job responsibilities. Road warriors are not industry specific. They can be found anywhere: easily spotted running through any airport wearing expensive silk suit and Nikes—clutching a flapping mobile office stuffed with fax, modem, laptop, portable printer, cell phone, beeper, and two changes of underwear hidden in a black zippered pouch.

Outsourcing: As defined by Pam Williams, president (formerly a senior legal assistant) of Landmark, a San Jose, California, legal staffing organization: Taking over a function of a company versus providing an employee on a temp basis. This function is not part of the core business of the firm or company (that is, practicing law versus outsourcing the copyroom function), is usually a nuisance for the company to run, but is important.

Examples of outsourced areas within a law firm are mailroom, legal research, human resources, accounting, copyroom, coding department, temporary staffing, in-house litigation support and MIS departments, janitorial, and library. Don't be surprised when firms outsource entire paralegal departments and even associates.

One management concept making its way through law firms is keeping only partners and key decision makers as full-time employees. All other staffing is outsourced allowing the firm or company to concentrate on the core business—what it does best. The concept of one-stop shopping for several related services is catching on. It is easier to deal with one supplier, and costs are usually fixed costs (agreed to up front).

Outsourced versus Temporary Staffing: As defined by Tom Cushing of Cushing and Bixler, a San Francisco-based legal staffing organization, temporary staffing refers to individual increments of producing capacity added at the margin of an organization (the "swing capacity" model). Outsourcing takes an entire function that is not among the core competencies of an organization and places it under management of a business whose core competencies do include that function. For example, a law firm's core competency may be delivery of top-drawer legal services. That does not imply that it is great at running its library, litigation support system, or other departments. By outsourcing the information management function, it may focus on core business, maintain cutting-edge capabilities, gain efficiencies, and reduce unit costs.

Outsourcing Potential: According to Peter Drucker, management guru, in 10 or 15 years, organizations may be outsourcing all work that is "support" rather than revenue-producing and all activities that do not offer career opportunities into senior management. (Source: *Wall Street Journal*, March 1995).

PARALEGAL INNER VIEW: JULIE HELLER—A TECHNOLOGY CAREER PATH SUCCESS STORY

Name: Julie Heller
Firm: Proskauer, Rose; New York, New York
Title: Practice Support Manager
Number of attorneys: 550
Education: B.A. from Yale, M.A. in social work from Columbia University
Prior history: I worked as a legal assistant for White and Case in New York from 1989 to 1990. During that period, I was a case manager on a large case that erupted and had a lot of databases. I decided not to go to law school because I burned out and wasn't getting more money for the work I was doing. I was getting the salary of a first-year paralegal, but I was doing more than that. I was managing complex litigation and had a large staff. I was also overseeing the summer interns.

I took about a year to figure out what I wanted to do. I decided to go into social work and got my master's degree in social work. During the time in grad school, I got to know the practice support manager and went to work part-time as a document coder for 5 years during nights and weekends. I was doing social work full-time. I got involved in new software as the field was moving toward imaging. Towards 1996, my last social work job lost state funding and the agency closed my program and offered a lesser position which I didn't want. I bailed and went back to White and Case on a big project. I was referred to a position at Skadden, Arps in New York in litigation support in the fall of '96.

I received a unique offer from Uniscribe and went to work for them in 1998. I was hired to be the on-site manager at White and Case. Uniscribe provided litigation support for the firm which was outsourcing the management and production staff of that department. I was the manager with a database supervisor and six coders. I met with attorneys, prepared project specs, coded manuals, trained coders, and prepared presentations to different groups about automation, software selection, consulting, converting data, and I worked with the information systems group on litigation support. We had an on-site imaging and scanning center and provided on-site bibliographic coding and updates. The political environment was challenging. I came into a situation where I was a vendor. The firm's expectations were very high.

This combination of vendor-on-premises sounds very challenging. Did you have to overcome any obstacles?

Politics. How do you play? I'm not a very political person. I tell people what I think and why. A lot of attorneys expect the nonlegal staff to kowtow to them which is not my nature. Sure, we're being paid by their revenues, but we have a value to add being an expert they are not. There is a lot of anxiety as an attorney when you are relying on someone to tell you something. There is always a need to justify automating a case. There's no way you can manually manage a million documents. The day-to-day project planning is easy. The difficulty is politics and personalities of a large firm.

What has been your most gratifying experience?

There have been a number of projects where we met our goals and came in on time. That, and knowing that when you train someone, they use the system well.

Where do you go from here?

I have a new position here at Proskauer which gives me a broader background in technology issues, away from litigation support and into IS management. Whether I stay in the legal field or move into the corporate environment is several years away. There is a big difference working for a vendor providing litigation support than working in a law firm. A vendor is one more step removed from the food chain. One step lower. That's a big consideration I didn't know about.

What's your opinion about where this profession is headed?

I think that there is going to be a dichotomy of the consulting end of electronic discovery and the opposite end where there are skilled people doing the processing. There will be less need for coding in the future. That's what people are waiting for—no coders. I think the tech people in legal are techies and generally don't understand what a lawyer needs. Those who do know are in a good position to provide a high level of service.

Are you making big bucks?

If I'm not working 60 hours a week, I'm making a good salary for the lifestyle I'm living.

Give us some words of wisdom.

For those looking to get into the field, working for a firm is a better place to start. You'll get broader experience and be treated better. There is a lot of opportunity for people who are computer literate to move into this area. There is a blurring now of what paralegals do and what junior litigation support people do. A lot of paralegals are working in this tech area in smaller firms. Be sure you learn all about databases.

CHAPTER 5

Paralegal Careers in the New Millennium

Basically, the only incentive a person needs to accept a job is to be shown another job where the work is the same but the pay is a little less.

Jerry Seinfeld, *SeinLanguage,* Bantam Books

OVERVIEW

Paralegals have infiltrated just about every position available in the legal field and beyond. What was once termed a "traditional" paralegal is now merely a segment of the market. Some paralegals translated skills into "alternative careers." Normal attrition, burnout, and downsizing forced some paralegals out of the field. Others crossed over into positions within the legal field but away from paralegal positions.

Some paralegal practice areas haven't changed too much over the years. What has changed is technology, levels of assignment (upward or downwards), more positive acceptance from lawyers, unprecedented client demand, increased hiring in corporations and the government sector, and more independent paralegals.

In discussing the many different career options you have, notice that some of the positions have overlapping descriptions and similar job descriptions. You may discover a position that sounds familiar but you know it by another title. These options are in both corporations and firms. Some positions may have cross-training requirements, while others are so highly specialized that you may have to dig deep to get one.

If the idea of learning new areas of law appeals to you, this chapter can introduce you to many alternatives. Cross-training (the act of learning more than one speciality or skill) has been the saving grace for many paralegals. As the economy rocks and rolls, cross-trained paralegals bring value to the firm through abilities to shift gears when specialities are gained or lost in the firms. Before getting too excited about a possible new route for you, consider:

1. Do you want to move out of your firm and need to expand your specialty to do it?

2. If you are not seeking employment elsewhere, are you certain these new areas are compatible with practice areas and needs of the firm?

3. Are you seeking to upgrade your position? If so, what does that mean?

4. Would you prefer to transfer to another area in the firm and need to learn more about other areas of law?

5. Have you investigated both the history and future for this specialty?

If you are toying with the idea of moving up, over, or out, the following topics are a few options to consider. REMEMBER: Hot and cold markets vary due to economic conditions of the general economy and region. Other factors influencing a specialty's viability are new government regulations, client demand, number of practicing attorneys in the specialty, available paralegal training, technology, and general interest.

TRADITIONAL PARALEGAL POSITIONS

Corporate Paralegal: Draft agreements, process Uniform Commercial Code (UCC) searches, direct formation and maintenance of domestic and foreign corporations, participate in bank closings, prepare deeds of trust and real estate documents. Areas of responsibility and knowledge include stock issuance, drafting legal agreements, blue-sky laws, mergers and acquisitions, securities law, preparing and filing corporate documents, EDGAR, preparing audit letters, assisting with closing commercial bank loans, due diligence on corporate acquisitions, regulatory and bankruptcy filings, and UCC searches. May need to know franchising. Knowledge of venture capital and financial institutions is helpful. Excellent business writing, drafting, communication, organizational, and interpersonal skills are necessary.

A subspecialty, usually paying very well, is *Securities Legal Assistant*. Positions are found in both law firms and in-house legal departments. Thorough knowledge of securities, merger and acquisitions, SEC regulations, Blue-Sky laws, EDGAR, compliance and real estate transactional matters usually required. Many employers require a 4-year degree and some require a paralegal certificate.

Corporate Maintenance Paralegal: Responsibilities include formation and maintenance of domestic and foreign corporations, partnerships, and joint ventures; executing corporate dissolutions and mergers; coordinating domestic qualifications of foreign corporations; preparing closing binders; drafting corporate resolutions; maintaining corporation database; researching ramifications and consequences of corporate and tax laws. The person must be detail oriented, have excellent follow-through, and communicate effectively with clients.

Transactional Paralegal: This position specializes in one or more of the following areas: ERISA, ESOPS, Corporate Tax, Securities, I.P.O. (initial public offerings), real estate, and finance. The paralegal may also work with firms representing individuals, privately held businesses, and banks involved in venture capital, real estate, acquisitions, financings, and formations. A tax and business background helps.

Bankruptcy Paralegal: This position is found in all sized firms. The paralegal works with Chapters 7, 11, and 13 bankruptcy and with workouts.

In-House Legal Department Paralegal Positions: (Sometimes referred to as "corporate" paralegals, not to be confused with the practice specialty.) In-house legal department paralegals' expertise can vary from corporate to litigation, real estate, immigration, regulatory, maritime, employment law, international law, intellectual property, and employee benefits. Specializations can include garnishments, corporate law, customs, trademarks, copyrights, environment, construction defect, franchising, securities, merchandising, financial services, and legal compliance (to name a few). Any of these in-house positions may also be found in law firms.

Mutual Fund Paralegal: Areas of expertise include initial and renewal registrations, mergers, compliance, risk management, management of litigation documents, and intellectual property.

FDA/Regulatory Paralegal: This paralegal specializes in FDA and DEA regulatory/compliance work; FTC and CPSC regulation, managed care, antitrust/unfair practices, work with outside counsel; initial trademark review; and real estate. Positions can be found within pharmaceutical companies, medical device companies, and health care products corporations.

International Holding Company Paralegal: This position requires experience in a wide variety of areas including mergers and acquisitions, securities, real estate, international law, customs, trademark, banking, and more. The paralegal needs strong communication skills, possibly multilingual abilities, and strong organization and analytical skills while possessing expert business acumen.

Patent Paralegal: This position normally does not have numerous openings, and when they do occur, there is a lack of qualified candidates. We have experienced a noticeable increase in openings as of late. There are two skill levels: patent prosecution and new patent filings, requiring knowledge of application procedures and pending applications. A more sophisticated level involves protection, infringement, and related matters, such as reviewing material transfer and confidentiality agreements. Various specialties include the emerging medical device companies, information technology, organic chemistry, and the pharmaceutical and biotechnic industries. Some paralegals work closely with research and development department staff to identify and protect new technology. Background in electrical engineering, materials science, electro optics, and/or physics is preferred. Superior legal and technical writing skills are required; education in mechanical arts is helpful. The paralegal can function as technical patent support to outside patent litigation firms.

Computer Law Paralegal: This position involves drafting and assisting in negotiations of hardware, software, maintenance, network, and software development agreements. Knowledge of the Internet, relevant legal issues, and thorough understanding of hardware, software, and software publishers is required. Additional experience may be required in general corporate law, business transactions (including licensing, merchandising, and distribution), and intellectual property. The paralegal needs excellent research and writing skills and the ability to work well with all levels of clients and management.

Intellectual Property Specialist/Corporation: This position can encompass a wide variety of experience, including patent procurement experience in mining, petroleum, biochemistry, biotechnics, medicine, pharmaceuticals, film publishing and music entertainment fields, agricultural chemicals, specialty organic chemicals, and health care technology. There can be involvement with foreign patents, including opposition, and work with corporations' domestic and international trademark portfolios, comprising mark selection, registration, and defensive measures. Responsibilities include contract negotiating and drafting for commercial legal matters, technology and trademark licensing, copyrights, acquisitions, and divestitures. The paralegal must have the ability to interface comfortably with corporate executives, paralegals, researchers, and outside counsel.

Environmental Paralegal: This paralegal works in litigation or with government agencies and lobbyists involved with environmental issues; toxic tort; and complex cases such as nuclear power plants, land use, zoning laws, agriculture, technology-related issues, and petroleum and energy issues.

Corporate and International Paralegal: Work with corporations in commercial, domestic, and international areas of law. (Position can also be found in some major firms.) Responsibilities include complex, legal, regulatory, and business matters such as international and domestic commercial transactions, joint ventures, mergers and acquisitions, securities laws, compliance programs, project management, corporate restructurings, corporate governance, and general corporate matters. A 4-year degree and paralegal certificate are generally required.

Employment Paralegal: Assist lawyers in employment law, employment litigation, health and safety matters, and contracts. Current demand appears to focus on insurance, high tech, HMOs, staffing organizations, and the automobile and banking industries. The paralegal handles employment discriminations, sexual harassment matters, ADR, unemployment hearings, and preparation of manuals.

Tax Paralegal: This position can require a wide variety of responsibilities. A 4-year degree is usually required. A few assignments may include assisting in mergers and acquisitions, finance, electric and gas projects, bankruptcy matters, leasing and general corporate work, reduction of costs, and corporate streamlining. Tax paralegals have also provided attorneys with research for articles and speeches (some even write for them). Positions may be found in many Fortune 1000 corporations (and some major and boutique law firms.) Strong communication, organizational, analytical, mathematics, and project management skills are necessary. Being bilingual with German, Mandarin Chinese, Spanish, French, Russian, or Japanese is helpful. The paralegal may work with various federal, state, and local courts and government and regulatory agencies. Excellent computer, communication, and interpersonal skills are necessary. Many corporations require a 2- or 4-year degree.

Litigation Paralegal: Some positions concentrate only on the discovery process; others range from "womb to tomb," that is, from filing of complaint through trial and posttrial. Some responsibilities are cite checking, document handling, trial prep, document production, drafting of legal briefs, legal and factual research, factual investigation, locating expert witnesses, preparing case budgets, assembling teams, and attending trial. Computer skills in WordPerfect, Microsoft Word, Word for Windows, Windows, spreadsheet, research (LEXIS and Westlaw), and database management programs are generally required. Litigation paralegal covers a multitude of subspecialties including:

1. **In-House Litigation Paralegal**
   These positions can take on a variety of tasks such as managing claims, insurance matters, patent and trademark, drafting real estate leases, summarizing depositions, computerized litigation support, trial prep, attending trial or settlement conferences. Toxic tort, general corporate, employment, products liability, biotechnics (litigation and patent), business and complex litigation, and medical malpractice are only a few areas of practice. The position requires a detail-oriented professional with excellent communication, computer, and organizational skills.

2. **Business Transactions**
   This responsibility includes business transactions, securities, and technology assignments. Excellent writing skills are required.

3. **Document Analysts and Coders**
   Usually an entry-level paying position involved in coding projects.

Prior coding experience is helpful. Strong computer data entry skills are required in programs such as WordPerfect, Word, Concordance, Summation, Discovery ZX, and Access (to name a few). These positions are concentrated in certain regions of the country, such as metropolitan areas. They are also found in second- or third-tier rapidly growing cities that have a significant college population, such as Tucson and Phoenix, Arizona; Herndon and Alexandria, Virginia; and the Silicon Valley in California. Other popular metropolitan areas are New York, Los Angeles, Minneapolis, Dallas, Washington D.C., and Chicago.

4. **Case Clerks**
   This is usually an entry-level position responsible for general clerical duties, such as numbering, organizing, indexing, entering documents, trial binder coordination, and summarizing depositions.

Senior Litigation Legal Assistant—Complex Litigation: Assignments can include large, complex case management and involvement in all phases of trial preparation (discovery and document production); trial and supervisory duties; at times, media-attracting cases, high-profile personalities, politically volatile issues. The position may require significant experience in litigating complex, multiparty cases involving issues of contract, tort, and statutory law. Excellent legal and factual research skills and strong organization skills are required. The paralegal primarily interfaces with firm attorneys and employees. Some positions do not offer client interfacing. Ability to work under pressure, work overtime, meet deadlines, and possibly travel is often required.

Senior Litigation Legal Assistant: This position requires experience in drafting documents, pleadings, correspondence; legal research; client interaction; preparing for and attending trial; preparing motions; preparing chronologies and outlines for depositions; locating witnesses; preparing witnesses; factual research; preparing settlement agreements; knowledge of ADR. The senior professional may also supervise and manage other paralegals and support staff. The position usually requires excellent computer skills, including database management, word processing, spreadsheets, knowledge of online services, and a solid litigation support background.

Midlevel Paralegal; 2 to 4 Years Experience: Due to the recent recession, many firms and corporations are having a difficult time finding the midlevel paralegal in several areas, including litigation, corporate, and some real estate.

Intellectual Property Paralegal: Involves a wide range of industries, such as film, publishing, TV, computers, and software programs. Litigation includes copyright, patent, and trademark prosecution. Responsibilities can include filing patents and foreign and domestic trademarks; handling renewals, legal research, patent and trademark searches and watches; and calendaring. Sometimes litigation experience is required.

Real Estate Paralegal: Real estate paralegals are showing up in firms and corporations. International hotels, commercial development, condominiums, resorts, and casinos are just a few of the highly specialized areas for which both firms and corporations are hiring. The paralegal must draft, assemble, and organize closing documents for real estate financing, acquisitions, commercial leases, and other transactions. Additional requirements may include knowledge of title and survey matters, strong written and oral communication skills, and computer literacy.

Probate Paralegal: This position is concerned with probate estate and trust administration, court accounting, and estate taxes. The paralegal should have word processing and spreadsheet knowledge and good interpersonal skills. The position is generally found in smaller firms. Major firms rarely provide these services anymore. Independent paralegals working directly with law firms can do quite well.

Entertainment Paralegal: These highly sought after positions are usually located in firms, studios, production companies, TV studios, radio stations, and distribution companies. They may require experience in merchandising, trademarks, copyrights, and trademark prosecution. Some paralegals negotiate simple contracts and location agreements and work with SAG (Screen Actors Guild), DGA (Directors Guild), Writers Guild, and others. Others specialize in music or music publishing and must know about distribution of royalties. These positions are found usually in Los Angeles, New York, San Francisco, Nashville, London, and other entertainment industry-driven markets.

Television Show Legal Assistant: This might go under the highly specialized unusual category. The paralegal will prepare AFTRA, Directors, Writers, and Producers Guild agreements; clear titles, prepare royalty statements; and work in business affairs or legal departments. Lately, legal assistants have received acknowledgment in the credits.

Labor Law Paralegal: This is a detail-oriented professional who can provide general assistance for employment matters. The responsibilities include analyzing pleadings, such as complaints, answers, demurrers, motions, and points and authorities, and performing factual investigation. Strong organizational skills and ability to maintain/update a litigation records database are required.

Construction Paralegal: This paralegal specializes in plaintiff or defense construction defect litigation. Knowledge of real estate, topography, construction, building industry, unions, approval committees, permits, electrical contracting, plumbing, condominium laws, and equipment is helpful. Organizational skills are required.

Insurance Defense Paralegal: This paralegal must be able to function in a high-pressure production-oriented environment. Responsibilities include management of large case load, trial work, multitasking, and drafting of complex legal documents. Responsibilities can include assisting attorneys in management of multiple cases through trial; subpoenaing medical records; preparing medical chronologies; preparing witness lists and trial binders; and summarizing deposition transcripts and discovery responses. This position usually requires knowledge of Microsoft Word, WordPerfect, spreadsheet, and database management programs. (Also found in in-house legal departments of insurance companies for complex general liability cases.)

UNUSUAL TRADITIONAL PARALEGAL JOBS

The following is a sampling of actual paralegal positions with unique specialty requirements.

Paralegal/Communications Advisor with Expertise in Employee Benefits: Responsibilities include IRS 5500 filings and employee benefits communications. Requirements are experience in benefits tax law, excellent writing skills, 4-year college degree, and analytical and interpersonal skills.

Litigation Paralegal Specializing in Minority Owned Businesses: A challenging position with experience in litigation, corporate law, or both. The position requires a flexible self-starter able to handle multiple tasks. Travel may be involved. Strong research and writing skills and an interest in assisting with entrepreneurs are helpful.

International Law: This position involves international trade and legislative assignments. Strong research and writing skills are required. Qualifications include a 4-year degree and related work experience.

Indian Law: Representation of Native American Indian tribes.

Assistant to County Counsel: County Counsel provides civil legal services and provides opinions concerning the actions, duties, and powers of represented entities. The paralegal assists at trial and appellate reviews; monitors legislation, regulation, and court decisions; researches and gathers information for attorneys to advise the Board of Supervisors and management on potential liability issues.

Air Quality Legal Assistant: This position assists attorneys in evaluating and planning for long-term air quality improvement needs. Experience in civil law working with or in public agencies or environmental law experience is helpful.

Credit Finance: The paralegal assists attorneys in structuring and restructuring credit arrangements on behalf of institutional creditors, leasing companies, finance companies, or other participants in various credit transactions. Prior industry experience is preferred. A 4-year degree may be required.

Hospital Specialty Paralegal: This position handles medical review board hearings; employment law, business, and contract litigation; medical malpractice claims; emergency room, psychiatric ward, surgery, ICU, CCU, and related hospital matters.

Eminent Domain Litigation Paralegal: Responsibilities include trial preparation, legal research, and drafting briefs and pleadings. The paralegal should possess excellent oral and written communication skills and be adept at handling case management responsibilities.

Energy and Natural Resources Assistant: This position requires an environmental background, research skills, factual investigation, monitoring of legislation, and attending public agency hearings.

Legal Assistance Program: Responsibilities include assisting attorneys who provide low-cost legal services in wills and estates, landlord-tenant and consumer affairs, real property, civil suits, taxes, nonsupport and indebtedness, civil rights, adoptions, domestic relations, and more.

Legal Assistant, Schools Specialist: The paralegal assists public or private schools, school districts, unions, and university and college general counsel. Some positions are available in school employee unions. Responsibilities include assisting attorneys in general corporate and employment law. Strong analytical and communication skills, public sector labor law experience, and benefits background are helpful.

Nonprofit Corporations Law: An international not-for-profit organization is an interesting place for paralegals. Cross-trained legal assistants for one particular agency were required to have a J.D. and 2+ years law firm experience in corporate law and litigation or 5+ years paralegal experience and ABA-approved paralegal certificate. The responsibilities include maintaining ongoing corporate matters, litigation support, coordinating donated properties, and life estate management.

Consumer Affairs/Lemon Law: The paralegal usually manages a high-volume caseload of warranty and "lemon law" matters for automobile manufacturers and importers, so experience with warranties is preferred. Responsibilities will be to draft discovery responses, perform legal research, and handle claims. The paralegal should have excellent writing abilities and computer literacy.

Professional Liability Defense: First-party coverage litigation (may include environmental, construction defects, advertising injury coverage) and bad faith litigation are highly specialized positions. Experience in First Amendment and media issues may be required. The paralegal should have excellent academic credentials and strong writing skills.

Transportation Legal Assistant: This position is within the transportation industry, usually in an in-house legal department. The paralegal assists attorneys in drafting pleadings, litigation, bankruptcy, claims, workers compensation, or commercial contracts. The person should have excellent communication skills and possibly environmental background.

Public Defender Paralegal: This paralegal assists in the public defender's office interviewing witnesses and inmates. It is a high-volume position in a fast-paced work atmosphere. The paralegal may work on capital, criminal, or white-collar crime cases and may work directly with incarcerated defendants. Academic and experience requirements vary.

Stock Compensation Paralegal: This position includes stock plan drafting and compliance work with responsibilities for private and public company bases. Strong communication and organization skills, computer literacy, and a bachelor's degree are required. A paralegal certificate is preferred. The position is usually highly compensated.

Nurse/Paralegal: A paralegal with nursing background is ideal for firms and corporations concerned with pharmaceuticals, medical malpractice, health care, insurance defense, products liability, and personal injury. The paralegal reviews medical records, testimony, medical analyses, and diagnoses.

Insurance Coverage: This position requires a strong understanding of coverage litigation. D&O, fidelity, surety, subrogation, property, or professional liability coverage experience is generally required.

HIGHLY SPECIALIZED, VERY NARROW MARKETS

Bikers' Firm: Very narrow, limited market, but it is interesting work with attorneys specializing in motorcycle accidents. The paralegal must know all about motorcycles and products liability law.

Travel Industry Specialists: This position requires familiarization with travel industry regulations, international law, business litigation, resort areas, tort law, contracts, franchising, and more.

Franchise Paralegal: The paralegal specializes in franchise contracts for large corporations in personnel, travel, mailbox, restaurant, hospitality, and other industries.

Products Liability—Pharmaceutical Specialist: This is a highly specialized litigation position within pharmaceutical companies or law firms with a products liability specialty. Responsibilities include assisting attorneys, medical analysts, and other legal professionals in analyzing and summarizing records, documents, and medical records; preparing time lines and deposition digests; corresponding with counsel, medical personnel, and police departments. There can be heavy interface with clients.

Resorts Specialists: These paralegals work for firms representing large resorts. Paralegals should know real estate law, environmental law, financing, litigation, mergers and acquisitions, and securities law.

Public TV Paralegal: Working for a nonprofit organization, the paralegal reviews SAG and AFTRA agreements, works with unions, researches facts, and handles scheduling and credits. Usually the paralegal duties are in the business affairs department.

Sports Law: Few positions in this area are available; however, it can be a very exciting position working with high-profile athletes.

Technology Licensing: Technology licensing is an emerging-companies practice specialty. It involves work in technology licensing, development, and distribution arrangements. Outstanding academic credentials and relevant law firm or comparable work experience are required.

CAREERS IN THE SMALL OR BOUTIQUE FIRM

These practice specialty areas are generally found in smaller firms. However, don't overlook the possibility that almost any of the positions under the other reference lists may be found here.

Family Law
Plaintiff's Personal Injury
Probate, Estate Planning, and Trusts
Business Litigation
Elder Law
Employment Law
Business Tax Law
Civil Litigation
Criminal Litigation
White-Collar Crime
Tax Law
Children's Rights
Automobile Accident
Workers Compensation
Admiralty Law
Maritime Law
Plaintiff's Insurance Coverage
Insurance Defense
Health Care
Environmental Law
Professional Malpractice Defense Law

ALTERNATIVE CAREERS WITHIN THE LAW FIRM OR IN-HOUSE LEGAL DEPARTMENT

The ability to translate your paralegal skills into other careers within the law firm or legal department provides a zig-zag approach to expanding your career. Just a few of those positions are the following:

Conflict Analyst: This position researches cases for conflict of interest. Conflict of interest software program experience and positive customer service skills may be required.

Systems/Network Administrator: Usually, at least 2 years plus network/computer experience are required to administer and provide long-term strategy for all aspects of extensive computer systems. Knowledge of LANs, WANs, document management, spreadsheet, and database programs is a must. Responsibilities include the design and implementation of firmwide training programs, evaluation and instruction of new programs, and troubleshooting day-to-day operational and systems problems.

Patent Database Administrator: This is an experienced database coordinator with knowledge of patent prosecution and databases.

Human Resources Director: This position requires employment law experience, recruiting skills, and excellent oral and written communication skills. It involves budget planning and recruiting new associates, paralegals, and support staff.

Paralegal Administrator/Manager: This position is responsible for supervising, recruiting, training, assigning workload, and evaluating paralegals within the firm or in-house legal department. In recent years, paralegal managers have bottom-line profit and loss responsibility. It is listed here because it generally falls under a middle- or upper-management classification. Financial, managerial, human resources, and training skills differentiate it from a paralegal position.

Some paralegal managers are required to bill time and perform administrative duties. The deciding factor is usually size of the program, turnover factors, temporary staffing requirements, and number of offices managed. Average salaries for major firms (New York, Los Angeles, San Francisco, Minneapolis, Chicago) range from $50,000 to $95,000 and are generally classified exempt. Bonuses can be based on profitability of the program.

Technical Trainer: This position oversees computer operations and training programs. It requires 4 to 5 years' experience.

Director of Client Development: The function of this position is to manage or direct the firm's marketing program, including hands-on coordination of promotional materials and editing, layout and design of written materials. It requires working knowledge of relational databases and spreadsheet software, marketing experience, law firm background, 4-year

degree, strong oral and written communication skills, and ability to interact well at all levels of the organization.

Records Manager: This manager is in charge of daily operations and
handling of files and file rooms. Excellent planning, organizational, supervisory, and communication skills are required, plus experience with a
management/file room.

Assistant Manager of Information Systems: This position helps support users and must identify and react to problems as they arise. Responsibilities include user training and telephone/voice mail administration.
Strong interpersonal skills are required. College degree and related law
firm experience are preferred.

Office Manager: Responsibilities of this position include budget planning; recruiting, hiring, training, advising, and evaluating support staff;
facilities management; assisting with summer associate program and evaluation; and overseeing MIS functions.

Office Administrator: A hands-on administrator for a midsized to small
firm should be computer literate, have experience with the general ledger,
employment law, policies and procedures, employee benefit packages,
partner compensation, human resources, time and billing procedures, lease
negotiations, facilities management, outsourcing, financial reports, payroll,
and accounts receivable and payable. Responsibilities include overseeing
general office administration.

Director of Administration: This management position is usually
highly compensated in a large firm and generally requires an M.B.A., J.D.,
or CPA, and comparable large-firm experience. The director is responsible
for all personnel and departments with the exception of attorney and paralegal staff. Must be techno-literate; knowledgeable of time and billing procedures and software, profit and loss documentation, and budgets; must
assist in long-term strategic planning. Salaries can range anywhere from
$65,000 to $250,000, depending on size, location, and prestige of firm.

Human Resources Manager: This position requires knowledge of
human resources issues, employment law, state labor laws, benefits, insurances, recruiting procedures, training and retention programs, payroll,

temporary staffing, and sexual harassment and discrimination laws. Excellent oral and communication skills are necessary.

Computer Trainer: The trainer should have at least 2 years' experience with curriculum development and microcomputer training to teach attorneys and support staff.

Information Services Paralegal: This paralegal trains personnel on recent changes in state and administrative procedures, assists attorneys and workers with legal issues, designs, and presents substantive law seminars for customers, and maintains an infobase consisting of the organization's accumulated knowledge. Experience may be necessary in preparing and filing corporate and/or UCC documents.

Computer Support Assistant: Provide technical support for network and computer system products and applications and support to end users. The assistant may be required to have current knowledge of many software programs. Experience is also necessary in configuring and troubleshooting PC hardware and peripherals; network experience may be preferred. The position also requires 1 to 3 years' experience in computer systems and a legal background.

Litigation Support Management: Here is a logical step for litigation paralegals, managing a full range of litigation support activities. Needed is an extensive knowledge of litigation support applications with emphasis on document database technology and imaging; ability to work effectively with a matrix organization; excellent communications skills; and ability to interface with all levels of management and support staff. Responsibilities include coordination of databases; training and overseeing personnel involved in coding, imaging, and scanning; developing and maintaining procedures based upon "best practices." Creativity is required in pursuing process improvements.

Business System Analyst: The ideal candidate for this new law firm position is responsible for system maintenance and database management; assisting in implementation and support of firmwide business software applications, including human resources (HR) information systems, financial systems, records, conflicts, and other software systems; analysis of

HR benefits and payroll procedures; design, coding, and processing of user-defined products. Required are business applications programming experience using a relational database; HR, payroll, or financial analysis experience; familiarity with client/server technology, networks, and word-processing programs. Excellent communication and presentation skills are also required.

Automation/Network Administrator: At least 1 year's experience is required to administer user and e-mail accounts on a network; troubleshoot hardware and software issues; oversee firm telecommunications; and maintain, evaluate, and upgrade systems. Database knowledge is necessary. Ability to train end users on software packages is preferred. The candidate must have strong verbal communication skills.

Legal Files Specialist: The legal files specialist must handle all aspects of records storage operations including transmittal of boxes, retrieval, and final disposition; maintain recordkeeping software function as a liaison with off-site vendors; train new employees on software; and monitor customer service issues. You may be asked to oversee department work in the absence of the legal files manager and assist the manager with special projects. This position usually requires experience in several fields such as records management, library, information services, or paralegal support. Excellent communication and organization skills are required as well as the ability to solve problems and handle a variety of tasks under pressure. Strong computer and database management aptitude are required.

Calendar Court Services Assistant: This employee must work with the Calendar Court Services department or team usually within a larger or midsized firm or corporation, and provide court services and support. Your responsibilities could include the filing of pleadings at local courts, retrieval of information from nationwide databases, providing of information on filing requirements, and documenting of possible impact of changes in court rules. You might maintain the calendar court database by entering or updating information daily, oversee the precedent files as an information resource, obtain Certificates of Good Standing, review court mail, and calculate due dates.

Contract Negotiator: This is a position found primarily in corporate legal departments. A research, development, and commercialization program for the natural gas industry recently advertised for a contract negotiator to negotiate, draft, and administrate all types of contractual documents, including sophisticated research contracts; technology licensing of intellectual property contracts; and grants and consultant agreements with government agencies, independent research and development facilities, universities, manufacturing corporations, and other cosponsoring organizations.

Trademark Docketing Specialist: A trademark docketing specialist maintains an active docket of U.S. and foreign patents and trademarks, produces client reports, manages PTO deposit accounts, and performs related docketing responsibilities. CPI knowledge plus outstanding oral and written communication skills are necessary.

Patent Searcher Supervisor: This person conducts patent searches, and usually needs a B.S. in related fields of biology, chemistry, or electrical engineering.

Litigation Technology Analyst: The litigation technology analyst assists with the design of the automated litigation support system; recommends litigation support software systems; trains lawyers and support staff on the systems; and coordinates, evaluates, and recommends outside services for lawyers. This position usually requires a degree in related area, as well as a working knowledge of database design, conversion, access, and data input and retrieval systems. Project management skills and knowledge of the litigation process, focusing on discovery or trial, are important.

Investigations: These specialists work with the public defender service, offering substantive administrative and/or managerial experience. They can supervise staff, and have knowledge and training in criminal investigations.

Director of Marketing Services: Directors of marketing services oversee a full spectrum of communication strategies and programs on a local, national, or international basis. They must have experience with legal business media, development of marketing materials, Web site development, and advertising and branding elements. They must be prepared to supervise departmental staff, oversee the execution of direct mail activities, maintenance of directory listings, event planning and development and monitoring of the firm's marketing budget. The job usually requires managerial experience in law firm marketing or communications, excellent written and verbal communications skills, and the ability to operate in a time-sensitive environment.

Financial Coordinators: Responsibilities of financial coordinators include various billing and receivables for the law firm. Financial coordinators work in the accounting department.

Schools and Colleges: Here is a unique position providing confidential and professional support to attorneys in a variety of matters including workers' compensation, subpoenae, liability claims, student bankruptcy, and FOIA requests. You may maintain and update the law library, file legal pleadings and other documents in federal and state courts as well as with governmental and administrative agencies. You may also conduct manual and electronic legal research using the law library, local agencies, and the Internet. Computer proficiency is usually required, including word processing and spreadsheets. You should be able to work well with employees at all levels and handle situations with tact, persuasiveness, and diplomacy. Excellent writing and verbal communication skills are necessary.

City Attorney's Office: The City of Evanston, Illinois, had an opening for an assistant to help with zoning opinions and ordinances; special assessments; property taxes; various court calls; drafting and reviewing ordinances and resolutions for City Council approval; and processing wage deductions and bankruptcy claims.

UNUSUAL TRADITIONAL POSITIONS

Energy, Environmental, Natural Resources and Transportation: These employees work on legal, legislative, and regulatory issues and should be familiar with FERC filings; proficient in cite-checking and bluebooking. Practice usually includes representation of natural gas distribution companies, natural gas and electric power marketers, electric utilities, power producers, and clients who have regulatory transactions issues.

ACLU Paralegal: ACLU paralegals work with accomplished, hardworking, tenacious, principled defenders of freedom and justice for all. They must have an excellent grasp of constitutional law, superb writing ability, and possess familiarity of legislature. They could be required to work in crime, reproductive rights, privacy rights, or in a variety of other areas.

Sierra Club: Sierra Club employees work with attorneys in key environmental lawsuits and help coordinate the club's large nationwide litigation docket. They should have excellent writing and interpersonal skills and political savvy.

Paralegal Technical Writer: A global software and development company focusing on the total automation of electronic trading sought a paralegal with 5 years' corporate experience to write resolutions, draft and file state-mandated filings, and assist in general corporate and contractual law issues. The candidate was required to have experience in intellectual property and ability and desire to write preliminary patent applications for software inventions.

Commodity Futures Trading Commission Paralegal: The CCFTC sought an experienced paralegal in its Division of Enforcement in Chicago for a litigation position.

TRADITIONAL POSITIONS

Corporate In-House Legal Assistant: These assistants are involved in the formation, formalities, and maintenance of corporations, partnerships, and LLCs; litigation management and responding to discovery requests; and drafting and review of general corporate legal documents and general legal research. They should have strong computer and oral and written skills, and possess the ability to respond to multiple requests for information in a timely manner.

In-House Technology Paralegal: In-house technology paralegals work in law departments supporting in-house attorneys. They perform legal and factual research using Westlaw, Lexis/Nexis and the Internet with emphasis on government contract issues; review various types of corporate contracts and agreements including software license agreements; review real estate leasing documents; document management for litigation related to contract disputes and protests; and respond to subpoenas, including locating, indexing, and preparing documents for production. They should be self-starters; have exceptional organizational skills and the ability to handle multiple priorities; and possess effective communication and interpersonal skills as well as the ability to work in a team environment.

Repository Manager: Litigation support companies seek paralegals with litigation case management skills, preferably complex litigation. Many repositories are now on-line. Excellent computer and organizational skills are required.

HOTTEST SKILLS AND SPECIALTIES

If Alan Greenspan can't predict where the economy's headed, how can mere mortals make such predictions? Those in-house legal department positions that most sources quote as "hot" depend on who you talk to. According to *Corporate Legal Times,* conflicting factors mean that the direction of the in-house job market is anyone's call. The rise in associate salaries and consequent increase in law firm rates forces legal departments to reexamine both costs and their decisions to make versus buy legal services. As outside costs rise, more legal departments will bring work in-house causing in-house hiring to expand. Acquisitions, international expansion, e-commerce—in short, everything corporations do today is more legal-intensive. It requires talented attorneys and paralegals in-house who understand the business.

As law firm salaries continue to grow, a number of attorneys and paralegals can be expected to jump ship from in-house departments back to the law firm. More in-house counsel and paralegal movement to law firms creates more vacancies in legal departments.

Despite an economy that's strong and growing, the rock-and-roll stock market has caused some jitters. Companies are reluctant to add positions if they fear that a weaker economy—and layoffs—are imminent. *Corporate Legal Times* is quick to point out that the booming economy means companies are less price-sensitive and are more likely to use law firms—and incur a cost that's higher than the cost of adding a new employee to the payroll. Low unemployment rates discourage some employers from undertaking a search for new employees because the search takes longer and is more expensive than when the unemployment rates are higher. Here are just a few takes on what's hot and what's cooling off at press time. Bear in mind, however, that things change quickly.

Acquisitions: Always getting hotter in a good economy. A paralegal who understands the art of the deal, contracts, closing documents, perhaps some real estate, mergers, due diligence, and more should do well in this arena.

ADA: *The Futurist*, a magazine forecasting trends and ideas about the future, predicts that as the workplace ages, more employees at all levels will have physical disabilities and more lawsuits charging discrimination will result. The push toward equal rights for disabled workers will be similar to the twentieth-century movements by African-Americans, feminists, and gays.

Antitrust: This practice specialty was triggered by increased merger and acquisition activity along with high profile matters involving Microsoft and Visa/MasterCard.

Transactional Corporate: Although there are fewer spots for transactionals than litigation, the transactional corporate paralegal at times leads the way in law firm demand. Harder to get, more costly to hire, fewer paralegal schools have offered this certificate than ever before. This position must work with securities, mergers and acquisitions, Blue-Sky research, and highly complex contracts and deals.

REITs: The real estate market is a roller coaster despite the economy. Right now, it seems to be waking up.

Bankruptcy: Chapter 11 filings are at this writing, not decreasing. Several reasons, despite a good economy, include high debt load, increased competition, and the use of reorganization through bankruptcy as an aid to ailing businesses.

Contracts: According to *Corporate Legal Times* (July 2000), 53 percent of general counsel respondents to the 11th Annual Corporate Legal Times Survey of General Counsel say they expect an increase in contracts-related legal work.

eHealth Law: Here is a new interdisciplinary practice combining health care with Internet law. More and more eHealth care sites have emerged including pharmaceutical sites, doctor "advice," and health and wellness. The practice specialty has also gotten hotter because the U.S. Health Insurance Portability and Accountability Act, passed in 1996, is just now being implemented, and businesses must comply.

Conservation: Easements that give landowners tax incentives to prevent development on their land are on the rise. North Carolina, Colorado, and

Virginia already offer such credits, and legislation is pending at press time or has just passed in Delaware, Hawaii, California, and South Carolina. This could give a huge spike to real estate practices even if the economy slows down.

Financial and Retirement Planning: One area expected to boom in the years ahead is financial and retirement planning as the nearly 77 million Baby Boomers begin reaching age 65 in 2011.

Intellectual Property: With the rise of the Internet and hardware and software, the demand for paralegals with expertise in intellectual property has risen as well. Few schools, if any, offer a certificate in intellectual property. (We know of only one at this writing—St. Mary's in Moraga, California.)

Nurse Paralegals: The demand for professionals to decipher medical records and events in legal proceedings is expanding, according to *Legal Assistant Today*. Nearly 50 paralegal programs geared toward the needs of the legal and health care industries are broadening paralegal career opportunities nationwide to include nurse/health care paralegal specialties. That number is expected to grow. Students with backgrounds in nursing or other health-science fields including physician assistant, occupational therapy, radiography, and applied health studies are considered for these positions. Nurse/health care paralegals and legal nurse consultants (LNC) may work in a variety of settings, including law firms, corporations, and government agencies on product liability, medical malpractice, and insurance-related cases. According to the Medical-Legal Consulting Institute's Web site, a resource center for nurses, LNC's can earn $60–$150 per hour. Contact the AAFPE (American Association for Paralegal Educators) for more information on nurse/paralegal programs.

Computer Skills: We've emphasized over and over the need for paralegals to expand their computer skills. Honest, folks, it's not going to go away. Just as most of us now cannot fathom life without TV, telephone, voice-mail and fax machines, so has the computer taken over our lives. You'll need to expand your knowledge to electronic evidence discovery; database management programs; time and billing; calendaring; spreadsheets; case management; desktop publishing; presentation; practice specific software; the Internet; and more.

Is It Hot or Is It Cold?

Insurance Defense: Insurance carriers continue to increase their in-house legal departments. The American Insurance Association, whose members are major carriers, strongly supports recent court rulings allowing the members to use their own staff attorneys to represent policyholders.

Growing Phenomenon

Law Actors: A growing phenomenon is professional actors who are hired to appear at trials to read prepared testimony for witnesses who cannot or will not appear. Lawyers and agents estimate that at least 200 "law actors" earn at least part of their living playing doctors, engineers, and accident witnesses in civil trials in Los Angeles and in other cities.

What's Slowing Down

As of press time, the growth of international legal work is slowing down. Seventy-two percent of general counsel respondents to the Corporate Legal Times Survey (for 1999) predicted an increase in international work. In the year 2000, only 46 percent of respondents expected an increase in the volume of international work.

The *Corporate Legal Times* survey pointed out that nothing was really "not hot." In no practice areas did a majority of respondents expect the volume of legal work to decrease. In fact, only in the areas of environmental law (12 percent) and litigation (13 percent) did a double-digit percentage of respondents predict a decline in volume.

If Relocation Is a Possibility

If you are seeking to relocate, *The Wall Street Journal* (November 23, 1999) has pinpointed the 13 hottest regions in America. Where areas are hot, particularly in technology, law firms are sure to follow if they haven't already. Hot areas also mean more in-house legal departments along with smaller firms that spring up to serve a booming economy. Get all your facts and information before you make a leap.

- Place: Billville. Washington state's Seattle-Redmond area is the Northwest's high-tech capital.
  - Specialties: Software, e-commerce and biotech. Microsoft alumni have emerged as important sources of venture capital for their own and others' start-ups in the region.

- Big players: Microsoft, Amazon.com, Vulcan Venture, RealNetworks, Inc., Nintendo of America, Immunex Corp., and Zymo-Genetics Inc., biotech divisions of major pharmaceutical companies.
- Hard data: The state of Washington is home to 10 billionaires. The Seattle area alone has 74,000 households with net worth exceeding $1 million excluding the value of their houses.
- Real estate horror story: $200,000 is a down payment in Medina, population 3,076, where the average assessed value of a house is over $1 million.

- Place: Multimedia Gulch. The collection of nose-ring-wearing neighborhoods south of San Francisco's Market Street—an area known as SoMA, the migration destination of new Web start-ups.
  - Specialties: SoMA was once the quiet home of auto-repair shops, small-time manufacturers, and blue-collar workers. But venture-capital-rich Netheads are slowly replacing them with loft homes and trendy offices. SoMA is home to the more creative Web types, such as ad agencies, content companies, and designers.
  - Big players: USWeb/CKS, LookSmart, *Wired* magazine and Spinner, a music company that AOL purchased for several hundred million dollars in stock.
  - Hard data: Investments in San Francisco's Internet companies are typically lumped in with the entire Silicon Valley region, which gets a lion's share of the cash.
  - Real estate horror story: Fourteen new lofts in SoMA priced above $500,000 sold out in one day.

- Place: Silicon Valley, California. (It's not on a map—locals say it's a state of mind.) Physically, it's a sprawling neighborhood from San Francisco to San Jose and beyond.
  - Specialties: Semiconductors, computer-networking equipment, and hundreds of Internet-related start-ups.
  - Big players: Hewlett-Packard, Intel Corp., Sun Microsystems Inc., Cisco Systems, Yahoo! Inc., Excite At Home, and eBay Inc.
  - Hard data: The region got $4.18 billion in high-tech venture capital funds for the first half of 1999—almost 40 percent of the funds available (according to Price-Waterhouse).
  - Real estate horror story: The down payment on a Palo Alto fixer-upper runs about $200,000.

- Place: Hollywood.com. The Digital Coast is a stretch of Southern California between Ventura County and Orange County. Its various high-tech pockets include Santa Monica, Pasadena, Irvine, and its own "Multimedia Gulch," Burbank and Glendale.

- Specialties: E-commerce and multimedia are the driving forces. Much of the activity springs from two renowned incubators—idealab! in Pasadena and EC2 at the University of Southern California in Los Angeles, but a third incubator has entered the ring: the Internet service provider Earthlink.
- Big players: Yahoo! Inc.'s GeoCities online community; Broadcom Corp; Gemstar, the online TV guide company; eToys Inc., Stamps.com, and Cooking.com.
- Hard data: L.A. and Orange Counties soaked up $640 million in high-tech venture capital in the first half of 1999 (according to Price-Waterhouse), or 6.1 percent of the U.S. total.
- Real estate horror story: A tiny fixer-upper in Santa Monica, the hottest place for Web start-ups, will set you back at least $400,000.
- Place: San Diego, California. Navy town and former defense-industry stronghold.
  - Specialties: The lively biotech and medical-devices industry is increasingly dwarfed by telecommunications and software. Companies are clustered in the Golden Triangle in La Jolla.
  - Big players: Qualcomm, Science Applications International Corp., Gateway Inc., and Agouron Pharmaceuticals.
  - Hard data: $311.3 million in high-tech venture capital investments in 1999 (Price-Waterhouse), or 3 percent of the U.S. total. High-tech employment is about 10 percent of the workforce.
  - Real estate horror story: A small homestead in the sprawling Fairbanks Ranch costs $1 million. Other upscale addresses include La Jolla and Rancho Santa Fe.
- Place: Dallas, Texas. Rooted in the defense industry, the technology base of Dallas-Fort Worth has diversified. Calculators, talking toys, airline reservation systems, Internet broadcasts, and the computer game Doom were all invented here.
  - Specialties: Semiconductors, telecommunications, defense electronics, computer services, entertainment software.
  - Big players: Texas Instruments, AMR Corp.'s Sabre Holdings, Electronic Data Systems Inc., i2 PageMart Wireless Inc., id Software.
  - Hard data: $54 million in high-tech venture capital investments in the first half of 1999.
  - Real estate horror story: In many parts of Dallas, $200,000 still goes pretty far. You can still get a three- or four-bedroom house with a two-car garage, and maybe even a swimming pool.
- Place: Austin, Texas. Once largely a manufacturing outpost for semiconductor companies, Austin's more than 450 start-ups are shifting the region's economic center of gravity to Internet software.

- Specialties: Semiconductors, software, and computers. IBM, Motorola, and Tracor laid the foundation for the current tech boom.
- Big players: Dell Computer, IBM, Motorola, Advanced Micro Devices, Applied Materials, Computer Sciences Corp., Trilogy Software Inc.
- Hard data: High-tech investments swelled to $218.7 million for the first half of 1999, or 2.1 percent of the nation's total for the period.
- Real estate horror story: Over the Travis County line, a three bedroom house in a cookie-cutter subdivision might cost $200,000.
- Place: Silicon Dominion. Northern Virginia/Washington D.C. Previously vast farmland outside Washington, now digital workers choke the freeways on their way to the high-tech suburban campuses in Dulles, Reston, and Herndon.
  - Specialties: Telecommunications, Internet service providers, technology consulting. The biggest companies here are in the bandwidth, not chip-making, business. There are plenty of high-tech Beltway Bandits, consultants, and defense contractors whose bread-and-butter business is government work.
  - Big players: America Online, MCI WorldCom, Network Solutions Inc. (the keeper of Internet domain names), Internet service provider PSINet Inc, Electronic Data Systems Corp.
  - Hard data: The D.C. area nabbed $392 million in high-tech venture capital investments in the first half of 1999, or 3.7 percent of the U.S. total.
  - Real estate horror story: A three-bedroom townhouse with a one-car garage in a Herndon, Virginia, subdivision runs about $200,000.
- Place: Research Triangle, North Carolina. Three university towns—Durham, Raleigh, and Chapel Hill—are the points of a triangle of real estate that is home to a growing number of high-tech start-ups.
  - Specialties: Telecommunications, operating-system software, biotech, life sciences.
  - Big players: IBM Corp.'s networking hardware and microelectronics divisions, software maker SAS Institute, Red Hat Inc., Nortel Networks Corp.
  - Hard data: $194.7 million in high-tech venture capital investments for the first half of 1999, or 1.9 percent of the total.
- Place: Silicon Alley, New York. A bevy of Internet companies lie in the shadow of the Flatiron Building in downtown Manhattan. Several miles south, the financial district is home to others, including CDNow and Mail.com, Inc.
  - Specialties: Internet advertising, publishing/content, design, consulting.

- Big players: DoubleClick, Flatiron Partners LLC, Latin American portal StarMedia Network, and iVillage, Inc.
- Hard data: Metropolitan New York area snared $759.1 million in high-tech venture capital funding in the first half of 1999, or 7.2 percent of the U.S. total.
- Real estate horror story: A thousand square feet of loft space might cost close to $500,000. Parking in a garage will run you another $350 a month.

- Place: Big Blue Country. Otherwise known as New York's Hudson Valley and Westchester County, the capital of IBM's empire.
    - Big players: International Business Machines Corp., Fujitsu Ltd., Prodigy Communications Corp.
    - Hard data: $55.8 million in high-tech venture capital investments went to upstate New York in the first half of 1999, or 0.6 percent of the U.S. total.
    - Real estate horror story: The average price of a single-family home in Westchester is $464,000. The farther north you go, the more house you get. For the Hudson Valley, the average price of a single-family home is $284,000.

- Place: Route 128. Digital Equipment, Wang, Data General, and other giant oaks that once lined Route 128 outside Boston have all been felled. But a new forest of Internet and networking saplings have sprouted in recent years. Massachusetts remains the No. 2 tech region in the country.
    - Specialties: Computer storage, Internet portals, Web development and software. MIT and Harvard have helped spawn a host of techie firms in and around Cambridge.
    - Big players: EMC Corp., CMGI Inc., and Lycos Inc.
    - Hard data: Massachusetts ranked second to California in high-tech venture capital investments in 1999 with $1.29 billion, or 12.3 percent, of the U.S. total.

- Place: Roboburgh. Pittsburgh is forging a new identity as Roboburgh, thanks to Carnegie Mellon University's Robotics Institute, a springboard for robotics companies.
    - Specialties: Robots that do hazardous waste retrieval.
    - Big players: McKesson HBOC Automated Healthcare, RedZone Robotics, Mobot Inc., Probotics Inc., and AssistWare Technology Inc.
    - Hard data: The Pittsburgh Technology Council says about $54 million in venture capital flowed in for technology-related industries in 1998.

- Real estate horror story: A restored Victorian mansion on Millionaire's Row near the Carnegie Mellon campus is for sale for $1.5 million.

The Wall Street Journal has also pinpointed Williamstown, Massachusetts, and nearby North Adams as Silicon Village. High-tech companies are multiplying in the Denver suburbs. Englewood, Colorado, is home to several players, including Rhythms NetConnections and Verio. Boulder, Colorado, hosts NetLibrary which recently raised $70 million from investors. Chicago has previously lagged behind, but start-up action is on the rise.

If you are trying to read the tea leaves, there seems to be no clear trend. When you've targeted a specific specialty, legal department, law firm, practice area, industry or region, talk to insiders—current and former employees, knowledgeable recruiters, and employees outside the legal field—to ascertain how the future looks. By putting all the pieces together, you'll be able to take your very best guess. The rest is up to you and, probably, a little bit of luck.

There's always a problem listing current hottest skills and specialties: One burp in the economy and the hottest jobs are mere memories, as evidenced by corporate and real estate paralegals. That is why cross-training can be described as "water wings for paralegals in a drowning economy."

The American Bar Association, along with various legal publications, targeted the following practice specialties as growth areas:

- Bankruptcy
- Communications
- Environmental law
- Health care
- Intellectual property
- International law
- Patent and trade law
- Entertainment law

Because nothing is set in concrete, always anticipate changes and follow lawyer trends. Legal publications, such as the *National Law Journal,* report "What's Hot, What's Not" in practice specialties across the country. If lawyers are needed, it follows that paralegal demand increases. Keep up by following the trades and closely watching events in the legal field.

Legal Assistant Today magazine is still, in my opinion, one of the best vehicles for paralegal information. The magazine is up-to-date with the latest in trends, concerns, salary information, and new specialties. *Legal*

Assistant Today frequently publishes salary surveys and "Hottest Jobs" information. This important professional magazine covers large, midsized, small, and boutique firms; in-house legal departments; independent paralegals; associations; and careers with legal vendors. According to *LAT*, there are more career opportunities in a corporate law department than ever before, particularly for senior-level paralegals. Law firms offer few promotions and emphasize paralegal profitability. Corporations, on the other hand, offer promotions, career advancement, and growth opportunities in other areas of the corporation.

At this writing, recruiters across the country report a shortage of experienced corporate paralegals with mergers and acquisitions, securities, and blue-sky background. Intellectual property paralegals are also hard to find.

Jobs and experience most in demand (at this writing) are the following:

- The midlevel, 2- to 5-year paralegal
- Some regions (such as San Francisco) seek top-caliber senior-level paralegals; other regions (such as Minneapolis) have 2 to 3 percent unemployment and candidates are hard to find (entry level still have to fight their way in, however)
- Information technology experts: database management; conducting online research; Internet experience; assisting in electronic discovery.
- Corporate paralegals with experience in venture financing, public offerings, mergers and acquisitions, securities, public and/or private company corporate maintenance, and EDGAR (electronic data gathering for SEC filings)
- Experts in imaging and scanning
- Experienced paralegals in almost any specialty with expertise in spreadsheets or settlement brochures
- Intellectual property
- Insurance defense
- Labor and employment law

Not hot but making a comeback:

- Real estate

Earmarked for substantial future growth:

- Electronic discovery

- Desktop publishing
- Computer forensics

We will most likely see increased use of:

- Temporary paralegals
- Project (or contract) paralegals (hired for the length of case only)
- Legal technicians (those paralegals providing services directly to the consumer)
- Paralegals used in outsourced legal research companies

Demand for marketing, sales, personnel, research and development, project management, and computerized litigation support professionals in the legal vendor arena is also expected to increase.

LAMA (the Legal Assistant Management Association) offers a Legal Assistant Utilization Survey presented from a manager's point of view. This survey can be ordered from the Association's headquarters. The survey compares legal assistant trends in law firms and corporations regarding organization/structure; billable hour requirements; marketing; and professional development, training, and education.

If you are thinking about expanding your career through specialization, the following practice specialities may be of interest.

Bankruptcy—Chapters 7, 11, 13, and workouts.

Computer law—Includes assignments such as leasing or purchasing hardware; assigning copyrights; negotiating with foreign companies; dealing with service bureaus and resellers; and protecting trade secrets.

Consumer rights specialist—Involves knowledge of consumer rights laws, including manufacturing and safety laws.

Copyright law—Works with the Copyright Office and performs assignments involving infringement and protection of copyrights.

Entertainment law—This position covers many areas and can include working with different media, such as music, film, television, radio, and publishing. Also includes working with various entertainers, authors, directors, producers, songwriters, and so forth on matters such as financing, constructing deals, royalties, and intellectual property cases.

Financial transactional paralegal—Manage complex financial transactions from negotiations through closings.

Franchising specialist—Requires understanding of franchise registration, trademark, or contract law.

Government—The government offers opportunities through agencies, the U.S. Attorney's Office, Department of Justice, Federal Public Defender's Office, Army, Environmental Protection Agency, Veterans Administration, and more. For information, write to Federal Reports, Inc., 1010 Vermont Avenue, N.W., Washington, D.C. 20005. For a fee, they will provide you with a monthly listing of opportunities.

Hospital liability—Includes assignments in the areas of liability of blood services, radiology, surgery, duty of care to the patient, and right-to-die issues.

Immigration—The number of immigrant visas available has significantly increased since a revision of the law in 1990. Some corporations have hired in-house immigration paralegals to cope with the volume of work. Knowledge of a foreign language helps.

International law—Knowledge of corporate structures overseas is necessary for firms representing international businesses. Multi-officed international corporations also have in-house paralegals. Some positions require background knowledge in import and export laws.

Labor and employment law—Covers areas such as wrongful termination, discrimination, sexual harassment, employee benefits laws, and occupational safety standards. Requires knowledge of National Labor Relations Board and National Labor Relations Act. There are paralegals in positions with unions who deal with collective bargaining issues and grievance procedures.

Legal clinics—Self-help clinics have sprung up all over the country and need experienced paralegals.

Litigation—A few areas of expertise:
- Discovery and trial preparation
- Trial expert
- Intellectual property
- Manager of complex litigation
- Complex litigation
- Antitrust
- Employment litigation
- Construction litigation
- Securities fraud
- Banking litigation
- Commercial litigation

Litigation support—This booming area has a high demand for litigation paralegals with information technology background. The area has created its own hierarchy.

Medical records—Analyzing medical records is a highly paid specialty position. Asbestos, environmental, and medical malpractice areas have a need for experts.

Patent and trade secrets law—This position deals with the U.S. Patent and Trademark Office. The paralegal needs knowledge of copyright and trademark laws.

Personal injury—Handling claims, interviewing witnesses, gathering facts, preparing interrogatories, and estimating and proving damages are only a few of the assignments in this specialty.

Products liability specialist—Involves government regulations, manufacturing, toxic tort litigation, factual investigation, technical knowledge, and federal legislation.

Real estate transactional paralegal—Involves knowledge of acquisitions and commercial leasing documents, drafting financing documents and partnership agreements, landlord and tenant laws, and environmental impact studies.

Sports law—Very few positions exist in this field, but if you love sports, you may want to explore this specialty.

Tax law—Involves working with the IRS. Knowledge of accounting is essential.

Travel law—Includes assignments in areas such as jurisdiction over foreign travel suppliers, contracts between operators and suppliers, and class action suits.

White collar crime—Includes assignments in areas such as RICO, mail and wire fraud, banking crimes, bribery and extortion, conspiracy, entrapment, government contract fraud, and criminal liability of corporations and their officers.

Other Practice Specialties:
- Administrative law
- Admiralty law
- Civil and criminal appellate practice specialty
- Corporate law
- Criminal law
- Environmental law
- Family law (including children's rights)
- Insurance defense
- Landlord/tenant disputes
- Lender liability and banking laws
- Medical malpractice
- Mergers and acquisitions
- Municipal bonds

- Oil and gas
- Police department defense
- Probate, estate planning, and trust law
- Public interest law
- Transportation law

CAREERS OUTSIDE THE LAW FIRM OR IN-HOUSE LEGAL DEPARTMENT

Pension Program Analyst: This federal agency position was spotted in Washington, D.C., for a federal agency that insures 55,000 pension plans covering 41 million workers and retirees. Requirements include in-depth experience and knowledge of the tax provisions of ERISA as applied to defined benefit pensions plans, and excellent writing and quantitative abilities. This government GS-13/14 competitive services position pays between $52,800 and $81,200.

Consultant/Project Manager: A position within a computerized litigation support organization, responsibilities include defining work scope schedules and budgets for projects; accomplishing tasks while maintaining levels of profitability; and providing sales support and day-to-day project support and client interaction. Requires 8 to 10 years' litigation support experience, extensive hardware/software database and imaging experience, and excellent client interaction skills.

Recruiter: This position in a staffing organization for temporary or full-time employment recruits candidates; develops new business; creates public relations programs; assists in trade shows; and teaches job-hunting seminars for attorneys, paralegals, or support staff. The position requires legal background, knowledge of the legal community, and membership in professional associations.

Sales/Marketing Representative: Many legal vendors seek paralegals for sales and marketing positions. Hot areas are imaging and scanning, photocopying, staffing organizations, hardware/software companies, litigation support companies, printing and graphics, publishers, microfilming services, and more.

Human Resources Director: This director must know all aspects of the human resources department, including payroll, personnel, insurance, and benefits administration. Requirements include detail oriented, excellent interpersonal skills; ability to interact with all levels of staffing and possibly with union relations; ability to be both a generalist and able member of a management team; and demonstrated skill in developing and operationalizing a responsive HR function. Computer experience with human resources software, outsourcing, and benefit programs is necessary. Call the Association for Legal Administrators (ALA) for more information.

Employee Relations Representative: This position applies the organization's policies and procedures, conducts internal investigations and exit interviews for disciplinary and resolution purposes, ensures legal compliance, advises on current legislation, implements substance abuse programs, and assists in the design and implementation of an ER training program for supervisors. An applicant must possess a proven ability to effectively communicate and interact with diverse individuals as well as all levels of management. A college degree is generally required.

Labor Relations Manager: Experience should include contract administration, grievance and problem resolution, and possibly contract negotiation.

Loss Mitigation Representative: This is a position found in financial institutions. The applicant should have background with loan administration and collections, foreclosures, bankruptcy, and loan workouts.

Legal Publishing Opportunities: Some possible positions are editor of legal publications, reporter, journalist, writer, and copyeditor. Many legal publishers hire paralegals to write, edit, or review paralegal articles and manuscripts. Responsibilities may include working with editors and outside authors in writing, editing, and reviewing manuscript and forms for a variety of print and electronic products. Seek out those publishers specializing in the profession, such as John Wiley & Sons, Inc., Delmar, Shepard's/McGraw-Hill, West Group, Bancroft Whitney, Lawyer's Co-Operative, Pearson/Prentice Hall, Clark Boardman Callaghan, *Legal Assistant Today* magazine, Law Office Computing, and Thomson & Thomson. You may also wish to use your talents for nonpaying positions with paralegal association newsletters.

Dispositions Closing Coordinator: Responsibilities include coordinating all aspects of property disposition processes, including due diligence, legal and reporting functions, and working with brokers in sale of properties. This position is found in real estate investment firms. Skills required include computer literacy; interpersonal, communication, proofreading, and editing skills; and ability to handle multitasks efficiently, independently, and under pressure. Experience in real estate closings is necessary.

Paralegal Educator/Instructor: Paralegals may teach in paralegal schools either on a full- or part-time basis. Most schools welcome experienced paralegals with excellent verbal communication skills and lots of war stories. Presently, there are over 800 paralegal schools in the United States. For more information, call the American Association for Paralegal Educators (AAFPE).

Marketing Director for Legal Vendor: Utilize your legal terminology, ability to maneuver around the firm, and contacts for a marketing position with providers to the legal field, companies that supply legal reference materials, software, personnel, legal research, deposition summarizing, and litigation support. The position entails management and supervision of a team of staff members in all aspects of marketing, including writing copy, editing, assisting in preparation of collateral pieces (brochures and literature), client contact, vendor contact, negotiations of advertising contracts, and setting up and attendance at trade shows.

Seminar Leader: Paralegal skills, characteristics, and experience lead naturally to lecturing in areas outside of the law. Think about your overall skills: organization, factual investigation, research, abstracting, drafting business letters and correspondence, and dealing with difficult clients and coworkers. These skills can translate into seminars for any industry, such as time management, great customer service, handling upset clients, writing memorable memos, and summarizing documents. You may be sitting on another career!

Electronic Discovery Paralegal (Information Technology): Fast approaching, not fully here, is the paperless society. Interpreted in litigation terms, hard copy is fast disappearing and documents in the future will need to be retrieved directly from computers. Here is the discovery-phase paralegal all over again. Same story but very different look. You read it here first!

Telecommuting Specialist: Someone is going to lodge a complaint, need specialized employment agreements, sue an employer, claim unfair business practices, slip and fall, lose original documents, commit fraud, or steal trade secrets in the new telecommuting world. Specialized positions will emerge focused directly on telecommuting issues. Law firms, corporations, and consumers will push for new legislation, research environmental impact, review utilities and transportation laws, need further protection of privacy and confidentiality, get involved in rezoning and land use agencies, and specialize in the various required insurances. This position may be a subniche speciality and require a zigzagged approach through various other legal and nonlegal experience.

GENERAL PRACTICE AREAS FOR PARALEGALS

Paralegals hold positions in almost every area of law. A very simple rule of thumb is this: Any area in which an attorney practices has room for a paralegal. Listed here are some of the practice areas you might consider if you are seeking to increase or expand your area of expertise:

Agricultural Law
Alternative Dispute Resolution
Antitrust Law
Arts, Entertainment, Advertising, and Media Law
Banking Law
Bankruptcy and Workout Law
Business Tax Law
Closely Held Business Law
Commercial Litigation
Commercial Real Estate Law
Contract Law
Criminal Law
Elder Law
Employee Benefits Law
Employment Law
Environmental Law
Family Law
Federal, State, and Local Government Law
Franchise and Dealership Law
Health Law
Immigration Law
Intellectual Property Law

International Business Law
Labor Law
Nonprofit Corporations Law
Personal Injury Defense Law
Plaintiffs Personal Injury
Probate, Estate Planning, and Trusts Law
Professional Malpractice Defense
Publicly Held Corporation Law
Real Estate Law
Securities and Venture Finance Law

INDEPENDENT CAREER TRACKS

What's sweeping the country, doesn't have a uniform name yet, has caused lots of controversy, takes guts, helps people, and needs attention?

The independent paralegal, of course.

This book would not be complete if we didn't at least address a trend that is occurring from west to east coast and up and down the middleland. This relatively new career is referenced in several ways: independent/freelance/public/legal technician paralegal. In some states, such as California, these professionals cannot technically call themselves paralegals or legal assistants. Translation: those who deal directly with the consumer—without benefit of an attorney.

Yes, folks, it's here. As a direct result of consumers' dissatisfaction and downright infuriation over excessive legal fees, consumers have created a market for low-cost legal services. No longer do consumers want to tie up all of their assets, empty their savings, or get second mortgages to pay the lawyers.

Why are we not surprised over the outcry from the legal community? "No to that!" say many lawyers unwilling to let go of portions of their business. "Absolutely not!" say many paralegals who openly acknowledge that many paralegals know very little about law.

As of this writing, the issue of licensing paralegals to provide some public protection has been bandied about. As hotly debated as this topic is, so far the licensing issue (in some states) has been aimed solely at independent paralegals. These licensing requirements are in specific areas such as bankruptcy, dissolution, landlord/tenant, and consumer complaints. These same states have dismissed licensing or standardization of paralegals who work directly for lawyers, arguing that these paralegals work under the supervision of a lawyer. Other states continue to actually arrest paralegals who work directly with the public, citing the unauthorized practice of law.

Deanie Kramer—Divorce Resource

One of the most enterprising independent paralegals is Deanie Kramer of Divorce Resource in Los Angeles. A vibrant personality with a good sense of humor and great interpersonal skills describes her. Possessing a B.A. degree, certificate from an ABA-approved school, and teaching credentials are only a few of her academic achievements. Her background includes strong experience as a paralegal, legal administrator, and adjunct professor of paralegal studies. It's not surprising her 8-year-old business is flourishing.

"The key to success," says Kramer, "is to gain experience in all phases of the legal process. You must understand the process from inception to completion and understand not only how law firms work but also how the court system works." Kramer also suggests that you do not attempt to become a legal technician until you have at least 3 years' experience in a law firm. "The formal setting of a law firm environment gave me a solid foundation to go out on my own," she says.

Warmth, compassion, and the highest quality of work product are imperative. Your clients are not generally calling you because everything in their lives is working properly. These are usually situations of a person in crisis.

Kramer's business is based on word-of-mouth referrals. She markets heavily through women's organizations, network referral services, and chambers of commerce, and takes referrals from psychologists, social workers, and attorneys. She has written several articles and has been the subject of many.

One of Kramer's secrets for top achievement is her years of managing a law office. She knew immediately what equipment, vendors, and support personnel were needed. "This is a business," she emphasizes, "and must run as cost-efficiently as possible with no exceptions. Outside services, such as accountant and attorney services, messengers, printers, and graphic designers, must be chosen with price, quality, and excellence of service in mind. These people reflect how well your services can be delivered to your client. I even engaged the services of a professional organizer so I could maintain evenness in paying my personal bills. This allowed me to focus more on my business."

Choosing the right office and location is critical. Easy access, free parking, and a nonthreatening atmosphere are necessary. Kramer's advice on choosing an office? "If the building looks like a million bucks, it's beyond your clients' means. Modest, yet comfortable four-room suite over Trader Joe's is great. However, having to keep the windows closed because you failed to find out the trash cans were right below you can be an embarrassing lesson."

Having a long-term solid foundation and legal training can enable you to know when issues present themselves that are ethically out of your domain. With proper training and expertise, you are aware of fact patterns that indicate that the matter is NOT for a legal technician. That is the time for immediate attorney referral. "Where people fall down," says Kramer, "is not admitting when it is time to step out and have an attorney step in."

Earnings vary widely. "Perhaps the question should be, 'What do I spend?'" laughs Kramer. "This is like any other business. For the first couple of years, the profits may not be a motivator. Every dime I make, I put back into the business." "In a perfect world," she says, "you should be able to make equivalent to what you were earning in the law firm in your first couple of years. There are reports of some paralegal firms generating revenues as high as $500,000 per year. Before you get too excited, understand this is the revenue line, not the bottom line. These firms could also have as many as six or seven legal technicians on staff. The general consensus is that many technicians are earning 'decent' money, but there are no real stories I know of pointing to huge salaries."

If you are considering a career as an independent paralegal, you must consider future consequences if you do not have an outstanding academic background and prior legal experience. If all indicators are right for the position, contact your local paralegal association and find out about the independent paralegal's section. Meeting those who can teach you, guide you, and give emotional support is a great way to start.

PARALEGAL INNER VIEW: TANDALA NOBLES— INTELLECTUAL PROPERTY

Name: Tandala R. Nobles
Corporation: Ventana Medical Systems, Inc., Tucson, Arizona
Title: Legal Assistant, Intellectual Property
Number of attorneys/paralegals: 1 attorney, 1 paralegal
Years of experience: I have been in the legal field for 18 years; 4 years in family law and estate planning; 13 years in defense litigation.
Education: A.S. in Paralegal Studies from Harper College; currently pursuing a B.S./IS (Bachelor of Science/Information Systems) degree at University of Phoenix
Job duties: I currently wear many hats simply because of the nature of the position. The legal department was only recently created within the company. Until October 1999, all patent matters were handled by outside counsel. Currently, I am responsible for monitoring the company's patent estate plan. I also draft most confidentiality agreements.

A typical day begins with review of the mail; a review of the patent matters due; drafting agreements; processing of invoices for the legal department; any other request by the attorney such as copying, filing, or searches for information.

Tell us about your most challenging assignment.

Actually, my most challenging assignment is ongoing. Since we have taken over from outside counsel and others, I am trying to centralize all the information from various sources. This is most challenging because many things have fallen through the cracks and I am trying to keep everything updated and current while having new things pop up from previous sources. This then puts me in a rush mode because it's an emergency and must be handled ASAP. The rush does not frazzle me. I work well under pressure but it is difficult to stay on top of everything with so many things going on.

What experiences make this all worthwhile?

My most satisfying paralegal experience was in my previous job as a litigation paralegal. I was instrumental in helping the attorney handle everything on a very high profile discrimination lawsuit—from start to finish—including drafting of pleadings, discovery, depositions, and settlement agreements.

What has been the most eye-opening experience for you?

There are so many things going on and the attorney is so busy, it's hard to review matters with him. I feel like I am grasping at straws trying to learn everything and keep everything in order at the same time.

What computer skills are you required to have on your job?

The Microsoft Office package including Word, Access, Excel, PowerPoint and Outlook. I also do research via the Internet.

What's in store for the future for you?

I am currently re-evaluating my career as a paralegal. I am studying the information systems field, and would like to link this area with the legal field. However, I will be paying close attention to the information technology field in the future.

Do you think that it is important for paralegals to have an education in paralegal studies or is on-the-job training sufficient?

I believe both are necessary. However, I would take nothing away from on-the-job training because that is how I got started in this career. I only recently received my certificate but I use what I have learned over the years much more than I do what I learned in school.

Where do you think this profession is going?

I think this profession still has a long way to go. Because so many legal secretaries are performing many of the duties that paralegals perform, it is difficult to say. I performed paralegal duties as a secretary and am now performing secretarial duties as a paralegal. I don't know how the two professions will be separated. It's ultimately up to the attorney for whom one works.

If you could change anything about the profession, what would it be?

I think a finite definition needs to be determined for paralegals and legal assistants. Perhaps one name would be a good idea, too. I hope the paralegal profession and those in it can become a group that helps each other as the attorneys do. We need professional organizations such as the NALA and NFPA to help accomplish this.

CHAPTER 6

When to Say "No (Thank You)" to Your Dream Job

Have you ever wondered what might have happened in your life if you had chosen one road over another? I mean, what *really* might have happened? I don't make a habit of writing about my own experiences, but, recently, while minding my own business (literally), I was approached by a major staffing organization (big players—a cool $3+ billion a year in revenue) to head up their $50 million legal staffing division. Now, I'm pretty happy doing what I'm doing. I love being an entrepreneur; I have a successful legal staffing organization; I'm my own boss; and I really wasn't looking to change. In fact, I subscribe to the old adage that you work 80 hours a week just so you don't have to work 40 hours a week for someone else. But the headhunter who called me talked a good game. I mean, I'm in the business, know the pitches, yet still I was intrigued.

The position involved heading up a national legal staffing division, expanding the client base, adding revenue and bearing the title of vice president. It sounded like a job that not only could I do, but also I had previous experience doing and enjoyed. It also involved a possible *very* comfortable housing situation, albeit in the cold abysses of the Hinterlands (i.e., *not* in California). I would have to uproot my home life and sell my business to this company. Well, shoot. I've been down that road before. But the challenge seemed tempting, and, frankly, when I started to weigh the upside, the idea of adding Vice President of Major Corporation to my bio along with the "financial security," and exciting challenging scenario seemed like a logical step in my 5-year goal plan. I tell myself that the dollars aren't anything to sneeze at either seeing as how rumors of my wealth have been greatly exaggerated.

Although my first instinct was to pass, I ignored my brief commune into my inner child and told the headhunter, "Sure. Here are my parameters. If they can meet those, I'll talk." Well, okay, so I sounded a little cocky. But at this stage in my career (having come from the ranks of paralegal to paralegal administrator to entrepreneur of thriving paralegal staffing company to national director of major staffing corporation to president of a division of major national legal staffing company to entrepreneur and author of eight books), I felt pretty confident that I could pick and choose. By golly, I wanted to do what I had been writing about and counseling paralegals for years: *Choose wisely, and, above all, make the change worth your while.*

I was willing to overlook the fact that I would have to move to a location where there was real snow in the winter. I'm from California—I have no clue that the stuff actually comes down from the sky. I was also willing to overlook the fact that a year ago, there was a huge splash in the *Wall Street Journal* when the person who had the job I'd been offered walked out mumbling something about "unreconcilable differences with top management." I was further willing to overlook the fact that I had a fast-track thriving business that was definitely going places. Along with a stellar team, I had sweated, toiled, and molded this company into the kind of experience I had always wanted. But gee, now that I think about it, I was actually getting excited about this opportunity.

Could I adjust from being a powerful "big fish in a small pond" to being a "little fish in a big pond?" (Okay, I guess I squandered too many Saturday nights of my youth watching the "Cliche Lady" on *Saturday Night Live* instead of working on my social life <sigh>.) Could I leave my exquisite view of the mountains and ocean in Los Angeles for the eerie chill of Eerie Lake (I think that's what it's called). And what about my boyfriend who obsessed every day about his rapidly decreasing hairline, his hives, and his love handles? Would he go with me? He was having a rough enough time adjusting to suburban California life after a lifetime of the hustle and bustle of New York City where he was a rock-and-roll journalist. He complained vociferously about crickets keeping him up at night. What would he say about behemoth Midwest mosquitoes and those elephantine June bugs? (And why was that little voice echoing inside my head asking, did I *want* him to go with me?)

I couldn't believe I was going through the exact same steps as our candidates. First, I interviewed via videoconference with the headhunter who had somehow convinced me to even consider this job. Him in New York, me in LA. Both of us plunging headlong into the latest technology—each of us acting as though this were just another day. Then I met with a VP who flies out here to see if my personality fits. Well, I don't know about my personality, but I sure did like his. Too bad about that wedding ring. (Okay, so I'm still single—geez, at my age, I'm *entitled*.) Then I'm flown across the country to meet seven top execs, one right after the other and hustled back on the plane. Somehow I manage to pass that round. A month goes by. I get a phone call. I have been summoned by the executive VPs, the CFO *and* the president of this $3+ billion *Fortune* 500 company. This time, they're waving lots of stock options, a new car, and a relocation allowance. <gulp> Geez, I think they're getting serious. I immediately consult everything that's ever been written about how to handle a third and fourth interview, what to wear, what to say, how to behave, how to breathe. I have long involved discussions with my partner, my advisors, my mentors, and oh, yes, my shrink. I worry once again about being overweight but notice that people in the Midwest seem a little chunkier than Californians so I stop at the local Dairy Queen. I'm all set. Then, <deep cleansing breaths> I get THE CALL. The offer is coming down. YES!!! I order up the snowmobile. I hop on Realtor.com and find out that for the price of a garage in LA I can have a mansion on a lake with my own personal boat dock. Not a bad deal—even if I *don't* know how to sail. One slight inconvenience: Two top execs are on their way out here to look over my business and make the offer on that. Oh, okay. I can't be bothered right now. I'm busy looking into designer muckaluks.

So, these major players fly all the way out to LA to visit us in our humble abode (office, that is) on a Sunday afternoon. These two (dare I, at the risk of sounding like a sour-grapes-politically incorrect female, these two charter members of—I hate to say, "the good old boys network") pay a polite visit on us. As Arlo Guthrie observed of his army physical in the whimsically autobiographical "Alice's Restaurant," "they were inspecting, dissecting, every single part of me, and they wasn't leaving *no* part untouched."

I have my whole staff in the office dressed up in their Sunday best. <Deep cleansing breaths, deep cleansing breaths.> Desks are clean, lean, and mean. You can smell the lemon Pledge all the way down the hall. However, this powerful duo felt they could have more leverage by interviewing me alone. *All* alone, that is—in a closed room with no windows let alone air conditioning. Suddenly, I experience the terror some of my candidates feel when they are sent to get the "once over" by a potential employer. But I tell myself, I'm ready. I've role-played. I've studied my answers. I am sure, confident, and meaningful. I have prepared a vision for them. I *am* ready. <Deep cleansing breaths, deep cleansing breaths.>

Things were going well until the duo decides to play "good cop and bad cop." Badly, I might add. They find a perceived mistake. I thought the little guy playing "bad cop" was a bit too gleeful. I really thought he was going to stand on the table and belt out "Anything You Can Do, I Can Do Better" from *Annie Get Your Gun.* "At BigCorp," the little guy who apparently enjoyed gnashing his teeth, spit out, "At BigCorp, we would have *FIRED* the person in charge for this! Not tomorrow—*today!*" Yeah, well, I saw it differently. I saw a learning curve, not a career buster. This makes me a bad manager? "What kind of leader *are* you?" he yells, swatting the table.

My heart suddenly pounded with terror. <Deep cleansing breaths, deep—oh, heck, I started to gag.> I can handle anything but yelling and swatting tables. I slunk back in my chair, stunned. Was this a proper way to treat a CEO they were considering to run a major division of their billion-dollar-plus company? Furthermore, was this the way *I* wanted to be treated?

At that precise moment, I felt a slight dampness. Oh, Lordy!—*sweaty palms*. I decide to ignore my own discomfort and rise to the bait. "Littleguy," I say, "Just what are you so angry about?" "**I–am–not–angry,**" he says through clenched teeth. "**I have been doing this for 19 years.**" I count to myself . . . five, six, seven, eight: "Yes," I say quietly. "I can *see* that." <Zoom> Right over his head.

After regaining my composure and understanding clearly that Littleguy is someone I would have to work with on a daily basis, I decide to withdraw my candidacy. In fact, I write the letter and fax it to the headhunter, the president of the company and the VP with the unfortunate wedding ring so fast, these two corporate wannabes haven't even mounted the jetway back to the Hinterlands yet. Would they still have wanted me? I'll never know. Is this the way they treat their employees? Frankly, I don't *want* to know. What I do know is where I draw the line: *I always want to be treated with dignity and respect. On that, I will not compromise.*

I'm re-evaluating my life here and reminding myself that I have created my ideal situation. I love my staff, my colleagues, my clients, my candidates, and my life. For me, this was a close call and an excellent reminder that I want to develop what I have. The "good guy" was kind enough to send a letter of apology. But I learned a good lesson. The grass is not always greener on the other side. (Thank you, Cliche Lady.) So now, it's back to the proverbial drawing board. I cancel the snowmobile. I put my bio back on the shelf. I forget about the affordable mansion with the boat dock on the lake. I take the air out of my floaties. And life is good. As for my boyfriend, well, girls and boys, we'll leave that for my next column.

The Despina Kartson Success Story

Success stories run rampant in this field, and the Despina Kartson story is a classic example of moving up a phenomenal career ladder. Kartson has never believed that the paralegal field is a dead-end career. With 15 years' experience, she has a motto, "Keep moving up." The high-profile executive with Bowne Business Solutions has had a career that exceeds the expectations of most paralegals, not to mention most professionals in today's workplace.

Starting as a legal secretary in Cleveland, she decided to finish her college degree and work during school breaks. Armed with a degree in journalism, Kartson sent out video tapes to TV stations, determined to be the next Barbara

Walters. Meanwhile, the Cleveland firm wanted her to train as a paralegal, temporarily, until she found her dream job in journalism. "I loved it," she says. "I had a great job with great projects. I felt like I was an investigative reporter. I was tracking witnesses." That "temporary" position lasted 3 years.

Moving to New York, Kartson landed a litigation paralegal position with the prestigious old-line firm, White and Case. "This was at a time when litigation support with mainframes and databases was done by tech guys for a created database," recalls Kartson. "In my spare time, I thought if I could learn this database system, it would be mine to run with. I worked in a basement on a dumb terminal and learned the application. Within a year, I formed the litigation support department and was a one-woman operation for a while. I then ended up working on the WPSS litigation case which plunged me headlong into litigation support."

At White and Case for 12 years, Kartson gained a national reputation as one of the foremost litigation support managers in the country. Topping out at the firm, she moved to another major firm as assistant director of IT. Seeing a way to broaden her skill set and learn more general technology, she enjoyed a brief stint in an enjoyable top-tier firm. Along came Uniscribe who recognized Kartson's talent and offered her a position as vice president. Her income skyrocketed. "My role was to oversee the litigation support facilities management (FM) with clients around the country and build that practice," said Kartson. "They added additional responsibilities in new product development which I really liked."

Success attracts attention and so does a great-selling book in the industry. After establishing herself as an authority at Uniscribe and authoring two well-known books, *Computerized Litigation Support* and *Designing Litigation Support Databases,* the phone rang with an offer she couldn't refuse. Bowne Business Solutions came calling with an awesome opportunity: the position of vice president, strategic solutions. "Litigation support is now only one of the five areas for which I have responsibility," beams Kartson. "I am responsible for strategic solutions: looking at new technology and innovative approaches to enhance outsourcing to law firms and investment banks. I handle IT outsourcing, word processing, presentation graphics, litigation resource management, and traditional services or office document services."

Her team is strategic in that they are the visionaries. They evaluate new technologies and work with sales and operations to price and implement offerings and help sell them. Kartson's biggest challenge is to stay ahead of technology. "There's so much changing and coming up on a daily basis, it's a whirlwind to stay on top of it—so much going on so rapidly. I have to continue to stay on top of things and stay focused so I can identify great technology that will make our clients happy."

Every organization Kartson has worked for, she's loved. "The book I wrote was right up there in my most gratifying experience," she says. "That was gratifying because I was a journalism major and wanted to write but I also loved legal technology and came full circle by writing a couple of books."

Where does she go from here? "I still have the next 10 years to build and grow. I have more to learn about the business world. When you spend a number of years in a law firm, you don't have exposure to being on the vendor side of the fence. I want to grow within an organization where I can be a major contributor and an owner."

Changes are not always easy—particularly if you are used to an environment that feels comfortable and safe. Once out in the vendor world, however, chances of returning to the law firm are slim, although they do exist. In the vendor world, you get the best of both worlds; staying in the legal field and working with intelligent people and creatively utilizing your background and skills. Always consider other options, too. There's something almost magical about it—another kind of challenge, another kind of dream.

If becoming an independent paralegal or legal technician is your career goal, there are several serious matters to consider prior to setting up shop. Before making any kind of move, research the career in the state in which you plan to work. Understand what is allowed, if anything. Just because there are paralegals who have hung out a shingle does not mean it is legal. No states allow paralegals to give legal advice or act as attorneys. Learn exactly what constitutes the unauthorized practice of law. Some of the areas of law in which you may be able to assist consumers include family law—assisting in uncontested divorce, adoptions, and guardianships; landlord/tenant disputes; wills; personal bankruptcy; and consumer affairs complaints.

CHAPTER 7

Cutting-Edge Legal Careers in the Virtual Workplace

> To boldly go where no (wo)man has gone before.
>
> *Star Trek,* film and television series

OVERVIEW

Scrap the office of the 1980s and 1990s! Today, one of the fastest growing segments of the workplace is go-anywhere workers—those who have traded in the security blanket of a law office for the great wide open of the virtual office.

Liberation! No longer tied to time clocks, overbearing supervisors, tattling receptionists, distractions, and long commutes, lawyers and paralegals alike have discovered the virtual office. What several years ago was called telecommunicating—working from home or another set location via computer—today encapsulates work that can be performed from virtually anywhere at anytime using technology such as fax, laptop, modem, e-mail, voice mail, videoconferencing, and cellular phone. Anyone can be contacted anywhere.

Once deskbound, cubicle-dwelling paralegals will be free to seek out computer-friendly work space wherever their jobs take them: off-site document productions, depositions, courtrooms, closings, client meetings. They can now perform the work on the premises. They can work from home, office, phone, airport, car, hotel, library, client office—virtually anywhere. To save time and money, they may meet at a local videoconferencing center to confer with colleagues across the country.

Unshackled from the 9:00 A.M. to 7:00 P.M. ball and chain, these paralegals are most likely to be more productive and profitable than in the past. Organizations such as IBM and American Express who have initiated virtual work arrangements point to harder working, more committed workers. While the virtual office place may not be for everyone, the trend toward this model is swiftly growing.

Large corporations that have adopted this new thinking about the mobile workforce have empowered employees. As a result, employees use their own discretion to determine where and when they work. The system encourages flexibility and increased productivity.

Tools for a typical day may include a laptop computer, hand-held computer, cell phone, and home office equipment such as fax, printer, and a two-line business phone that transfers unanswered calls to the company's branch office voice mail system. Employees may split the work week or mornings and afternoons between office and home, saving time by avoiding rush hour traffic. Mobile workers jump out of bed and can immediately start their workday.

The mobile workforce saves the organization time, costs, overhead, and expenses. Advantages to the mobile workplace include:

1. Decreased real estate costs and office equipment expenses: less office space is needed
2. Decreased overhead: fewer support staff and supplies are needed
3. Improved response time to urgent matters, clients, and deadlines
4. Improved face-to-face time with clients
5. Increased individual productivity
6. More bottom-line profitability
7. Improved technology skills
8. Improved employee morale through empowerment.

If they choose, mobile workers may work at the company's local productivity center. These are branch offices converted into temporary offices with an emphasis on the corporate mailroom. This unorthodox service center allows employees to check their mobile mail slots for hard copies of mail, faxes, and printed computer documents originated from home or a client's office. At the same time, workers can use a desk, work space, or conference room. Clerical support is usually provided.

It isn't always possible to satisfy all personality types with the new mobile arrangement. If an attorney or supervisor is more comfortable with you *in* the office so she can oversee you, creating a comfort zone may be impossible. The legal field is usually last to join new cost-saving ideas and technology; let us not forget the slow, cumbersome emergence of computers on lawyers' desks. Lawyers fought tooth and nail against using computers personally. One hushed, rarely acknowledged defense was simply image—no one wanted it because it required the attorney (of all people) to type. That was, of course, the legal secretary's job.

The mobile worker concept widens availability of good candidates in the marketplace. Working mothers and fathers, those caring for aged or disabled parents or family members, workers with disabilities, independent contractors, and more are able to devote more time instead of less to the job.

Don't overlook the possibility that the experiment could backfire. For instance, a paralegal with small children at home and who is expected to travel may find herself unable to leave the home. Others may find that lack of daily interface with coworkers is isolating and depressing. Still others may need stricter supervision, guidance, and counseling, which may be accomplished only through a traditional office environment.

SETTING UP THE EXPERIMENTAL VIRTUAL OFFICE

10 Guidelines for a Successful Launch

Your firm or corporation may be toying with the idea of the virtual office. As often happens in an organization governed by committee, consensus is hard to reach. To move your firm along in its decision-making process, you might suggest that the concept is implemented as an experiment rather than set in concrete. In today's tumultuous work environment, no one has the luxury of making costly mistakes.

If you get approval, make sure that the virtual office rollout is conducted smoothly and with plenty of forethought, planning, and resources committed to start the project. Here are a few tips for a steady transition:

1. Mix senior management with remote workers. Rarely do executives go virtual. They don't want to be out of sight. Years of training executives about walk-around management now has to be undone. Executives value face time. It's a little like training people to drive on the left side of the street instead of the right. All of your instincts say "stay right! stay right!"

2. Management committee buy-in is essential to make virtual offices work. Attorneys and administrators need to demonstrate buy-in by participating in the experiment.

They need to clean out their desks, shake hands, and head for home with laptops tucked under their arms.

3. Training and education of how to work in a virtual office is mandatory. Behaviors, years of conditioning, and certain measures of performance, such as attendance, punctuality, and cheerfulness on the job, now go out the window. The home distractions of babysitters, the home phone ringing, interruptions at the front door, sick kids, managing time, and setting up an efficient and cost-effective

work space must all be addressed. Expectations, goals, and objectives need to be clearly defined. The scope of work, where to get help, and how often to check in must all be established prior to setting out for virtuality.

4. Trust must be established with other virtual workers. Managers have to be less concerned with eye-ball management and more concerned with what tools, training, and support the virtual workers need. Managers will have to be re-trained to get away from observing activity and focus intensely on re-sults and processes. No matter how flexibility is emphasized, managers have strong convictions that people should be working during the day. Attorneys will need paralegals working with them side-by-side as situations and issues develop. However, studies show that 50 percent of people say that their most effective work hours are outside the 9 to 5 norm. This half feel their best time is early morning or late at night. Body clock monitoring has a great deal to do with peaks of productivity.

5. Productivity is the litmus test. Those without organizational capa-bilities may not succeed in this type of environment. Poor per-formers stand out.

6. Conquer the isolation jitters. A sig-nificant number of people do not want to work at home because of the isolation, and many view the workplace as their primary social-izing activity. In fact, they may not spend large chunks of time alone,

considering their increased use of videoconferencing, computers, phones, and more client visits. Workers form new relationships and develop new social lives. Per-haps for the first time, paralegals may get to know others outside of the legal field.

7. Take steps against burnout. Experts say employees, especially those re-cently released from the corporate harness, tend to go wild in their new playgrounds. Technology al-lows people to work more, get more accomplished, and become more motivated to get on to the next project. Saturday mornings are available and sometimes tempting. The worker is no longer distracted with unrelated business and may concentrate fully on the job at hand—sometimes overdoing it.

8. View stress differently. There will be different kinds of stressors. Ac-cording to the Institute for the Study of Distributed Work, 72 per-cent of virtual office workers re-ported decreased levels of stress, while only 11 percent reported in-creased levels. The other 17 percent may have been too stressed to fill out the survey.

9. Create a purchase program with volume discounts. Purchasing equipment at retail is unnecessarily expensive. Develop a program where volume discounts are given, trade-ins accepted, and firm-approved, low-cost quality providers are easily accessible.

10. Gain firmwide support by calling the project an experiment; don't mandate the program. That way,

no one loses face if the experiment doesn't work. Productivity and increased billables are not the only things that will be reviewed if the program is bumpy, expensive, and difficult to manage. Set time limits, boundaries, and regular reviews, and benchmark performance. In experiments, no one really fails; the program is attacked with a learning process mentality. It is openly refined, discussed, and tweaked. In the unlikely event it does fail, no one's ego or career is at stake—it was just an experiment!

PARALEGAL INNER VIEW: SAL ZURZOLO— IT'S NOT ALWAYS ABOUT BIG BUCKS

Name: Sal Zurzolo

Firm: Sills Cummis Radin Tischman Epstein & Gross; Newark, New Jersey

Title: Practice Support Manager, MIS Department

Number of attorneys/paralegals: 160 attorneys, 50 paralegals

Years of experience: Litigation support, 13 years. Started as a paralegal.

Education: B.A. in Political Science from Brooklyn College; one year law school. Paralegal certificate from University of West Los Angeles, California, ABA approved

Job duties: I'm responsible for litigation support mostly. I'm trying to branch out. Litigation support keeps me busy 99 percent of the time. We maintain an imaging system of over 3 million images online right now. We've got several large cases and small ones on the imaging systems and over the last year, we've been more involved in trial support. In the MIS department, I have one person who works for me and we're a subset of the MIS department called Practice Support. Trial Support is also an element which is everything technological that has to do with the trial. We go to the courtroom, do a diagram of the courtroom and give the attorneys options on whether to use projectors with screens or monitors for the judge and jury. We help decide the software depending on presentation and maintain software—everything from renting equipment to scanning documents. We can be in the courtroom when the trial is going on. I was recently on a case in the courtroom for a month and a half assisting a partner with his first foray into technology.

Prior experience: I've been in litigation support for 13 years. I got into it while I was at White and Case in New York City for 11 years. I started as a senior paralegal coming from Los Angeles. I went to law school for a year but didn't continue. I went into paralegal work, met my wife, and moved back to New York.

In 1982 through 1985, when I was in a small firm, we did everything on paper and word processor with typewritten indices to documents. I could control this in a direct way. When I got to White and Case, they were plunging headlong into technology. I was on the WPPS litigation—a huge case. We had four or five databases with no imaging at that time. The firm formed a litigation department and chose Despina Kartsen to head it up. She thought I had the most familiarity with technology and chose me to help run it.

Tell us about meeting challenges in this position.

That would be getting attorneys over the tech phobia even in this day and age. Even people who have computers at home. For some reason, they are gun-shy when it comes to doing things at the office. There's pockets of resistance. Breaking through is sometimes tough. The best way is to have the lead attorney supporting the technology or a strong junior attorney so you'll get the others involved. There are those who will say, "You'll make me so efficient, my billables will go down." Trying to get them to buy that they will be able to use the time in other ways is a hard sell.

Can you share a great experience with us?

This trial I recently attended was a rewarding experience. It was the first time I actually went into the courtroom to that extent. Just being Johnny-on-the-spot and getting things done and working with a really good group of lawyers, particularly the lead partner, was a great experience. You'll go the extra mile for people like that. At a recent litigation department meeting, that partner got up and said, "Don't hesitate to work with Sal and Mike" in front of the entire department. Now that was a rewarding moment.

What kind of skills do you need to get a position like yours?

You have to know the legal side of things and what's involved in a document production, cutoff, trial, and motions probably more than the technology. To me, if you're going into management, you need to be tech savvy but if you don't know the legal side, lawyers are leery of coming to you. When I meet a lawyer for the first time, I mention that I worked as a paralegal to build confidence in my abilities.

Are we talking about good dollars here?

It's not as good in New Jersey as it is in Manhattan. But the commute to New York City is 2½ hours round trip by bus. The commute now is a 30- to 35-minute car ride. It's worth it to me. I couldn't coach my kids if I still worked in Manhattan. Every couple of months, I get tapped for New York. I could make $20,000 more, but family is more important. I don't work as many hours as I used to.

What advice can you give to paralegals?

Bone up on the legal side of things. Get familiar with as many different litigation support packages as you can and learn what the differences are. There are a zillion packages.

Where is the legal technology field going? How will it look in the next five years?

I don't think it will change all that much in the next five years. Machines are getting faster and better. I think it will become more efficient. I don't know that any of the basic underlying strategies in litigation support will change. We're talking about automatic OCRs and auto coding software will get better. Coding departments will become smaller. I'd like to expand from litigation and trial support into other practice areas like real estate or corporate.

CHAPTER 8

In Pursuit of Success

It's tough measuring success, particularly in a field that has little upward mobility and no designated titles of excellence at a level of work other than manager. Despite its rumored high job satisfaction, the paralegal field has yet to develop an achievement hierarchy. Career moves tend to be more lateral than vertical.

How can you get the recognition that communicates success? You can, I suppose, make a lateral move to a position outside of paralegal, such as marketing or recruiting coordinator, or move into an office management position. You can also move out of the traditional paralegal role and into one that is strategically aligned, such as litigation support department head, or into one of the newly developed practice management positions commonplace in today's legal industry. (In fact, some former paralegals across the nation are earning upwards of $125,000 in those coveted jobs.)

But the hazard of aspiring to an alternative or strategically aligned career is that there is usually only one of those positions within a firm or corporation. If your desire is to remain a paralegal yet move upward you might have to look outside the law firm environment.

Other positions, such as legal analyst, designate status and tenure in the field. In some firms, the title legal assistant versus paralegal denotes a claim to fame. But other than those few positions, no real climb up a career ladder in a law firm actually exists. Of course, there are more upward opportunities in a corporation. You've just got to be savvy about working for the company store. Woe be unto those who lack the foresight to figure out that the organization in which they have just withstood 5 days a week, 9 hours a day, 12 months a year considers the legal department a stepchild from which a VP will never rise.

For most paralegals in law firms, there are career designations by years of experience rather than performance or achievement. These rewards can bear the title senior paralegal complete with a window office or attachment to a name partner. Access to the sacred senior paralegal status is often no more than hard-earned years in the field. All you have to do, in some cases, is suit up and show up and eventually you are wearing the title. And while the buzz or verbal recognition throughout the firm is important, it is sometimes the *only* way paralegals fully enjoy star status. These career achievers garner better assignments or opportunities to team with more highly recognized lawyers.

But beware the difference in interpretation of recognition bestowed through "increased responsibilities." The firm says, "We love what you do and we're going to give you more responsibility." "YES!" is your enthusiastic response. "Finally, great challenges." This challenge could take the form of research and drafting assignments or attendance at depositions or trial, and, in many instances, that's what happens. But being told your responsibilities are about to increase can have an entirely different meaning than what you may fantasize. Paralegals sometimes find themselves victims of "empty-loading": your increased responsibilities may change from organizing 10 boxes of documents with one assistant, to organizing 100 boxes with two assistants. Rather than graduating to more sophisticated assignments, you are handed additional similar routine and repetitious tasks. *Yikes!*

The good news is there is always the silent recognition of success, the unspoken yet real acknowledgment between you and the firm: more money. But as far as I can tell, it is still in poor taste to brag to your colleagues just how much increase in salary you received or how large a bonus popped out of that envelope. Public or peer recognition becomes difficult to achieve.

Rest easy, though. The outlook for those seeking success isn't really so gloomy nor is cynicism necessarily the right avenue. Those who seek outward recognition and rewards in this field *can* achieve their dreams. It's a matter of defining your individual success, recognizing your goals, visualizing where you want to go and designing the steps to get there. The first important step is to know where you're headed. How do you get *there* if you don't know where *there* is?

I talked with Jay Pooler, Ph.D., a Los Angeles-based clinical psychologist who coaches clients in the process of achieving success. During our interview, Dr. Pooler, a youthful 49 with a delightful twinkle in his eye, conveyed instantly how to teach paralegals some valuable pointers. Creating a structured process for identifying and achieving victory in the pursuit of success, Pooler has taught professionals at all levels how to achieve their ideals. It is apparent that this likable, insightful, intelligent success mentor draws from all walks of life, value systems, and experiences to formulate his success program. "What qualifies as success for one individual does not necessarily work for another," he says. "Don't buy into someone else's definition of success. You have to stay true to your own needs when determining what's really important." Dr. Pooler assists his clients through five levels of consciousness so that even the highest mountain feels easy to climb. The interview revealed a rare authority who really understands the trials and tribulations of achieving success in the paralegal world. I found myself captivated as he explained his simple technique. The following section discusses how he turns corporate contenders into winners.

THE POOLER FIVE-STEP GUIDE
TO ACHIEVING SUCCESS

Step 1: Create and list your options and satisfactions. Diving deep into your inner world and thoroughly understanding your chosen field, you must first realistically assess your current situation. List options and define your version of job satisfaction. Buttressed with money and job satisfaction quotient, you have to be satisfied with levels you can achieve within your given field and be able to convey a sense of urgency when negotiating your goals. So many people know what they *don't* want. It's sometimes harder to pinpoint what you *do* want.

Step 2: Hammer out a job description of how you want your job to look. Visualize the components important in your restructure. Presenting your redesigned job to your supervisors isn't as important as claiming the job in your inner world. Such a restructuring of your job can be essential to your career success. You may want to use this redesign of your present position to transition to a more meaningful job, one where success is easier to attain. Let's look at what components apply in the career of a successful paralegal:

- Highly paid
- Title based upon skill, abilities, and past performance
- Sophistication of assignments
- Structure of workload
- Confidence of attorneys in your ability and capability
- Recognition by peers, supervisors, and the firm in general

Don't be afraid to create a new title for your position and present it. You may find your value and status elevated simply by structuring a new title for yourself. Internet specialist, trial consultant, research assistant, and mergers and acquisitions specialist are just a few of the titles which might exemplify your achievement level. The firm should immediately recognize that with a "specialist" title, the billable rate might just have gone up substantially.

Step 3: Ability to communicate. In order to be successful, you must have a strong ability to communicate what you want. Convey the importance of structuring your niche into the organization by emphasizing its importance to each department. Communicate how the change benefits the firm either through profitability, cost or time savings, or even reduced people power. How would your redesigned position give you a level of satisfaction that maximizes the ability to perform well and meet the needs of both the firm and yourself? Start negotiations for an understanding of tasks. The organization chart or job description may have to be reorganized along with questions of title and monies. Go deep into your soul and ask yourself:

- Will renegotiating afford you the kind of personal flow so you feel fulfilled? Will you be able to interpersonally relate on the job front, in the community, or in your social life? Are you financially and physically able to sustain such a lifestyle?
- Can you communicate the content of the assignment and workload?
- What is your ability to structure your success? How can you communicate those desires?
- Do you seek out the person with power who can implement those changes? Is it better to go to the conduit to the power: those who have the administrator's or the attorney's ear?

Step 4: Execute, implement, and reiterate your expertise. Imparting knowledge to others establishes you as an expert. Be careful, though! You really do need to have superior knowledge and expertise before you can be considered an authority! Don't make the mistake of having just enough information to make you dangerous. Your goal is to become someone who can be relied upon for the answers. People want information that facilitates their work or department needs. One good way to impart knowledge is through the written word: articles by or about you or the ability to write for others. Another excellent method for establishing credibility is teaching. It's a simple correlation between "expert" and "teacher or writer" in the minds of most people.

Step 5: Establish solid relationships. Success is relationships within one's field. Women, in particular, are great at establishing relationships. And although the term "networking" is overused, it is a highly effective technique for leveraging and communicating success. Consider establishing a networking support group—one that shares new developments in the field. Paralegals can get together to share information about job responsibilities and give you fresh ideas as to direction and possibilities in the field. Set monthly meetings for brunch or lunch in a roundtable atmosphere. Share the experiences of in-service that might help others perform tasks more successfully.

Success affects home life, significant others, and your ability to maintain those relationships in the community without becoming overwhelmed. Don't expect instant gratification. It takes hard work, vision, and commitment to change to bring about success. While no one can predict every roadblock that you will run into, you sure can decide how to react. Prepare, prepare, prepare. Success is not an accident: It is the result of a carefully thought-out program. As for me, hey, I'm headed back for another session with Dr. Pooler. Like success itself, sometimes you just can't get enough of a good thing.

CHAPTER 9

Shifts in Legal Temporary Staffing Trends

> You can't learn anything from experiences you're not having.
>
> Louis L'Amour

LOOKING AT THE WORKPLACE OUTSIDE OF THE BOX

Long before paradigm shifts were in vogue, my dad taught me a good lesson. I was 19 years old and desperately needed a car. So Dad and I went down to the local Chevrolet used car lot to pick out the vehicle that was to announce my social status to the world. We picked out a 1961 white Corvair (most of you may not have heard of this short-lived classic) for a great price of $400. It was a small car with the motor in the trunk and the trunk where the motor should be.

"It's perfect," I sighed. "We'll take it," said my dad. "By the way, Bob," he said to the used car salesman, with whom we were now best friends, "just why is all that oil blowing out the back?"

"Fifteen cent part," said our pal, Bob. "We'll have it fixed in a jiffy." (There was a time when people talked like that.)

I drove away, excited, fully liberated, and loving every second of my newfound independence. Driving down the street I suddenly spotted a car right in front of me about to make a left-hand turn. I stepped on the brakes. Nothing much happened except that my entire life flashed before me. Two milliseconds later, I ran smack dab into the car in front of me. The Corvair, with the trunk in the front, motor in the back, curled up and died in the middle of the street. Fortunately, no one was hurt.

After all information was exchanged, I hiked over to the nearest convenience store and called my dad. (There were no cell phones in those days.) Sobbing into the phone, I tried to grasp how the car I owned for a total of

16½ minutes was now a mere memory of itself. I felt terrible. Nothing could console me.

"Dad," I wailed, while looking at this crumpled mess now attracting attention from the entire neighborhood, "I wrecked the car. I stepped on the brakes. It . . . didn't stop! I rear-ended the car in front of me."

"Honey," my dad said after hearing the story, "it's not your fault. She was in your way."

Thank you, Dad.

He taught me a valuable lesson, one I will remember for the rest of my life. Keep an open mind and see if there isn't another way of looking at things. Shift the thought patterns. Flip the thinking.

Which is precisely what happened when the legal field threw out its myopic thinking and joined the rest of Corporate America in new staffing hiring trends. The terminology we use has also changed. We no longer say "permanent employee," because no one is hired for life. The new term is full-time employee. On occasion, "part-time employee" can refer to a temporary employee rather than someone who works fewer than 40 hours per week. Keeping up? Outsourcing, temporary staffing, contract employees, leased employees, job-sharing, professional employer organizations, project employees, virtual departments, full-time employment, regular employment, contingent workers, supplemental staffing are just a few of the new labels employees face today.

Only 35 percent of the twenty-first century workforce will hold traditional, full-time, on-site jobs; 25 percent of all U.S. jobs will be contingent; 15 percent will be contract professionals or specialists; and 25 percent will be support services such as transportation, food services, custodial, and maintenance. These predictions were announced at the 1996 Staffing Industry Executive Forum and were credited to David Pierce Snyder, a renowned social and future forecaster who used history to predict how the evolutions we are currently living through will affect our future. According to Snyder, we are in the midst of reengineering the workforce to sustain the American economic advantage as we transform into a technological and information-based society.

Corporations and law firms have already cut back on permanent staff and are instead using temporary staff as a means to provide a broad scope of services without incurring increased overhead and salary costs. Since 1991 there has been a fourfold increase in the use of contract attorneys and paralegals. Contract attorneys have been estimated from 10,000 to 40,000 according to the American Staffing Association.

Corporations and law firms are creating "virtual departments" built entirely around temporary employees working on litigations projects. One major U.S. defense contractor set up an in-house litigation support department with full-time supervisory personnel only. It used a temporary staffing organization to fill all nonsupervisory positions on an as-needed basis. The estimated savings: $1.4 million annually.

Outsourcing, contracting another company or firm to provide personnel or services, has caught on in some law firms historically known as conservative, slow-moving, blue-chip, staid organizations. Outsourcing in many corporations is now standard operating procedure. Some corporations will outsource all of the temporary help needs to one staffing vendor, who, in turn, staffs all departments—legal, engineering, clerical, accounting, and more.

Staffing organizations may place a coordinator on-site. This manager is usually housed on the client's premises. The coordinator is responsible for recruiting, testing, training, managing, and paying the temporary. Some outsourcing organizations have created elaborate orientation programs, complete with customized videos and corporate personality compatibility tests. The corporation is linked to the vendors' accounting and recruiting systems.

For many years, firms and corporations have contracted outside firms to provide services such as payroll, mailroom, photocopying, and data processing. Today, as outsourcing has become a widely recognized business, other services that are commonly outsourced include information technology, accounting (including billing and accounts receivable collection), human resources, and facility management.

Firms are now experimenting with concepts such as outsourcing entire associate and paralegal departments. Associates surveyed in one large firm spent 80 percent of their time on legal research. Paralegals in the same firm billed an average of 1,100 hours per year. A few had been with the firm over 10 years with no visible growth pattern. A new CEO, wielding a mighty sword, slashed, scorched, and cremated the infrastructure. Only partners and key personnel covering the core competencies were to remain. All other departments were outsourced. A contracted legal research firm touted over 1,200 researchers across the country. Their database consisted of superior court clerks, managing partners, and high-level associates. The paralegal department was cut to the bone. Temporary paralegals were hired on an as-needed basis. Human resource functions, accounting, and MIS departments were outsourced. While the firm plans to spend around $30 million per year in outsourcing, it expects to save significant dollars on the bottom line. This experiment may render a tremendous impact unlike any other on the legal community's staffing plans.

Outsourcing has caused considerable debate. There is a profound difference between outsourcing, downsizing, and cleaning house. Replacing poor performers is one thing, but outsourcing and downsizing can eliminate talented lawyers and paralegals. Targeted professional librarians worry that bargain-hunting firms will look to outsourcing the virtual library as an answer to saving costs, ultimately sacrificing quality. Leadership, which must be groomed from within, is at risk.

Naysayers claim overload of outsourcing can lead to top-heavy organizations steeped in a bureaucracy of decision makers who have confused the issues. The real definition of "lean and mean" is highly functioning teams, engaged in creating better legal services.

Then we have those middle-of-the-road trend watchers who make us stop and think. Outsourcing is a new concept with a history that includes relatively few companies. Midroaders are asking questions such as, "Outsourcing: death knell for the profession or an idea whose time has come?"

An interesting trend for paralegal hiring is the contract paralegal. Rather than hire paralegals fulltime, firms now contract paralegals for specific cases or matters. When the matter is over, the paralegal moves on to another job.

The monumental transformation occurring in Corporate America directly affects the legal industry. There is a fear that efforts to capture a healthier bottom line may devalue a law firm's greatest asset—people. The paralegal career, still in its infancy, is particularly vulnerable. Although paralegal jobs should increase (the field remains on the Department of Labor's top-ten growth lists), workplace relationships as we know them will change.

The healthy side of the picture is that these various hiring trends lead to opportunities you might otherwise not have experienced. It is no longer considered a career-limiting move to work on a project-by-project basis. The temporary career has arrived.

TIPS FOR TEMPING

There's lots of movement here. Status has changed. No longer is a temp position considered a job "in lieu of." Many workers are now permanent temporaries. Benefits have been added. Many are enjoying the same perks as full-time employees: workers' comp, group insurance, retirement programs, and 401k plans. Choice of work has improved. Because temporary work is more valued than in the past, the temp isn't always receiving the worst assignments. Assignments can last from 1 day or longer, sometimes up to 2 or 3 years. Many firms have chosen temporary staffing organizations rather than hire independent contractors, lessening firm liability. One of the most popular hiring trends today is temp-to-full-time. Employers want the opportunity to evaluate job performance before deciding whether the candidate fits with the firm. Employees have a reciprocal attitude: It's always nice to be able to evaluate the potential employer.

Tips to Temping Checklist

___   Always be ready to work on short notice. Make up your mind, yes or no, *before* the phone rings. Tell the staffing organization if you need a day's notice.

___   Be prepared to interview for long-term assignments. Firms are seeking personality fits as well as skill matches.

___   Politely inform people when lengthy explanations for simple procedures are unnecessary. On the other hand, be sure you know how the firm does it, simple or not. Everyone has a different way of doing things.

___   Don't feel left out if you are excluded from office social functions or not asked to lunch. People sometimes don't think beyond their normal habit patterns. It doesn't occur to them that you might get your feelings hurt.

___   Don't expect to temp at every job for the sole purpose of finding a permanent position. While the trend leans toward temporary-to-full-time hiring, some firms still frown on it. Find out, if you can, which firms are open to the idea.

___   If the firm has a strong hierarchy, temps may be viewed as circling the bottom of the totem pole. Don't let it bother you. If you think about it, people with that kind of prejudice end up losing in the long run.

___   Be prepared to fill out conflict-of-interest and confidentiality agreements. You may also have to be a U.S. citizen to work on some government sites.

___   If the firm does not provide a point person, seek out the office manager or senior paralegal. Get someone to demonstrate how to use the phones, library systems, photocopying, faxes, e-mail (if necessary), computers, office supplies, couriers, access codes, and client matter numbers. Additionally and critical to doing a good job, find out who you can turn to for help.

___   Get the billing system straight. Be sure to use correct key codes, lingo, measures of time, and client matter numbers. Understand what is, and more importantly, is not billable. Every firm is different. Find out if you are expected to bill a minimum number of hours. Get very specific about administrative time.

___   Get correct signatures for time cards. Otherwise, paychecks may be held up.

___   Find out absolutely, positively when that time card is due and where. Is faxing okay? A phone call? What's the deadline? Failure to follow instructions causes late paychecks.

___   Certain information is always needed to complete the assignment. Be sure to get all the details. Discuss background information, case status, and so forth with the supervising attorney or paralegal.

___ Work within the boundaries of the job in the beginning. As you progress and prove yourself, chances are that more sophisticated assignments will be delegated.

___ Establish a rapport. Get acquainted. Clients are more relaxed when they see a great attitude.

___ Say no when self-respect, health, or safety is jeopardized.

___ Bring a resume to the job even if one has been forwarded. Never trust it was received by those who will be working with you.

___ Create a box office if you are unsure of necessary support items such as a copy of local court rules, manual to an unfamiliar software program, extra office supplies (if you are offsite), and list of trusted vendors.

___ Make sure to receive a competitive salary for the work. However, discussing salary with the temp next door is probably not a good idea.

___ Reaffirm length of the assignment. Find out whether overtime has to be approved before starting.

___ Get "kudos" letters from supervisors when possible. These are great tools for finding other temp or full-time positions.

___ Above all, have a good time, make some great contacts, and use this opportunity as a learning experience.

TEMPING VERSUS FREELANCING

There are very distinct truths and myths to working on your own:

Truth	Myth
1. You can work when you want.	**1.** You can work when you want.
2. You earn more money.	**2.** You earn more money.
3. You are your own boss.	**3.** You are your own boss.
4. You are in charge of your career.	**4.** You are in charge of your career.
5. You have less stress and responsibility.	**5.** You have less stress and responsibility.

Firms that hired too many associates and have experienced a decrease in new business are reportedly using first-year associates for paralegal assignments and cutting back on the number of permanent paralegals hired. Firms would rather reduce the staff than let on to the legal press that they are laying off associates. Other firms have decreased their permanent staffs but have budgeted for temporary employees.

How Do You Know If It's Right for You?

In the past years, the temporary paralegal position has become a legitimate segment of the field. There are paralegals who are considered career temps and earn very decent salaries. Attitudes among many employers have changed over recent years. You may no longer be considered to have a less marketable resume or less stable work history if you have been temping for awhile. This attitude is more prevalent in the major metropolitan areas where temporary paralegals are used more. In fact, some employers consider temping an asset because the paralegal has honed certain skills, such as the ability to adapt quickly to a firm. A skilled temporary can take less training time and understands a variety of firm procedures. This is due, in part, to temporaries' ability and past experience in quickly analyzing the assignment and starting with a minimum of instruction. They are expected to jump right in.

If you have less than 1 year's experience as a paralegal, don't try becoming a freelance paralegal, marketing directly to the law firm without benefit of an agency. Chances are you haven't set up enough of a network to keep yourself going and haven't attained enough experience to bill yourself as an expert in the field.

As a freelance paralegal, you present yourself to the firm as an expert in the field and can command a higher hourly rate (generally) than what the firm will pay for its permanent employees. Because of your expertise, the firm has higher demands of you in a shorter period of time than one of their permanent employees. In reality, they will be less tolerant of any mistakes. The firm expects to train its permanent employees. They do not expect to hire you as an expert, pay a premium, and then train you to boot.

On the other hand, some of the paralegal temporary agencies will take you if you have less than 1 year's experience. They control where they send you and do get assignments that call for little or no experience.

If you are security conscious and feel that you need that weekly check, then this probably isn't for you. If, on the other hand, you can afford to be off for a couple of days or weeks, you may have a great time. Temporary/freelance paralegals take on a certain mindset. These are generally people who have less need to belong—it is not so important that they have a family at work; they have little or no problem moving on. They like the feeling of freedom and being able to pick and choose where and when they work. If they don't like a particular employer, they can simply arrange for another position. Needing and enjoying flexibility and variety are two key factors in determining whether to enter this segment of the field. Other determining factors are financial considerations, whether you are in school, or whether you are new to the area.

This is also a good way to learn what's right for you. Working for short periods of time at several different firms or companies gives you an opportunity to experience various types of environments, specialties, locations, and firms. You are, in effect, job-hopping and getting paid to do so. You can expect to stay at any one firm anywhere from 1 week to a year or even more. I know of one "temp" who was named the "permanent temporary." He was a temporary on one large-scale litigation for 2 years, until the case settled. This is not an uncommon situation.

The temporary/freelancer position can be found in almost every specialty. The most demand is found in litigation, particularly large-case litigation and computerized litigation support. There are also a number of highly successful probate paralegals across the country with lucrative businesses. You need to be confident of your skills because most of the time you will have very little or no training on the job. You will be called in when firms

- have an overload of work
- do not have the necessary personnel to cover the normal workload
- have need of an expert for which they do not have a permanent slot
- need someone to cover for an employee on a leave of absence, or while the firm is searching for a permanent person for an open position.

THE TEMPORARY PARALEGAL: WORKING FOR AN AGENCY

If there is more than one paralegal temporary agency in your city, you may want to sign up with several to increase chances of getting called for work. You may be told by an agency that it does not want you to sign up with any other agencies. Some may go so far as to tell you that to do so puts you in a potential conflict of interest situation. As of this writing, some issues are emerging regarding temporaries and conflict.

If you are reasonably assured that the one agency can keep you as busy as you want, you may choose to sign only with that particular agency. On the other hand, you have the right to work and the agency should not restrict your ability to seek work. If the agency puts you on its permanent staff (it pays you whether it has assignments for you or not), then you may need to abide by this request. Also, if you are working for a service that produces a product, such as a deposition summarizing service, that service may expect you also to honor this request due to potential conflict of interest. Other than that, you can sign up with several agencies. As of this writing, I am unfamiliar with any cases that prohibit paralegals from signing up with more than one agency. However, because this book will reach all 50 states, to be on the safe side, research in your own state just to make sure. Extend your research cases involving temporary attorneys to see whether paralegals were included in those rulings.

Each agency operates differently. Some stay more closely in touch with you so they can place you more effectively. If you expect to work on a regular basis, here are a few suggestions:

1. Find out whether the agency wants you to call on a regular basis to check for available assignments. Some will put you on active status and prefer to call you when they have an open job order. Others need to know on a daily or weekly basis whether you are still seeking assignments.

2. Keep the agency posted when you are on an assignment. Let the agency know as fast as you can when an assignment may end. The more advance notice the agency has, the more time it has to look for something else. Paralegal assignments are not like clerical assignments. Firms don't generally call because someone is out sick that day. Temporary assignments are usually project-oriented and need advanced planning.

3. Keep your resume updated. You never know when you will need it to compete for a temporary assignment or when it is time to look for a permanent position. Oftentimes, the agency needs to send your resume. The employer may select a candidate strictly from resumes. The myth is that the agency chooses all the paralegals. This is not necessarily so.

4. Find out from the law firm whether it is happy with the agency's service. The agency should appreciate this feedback. If you are not getting assigned to very many firms and you know your performance is good, it may be because the agency is not serving clients as it should. You may want to consider another agency or help the agency in straightening out the problem, if you can.

5. Turn your time cards in on time. Make the agency enjoy working with you. The happier it is with your relationship, the more likely it will want to work for you.

6. Let the agency know if you have picked up a new skill. Most agencies keep strict records. Toot your own horn (don't wait for someone else). Call the agency if you learned a new software package, new area of law, language, technology, form or procedures, or a subspecialty. Let it know about all new developments, such as completing a course or seminar, getting a degree, or completing your paralegal certificate. These new skills can enhance chances for better assignments.

FREE AGENTS: THE LATEST IN
TEMPORARY/CONTRACT WORK

There is a deeper change shaking the old employer-employee temporary-help paradigm. Today, with the transition to a knowledge-based economy and global connectivity, the power is shifting to those with skills. Supplies of talent needed to fuel the new economy are expected to remain scarce for the next 20 years, according to *Business Week* (August 2000). At the same time, the amount of work hasn't decreased but the need for law firms and corporations to grow and shrink according to the demands of the global marketplace has increased. That's why, in place of the twentieth century labor model, something new is emerging.

Business Week discusses the Human Capital Exchange (HCE), a market for skills and talent that fits the bill for the twenty-first century. In the HCE, much like the Nasdaq and the New York Stock Exchange, the value of free agents is determined by the open market—lawyers down $2, doctors up $3—rather than by a hierarchical organization. The old salary-plus bene-fits structure just doesn't cut it anymore as a way to realize one's true eco-nomic value.

These contingent workers keep their resumes permanently posted on job boards—the first sign of the shift toward skilled new economy workers day-trading their careers. More and more companies from job-posting sites to bounty-paying referral services are popping up on the Web, creating a sort of labor auction where workers can sell their skills to the highest bidder.

A few sites now cater to lawyers, and we expect that paralegals will soon follow. Sites such as www.guru.com represent the tip of the iceberg. This concept is primarily project oriented which is why paralegals will fall into the trend. *Business Week* cited the growing ranks of free agents from 22 percent of the workforce in 1998 to 26 percent in 2000 according to a poll by Lansing, Michigan, market research firm EPIC/MRA. By 2010, 41 per-cent of the workforce will be working on a contract basis, the firm predicts. The prediction is that business superstars will have agents as do actors and athletes.

Changing jobs or working on a project basis will become standard oper-ating procedure. According to the Labor Department, a typical 32-year-old has already held nine jobs and could have as many as 20 different positions in her lifetime. These MVPs will constantly bargain for better deals within their organizations—deals such as new projects, Tuesdays and Wednes-days off, or the entire month of December off.

The upside to free agenting is the possibility of more dollars, more free-dom, and the ability to sell your skills around the globe thanks to the wired world. Free agency offers lifestyle perks. But the downside could mean late paychecks, costly health insurance, and the pressure of hunting for every gig, plus the distractions of a home office. If the economy sours, free agents could wind up pining for security. However it turns out, there is no going back to the old cradle-to-grave cocoon corporations came to provide in the century just past.

THE FREELANCE PARALEGAL: MARKETING YOURSELF

If you choose to work as a feeelance paralegal and not through an agency, have a different technique for marketing. Think as though you are a business, even if only a business of one.

Preparing Your New Client Materials

Your new client package can contain all or part of the following:

- Resume (can be used in place of a brochure)
- Business card
- Brochure (can be used in place of resume)
- Articles by or about you
- Letters of reference
- Client list (only if you have permission from the firm or corporation)
- Rolodex card
- Home page or Web site
- Sample work product

Networking

Countless studies have shown that the majority of jobs are filled by people recommended informally to the employer. This is the hidden job market which also exists for freelancers. Continue to reinforce your network of associates, colleagues, clients, teachers, students, past clients, former employers, friends, and other freelance paralegals. Some networking ideas follow.

Solicit business through meetings.

1. *Attend the local bar association meetings.* Many bar associations have membership or associate membership for paralegals. The idea, of course, is to talk to attorneys in casual conversations about what you do. You may find one or two have a need for a freelance paralegal, or they know someone who could use your services. Take plenty of cards.

2. *Attend paralegal meetings.* Enough cannot be written about the positive results of networking. Paralegals not only know where the jobs are, but many also have the hiring power.

3. *Attend city council and other political arena meetings.* You just never know who you will meet and how they can use your services.

Network where attorneys network. Join organizations that attorneys in your city tend to join. For example, in Los Angeles, the Jewish Federation has a legal division. That legal division is comprised of more than 400 attorneys. They have many social functions and fund-raising events for the division alone. At some of the functions, law firms pay for entire tables. What better opportunity to network with attorneys on a social basis! Other organizations or functions you might attend are town hall meetings, political rallies, continuing education courses for attorneys, business council meetings, chamber of commerce meetings, and Rotary clubs. In other words, go where attorneys go.

Go to legal trade shows, state bar conventions, ABA conventions. Attorneys, paralegals, and administrators love to attend good trade shows and conventions where seminars and booths update them on the latest. Go as a participant and get involved in their conversations. Also introduce yourself at booths at the trade shows. Vendors know where the work is. They enjoy being able to recommend a good paralegal. When you are well-versed in their product or service, they don't hesitate to recommend you. No one expects money to change hands or exclusives (you recommend only each other). Lots of business can bloom from this avenue.

Attend paralegal seminars. Even if the topic doesn't quite fit, it's worth getting out there and meeting as many people as you can. Besides, there's always at least one new idea to learn.

Get on the Internet.

Research Sources

Track the newspapers. Some law trade journals have sections such as "new cases filed," or "what's happening," or "mergers and acquisitions." Send a letter directly to attorneys stating how they may best be able to use you.

Look for law firms and corporations that are laying off. Often they have to lay off permanent staff but are budgeted for temporary help. They don't have to keep you on past the project completion or pay any benefits, not even parking. This is a great source of potential business that often is overlooked.

Go down to the courthouse and see what's been filed. Just as a reporter would do, you, too, can research the files to look for cases that may need your services.

Look in the want ads. Check for firms and corporations seeking to hire permanent employees, particularly if you have a specialty that may be hard to find. Sometimes firms have not considered hiring a freelancer while they launch an extensive job search for just the right employee. They may appreciate a temporary employee so that the workload doesn't pile up too drastically.

Read promotion announcements. Find out about associates promoted to partner, lateral moves, paralegal promotions, and newly hired directors of administration or office managers. These people may want help in their new positions and can use you during the transition period. Fire off your new client letter or call them on the phone directly.

Following Up

Following up is divided into two categories:

1. Follow up on the new client materials sent. If you used direct mail, call or send another letter to spark interest in your services. If a potential client told you to check in with the firm at a later date, don't dismiss this as a rejection. Follow up when asked. Circumstances may have changed and the firm may now need you. You may want to follow up on a case when it is in a particular phase, such as discovery.

2. Follow up with past clients, colleagues, teachers, students, and events. Drop a friendly note to a client who hasn't used you in a while. Send a letter congratulating someone on winning a case, settling a probate, spearheading a deal, or to remind him that you are there for the next case. As you finish an assignment, send a letter thanking colleagues for using your services. Urge them to contact you in the future. Be sure to include business and Rolodex cards. Anything that reminds the client you are ready for work, even at a later time, is good marketing.

Sending Holiday Cards and Gifts

It's just good business to send clients holiday cards. If you do not wish to send Christmas cards (too religious), send "happy holiday" or "happy New Year" cards. Some businesses, in an attempt to separate themselves from the crowd, are sending Thanksgiving or Fourth of July cards. Use your best judgment. Remember, for the most part, law firms still think conservatively.

If you decide to send a gift, do so wisely. Holiday gifts, if too extravagant, will give a bad impression. On the other hand, something that looks cheap will give just as bad an impression. Look for a company that specializes in corporate gifts and be sure the gift is in good taste. Give gifts to everyone in the firm who should receive one. If you worked for only one attorney, then perhaps he or she receives the gift. If, however, the paralegal administrator was responsible for hiring you, supervised your billings, and made sure you got paid on time, don't forget this person!

Be aware that some corporations have very strict policies about accepting gifts of any kind. If there are government contracts involved, chances are they will return the gift with an apology note. Try not to put anyone in that situation.

Other Marketing Tools

Lunch and brunch. A standard but effective marketing tool is to take clients, new and old, to lunch or breakfast. In some regions, dinner is not always appropriate. Find out what best applies. Choose an upscale restaurant, but not excessively expensive. Coffee shops simply will not do. ("Is this all you think of me?" the client will be apt to wonder.) Overpriced, exclusive restaurants also give the wrong impression (no wonder your fees are so high). Certain corporations may also have rules—employees may have to pay for their own lunches. Most companies with restrictions will reveal this to you.

Hold seminars. Nothing works better than to establish yourself as the expert in the field. Try to hold the seminar in conjunction with someone else, possibly a school.

Take a course in sales techniques. Excellent courses, books, and tapes are available that teach how to solicit business and overcome objections. Many paralegals frown on the "S" word, sales. However, you are selling your services to the law firm. Be ahead of the competition when the law firm or corporation sits down to select a freelancer. Stop wondering when or where the next job will be. Some books to consider are *Zig Ziglar's Secrets of Closing the Sale* (or any of Ziglar's books); *Swim with the Sharks* by Harvey

MacKay; and *What They Don't Teach You at Harvard Business School* by Mark H. McCormack.

Market for the next job before this one ends. Many freelancers have down periods because they were too busy working on one assignment to market for the next. You need to market on a continuous basis. It's much better to present yourself to a firm as booked up and looking ahead for the next assignment, than willing to take almost anything. In the legal field, decisions take time. Continuous marketing means you won't be idle while the law firm or legal department makes up its mind or waits for a client to act.

Market to other attorneys and paralegals in the firm while on assignment. These attorneys and paralegals are already familiar with your personality and quality of work product. As one case winds down, other attorneys and paralegals may leap at the chance to have you on their team. They may not be aware that your assignment is about to end. Get the word out within the firm or legal department.

Write, Write, Write. Send copies of articles written by or about you to your clients with a note: "Just to keep you updated on the latest in . . . ."

Getting Paid

When you work for an agency, you will generally be given an opportunity to work for an hourly rate. Some agencies will specify a range according to job skill level, specialty, years of experience, and client base.

If the agency quotes a pay range and states that most of the assignments pay *between* a certain amount, say, between $15 and $20 per hour, find out what amount most assignments pay. It's tough to work on one assignment for 6 months at $19 per hour and then take a significant drop to $15 per hour. Tell the agency the lowest rate you'll accept. The agency may claim you are limiting your opportunities. Maybe so, but chances are, if you're good and they're good, they'll keep you working.

If you are freelancing, you will have to establish your own hourly rate. Research what the market will bear. Freelance paralegals have reported earning anywhere from $15 per hour to $100 per hour, depending on expertise, region, experience, reputation, and ability to provide the necessary services.

If a firm insists on lower rates, follow the lead of many consultants and negotiate the amount of time the project will take. In other words, if you are charging $35 per hour and the firm wants lower fees, you might say, "I would very much like to undertake this assignment. However, lowering my fee that drastically is not possible. Let's do it this way. This project will run about 3 weeks. Why don't you hire me for 2 weeks, and we will get someone in for $25 or less to tie up loose ends. The person you get for

$25 or less will not have my level of experience or my years of experience. Let's have that person do the 'grunt' work."

Now, chances are the firm may want you and only you. However, you have presented an option and opened up negotiations.

Payday

For those choosing to work with an agency, you should be paid on a regular basis on a specified payday. Freelancers should insist on the same payment schedule. Before starting the project, establish on what day you will get paid. Find out how the firm wants to be billed: time sheets or invoice. Then establish on what day you will pick up your check. There is nothing wrong with asking to get paid the same day the firm pays all of its other employees. I have witnessed freelance paralegals experience severe financial and cash flow problems because they bill and then sit back and wait for payment. If you are on the firm's accounts payable list, they will most likely not pay you before 30 days and probably closer to 45 to 60 days after receiving the invoice. This just isn't necessary.

If you are working on contingency, probate, or any other type of matters where the firm must wait to get paid, it is not your problem! You are considered an out-of-pocket expense. Most firms can pass your billing on to their client. They can pay you first while waiting to get reimbursed from their client. It is simply the firm's cost of doing business.

Freelancing and Payroll Taxes

Before venturing into freelancing, check with your accountant for payroll and tax information. If you are thinking of categorizing yourself as an independent contractor, be very clear about the IRS rulings. In order to become an independent contractor, you must abide by strict rules. Most freelancers do not meet the lengthy criteria, some of which are that you must have a federal I.D. number and a certificate of compliance for workers' compensation insurance. While I cannot advise you on how to file taxes or interpret the IRS code, be sure to check with a bona fide CPA. Each person can set up business differently. If you are an employee, talk to the firm about being paid through their payroll, and have the firm deduct appropriate taxes. However, you still need to reconcile at tax time like the rest of us.

RESUME WRITING

As a temporary paralegal or freelancer, your resume should be the same as if you were a candidate for a permanent position. It should have the same professional look and feel. Use either the functional or reverse chronological formats. If using the chronological format, be sure that it is in *reverse* form. One freelancer I know used this format, but listed all of the firms in chronological order. Unfortunately, the first firm dissolved several years ago. Potential clients assumed she hadn't worked since. Her resume was hindering her job search. The fact of the matter was she had a highly successful business.

Following is a sample functional resume for a temporary or freelance paralegal.

SAMPLE: FUNCTIONAL RESUME FOR TEMPORARY OR FREELANCE PARALEGAL

NAME
ADDRESS
CITY, STATE AND ZIP CODE
PHONE NUMBERS
E-MAIL ADDRESS

HIGHLIGHTS OF QUALIFICATIONS

- Self-motivated, focused, detail-oriented
- Successful in mastering new skills
- Proven ability to obtain objective conclusions involving massive documents

SKILLS AND ACCOMPLISHMENTS

Knowledge of Real Estate and Finance:

- Mastered real estate procedures, forms, and contracts
- Authored prospectus for multimillion dollar shopping center
- Prepared abstracts for real estate syndication deals

Analysis of Feasibility:

- Transformed form file system into highly efficient and cost-effective operation
- Implemented and modified new systems until results were achieved

- Increased client satisfaction through new documentation system
- Appraised feasibility and cost-effectiveness of proposed expenditures of new equipment and facilities

Project Planning/Management:

- Successfully assisted in start-up of new developments
- Oversaw staff, prepared evaluations
- Developed status report systems

EMPLOYMENT HISTORY

Feb. 1997–present

Freelance Legal Assistant
Clients include: Smith & Smith; Green and Green; Perry & Berry; Hygh & Low; Brown, White and Jones; King, Joseph, Polk and Kramer

March 1994–Nov. 1994

Real Estate Legal Assistant
Perrins, Perino and Parkins

Jan. 1992–Feb. 1994

Administrative Assistant
Security Atlantic Bank

EDUCATION AND TRAINING

Paralegal Certificate—St. Mary's College
San Francisco, CA 1994
With Honors

B.A., English—University of California at
Santa Cruz, CA 1993
Dean's List

CONCLUSION

Many paralegals fantasize that by working on a temporary basis they will have less stress and responsibility than in their present positions. To some extent, this is true, but don't overlook the fact that deadlines remain the same, work quality must be superior, marketing for new jobs or new clients is constant, hours can be long (although ability to control the hours is sometimes easier), and you must still negotiate for dollars. If none of that is particularly bothersome, then you may have found a new and exciting job avenue.

PARALEGAL INNER VIEW: GINNI HANKS— NIKE WAS RIGHT—SHE JUST DID IT

Name: Ginni Hanks
Title: Litigation Coordinator
Corporation: Nike, Inc., Beaverton, Oregon
Education: Went to business college in 1979 as a paralegal before ABA certification
Years of experience: 20+; at Nike over 2 years
Number of attorneys and paralegals: 17 attorneys, 5 paralegals
Job duties: Mainly, I interact with outside counsel and help them answer discovery requests; conduct witness interviews; keep track of documents. In addition, I process service, route, track, and follow up on cases. I was surprised at how varied the cases are here—wrongful death; employment; labor practices; personal injury; advertising or breach of contract; and product liability are just a few. For the last 2 years, I've dealt with product liability claims. I just moved to risk management department which I enjoy tremendously. I was a litigation paralegal in insurance defense, and before that, I worked in family law.
Biggest challenge: Motivating people to get things done, like get documents to me. We have designers who are working on footwear that goes to market 2 years from now, getting them to think back 3 or 4 years is difficult.
Most gratifying experience: I once caught someone who changed a date on an important document which made a big difference in the case. We subpoenaed the notary whose testimony was quite different.

How does a law firm compare to an in-house legal department of a corporation?
   The corporation is much better. I came from a midsized law firm. Here, there are resources available. When a computer breaks down, there is someone to call. There isn't nearly the caste system in a corporation that there is in a law firm. This is helped by our dress code which is casual everyday. Oh, and no billable time which is another wonderful thing.

What's it like to work at Nike?
   Nike is a great place to work. They place a high premium on fun. For instance, Pete Sanford will be here tomorrow to play with the employees. The Olympics are coming up and someone will be chosen to go. There was an essay contest for that.

What's the market like in Portland, Oregon?

The market is excellent. Intel is here and there are lots of law firms and in-house positions.

How's the pay?

It could be better. However, I have a tremendous amount of job satisfaction, so I wouldn't leave for money.

What are your career hopes, dreams, and desires?

I can see myself here for awhile. I developed databases that were not in place here and I'm getting more into database design and management. I've also developed timelines and chronology and cast of characters which I turn over to our outside counsel. I'd like to go further with that.

What's your crystal ball say about the future of the paralegal profession?

I think technology will play more and more importance.

CHAPTER 10

Careers with Legal Vendors

> You've forgotten the grandest moral attribute of a Scotsman, Maggie, that he'll do nothing which might damage his career.
>
> Sir J. M. Barrie, 1860–1937 (*What Every Woman Knows*, Act 2)

INTRODUCTION

There are times in your life when you just don't feel like jumping on the traditional bandwagon. It's during those times that the dream machine pumps very hard and the traditional law firm environment loses its appeal. Something different, you think, that's what I want. Somewhere I don't have to bill time, chase billable hours. Someplace I can go up the career ladder with a sure foot instead of slip'n'slide; where I'm not involved in daily adversarial situations. A place where the definition of an office is something other than three 6-by-9 covered movable walls.

Have you ever considered life with a legal vendor? If so, were you afraid to move because you thought you would be leaving the profession? Wasting your legal education? Making less money? Have you investigated opportunities within the vendor community? Used your network to interview successful paralegals who made the jump? Are you afraid you might limit your opportunities?

The paralegal background is highly sought after for many positions within legal vendor firms. A vendor, as you probably know, is a company producing products or services directed toward the legal community. In case you're not sure who that may include, consider these vendors: IBM, Xerox, Prentice Hall, Martindale-Hubbell, Kodak, Mitsubishi, and LEXIS. If working for a vendor frightens you because you think you lose professional status, think again.

Positions with legal vendors can be stimulating, lucrative, and goal-oriented. There is nothing wrong with utilizing your paralegal background and making a leap into the vendor world. It simply means capitalizing on your paralegal framework and leapfrogging into another area that might bring a different kind of career satisfaction.

Legal vendors recognize that paralegals bring a unique perspective to their companies. Some positions are in sales and marketing; some are more of a consultative sale where paralegals have been known to excel. Other positions utilize paralegals in administrative capacities, project management, or research and development. Vendors seek your legal terminology expertise; knowledge of the legal system; investigation, interpersonal, and communication skills; and law firm familiarity and contacts. The following is a list of the types of companies hiring professionals with paralegal background:

1. Software technology
2. Computerized litigation support
3. Document imaging and scanning
4. Legal publishers
5. Office supplies
6. Legal photocopying services
7. Coding services
8. OCR services
9. Information technology
10. Public record access companies
11. Asset search companies
12. Film and television
13. Litigation support software
14. Trade journals and magazines
15. Paralegal schools
16. Travel agencies specializing in law firm travel
17. Temporary and full-time staffing organizations
18. Printing companies specializing in the legal field
19. Facilities management corporations, such as Pitney Bowes and Merrill Corporation
20. Legal support services
    - Conversion or image capture
    - Case management/planning
    - Document retrieval and reporting
    - Database design
    - Application software and systems
    - Trial support
    - Data entry
    - Electronic evidence
21. Trademark and copyright search services
22. Corporate services, including
    - Qualifications
    - Incorporations
    - U.C.C. searches and filings
23. Legal research firms
24. Medical records summarizing services
25. Deposition digesting services
26. Association administrative headquarters
27. Seminar companies
28. Research firms
29. Law librarian outsourcing companies
30. Courier services
31. Fax filing services
32. Information brokers
33. Legal marketing and public relations services
34. Advertising agencies specializing in the legal field
35. Notary services
36. Document and records management companies
37. Training services
38. Calendaring systems management services
39. Court reporting services

CHAPTER 11

Learning the Secrets of Quality Service

You want it when??

Anonymous

IMPORTANCE OF QUALITY SERVICE

With tough competition for clients, firms no longer sit back waiting for clients to appear at the door. Gone are the days a firm can expect clients to remain with them forever. Competition has forced firms to give quality service along with lower legal fees.

Many law firms fail to concentrate on the service side of the business. Rather, an emphasis is made on the technology, skill base, and job performance. Too little time is spent on the "people side" of the legal business. Service training (known as "customer service" in all other industries) is either nonexistent or catch-as-catch-can because of limited resources and time, people power, busy schedules, and constant deadlines. Although most attorneys, administrators, and paralegals are exceptionally skilled at their jobs, they are not trained in effective client-relation skills. Presently, seminars and schools teaching law firm customer service are hard to find. Several reasons quality service is so significant for competition in the legal field today are:

Growth of the industry. The overwhelming number of attorneys and firms today illustrates the extreme litigious nature of Americans. More lawsuits are filed in the United States than anywhere else in the world. Technology has created an easier system for filing lawsuits than ever before, and, of course, we still have media influencers. Law schools report admissions rise every time a lawyer TV show such as "The Practice" scores high in the Nielsen ratings.

Increased competition. Not very long ago, just a few years in fact, clients tended to engage one firm for all legal needs. Large corporate clients rarely questioned law firm billings. Few details were provided; sometimes even precise hours were left out on bills. Stories flourished (some perhaps embellished) about outrageous pass-throughs by attorneys, such as caviar, unused hotel rooms, first-class airfare, bagels, cream cheese, gourmet goodies, or shirts bought on the road.

During the early 1990s recession, corporate clients demanded lower legal fees. When competition for long-term clients threatened survival, law firms finally understood that quality with efficiently priced service and delivery was essential.

Greater understanding of the legal process by clients. Whether you agreed with the procedures used by the Dream Team or the prosecution, broadcasting the O.J. Simpson trial was a great way to educate the general public about how a trial proceeds. It also gave the general public a glimpse into the high costs of legal fees. Increased public awareness continues to force the issue of a fair, just, and *affordable* legal system.

Corporate clients had already become familiar with the necessity of lowering fees. To enforce that effort, corporate executives took it upon themselves to learn the kind of job tasks corresponding to skill and educational level. They demanded delegation to the lowest competent level and "beauty contests" to select the best firm. They no longer accepted invoices without questions.

Clients all along have wanted to be treated fairly. Sheer economics forces clients to change their passive acceptance of "big daddy." They want to repeat business with firms that not only produce the best work product but also emphasize service and lower fees.

In response, lawyers were forced to acknowledge the marketplace. The arrogance of the elite had been smashed. Firms recognized that repeat business, the lifeline to continued existence and expansion, could no longer be taken for granted. Survival of law firms relies on client expansion and retention. No clients = less work = no growth = fewer partner profits.

Despite recent acceptance of sophisticated law firm advertising, word-of-mouth referrals are still the most effective resource for business leads. And, no one wants to refer a firm where he has been treated poorly.

In-house legal departments face a similar challenge. The legal department often refers to the company and its divisions as "the client." The core function of an in-house department is to save the corporation legal fees. By not providing excellent service to their clients, in-house attorneys face boycott and possibly higher outside counsel fees, culminating in fewer budget dollars for the department. Quality client service can help retain and attract new clients.

Let's define quality customer service for the legal environment. Two primary dimensions make up quality client service: the *procedural* and the *personal* dimensions. The procedural side consists of established systems and procedures to deliver the service. The personal side of service is the verbal interaction between you and the customer (your clients and coworkers). Quality service combining excellent procedural and personal service enables the paralegal to further champion the profession:

1. The client continues to use the firm and you are a key component for repeat business, and

2. Attorneys continue to request paralegal services because repeat business is captured through excellent product quality and attitude.

Excellent client service requires emotional labor, which takes a toll on energy level in the same way physical labor does: *You can get tired. Very, very tired.* Tired paralegals often exhibit an overload syndrome through physical and emotional signals:

- Bleary-eyed
- Grouchy
- Weepy
- Less motivated
- Late for work or meetings
- Slaphappy
- Caffeine addicted
- Even bumbling

These conditions reduce abilities to deliver quality service, affecting job performance, capabilities, and, ultimately, promotion and raises.

LACK OF CUSTOMER SERVICE

Everyone knows the Nordstrom service story. A customer can bring back almost anything to be returned, even if the item wasn't purchased at Nordstrom. Salespeople will go the extra mile to provide exceptional customer service. The Nordstrom way has become a standard by which other stores are compared.

Unfortunately, in all my years in the legal field, while I have certainly heard heartwarming stories about many, many firms, I rarely hear clients bragging about how well they were treated! A few client service complaints frequently heard are these:

- "I can't ever get through to the attorney; getting her to call back or e-mail is a monumental event."
- "Calling the firm is a game; the phone rings and rings and when finally answered, I have to talk fast to avoid getting put on hold until lunch."
- "I have to spell my name every time I call. With the fees I pay, you'd think the least they could do is know who I am."
- "This is *divorce* I'm going through! Don't they understand I was married to the jerk for 27 years?"
- "They have me come in to meetings just to plan other meetings."
- "Just try getting someone at the firm after 5:00."
- "The voice mail system takes a genius to figure out and I'm not so sure my attorney or paralegal even *gets* the message."
- "When they tell me it'll get done by Tuesday, I have to ask, 'what week?'"
- "I never hear a word unless my payment is late."
- "Every time I sense the bill is wrong, I am told it's all the fault of the new accounting system. Isn't anyone in charge?"

Attorneys complain about paralegals, support staff, and even other attorneys in much the same manner:

- "No one told me the assignment would be handed in late."
- "After 5:00, it's deserted around here. I can't get any help."
- "Whose hire was that?"
- "I wouldn't know how to reach anyone anywhere after hours."
- "I never know the status of things."
- "Asking [so-and-so] to get my work done is like pulling teeth!"
- "It would be nice if they got the assignment right the first time."
- "No one asks, 'how much'; they just go out and spend the money."

Vendors providing services or products to the legal field have great stories of mistreatment. It may be true that some alienate firm personnel by hounding them in a desperate attempt to win the account. However, sometimes vendors are simply not considered part of the elite and, as such, are treated as though they can enter only through the servants' door. Whatever the cause, a good relationship with a vendor is indispensable. It enables you to get the job done quickly and efficiently. The ability to get people to work *with* instead of against you is pivotal.

And for heaven's sake, don't underestimate the power of the vendor! Just as law firms and legal departments are limited in number, so are legal vendors. The attitude that you can just get another vendor anytime is naive and narrow-minded thinking. Vendors do talk to each other, and the word is out on who is outstanding to work with and who should be avoided at all costs.

26 TIPS FOR OUTSTANDING CLIENT SERVICE

Here is a list of tips to provide exceptional service inside and out of the firm (clients and coworkers are referred to as "client"):

1. Expand awareness of your abilities so clients know how to get a full range of services.

2. Explain the benefits of your services, for example, "By scanning these documents on-site and in three shifts, we can save even more time and money. A guesstimate of the savings is around $_____. I think that might make your client happy."

3. Anticipate the clients' needs:

    If Attorney B is always missing deadlines, is there any reason to expect that behavior to change? Make sure you take steps to expedite delivery.

    If you are assigned to a traumatic marriage dissolution matter, is it reasonable to expect the client may call in an emotional state from time to time? Are you prepared to deal with heavy emotions? Do you know what to say?

4. Learn to be effective over the telephone:

    Relying only on your voice to convey a message means being as pleasant over the phone as you are in person. Barking into the speaker phone in an effort to sound important only turns people off. Sounding rushed causes people to feel they are bothering you.

    Remember—The client sees you as a paralegal representative. You *are* your organization or department. Learn to:
    - Smile as you talk. You can't help but communicate a positive attitude.
    - Return all phone calls promptly. Determine in your firm what promptly means—I guarantee it's not tomorrow.
    - If someone is snippy, do not respond likewise.
    - End all conversations in an upbeat manner with a summary of the action to be taken.
    - Avoid keeping callers on hold. It's just bad business.
    - Keep personal calls to a minimum.

5. Keep voice mail up-to-date. Change the greeting daily, if

necessary. A good message to clients that you care is:

"Hello, this is Sue Smith. Today is January 18th and I'm in a meeting out of the office all morning. Please leave a message and I will get back to you promptly. If you need help immediately, please dial 322 to reach Tim Jones, my assistant, or dial zero to reach the operator."

Using voice mail properly reinforces great client service by sending the message, "Your call is important to me." If you are not available, make sure your voice mail says how you can be reached, when you will return the call, or whom to call instead.

6. Know the names and pronunciations of all members of the firm and its clients. Nothing is worse than to have the client reintroduce himself time and time again.

7. Always let clients or attorneys know if you are late—for work, with couriers, appointments, or assignments.

8. Find ways to expedite delivery of assignments.

9. Offer to save attorney's time by handling the client when they are busy. (Be sure not to offer legal advice.)

10. Meet the computer challenge: If you are unfamiliar with a software package or system, take time outside of work hours to learn it. Don't take training time at the expense of clients or attorneys.

11. Make sure backup clerical duties run smoothly. These include:
    - All office supplies are in place
    - Filing is up-to-date
    - Mail goes out on time
    - Temporary help is adequately arranged ahead of time
    - Computers are maintained
    - E-mail is read regularly
    - Voice mail is checked consistently
    - The best vendor services have been attained: photocopying, messenger service, staffing services, court reporters, online services, Web designers, and so forth.

12. Don't overpromise or underdeliver. If you say you can do something, make sure you can do it competently the first time.

13. Don't tackle any assignment without letting attorneys or supervisors know if it's your first time.

14. Know your competition. If you are involved in a "beauty contest" and know, for example, a competing firm utilizes paralegals more efficiently, find a way to implement the same benefit.

15. Make clients feel important. The more important they feel, the better they feel about using you.

16. Develop a good rapport, a key to effective communication. Use the client file or contact manager program to notify clients about important deadlines, dates, events, appearances, preparation materials, or even to wish happy birthday. A "welcome back from vacation"

call inquiring about any immediate assistance is always appreciated.

17. Expect excellent performance from yourself and those around you. Set expectations high. Good enough just isn't.

18. Let clients know you care. Send holiday and birthday cards, if appropriate. Ask to visit their offices to meet all the players. Don't let them forget that you exist. Teach them they can count on you, no matter what.

19. Conduct internal assessments. Constantly evaluate what clients (and employers) think of you. Don't wait for review time. Ask coworkers, supervisors, and clients what more they need and use this information to improve.

20. Know what clients want and expect. Gaps in perception only lead to disappointment.

21. Always be easy to reach. Clients expect to find you, particularly if they are in crisis. Wear a beeper, get a cell phone, forward voice mail, get e-mail, have a backup. Do use discretion, however. Don't inadvertently reveal confidential information.

22. Turn gripes into opportunity. For example, a partner states she doesn't use paralegals because she can never get one. Offer to form a team and an easy access system. The message to clients, coworkers, attorneys, and supervisors should *always* be, "I'm here to help you."

23. Conduct market research. Know your clients.
  * Find out how long clients have been in business; get an annual report, if available; and find out hiring requirements. Get information on services/products provided, names of key personnel, market size, locations, potential industry threats, and competitors.
  * Learn about coworkers' and attorneys' professional attributes: published articles or books; pro bono work; other practice specialties; honors awarded; professional associations. Establish good rapport so you have something you can talk with them about besides the case or a business matter.

24. Go the extra mile while always using good judgment.

25. Resolve concerns or complaints quickly. Stringing out decisions, resolutions, or conflicts only exacerbates the situation.

26. Train, train, and retrain. Get on-the-job training; attend seminars; cross-train; read books and listen to tapes; audit in-house attorney training sessions; read customer service how-to books; surf the Internet; increase cultural awareness; learn more about business practices; find out the hottest practice specialties and how paralegals fit into the picture; encourage local paralegal schools to provide up-to-date classes relating to current trends.

SETTING UP A WIN-WIN RESOLUTION

When you can't appease clients or attorneys or give them exactly what they want, consider using some alternatives. Here are a few phrases:

- "Another possibility is . . . ."
- "I will investigate this right now and get back to you within the hour."
- "I will speak with [so-and-so], get another viewpoint, and get back to you by tomorrow afternoon with new alternatives."

One surefire way to agitate some people is to use phrases such as, "that's company/firm policy"; "no one told me to . . ."; "there isn't anything I can do"; or "that's not in my job description." When a solution is unlikely, expressing that you do care may help:

- "I will check the air courier again for you tonight."
- "To prevent further problems, let's . . . ."
- "Let's double-check what you need from here on out."

PARALEGAL INNER VIEW: MELISSA COHON—
MOVING FROM WEST TO EAST

Name: Melissa Cohon
Title: Paralegal
Firm: Michael, Best and Friedrich, Chicago, Illinois
Number of attorneys and paralegals: 30 in Chicago; 100 in 4 offices; 2 paralegals in Chicago; 35–40 nationally
Education: B.A. Political Science/Journalism from CalState Northridge; Paralegal certificate from UCLA, June 1997
Personal background: 30 years old, from Los Angeles, California
Job duties: Litigation Support and Employment litigation support. I have a couple of cases going that are very large and headed for trial. I'm doing everything from file management to comparing exhibits for depos for trial, witness binders, and trial support. We have mostly commercial/business litigation matters. I have an office and use of a secretary if I need it. I've only had one other job besides this. My first job at the county was substantially different because you didn't have the layering of attorneys. Attorneys worked every facet of the case and they were overworked. I drafted pleadings, discovery, and correspondence. I was heavily involved in substantive parts of the case. Here, it's private

practice—the associates, junior partners, etc., are all stratified. There is less of an adrenaline rush on projects. I'm pushing for more work but it's a slow process.

Biggest challenge: Moving from California to Illinois and learning the new rules and procedures. When I first came to Chicago, I had held just one other job. I went to a temp agency and found out that all the work I did in L.A. didn't count. I was told I was going to make $20.00 an hour and you're going to do nothing but Bates stamp for 5 years! I couldn't believe it. So I went to other agencies and got temp work within a week which led to a great job.

Most gratifying case: That was my first job out of paralegal school. I worked for the County of Los Angeles in public works doing eminent domain for the MTA for the Redline. I assisted at a trial for a week and sat at the counsel table. I assisted the attorney in taking notes, managing documents, and exhibits. It was a total adrenaline rush! And, we won.

What do you like best about your job?
   The people. I landed in a really good office.

How's the pay?
   The pay is good. I've compared it with the salary surveys.

What are your career hopes and desires?
   I would like to go from paralegal to judge and skip the whole lawyer thing. I want more responsibility and more facets of the case, writing, and more in-depth research. I don't have many complaints.

Any advice to students?
   Students have to be prepared that they're going to get stonewalled and it's not true. I had a full-time job within 3 weeks of when I graduated.

What do you do for fun?
   I'm married. I go to the movies, visit friends. There's always something to do here. It's so different than Los Angeles.

What do you think is the future of this profession?
   That's a difficult question. It's so hard because some of the attorneys have a clear grasp of what I can do for them and some don't. I do more than just file management. I don't do pleadings here, but I do research which I'm being asked to do more and more. As attorneys discover my abilities, my assignments will grow. Hopefully, that will happen throughout the profession.

CHAPTER 12

Baby Boomers, Meet Generation X

> The day I knew I had officially entered middle-age was the day I heard "House of the Rising Sun" in the elevator.
>
> One Baby Boomer confesses to another

HOW TO COPE WITH PARALEGAL GENERATIONAL DIFFERENCES

If you have been in this field for more than 10 years, you have probably witnessed some newcomers recently invading your scene: Generation Xers. While some of us are barely keeping up with e-mail, these Xers parachuted into the profession with computer skills they gained when they were 5 years old, with attitudes that jobs last no longer than a TV commercial.

In a *Los Angeles Times* article about generational differences, Bruce Tulgan, founding principal of Rainmaker, Inc., a Connecticut firm studying work habits of twentysomethings, was quoted as saying, "They're pursuing a new kind of career model that we call 'self-building.' Instead of allowing the learning and the creative opportunities to be mediated by a large institution, they're pursuing these things on their own."

Xers watched as their parents became victims of Corporate America. They were laid off, downsized, or merged into oblivion. Xers did not learn about loyalty to the law firm or corporation. Instead, they witnessed examples of stellar performance rewarded with less than stellar remuneration. Xers learned to make their own breaks.

Baby Boomers, on the other hand, exiting the 1960s' free-spirit, free-love society, plunged feet first into the yuppie generation and the divine decadence of the 1980s. Boomers descended from parental role models who understood a different value system. Longevity and loyalty to the firm were continuously rewarded. The patriarchal law firm and corporate environment ruled. What the boss said was always right; after 30 years of service the company gave you a gold watch and a retirement party. Hopefully, you've saved enough nickels and dimes to get through the next phase: false teeth and orthopedic shoes.

Generation X paralegals enter the field with computer skills as a second language while many Baby Boomers did not touch a computer until after college. Both generations struggle with attorneys who entered the field with only legal secretarial and associate support. This generation learned very late in their careers how to utilize paralegals. First year Generation X associates entering today's practice *expect* to work with paralegals.

Self-builders make a priority of expanding their own skills. An Xer reading this book has probably been very curious as to why emphasis on taking charge of your own career is even in this book. In a conversation with 23-year-old Shavondra McCutchen, a recent paralegal graduate, I learned more about the Xers' way of thinking. Shavondra laid out her career growth plan through achieving a higher level of communication and interpersonal skills. She knew precisely how she was gong to go about it. She never assumed it was the firm's responsibility to provide continuing education. It didn't even occur to her. "No one is going to knock on the door and give you anything," she says. "You have to go out there and get it yourself."

Xers ask for extra assignments, expect to remain on a learning curve investing in themselves rather than in a firm. They don't expect to nest. A lifetime of employment in one firm is, as far as they are concerned, weird. They may take a "slacker" job, a position that is transitional, to get money while they focus attention on activities they hope will lead to more fulfilling employment. Many demonstrate entrepreneurial characteristics. According to a 1995 study by Marquette University, 71 percent of people trying to start businesses are between 25 and 34 years old, and 8 percent are between 18 and 24.

Forget about lifetime employment. Many Baby Boomer paralegals are so consumed by the firms' restructuring efforts to be low-cost providers, they can't focus on the future. Tomorrow's paralegal expects to be hired as a free-lancer, project paralegal, or virtual office worker. Mobility and flexibility are the new watchwords of the twenty-first century. Get ready for intergenerational conflicts as anxious but aging Baby Boomers seek to throttle back, and ambitious Generation Xers strive to zoom ahead in a world with fewer managers and more empowered employees.

Brought up as a TV-fed, video-game-bred, computerized generation, twentysomethings' attention spans are generally shorter than Baby Boomers'. They are eager to get on to the next project or assignment. They may not need long explanations or detailed instructions. These self-building paralegals take advantage of the resources within their firms. It is not unusual for supervisors to receive calls complaining that the employee is using dormant computers in the office or staying late to ask unrelated work questions of the star associate. Even clients are fair game for twentysomethings in search of brains to pick.

Baby Boomers and Generation Xers: Learn from each other. Listen and assimilate what the other generation has to say. There has never been a time when so much technology has moved into the workplace so quickly. There has never been a better collection of combined talent and expertise. Maximize, maneuver, and manage it. Rare opportunities don't come along that often.

10 TIPS FOR GRAPPLING WITH GENERATION X

If you are a Baby Boomer supervising or working with a Generation Xer, or an Xer supervising or working with a Boomer, here are some guidelines that may help when speaking to each other in different vectors:

1. Baby Boomers beware: Xers may be much more computer literate than you. Don't shut them out because you think their age means inexperience.

2. Xers: A few wrinkles and a little gray hair do not mean the Boomers are ignorant or unsophisticated around computers. They may have written the very software program you are currently using.

3. Baby Boomers: Xers did not learn through step-by-step processes. When training Xer attorneys or paralegals, don't overlook that their learning process was different than yours. Old-fashioned methods of learning may ultimately be recognized as more effective than high-tech simulations, which do not always convert to effective learning and retention.

   Xers relied upon computers, calculators, and interactive videos. You learned multiplication tables by rote, carried a slide rule, and watched TV in black and white. Embrace the generational differences.

4. Xers: you think *Boomers* are old???? You should have seen *our* parents. Use Boomers' knowledge and expertise as a learning tool. Major conflicts are likely to develop in the future as Baby Boomers age and Generation X balks at supporting a growing number of retirees.

5. Baby Boomers: Xers are building a career outside their job. You, on the other hand, depend on your job to teach you what you need. Don't get offended if Xers tackle the job scene differently than you.

6. Xer attorneys and paralegals seek a life outside the firm. They expect it. Boomers evolved from hippies and flower children to upwardly mobile and yuppie to lifestyle choices and meatloaf. They continue to reengineer an entire generation. Xers believe that family and life outside the firm are automatic.

7. Boomer: Xers are wary about depending on employers for the assets they will need to build successful careers, so they create their own breaks. We used to think that was "cheating" to get ahead, or they were the kind of employees who blatantly sought our job. Now, some of us would happily give it to them.

8. Xers do not expect long-term reward systems. They don't plan on staying with the firm for life. With the trend toward temporary or project help, downsizing in their blood, and traditional relationships diminishing, Xers are more likely to respond to instant gratification. Build contingency rewards into the system, such as paying a bonus for efficiently delivering the project.

9. Boomers are familiar with the typical old-fashioned hierarchical pyramid. They are used to a caste system. Xers, on the other hand, expect the manager to be working for his or her "subordinates," as the manager's role is to coach and guide people in how to do a task and get them the resources. The new generation is empowered.

This concept of flipped management was illustrated by Joanie, a Generation Xer at a small firm. When cocounsel called, prepared for battle over missing documents, Tom, a Baby Boomer took the call. He put the attorney on hold in order to find the billing partner. When he couldn't find the attorney, he listened carefully to the complaint and promised to get back to cocounsel as soon as the billing attorney returned. Joanie took over. She immediately soothed the caller by promising to deliver a duplicate set of the documents within the hour.

It wouldn't occur to the Xer to solve the problem by asking for approval. The Boomer, on the other hand, has been trained to automatically move this kind of problem up the hierarchical ladder.

10. Baby Boomers have seen advancement opportunities wrestled away. Middle managers are expendable. No longer can employees count on a steady rise up the career ladder. The implied social contract—work hard, be loyal, move up—is extinct. The message is clear: Work harder to make up for lost colleagues, and expect little in return. Xers view managers in the new era as process integrators, not people integrators.

Just in case you weren't feeling too old today, this will certainly change things. Each year the staff at Beloit College in Wisconsin puts together a list to try to give the faculty a sense of the mind-set of that year's incoming freshmen. Here is a recent list making the rounds on the Internet:

- The people who started college the fall of 2001 across the nation were born in 1983.
- They have no meaningful recollection of the Reagan Era and probably did not know he had ever been shot.
- They were prepubescent when the Persian Gulf War was waged.
- Black Monday 1987 is as significant to them as the Great Depression.
- They were 11 when the Soviet Union broke apart and do not remember the Cold War.
- They have never feared a nuclear war.
- They are too young to remember the space shuttle blowing up.
- Tianamen Square means nothing to them.
- Their lifetime has always included AIDS.
- Bottle caps have always been screw off.
- Atari predates them, as do vinyl albums.
- The expression "you sound like a broken record" means nothing to them.
- They have never owned a record player.
- They have likely never played Pac Man and have never heard of Pong.
- They may have never heard of an 8 track. The compact disc was introduced when they were born.
- As far as they know, stamps have always cost at least 33 cents.
- They have always had an answering machine, or voice-mail.
- Most have never seen a dial TV set with only 13 channels, nor have they seen a black-and-white TV. They have always had cable. Tin foil on antennas means nothing to them.
- There have always been VCRs, but they have no idea what BETA is.
- They cannot fathom not having a remote control.
- They were born the year after the Walkman was introduced by Sony.
- Roller-skating has always meant in-line for them.
- Jay Leno has always been on the "Tonight Show."
- They have no idea when or why Jordache jeans were cool.
- Popcorn has always been cooked in the microwave.
- They have never seen Larry Bird play.
- They never took a swim and thought about *Jaws*.
- The Vietnam War is as ancient history to them as WWI, WWII and the Civil War.
- They have no idea that Americans were ever held hostage in Iran.
- They can't imagine what hard contact lenses are.
- They don't know who Mork was or where he was from.

- They've never heard: "Where's the beef?," "I'd walked a mile for a Camel," or "de plane, de plane."
- They do not care who shot J.R. and have no idea who J.R. was.
- The Titanic was found? They thought we always knew where it was.
- Kansas, Chicago, Boston, America, and Alabama are places, not groups.
- McDonald's never came in Styrofoam containers.
- There has always been MTV.
- They don't have a clue how to use a typewriter. And:
- Paralegals have always been around. (Okay, we added that.)

CHAPTER 13

The Experienced Paralegal: Climbing the Invisible Career Ladder

> No rush on this. Take all night if necessary.
>
> Litigation department head to paralegal

PLANNING YOUR OWN CAREER DESTINY

When we accept a new position, we are accepting the dream that life will somehow be better with this new position and the upward mobility it is sure to bring. Rarely do we attribute disappointment or growing frustration in the position with our own lack of personal responsibility for career planning.

The purpose of this book is to help you break through those barriers that may exist in your career by sharing with you techniques and suggestions that have worked for other legal assistants. Compared to the practice of law, which is hundreds of years old, the paralegal field is still only a small dot on the map, but it has made a major impact on the way attorneys practice law and consumers view their bills. Nevertheless, procedures, practices, career paths, systems, job descriptions, hierarchies, and the need are still in the process of developing. Consequently, the field is in a state of flux, constantly defining and redefining itself.

Part of the process of making changes in our careers includes asking ourselves hard questions. If you consistently experience boredom, stagnation, or a feeling that you are outgrowing your position in any way, it is time to take a good look at what you are doing and why. The response to "why do you do it this way" is often, "because I (or we) have always done it this way." This is really not a valid justification. It is an indication that no new thought or creative process has been applied for a long time. Perhaps you feel you have fallen into a rut. You may feel it is because your firm or corporation has not attempted to change the way they utilize paralegals since their first hire. Or perhaps you find that you are doing the same kinds of assignments over and over and are craving new stimulation. You may not be sure exactly what that entails. You may feel that moving up is not an option because there is simply no place to go.

You may be one of a large group of paralegals experiencing tremendous job satisfaction, but you are wondering just how to advance in a field that is only in the beginning stages of defining career paths. Many legal assistants repeatedly state that they enjoy an intellectually stimulating environment, have challenging work, and are part of a team. It is the push forward to other areas that many paralegals find difficult. These areas include higher salaries, moving up in a firm with no vertical climb, negotiating for more sophisticated assignments, breaking that glass ceiling, or getting off the sticky floor.

Many of the techniques and processes outlined in this book will help you define your position and give you a foundation from which to mold your career, whether you are at the senior, intermediate, or entry level. Other techniques will plant a seed from which new ideas will begin to take shape. Some techniques will work for you or your firm, others will offer you a starting point. It's up to you to remain open-minded and learn to create new ideas around these suggestions. Take what works, leave what doesn't. The rest may work at a later time.

Forming a Plan of Action

Poorly thought-out job planning has caused many legal assistants to leave otherwise satisfying positions. What is your plan of action? What do you intend to do to ensure that you have continued job satisfaction? If you are looking to upgrade your assignments, how do you plan on proceeding? The very definition of a paralegal, "performs routine and repetitious tasks," can incorrectly position you by making upward mobility appear unreachable. By having a plan of action or guidelines, you may redefine the niche between the attorney and secretary and break through any perceived glass ceilings.

In order to increase responsibilities and receive upgraded assignments, first target specific job duties that will enable you to move up. Expecting to climb a nonexistent ladder utilizing vagueness is as effective as receiving a nondirective from your supervisor to improve. "You'll have to improve your job performance," she says. "Great," you respond, "I'll do just that." What on earth was actually said here? Improve what? Writing skills? Ability to use the computer? Research skills? And further, which research skills? Computer skills? The same vague and useless exchange happens when you ask supervisors or attorneys to upgrade your assignments. Upgrade? Increase? "Okay," says attorney Jones, and nothing happens. Why? Because not only have you now given control of your job over to someone else, you gave that person permission to handle it without specific directions on how to proceed. You have made the assumption that that person will know what to do with your professional life.

Taking a proactive rather than a reactive approach can enable you to direct your own career. Being proactive does not translate into rebelling. It simply means that you take charge of those circumstances that are within your control. Yes, there will be instances in your career you cannot control, as in any other aspect of life. However, being master at the helm can allow you to enjoy, profit from, and steer your career at your own choosing. Let's explore a few of those options, techniques, and new possibilities.

HANDLING ASSIGNMENTS: TECHNIQUES FOR MOVING UP

Abilities and characteristics, such as teamwork, willingness to learn, attention to detail, promptness, and amount of billables, all take a backseat to the skill upon which you are most critically judged: your ability to handle and deliver quality work product.

A senior-level paralegal once told me that her opinion on handling assignments was this:

1. Did you find out *exactly* what the final work product is supposed to look like?

2. Did you find out *exactly* when the final work product is due and why?

Unless you slept during the last decade, snoring soundly into the next, you have heard, read, and practiced open communication techniques. Yet, in a law firm environment, a good percentage of write-offs (or write-downs) of billable time occurs because of failure to issue clear directions or to interpret those directions correctly. Paralegals can be victimized by these poor communications, and law firms lose profit, attorneys lose time, and clients lose confidence as a result.

15 Warning Signs of Poorly Managed Assignments

Here are just a few warnings signs that you or your firm/corporation, or both, are not managing assignments effectively:

1. You miss deadlines because you are handling too many matters.

2. You are receiving assignments from more than one attorney and cannot prioritize them.

3. You are consistently receiving assignments that you don't know how to complete.

4. An attorney stops you in the hallway and demands your immediate attention to a matter. You drop other assignments, causing delays.

5. You are routinely given ASAP and RUSH deadlines. A difference of opinion emerges regarding interpretation of these deadlines.

6. You are trying to complete an assignment and need additional legal assistants to help you. However, there is either no one available to assist you or not enough time to bring someone else up to speed.

7. Had you known about an impending event (a closing, a deposition, a filing, meeting, and so forth), you may not have allowed yourself to get overloaded. Or, you could have anticipated an assignment and completed it last week when you had more free time.

8. You are afraid to go on vacation because you are sure to be called by the firm. No one else but you knows anything about the exhibits, factual investigation, status of a document production, or like situation. Furthermore, no one else but you knows enough about the database.

9. You can't seem to get enough assignments, or you can't seem to get the kinds of assignments you would like. You find yourself frequently having to knock on doors looking for work.

10. Your access to LEXIS, Westlaw, the Internet, or other services is restricted, limiting your ability to complete assignments.

11. Your time is written off or you are criticized because the assignment took you much longer to complete than the attorney anticipated.

12. You are criticized for having too much administrative (non-billable) time.

13. Because so many different paralegals have been assigned to a matter during different phases, no one particular paralegal knows the case inside and out, making it difficult for you to complete an assignment.

14. Because you are a star, attorneys seem to always request your services, and not those of a more junior member of your staff. Consequently, you are performing assignments below your level of expertise and you are overloaded.

15. You are asked to redo an assignment.

Using Calendar Memos

Whether you are in a law firm, an in-house legal department, or with a legal services vendor, if a centralized and uniform system of assigning projects to legal assistants does not exist, your firm can experience chaos, loss of profit, and turnover. Many times, systems are set up only to be abandoned because:

- People lose interest. No one person is responsible for continuation of the system.
- The system is too difficult.
- One or two people decide not to conform to the system, destroying confidence.
- Bypassing the system results in faster response.
- There are too many forms to fill out over a simple request.
- The system is too costly.

It is difficult to juggle assignments when you are not sure when and from whom the assignments will arrive. Although not usually written in your job description, part of the job of a legal assistant is to assist attorneys with their work plans. Because of the nature of a law firm environment (its pace, workload, hours, stress), it is incumbent upon you, as a paralegal, to take charge of your own destiny involving assignments.

A calendar memo is one of the most important tools for saving time, scheduling, upgrading your assignments, and educating attorneys about your capabilities in a nonconfrontational manner. Presenting a memo on a regular basis reinforces your position, telling attorneys (1) what you can do, and (2) exactly when you expect to do it.

A calendar memo is based on the firm's master calendar. If you are not receiving the master calendar or a departmental calendar on a regular basis, immediately rectify this. Why many firms give copies to attorneys and secretaries but exclude paralegals remains a mystery.

By checking the master calendar, you will be aware of all events well in advance of their occurrence. You will also see events that could involve paralegals. If the events do not involve paralegals in your firm and you are seeking to upgrade assignments or receive better utilization, here is an excellent way to do so.

Let's say that you see that a deposition in the Acme case will occur in 3 weeks. Send a standard deposition calendar memo to the attorney on the case. The memo lists all of the assignments a paralegal in your firm can perform in regard to a deposition. The memo also includes assignments that paralegals in your firm do not yet perform but could.

You can use a calendar memo in every area a paralegal can and should be involved with, such as trial, pretrial, pleadings, posttrial, closings, meetings, mergers, document productions, securities transactions, probate filings, hearings, motions, tax court, witness interviews, client intakes, and more. By keeping the form extremely simple (all attorneys need to do is check off those areas in which they may need assistance) the form does not become time-consuming. The memo form itself can be sent via e-mail. The memo:

- Acts as forerunner to a work plan
- Gently gets the attorney to think ahead regarding your involvement, and
- Alerts you in advance of what's coming.

The memo is an effective tool for advance planning and crisis management for firms of all sizes. The trick is to keep sending the memos on a regular basis. Depending on how your firm's paralegal program is structured, someone needs to be appointed to review the calendar on a regular basis. The reviewer may be a team leader, paralegal manager, senior paralegal, you (if you are the only paralegal in the firm), or anyone else who will be able to follow through on a consistent basis.

Be creative and design your calendar memos in accordance with your firm's job descriptions, paralegal specialties, and assignments you would like to have, but so far have not yet been assigned. Since each firm has different policies and practices, conform your calendar memos accordingly.

I remember the first time I used a calendar memo. One of the attorneys came running out of his office, waving the form and yelling, "I have a deposition when????" Gradually, the firm got into the habit of using the forms, learning to automatically incorporate paralegals in their master plan. The second firm was more resistant. I sent out the various forms to about 75 attorneys and received absolutely no response. I persisted. Gradually, I received a few responses that said, "See me." Hallelujah! That meant assignments. It took about a month before most attorneys got on the bandwagon. At one point I held back sending the memos because we were getting so much work, and I needed time to hire more legal assistants. At a litigation department luncheon, a few attorneys complained they weren't receiving memos anymore and needed them to plan ahead. Other paralegals from various firms initiated these forms and have reported great success in solving many of the problems inherent in assignment juggling. You can anticipate the workload ahead of schedule and adjust accordingly.

Sample calendar memos for various situations are shown on pages 146–151.

Preparing a Legal Assistant Assignment Request Form

Once alerted work is coming down the pike, you need a method for obtaining clear directions on exactly what is expected. Now, before groaning, "Oh no, another form," or "My firm will never go for this," let me introduce a simple, clean-cut method that can clear up problems such as:

- Finding out exactly when an assignment is due
- Spending too much time on an assignment
- Producing a work product that did not meet expectations
- Prioritizing
- Expending unauthorized costs.

The Legal Assistant Assignment Request is a simple form designed to ensure clear, concise directions. It can be completed by either the paralegal or requesting attorney. If filling out a form seems to be too much trouble for your firm, take out the form when you go in for verbal instructions and simply fill it out as you receive directions. That way, all of the questions regarding the assignment are answered. When completed, tear off a copy for the attorney. Don't wait for approval or sign-off before beginning the project.

Make sure the firm understands the attorney has responsibility for reviewing the form for miscommunications or changes in the original assignment. Reviewing the assignment request allows the attorney the luxury of advance planning, crisis management, and room for necessary changes before you get started and waste any precious time.

CALENDAR MEMO FOR DOCUMENT PRODUCTION

<u>Calendar Memo</u>

To:
From:
Date:
Re:
Client No.:

Document Production

According to the Master Calendar, there is a document production scheduled in the above-referenced matter on _____ at _____ a.m./p.m. at _____.
                           (Date)   (Time)   (Location)

In order to schedule adequate paralegal support, please check the areas in which you may need assistance.

_____ Prepare objections
_____ Attend production
_____ Inspect and categorize documents
_____ Prepare response to demand for inspection
_____ Prepare privilege list
_____ Prepare motion for protective order
_____ Prepare subpoena for _____
_____ Document management assistance
_____ Computerized litigation support required
_____ Number documents
_____ Bar code
_____ Redact documents
_____ Prepare stipulation for confidential documents
_____ Prepare indices
_____ Arrange for photocopying services and quality control check
_____ Investigate and price _____ imaging _____ scanning or _____ virtual repository services
_____ Other: _____
_____ See me

CALENDAR MEMO FOR DEPOSITION

<u>Calendar Memo</u>

To:
From:
Date:
Re:
Client No.:

Deposition

According to the Master Calendar, there is a deposition scheduled
for _____ on _____ at _____a.m./p.m., in the above referenced
     (Name)   (Date)   (Time)
matter. In order to provide you with adequate paralegal support, please
check the areas in which you anticipate needing assistance.

_____   Organize or index documents/exhibits
_____   Attend deposition
_____   Prepare graphics
_____   Prepare chronology of events
_____   Arrange for court reporter or video
_____   Prepare client for deposition
_____   Prepare outline or questions for deposition
_____   Coordinate factual investigation
_____   Prepare objections to notice of deposition
_____   Prepare deposition summaries
_____   Other: _____
_____   See me

CALENDAR MEMO FOR POST-DEPOSITION

<u>Calendar Memo</u>

To:
From:
Date:
Re:
Client No.:

Post-Deposition

According to the Master Calendar, the deposition of
_____ was scheduled on _____ in the above-referenced
  (Name)   (Date)
matter. In order to receive adequate paralegal support,
please check the areas in which you will require assistance.

_____   Summarize deposition
_____   Prepare motion to compel attendance/oppose attendance
_____   Locate witness
_____   Prepare meet and confer letter
_____   Prepare analysis of testimony inconsistencies
_____   Prepare subpoena duces tecum for Custodian of Records
_____   Locate expert witness
_____   Utilize software such as _____
_____   Notify _____
_____   Prepare Notice of Deposition for: _____
                                      (Name)
_____   Other: _____
_____   See me

CALENDAR MEMO FOR PRETRIAL

Calendar Memo

To:
From:
Date:
Re:
Client No.:

Pretrial

According to the Master Calendar, trial in the above matter is set
for _____ at _____ a.m./p.m. in _____ court. In
      (Date)   (Time)   (Branch)
order to prepare early, please indicate the areas in which you will
need paralegal assistance.

_____ Prepare exhibits
_____ Prepare graphics
_____ Arrange for war room
_____ Arrange video
_____ Arrange for computers in courtroom
_____ Prepare graphics technology
_____ Attend trial
_____ Prepare at-issue memorandum
_____ Prepare request for jury trial
_____ Prepare offer to compromise
_____ Prepare rejection
_____ Prepare settlement conference statement
_____ Prepare settlement documents
_____ Prepare discovery analyses
_____ Organize pleadings correspondence for trial
_____ Prepare witness files
_____ Prepare exhibit list
_____ Prepare trial notebook
_____ Prepare witness list
_____ Prepare notice to appear at trial
_____ Computerized litigation support
_____ Prepare trial subpoena
_____ Arrange witness interview
_____ Other: _____
_____ See me

CALENDAR MEMO FOR TRIAL

<u>Calendar Memo</u>

To:
From:
Date:
Re:
Client No.:

Trial

According to the Master Calendar, the above-referenced matter is scheduled for trial on _____ at _____ a.m./p.m. in _____
                (Date)   (Time)   (Branch)
court. Please assist the paralegal department by checking the assignments you will need completed. Providing this information will enable us to assist you better.

_____ Arrange for travel
_____ Arrange for additional personnel, such as _____
_____ Attend trial
_____ Prepare jury questionnaire
_____ Prepare jury instructions
_____ Assign exhibit numbers
_____ Prepare exhibits
_____ Prepare exhibit lists
_____ Prepare list of exhibits admitted into evidence
_____ Prepare summary of transcript dailies
_____ Prepare deposition excerpts index
_____ Prepare witness testimony index
_____ Arrange for travel and hotel for witnesses
_____ Arrange for computerized litigation
       support during trial
_____ Other: _____
_____ See me

CALENDAR MEMO FOR POSTTRIAL

Calendar Memo

To:
From:
Date:
Re:
Client No.:

Posttrial

In order to provide you with continuing paralegal support in the above-referenced matter, please indicate the areas in which you will need assistance.

_____ Prepare judgment
_____ Prepare memorandum of costs
_____ Prepare posttrial motions
_____ Close files
_____ Prepare files for storage
_____ Return original documents
_____ Destroy duplicate sets of documents
_____ Index documents
_____ Prepare documents for appeal
_____ Other: _____
_____ See me

Understanding the Assignment Request Form

Following this section is a sample assignment request form. Here is how to use the form to its greatest advantage.

1. *To:* The request goes to the supervising paralegal or attorney responsible for assignments.

2. *Requesting attorney:* The attorney making the request.

3. *Client and client matter no.*

4. *Nature of assignment:* What kind of assignment is this? Be general in nature. Is it a summarizing project, indexing project, document production, closing, or deposition?

5. *Number of case clerks or paralegals needed:* How many paralegals are necessary to start this project?

5a. *Levels:* According to your job descriptions, is this a project for a senior, intermediate, or entry-level paralegal, or for a paralegal assistant or document case clerk?

6. *Estimate of time involved:* Probably one of the most important questions on the form. How long does the attorney estimate this project will take? You will find that you can stop most misunderstandings right here. The attorney may feel that the project will take 2 hours. After reviewing the assignment, you may be certain it will take 2 days. Here is where you can avoid write-offs or miscommunications.

7. *Date needed:* ASAP or RUSH are *not* acceptable because they mean nothing. One person's interpretation of ASAP may mean 2 weeks, another person's may mean tomorrow. Get the exact date.

7a. *Time:* This question can eliminate potential problems if the attorney intends to use the project the day it is due. Does she need it at precisely 10 A.M. because there is an important meeting involving the assignment at 1:00 P.M.? Find out.

8. *Priority:* Help yourself to prioritize. Is this a drop-dead deadline? Is there flexibility if you complete it 1 or 2 days later? 1P (first priority) tells you the attorney absolutely must have the assignment on the date given. 2P (second priority) tells you there is some room on the deadline. If you receive two 1Ps for the same date from two attorneys, bump the question over to the attorneys. Go to both and tell them you have a 1P from each. Leave it up to them to decide between themselves who can be flexible. Have them get back to you. Be sure and tell them how soon you need to know and to get back to you quickly.

9. *Is this matter billable?* If you are accountable for a certain amount of billable time and continue to receive requests for nonbillable time, you can control what you receive. If you cannot turn down the request, at least you have a paper trail documenting where the nonbillable time originates. If you are questioned about having higher nonbillables than allowed, you can

alleviate a potential problem. The supervising paralegal or attorney should also review the amount of nonbillable time requested of you and step in if necessary.

10. *Is this assignment:* __ one-time project __ permanent assignment __ as-needed basis __ full-time assignment? You need to know whether you will be performing a one-time assignment and never seeing the matter again, such as a letter, settlement agreement, and so forth. Is this a permanent assignment where you will be called on an as-needed basis or will this project consume most of your time?

11. *Overall length of permanent assignment:* Just how long will this assignment continue? You need to know in order to allocate your time and availability for other assignments.

12. *Authorized:* LEXIS/Westlaw __; Nexis __; Internet services __; such as __; trademark search __; other online computer services as needed; other __. These online computer services result in charges to the client. Most bill the firm by the hour or the minute. Are you authorized to expend these costs on behalf of the client? Find out ahead of time before you run up the bill.

13. *Authorized:* Backup paralegals __; temporary paralegals __; additional secretarial support __; case clerks __; other __. Find out ahead of time what you can do in order to get assistance. Don't wait until the last minute when your deadlines are imminent to find out whether you have the authority to get help.

14a. *Authorized:* __ Computerized litigation support (in-house). Many firms now have in-house automated litigation support, so find out ahead of time whether this project will utilize this department or even the system. You may have to find a new software program or call in a consultant. Budget your time accordingly.

14b. *Authorized:* __ Other outsourced services. Are you authorized to use an outside photocopying, imaging, or scanning service or to hire an investigator or corporate search firm, or to conduct an asset search? If so, are there budget constraints?

15. *Describe specifics of the assignment. Attach background information if necessary:* Here is the opportunity for the requesting attorney to tell you exactly what the assignment should look like. For example, if this is an analyzing project, what are the pertinent issues? How should the analysis look? What format should be used? Who are the key players? What is the analysis used for? Attaching a synopsis of the client history or the case should help you. Don't hesitate to ask for one if the matter or client is new to you.

16. *The file:* Original file attached __; copy of file attached __; Complaint attached __; other documents attached __.

17. *Assigned to:* This space, either filled in by the supervisor or attorney, may request a particular paralegal. You may also enter your name.

18. *Date:* Date assigned.

19. *Prepared by:* Who filled out this request?

LEGAL ASSISTANT ASSIGNMENT REQUEST FORM

Legal Assistant Assignment Request

To: Date:

Requesting Attorney:

Client: Client Matter No.:

Nature of Assignment:

Number of paralegals or case clerks needed: _____
Levels: _____

Estimate of time involved: _____

Date Needed: _____ Time: _____ Priority: _____
(Priority: 1P = 1st priority, absolutely need on this date; 2P = 2nd priority, some flexibility on this due date)

Is this matter billable? Y _____ N _____

Is this assignment: one-time project _____; permanent assignment _____; as-needed basis _____; full-time assignment _____

Overall length of permanent assignment: days _____;
wks. _____; mos. _____; yrs. _____

Authorized: LEXIS/Westlaw _____; Nexis _____; Internet _____; trademark search _____; on-line services as needed _____; other _____

Authorized: backup paralegal _____; temporary paralegals _____; additional secretarial support _____; case clerks _____; librarian _____; other _____

Authorized: _____ computerized litigation support (in-house)
                _____ outsourced services _____

Describe specifics of the assignment. Attach background information if necessary.

_____

_____

_____

_____

_____

_____

Original file attached _____; copy of file attached _____;
Complaint attached _____; summary attached _____;
documents _____.

Assigned to: _____
Date: _____   Prepared by: _____

Using the Request Form at Review Time

By saving copies of the request form, you will be able to track progress during the year. Does it feel as though you are making progress? Check your completed forms. Getting too many of the same types of assignments? Review your request forms to be sure, and then seek out other types of assignments.

At review time there will be little question as to what you have accomplished during the year. Usually, when supervisors conduct a review, they are only able to go back in their minds 2 to 3 months at the very best. Chances are unlikely they recall precisely what you did at the beginning of the year, which undoubtedly counts for a portion of your review; however, if there were any major problems, they will be sure to recall "last March when the paralegal made that horrendous mistake." Be sure everyone remembers all the excellent assignments. By keeping copies of request forms, you have a ready-made file.

Upgrading Your Assignments

Here is the perfect opportunity to ask for and receive an upgrade in assignments. A few techniques are:

1. Ask for an assignment that is one step above what has just been given. For example: You have just been given an assignment to summarize depositions. Tell the attorney, "When I finish summarizing all ten

depositions on this case, I can put together an analysis of testimony inconsistencies to help us track this case. Would you like it on Tuesday or on Wednesday?" Asking for an upgrade and then "closing" the sale by giving a choice of when instead of waiting for a yea or nay is highly effective.

2. Do not become a victim of empty loading, a technique inadvertently used by law firms when they confuse "increasing responsibilities" with "upgrading." The law firms says, "Sue, we are going to increase your responsibilities," and Sue thinks, "Great!" Then she finds out that instead of summarizing six depositions per week, she is summarizing twelve. Repetition versus innovation, or more of the same instead of upgrading, leads to boredom, stress, and job dissatisfaction.

3. Use your calendar memos twice. When completing one assignment, for example, an indexing assignment, return the original memo to the attorney with a handwritten note such as: "Now that we have found these 'smoking guns,' let's get those documents from Jones. I can handle that production for you next Thursday with two document clerks." If sending back the memo is too formal, then go right in and ask for the upgrade by telling the attorney,
   - What you can do
   - When you can deliver it
   - How you can deliver it
   - Time and cost estimated.
   You decide whether you are ready to upgrade, not the attorney. They only affirm your decision.

Sometimes you just have to stick your neck out! If you do get a "no," don't worry; keep trying. Eventually you'll get some "yeses."

4. Trade billable time for training time. This method is one of the most effective tools around for upgrading your assignment level. Remember, the reasons you don't get upgraded may be a result of simple apprehension from attorneys because (a) you will take too long performing the assignment, resulting in write-offs, and (b) they just don't have enough time to show you what to do (or so they think).

   Understand the mind-set of the attorney. Remember, attorneys are trained to negotiate. If you present your request in a manner that sounds confrontational, threatening, or like begging (indicating weakness), you will probably not get what you want. Some unhelpful techniques paralegals use without even realizing it are
   - "I learned how to do that kind of assignment in school."
   - "My job description says I am supposed to do this."
   - "If you could just show me how to do it, I'm sure I could catch on."
   - Circulating a "uses and abuses of paralegals" memo (generally originating from frustrated employees). The memo describes what paralegals are trained to do. Most of the time, the memo goes into the circular file.

   A better way to negotiate for assignments is trading for training. A common objection attorneys voice is, "You don't know how to do it."

A perfectly acceptable response (be sure you learn to recognize objections) is, "You're right. Now is the perfect time to learn." Then ask, "If a senior paralegal or an associate were to perform this assignment, how much time would it take to complete the assignment?" Let's say the attorney answers 4 hours. "Okay," you respond, "let's do this. I think I can complete this assignment in 6 hours. I will need about one-half hour of your time to go over the project. When I complete the project, *if* you approve of the job, we will bill the client for 4 hours only and put the other 2 hours under nonbillable time. Or, if accounting for the time as administrative is not satisfactory, I will take my own time. I can meet with you in the morning before office hours to review the project. I will even bring coffee and croissants." Then sell the dollar benefits of your training. "The advantages to the firm are that an associate no longer has to perform paralegal work; I am now trained to do this type of assignment; the client gets a quality work product and saves fees; and you can call on me again for this type of assignment."

What you have accomplished is a safe and well-thought-out method to shift the workload. You have em-phasized benefits to the firm and the client. And most importantly, you have given the attorney the problem *and* the solution.

5.   Use the problem and solution technique to enhance your assignments; the image you will present is that of a capable, competent person who is a problem solver.

Perhaps you run into a complication working with Attorney A on one of your assignments. Approach the situation with solution in hand. For example, you are assigned to a document production that will extend 1 week more than anticipated putting you behind in other assignments. Call Attorney B immediately and say, "I am on the *Jones* document production which has extended 1 week. I can do one of two things regarding your assignment: complete it when I return, or Marcia can step in and complete it by tomorrow evening. Which would you prefer?" Present the problem, then solution or choice of solutions. You will eliminate the attorney's anxiety (taking away her need to solve *your* problem); your professional image is intact; and you will have handled the situation competently. If the attorney offers his own solution, fine. You took your best shot and got the ball rolling.

10-4 MEMOS

Now that you have a systematized manner to handle and upgrade assignments, don't drop the ball because the supervising attorney doesn't know what you are doing.

Some time ago, an article in one of the business magazines talked about a CEO who had her staff prepare status memos every Friday. The memo took 10 minutes to write and 4 minutes to read (thus the name, 10-4 memos). This simple technique eliminated crisis, miscommunication, and the dreaded feeling of (a) nothing is being done, or (b) everything must be okay, otherwise I would have heard.

At the end of this section are two sample 10-4 memos. You may wish to draft your own version. Particular attention should be paid to the following:

- *Update:* Give a concise update on what has occurred. Example: "Completed minutes for fiscal year end. Sent to client for signatures."
- *Needed to complete this assignment:* What do you need in order to complete this assignment? Are you waiting on someone else before you can finish? Example: "Have not received revised minutes from Edward. Need your approval before sending to client who expects it by Tuesday."
- *Estimate of time billed:* 8 hours.
- *Estimate of total time to be billed:* 15 hours.

Organizing a Backup Paralegal System

Ideally, strategic and organizational skills will enable you to handle and juggle assignments with a minimum of effort. However, even the most experienced senior legal assistant cannot predict the waves of work that result as a case or client matter develops. How many times have you been caught in a flurry of unexpected work when a client delivers not 10 boxes of documents as anticipated, but 100 boxes? Or, when the case absolutely everyone, from the managing partner on down, thought would settle is now going to trial in 2 weeks?

A backup paralegal system is designed to cover unanticipated peaks of workload without hiring and updating a new recruit, pulling someone off one assignment to fill in for a crisis, or leaving you stranded. It also eliminates the pressure to be at the firm all hours of the day and night, afraid to take a vacation because you are the only person who knows where everything is.

Here is how it works. If you are in a law firm or legal department with anywhere from 2 to 200 paralegals, you can have a backup system. When assigning a case, client, or matter to a lead paralegal, a backup paralegal is automatically assigned. Everyone leads and everyone is a backup. The backup paralegal is informed of the history of the client or matter, where documents are located, computer/software system, significant dates, and status of the matter. It is the lead paralegal's responsibility to keep the backup paralegal well informed. This may result in a 5-minute meeting every week, a 15 minute meeting every 2 weeks or a meeting once a month, depending on the activity. The backup paralegal is copied on all correspondence and legal documents and can step in at a moment's notice to assist when the workload peaks.

The backup paralegal can be junior in status, such as an intermediate if you are a senior, paralegal assistant, or entry-level paralegal. The team concept is effective in saving costs for the client and most importantly as a stress saver to you. Perhaps you find yourself in a situation whereby an increase in workload on one matter will cause you to work again until 12:00 A.M. You will work 6 extra hours that day. Two paralegals (working up to speed) can complete the job in half the time. In this instance, it is far better to have two paralegals work until 9:00 P.M.

To demonstrate how two paralegals can save the firm's paralegals from burnout and with no increase in fees to the client, review the following calculation.

One paralegal: Works overtime from 6:00 P.M. until 12:00 A.M.:
                 6 hours at $90 per hour to client = $540
Two paralegals: Work overtime from 6:00 P.M. until 9:00 P.M.:
                 $90 per hour × 2 paralegals = $180
                 (X 3 hours) = $540

As you can see, two heads can be better than one. It is critical to missed deadlines and burnout of your staff.

Generating Department Status Reports

Someone needs to now what the paralegal department is doing. Someone needs to be able to spot trends, predict fluctuating workloads, look for overloaded employees, and prevent turnover. That someone can be a department head, a supervising paralegal or attorney, a paralegal manager, or a team leader. Status reports know no boundaries as to size of paralegal programs. One paralegal in a firm should generate status reports. Twenty-five paralegals and you are in hot water if you don't have them.

Informing attorneys and paralegals as to who is available, where to route a project, which attorneys are more apt to use paralegals, and who is backup on what matter are all bits of information necessary to run a smooth department.

Create, design and implement status reports according to the firm's environment and culture. Reports can be generated once a week, twice a month, or monthly and should be circulated to all attorneys and paralegals. The report can be sent by e-mail. Case, client matter, due dates, paralegal, attorney, backup, and assistant should be listed.

FORM: 10-4 MEMO

<u>10-4 Memo</u>

To:

From:

Date:

Matter:

Client:

Week of: _____

Update:

Needed to Complete this Assignment:

Estimate of Time Billed on Project:

Estimate of Total Time to be Billed on Project:

FORM: 10-4 MEMO

10-4 Memo

To:

From:

Date:

Re:

Matter	Status	Needed to Complete	Time Billed	Anticipated Total Billing time
1.				
2.				
3.				
4.				
5.				
6.				
7.				
8.				
9.				
10.				

SAMPLE: STATUS REPORT

<u>Status Report</u>

To:

From:

Date:

Subject: Paralegal Case Load as of 6/1/20___

Department: Litigation

Case	Type of Assign.	Due Date Priority	Atty.	Para.	Backup	Assist.
Downs	Doc.Pr.	1p 6/15	RHR	PS	JW	EC
Happy Films	Trial All nec.	1P 7/15	FRR	JW	PS	EC
Ofc.	Audit Ltrs.	2P	JSS	ST	CE	——
Doe Dissol.	OSC	1P 7/15	MLG	EW	JW	EC
Patrick	Depo	Hold	MLG	JW	EW	RR

PARALEGAL INNER VIEW: WENDY STECHMANN—HER CASES MAKE HER LEERY OF HOSPITALS

Name: Wendy D. Stechmann
Title: Paralegal
Specialty: Defense, some plaintiff work
Previous experience: Medical malpractice defense cases
Education: B.A. Legal Studies; Paralegal Certificate from Marywood University, ABA-approved, Scranton, PA
Years of experience: 13 years
Firm: Leven, Gouldin & Thompson, LLP; Vestal, New York
Size: 46 attorneys, 19 paralegals; 2 offices
Job duties: Respond to Requests for Bill of Particulars; discovery demands; analyze documents and medical records; interview witnesses; obtain medical, employment, education, and military records; summarize depositions; interview pro bono divorce clients and draft divorce papers; work on paying divorce cases. Currently working on converting firm's entire library into CD-ROM, and other interesting and various duties.

Tell us about a tough assignment.

Working on a very large, complex international litigation case. We would get thousands of documents in at a time, almost daily, and it was difficult to catalog them because the subject material was pig genetics, which was not a familiar area to me.

What has been your most satisfying experience?

Working on a plaintiff's case. It was satisfying because our clients were very special people who were legitimately injured. I was the one who had the most contact with them and would update the attorney on their status. They were a pleasure to work with and it was so nice to see things turn out well for them. I had almost daily contact with them, but they weren't a nuisance. (They would send me a piece of candy every time that they sent me a medical bill, etc.)

What has been your biggest eye-opener in this field?

The medical malpractice that occurs on a daily basis! It scares me to think about having a baby, surgery, etc.

What computer skills do you need here?

I don't think that there is a computer requirement. They asked me if I used WordPerfect, but that was about it.

What are your plans for the future?

I plan on staying at my present firm for the rest of my career. I hope to broaden my position once I show the firm my abilities. (I just started this position.) I hope to take on more responsibilities in my job, and in my professional associations.

Do you believe a paralegal education is necessary?

I think that an education is paramount. I know many legal secretaries who have been doing the job for 20-plus years who know much more than I do. But I think that everyone needs an education now, if for no other reason than the satisfaction that it gives you knowing that you have an education. I would go get a master's in paralegal studies. Education is so necessary today.

What would you tell your colleagues out there?

Don't get discouraged with the job. At times, it can be very stressful, especially if you are really busy, working extra hours and feel unappreciated. It will get better. Don't worry about the attorney who doesn't seem to appreciate you at times and is condescending. They are under a great deal of stress and tend to take it out on the paralegal. Most of them really do appreciate you and will let you know under less stressful times. It's a really rewarding career.

Where is the profession going?

I'm not sure. It seems to be taking a bit of a regression right now. When I graduated from college, there were many positions paying a top salary with many perks. My first job was for a great firm. The potential salary was great, I had my own secretary who did all of my typing, and the paralegals were treated as professionals. You had to have graduated from a 4-year ABA-approved program to work as a paralegal [at that firm]. Right before I got married and moved, the firm began to change. Secretaries were given paralegal positions, even though they didn't meet the 4-year, ABA-approved requirements. (The firm was able to pay them less and not provide them with a secretary.) Now, the paralegals there do all of their own typing and don't really use the secretary for much. The respect isn't what it used to be. The only thing on their minds now is for the paralegal to bill, bill, bill, and make the partners lots of money. Since that position, I have found it more difficult to command a decent salary, even with experience. At my previous position, I was more of a secretary/paralegal. I had no secretary, had to do my own copying and faxing, scheduled depositions, did personal things for the attorneys that I worked for and more. (And that was the best firm to work in where I was living!)

Now, I have a better position with a secretary and more prestige, but there is still no real division between the paralegals and legal secretaries. We have our own offices, unlike the secretaries. And, we bill our time, unlike secretaries, but there doesn't seem to be any more distinction other than that. I think that it seems like firms are changing. They want good help but don't want to pay for it. They want you to bring in lots of money for the firm, but don't want to compensate you for your hard work. They want the money in their own pockets and don't want to share the wealth.

The paralegal profession was once the up-and-coming career that everyone wanted. Now, it seems that the prestige of the position has worn off. Paralegals aren't really thought of as professionals anymore, just glorified secretaries. I've noticed that law firms, in my experience, don't care if you are certified. It means nothing to them. They don't think that it gives the firm more prestige and aren't willing to pay for you to obtain certification. It doesn't mean more money for you. It seems like it is a waste of time because it only means something to you but not the firm. Again, I think that the paralegal professional is regressing. Hopefully, we will start going on an upswing again.

What would you change about the profession?

I would make paralegals be treated like the professionals that we are. I would try to make attorneys understand what we are capable of and that we aren't just people who couldn't get into law school but rather, people who chose the paralegal profession over being an attorney. So often I am asked when I am going to law school, as if I am using this as a stepping stone. I want to bring the prestige and professionalism back into the paralegal field.

CHAPTER 14

Using Vendors to Upgrade Your Career

Businesses are just now awakening to the fact that legal assistants have tremendous buying power. While the extent of that authority varies from east coast to west coast and firm to firm, no one can deny that paralegals influence the firm or corporation in the selection of suppliers of services and goods. This is verified through the number of exhibitors at paralegal conferences, increase in advertising in newsletters and trade magazines, and number of direct sales calls paralegals now receive.

By giving you buying power, firms bestow an additional responsibility: to wisely and prudently spend dollars to maximize productivity and profitability of the firm. When choosing a vendor, it is your name on the recommendation, your research into the service or product, and your reputation on the line. As with anything else, when the selection is great, such as a responsive new software package, the firm responds with "Boy, did we pick a winner!" When the selection is bad, the firm responds with, "Who selected that rotten package anyway?"

WHO ARE VENDORS?

Vendors come in all shapes. A vendor is anyone who sells products or services to a law firm or legal department, such as the following:

- Office supplies
- Software and hardware
- Online services
- Books and training manuals
- Automated litigation support
- Staffing services (including temporary help)
- Imaging and scanning services
- Professional services, such as accounting, insurance, legal, investigators, health care, interior design, and asset searches

- Office equipment and furniture
- Corporate services, such as incorporation
- Research services
- Court reporters
- Graphics
- Photocopying services
- Schools and seminar companies
- Facilities management services
- Electronic evidence
- Printers
- Publishers
- Marketing consultants
- Trial consultants
- Caterers
- Database management
- Messenger and courier services
- Video services
- Court services (that is, filing and fax services)
- PR—public relations
- Advertising or collateral materials
- Travel agency services
- Repositories

These businesses target paralegals as a buying power of influence in the firm. Maybe you have been contacted by some or all of these companies. Perhaps your firm has, at one time or another, told you to go out and find a particular service, such as a litigation support company to assist in a case that's heating up, or to hire a few temporaries to finish a project. Perhaps you were handed the task of finding the right software package to speed up production of wills or incorporations. All of these peripheral assignments contribute to the firm's evaluation of your management skills.

CHOOSING THE RIGHT VENDOR

"The two most important factors in choosing a vendor are people and quality," claims Rich Finkelman, formerly Director of Technology for the 200+ lawyer firm of Phelps, Dunbar in New Orleans, and consultant with Arthur Andersen. Finkelman offers sound advice when setting out to choose a good vendor: "Law firms are a crisis-driven business. You need to know if the vendor can respond to the crisis. Can they work the hours a law firm works? If there is a problem on a Friday night at 8:00, can the vendor take care of it? If not, you don't have a law firm-compatible vendor."

The quality of the product or service cannot be overlooked. Law firms are extremely conscious about producing high-quality work product. Do the vendors' references check out? You can get a good feel about the vendor by talking with clients who have had firsthand experience using the service or product.

"The two biggest mistakes that are made when selecting a vendor," says Finkelman, "are selecting on the basis of price or selecting friends to do the job. Letting a partner convince you that his cousin can do the same job is automatically asking to have the job redone. Stick with people whose job it is to do what they do."

People who service law firms are generally exceptionally bright, otherwise they would not be able to respond to the special needs of the legal profession. These vendors are willing to share their knowledge with you. Here is an excellent way to learn about a new area of expertise and bootstrap into an upgraded position through the use of the vendor system.

"Don't confuse a consultant with vendors," Finkelman cautions. "The vendor has the same knowledge as a consultant. The difference between a consultant and a vendor is that the consultant will charge you for his knowledge and refer you to a vendor anyway. Generally, that vendor will be someone the consultant prefers."

Finally, remember that the vendor with the lowest cost is not always the best for the job. If you are buying paper clips and do not care about the quality or where they come from, then buy according to cost. If you are purchasing a product or service where quality is of utmost importance, particularly if it involves the client, then cost is only one of your considerations.

"If you are choosing a service or product based solely on cost," says Finkelman, "then remember, you get what you pay for. When you have determined the two or three finalists for your project or product, you will find that they are within 20 percent of each other. If someone is out in left field with a cost projection, something is wrong with the picture."

HOW TO INTERVIEW A VENDOR

If possible, start with five or six vendors. You might start with a list as high as 10, buy beyond that may confuse or exhaust you. Compile your list from vendors the firm has previously used with satisfaction, and ones recommended through your network. Call other firms to find out who they recommend. Word-of-mouth in the legal field is still the most effective recommendation for quality services and goods. A rule of thumb is if the vendor services major firms and corporations, it may be a business worth reviewing. The following are questions to ask the vendor:

1. *How long have you been in business?*

The vendor who has been in business the longest does not necessarily produce the best product or service. However, if you are looking for stability for a long-term project, you want to make sure that they will be around when the project comes to fruition, that is, when you go to trial in 2 years.

2. *Where are you located?*

If this is a vendor that you need close by, for example, a temporary help service or computer hardware vendor, location may be a factor. On the other hand, some vendors, such as computerized litigation support companies, may be located in another city or state. This is usually done because costs of labor and real estate are cheaper. Many times it doesn't really matter where they are, particularly in this day of electronic transfers, 1-day freight, CD-ROM, and video-conferencing.

3. *Where is the project completed?*

Some companies, such as litigation support vendors and document imaging and scanning companies, will complete their projects out of town, out of state or even out of the country. This may be a factor for you if for some reason you need to visit the vendor every day. Others see no problem provided they can send a paralegal to the site to oversee the project and confidentiality is guaranteed. Paralegals have been sent as far away as the Philippines to oversee document coding projects. Others will be allowed to travel uptown to review the work only on a regular basis. Find out what your firm will accept.

4. *What are the qualifications of the people doing the work?*

Who do the vendors hire? Depending on the service or product, it is critical to know who is producing the work product. For example, if the vendor is

- A training company: Who does the training or writes the materials?
- A court reporting service: Do they meet state requirements?
- A litigation support service: Who does the coding? What are their academic credentials?
- A software program vendor: Does the programmer understand the needs particular to the legal community?

- A deposition summarizing service: Are the summarizers experienced paralegals with knowledge of the practice specialty? Do they use the latest technology?

5. *What is the history of the company?*

Who founded the company? When? What is their track record? Are the principals familiar with legal terminology? How many offices do they have? How solid are they? What is their turnover rate?

6. *Can you provide a copy of your annual report?*

Check their financial history. Can this company financially sustain the project? If the company is financing a payroll to complete your project, do they have full funding?

7. *Who are your references?*

Don't *ever* be shy in asking for references. When you do receive a list of references, ask to speak with the person who actually used the product or service, not just the name given to you. Ask if she knows anyone else who has utilized this vendor and search out information other than what has been provided. You are looking for reputation in the field. The vendor may have given you only references of businesses that were pleased with the service. Find out if someone wasn't pleased and why.

8. *Why are you different from your competitor?*

Be careful on this one. They will all tell you *why* they are better, and they believe it! What you are really looking for is how well they know this industry and their own product or service. Do they speak the language? Use the proper terminology? Understand what you are saying?

9. *What are your quality control procedures?*

Find out the steps the vendor takes to ensure quality control. Nothing is worse than spending big bucks for something that doesn't work or is inefficient. What is their quality control rate?

10. *What assurances or guarantees do you provide to meet my deadline?*

Maybe they can't. Maybe they need your cooperation. If so, what do they need? It may be something you find too cost prohibitive to provide.

11. *How often can I visit the project site?*

Good vendors will tell you that you can put a bunk in their offices and stay until the project is done.

12. *Is there a conflict of interest?*

If you are requesting a service of any kind, be sure that there is no conflict of interest with another firm.

13. *What guarantees can you give me regarding this product or service?*

Look for vendors that will stand behind their service or product. Where will they be if something goes awry? Who can you call if there is a problem? Are you history once you buy? What are the hidden charges?

14. *What guarantee of confidentiality can you give me?*

It is important that there is no breach of confidentiality.

15. *What are your hours of operation?*

If you need this vendor at 2:00 A.M., is there someone who will respond? If you are working over the weekend and need their services, do you have to wait from Saturday morning until Monday morning when someone is there to take your call?

16. *What percentage of your business is directed toward the legal field?*

Is this a vendor who understands the unique needs of the legal field? Do they understand necessary terminology?

17. *What projects have you completed that were of a similar nature?*

You are looking for experience and expertise.

18. *What is the largest project/farthest distance/largest number of people/most volume/you have provided?*

Without revealing confidential information, ask the vendor to describe the project to you.

19. *Please provide a cost estimate breakdown.*

20. *Please provide a list of additional (hidden) charges.*

21. *How often do you increase prices? Can you guarantee this price for (length of time)?*

If a decision from the firm will not be made immediately, how long can the vendor guarantee that quote? If you are on a project where you will not need the vendor for another 6 months or so, will the cost quote you are getting today remain the same?

22. *What are your billing practices?*

Arrangements need to be made with your accounting department for payment. If the vendor expects payment every 7 days, but it is firm policy not to pay any bill for 30 days, you may have an unhappy vendor on your hands. Unhappy vendors who are not getting paid tend to drop the quality level of services. This is precisely what you don't want. Get a clear understanding of billing practices and payment procedures ahead of time.

23. *How much advance notice do you need from this firm in order to gear up for the project/order the product?*

If you expect a vendor to deliver immediately when advance notice is needed, you are setting both of you up for failure. Find out ahead of time what's expected.

24. *What kind of follow-up do you practice?*

This is a necessary question for certain products and services, such as software packages (training purposes), temporary help (checking up on the paralegals on the job), training seminars (did anyone learn anything?), and litigation support projects. Make sure the services are thorough.

25. *Do you offer a discount for volume?*

It never hurts to ask.

26. *Are the people on your staff employees or independent contractors?*

Find out. Don't get caught in a cross fire between the vendor and the IRS.

PREPARING A REQUEST FOR PROPOSAL

A request for proposal (RFP) is a letter to a vendor who provides services or products, generally over a length of time. You are asking the vendor to bid on the job and to provide details of how they propose to supply the service, key personnel employed, and a cost estimate. In the legal field, a request for proposal is generally used to engage the services of a computerized litigation support company, consulting service, on-site personnel (temporary) services, facilities management services, computer equipment, technical services, photocopying, imaging, scanning, and records management. Today, drafting an RFP is a standard assignment for many paralegals. The example on page 174 is a hypothetical letter to a litigation support company asking several companies to bid on development of a computerized litigation database. Details in the request actually could be expanded, but for teaching purposes, a shortened version is offered.

SAMPLE: REQUEST FOR PROPOSAL

April 30, 200X

Acme Litigation Support Company
1234 Main Street
Metropolis, USA 55555

RE: A-B-C Case

Dear Vendor:
   This firm is in the process of retaining a litigation support services company to assist us in the development and management of a plaintiff's litigation database.
   We will use the database for deposition preparation; trial preparation; witness preparation; pleading preparation; tracking trial and deposition exhibits; constructing chronologies; subject matter research; and prioritizing documents.
   This request is structured to include known quantities, issues to be addressed, and cost estimates. Your response to this proposal must be in writing to our offices no later than June 1, 200X. Please include the background of all key personnel expected to be involved on the project. A sample contract and references from at least three firms or corporations are required.
   Please confirm that your company is not now nor has in the past been involved in providing services to any parties in A-B-C case, filed in Anytown, USA, or Jones case, filed in Anytown, USA, or related proceedings. Also confirm you are not providing services for the firms of Jones, Jones and Smith, or Smith, Smith and Jones.

I.   Background of Case

   This suit is a declaratory judgment action filed by A-B-C company against its insurance carrier seeking coverage for alleged property damage. A-B-C company is a chemical manufacturing company. The suit involves claims for the environmental cleanup of a toxic waste dump.

II.   Scope of Project

   We anticipate all documents selected during the discovery phase of the litigation will require coding and entry to the database. We estimate that the number of documents* to be produced will be around 1 million.

Please provide bids for:
- 300,000 documents
- 500,000 documents
- 1,000,000 documents
* (We estimate 3 pages to equal one document.)

III.   Database Design

The following fields are preliminary suggestions for design of the database. We welcome suggestions for improvement:
1. Beginning document no.
2. Ending document no.
3. Attachments: must indicate relationship between documents, i.e., en-closure, appendix, chart.
4. Document date: Must indicate date document was created or signed.
5. Document type: Memo, letter, telegram, e-mail, handwritten note, transmittal, invoice, policy, minutes.
6. Document title: Must indicate re: line.
7. Author
8. Recipient
9. cc
10. Duplicates
11. Names mentioned
12. Dates mentioned
13. Places mentioned

IV.   Document Repository

Please provide information for management and pricing of a repository for 1 million documents. Cost estimates should include equipment, personnel, fur-niture, space, and terminals or host server.

V.   Hardware/Software Specifications

Please indicate the hardware and software provided by your company. Once the database is static, we require the option of transferring some or all of the database to a laptop computer.

VI.   Training

Please provide a training manual and describe the duration of your training for use of the database along with costs, if any, of a trainer.

VII.   Quality Control

Please provide a detailed description of your quality control system for identifying and removing duplicate documents. Indicate the expected error rate for each field.

VIII.   Pricing

Please provide a cost breakdown that includes:

A. System design, including cost and time of design meetings and manuals.
B. Personnel costs
Please include the number of people required and hourly rate, when appropriate:
- IT personnel
- Project manager
- Document coders
- Quality control personnel
- Web master
- Web designer
- Programmers
- Data conversion operators
- Systems analyst
- Supervisors
- Trainers

C. Any additional costs
Please provide a detailed list of all additional charges such as online costs and reports generated at our request. Please include how and when billings are generated.
D. Start-up estimates
Include consulting services to design the database, initiate project, install hardware and software, design user manual, and train users.
E. Per document costs
F. Monthly costs

Estimate the monthly charge for the coding phase, such as photocopying and facilities.

Please confirm that the information contained in this request for proposal will be held in strictest confidence. We expect our first wave of documents on or about July 15th. Your proposal will be reviewed by our executive commit-

tee on or about June 10th. We expect to interview no fewer than three finalists during that week. Please advise us as to your schedule and availability for
meeting on June 12th.

Sincerely,

Sara Lee, CLA
Sr. Legal Assistant

cc: Executive Committee

COMPARING VENDOR RESPONSES

After you have interviewed and researched prospective vendors, it is necessary to compare the bids. Prepare a chart outlining the pertinent points of
information critical to making a decision. By having all of the facts in front
of you, you will be able to select a vendor based on data and remove any
emotional aspects of the selection, such as the Smith Company was friendly
and fun to work with. The following form is geared toward a litigation support company, but you can prepare a chart for any type of comparison by
simply changing the headings.

FORM: VENDOR COMPARISON

Vendor Name: _____

Comparable references	Ease of access to project	Price per page
Qualifications	Time necessary to complete	Additional charges
Location of project	Quality control procedure	Online storage costs
Location of company	Hiring criteria of key staff	No. of pages for doc.

Applying the Vendor System to Your Career

By walking through the vendor process, it is possible to add yet another line of accomplishment on your resume. Parlay the experience into an achievement in the eyes of the firm. For example, if you were in charge of organizing the expansion of space for the paralegal department, you contacted many different vendors, coordinated the move, compared costs, researched several products and services, and negotiated on behalf of the firm for the best price. You also wrote many memos to members of the firm, had several "meet and discuss" meetings, and, in turn, demonstrated your ability to manage, coordinate, supervise, organize, take initiative, use good judgement, and set yourself apart as a leader and good manager. Don't overlook this opportunity!

PARALEGAL INNER VIEW: DIANE GAGNER—INTERN

Name: Diane Gagner
Position: Intern
Firm: D.A.'s office in Castle Rock, Colorado, and part-time for a firm in Denver.
Size: Denver firm has 2 attorneys, 3 paralegals, a few ghosts, and two small dogs.
Education: In process of receiving paralegal certificate from Arapahoe Community College, Littleton, Colorado. Plans on transferring to Regis University upon completion and hopes to receive B.A. in 2 years. May attend law school.
Specialty: Criminal Law
Job duties: Filing, Bates stamping documents for court; calling the sheriff's department to confirm if a witness was subpoenaed for court; legal research; and watching a court proceeding pertaining to discrimination.

What's put you between a rock and a hard place in your internship?
   Answering client's questions over the phone. Many were hyper-verbal and it was important to calm them down and reassure them that the attorney would call them as soon as possible. My job at the D.A.'s office requires me to interview women who have been assaulted by their boyfriend or husband. I orally walk them through the whole process and leave them with brochures on domestic violence and what to do if the defendant violates the restraining order.

What has made you glad you're entering this career?

Knowing I have taken care of the victims who are very emotional at this time. I try my best to calm them down.

Has anyone told you what computer skills you'll need?

WordPerfect and Microsoft Word. I am learning Westlaw at the moment and finding it quite rewarding.

What suggestions can you give your colleagues?

Since I'm not a paralegal quite yet, I feel I should only give advice to interns. I would say, "Hang in there." Many lawyers confuse us with law clerks and think we know everything! Many of us know nothing! I've read 200 law books but can I put a trial notebook together? No! Lawyers expect performance and how does one obtain that when you only read books in school? The program lacks hands-on experience which I have talked over with my instructors.

What education do you think a paralegal needs?

It's necessary that a paralegal has an education, absolutely! Some are lucky enough to start as a secretary and move their way up, but I have found most lawyers don't have the time to teach what a paralegal needs to know.

What is your scariest or most eye-opening experience?

A scary adventure at the Denver firm involves a ghost or ghosts that seem to enjoy haunting and hanging around the firm. I call him the doorbell ghost because he loves to ring the doorbell. Some view him as a client who was long ago overcharged and is now seeking revenge. One evening a paralegal was left alone to engage in some legal research in the library. Out of nowhere came a voice to "Get out!"

The paralegal never returned or took the time to lock the doors. We have heard strange voices and all agreed it was hard to rationalize the odd occurrences we were encountering. One afternoon, our doorbell kept ringing. A paralegal, hearing the door open from her office upstairs, leaned over the rail and caught a glimpse of a man wearing an old wool coat. She ran downstairs but he had vanished. One of the lawyers has a couple of small dogs that start growling and barking for no reason. It gave us a clue that we have visitors. I was told the ghost didn't like the changes. Since I was a new intern to the firm, I was always on my best behavior. The old house we use as a law firm is 120 years old. We think it possesses two ghosts.

How's that future looking?

My future holds an area of criminal law that is somewhere out there waiting for me. I start job hunting soon and hope to pick up a position quickly. I think there is a high demand for qualified paralegals. A lawyer will give you a month's vacation and use of a limo if you can excel at your job. They depend on us and that's a darn good feeling.

What would you change in the paralegal profession?

I would definitely change the classroom. Lawyers expect interns to perform on the first day as if they were seasoned paralegals with 5 years' experience. Our schools for paralegals really lack hands-on training. I would have a class in school that would specialize in paralegal duties—a class where we learn to put trial notebooks together and one that pertains to courtroom drama. I'm tired of READING about it, let's just DO IT!!

CHAPTER 15

Billables: A Win-Win Situation for Everyone

> How many hours did you say I have to bill??? Does that make me eligible for partner?
>
> Overheard at a paralegal school orientation

The firm has a wonderful way of sending a message as to how hard it expects you to work. The method is called "minimum billable hours requirement" or "suggested" or "recommended" hours. Since the billable hour is the unit produced, it is, in effect, the law firm's "widget." No hours produced, no profit to the firm.

To skirt possible legal issues, some firms now refer to "minimum billable hours" as "suggested hours." Rarely, though, does a firm set its billable requirement without expecting that minimum. Flat fees, value billing, and task-based billing are only a few of the new systems that have emerged in the legal field. These methods theoretically no longer bill the client on an hourly basis. Instead, the client is charged one fee (as for flat fees); charged one fee if the firm wins a case, another if it loses (value billing); and charged so much for each task, such as taking a deposition (task-based billing). Under this methodology, firms exceeding the quote may have to absorb the loss. More often than not, limited fee arrangements are based upon average time to complete the assignment.

Even as law firms slowly change, the concept that the billable hour will "go away" altogether remains unthinkable. Paralegal profitability is based upon the amount of work "sold," that is, the billable hour. "Sold hours" include real time (absent write-offs) met within the firm's required realization rate (hours minus write-offs minus uncollectible accounts). The billable hour expectation is part of the formula measuring employee worth.

Holding a position within an in-house legal department does not necessarily eliminate keeping time records. Many corporations now request that all time is tracked on each matter. The legal department internally "bills" their charges to relevant divisions. The company determines dollars saved in outside counsel fees—a justification necessary to enhance in-house budgets.

Today, legal assistants in law firms are acutely aware that they hold revenue-generating positions, and legal assistants in corporations know that their department saves the company thousands, possibly millions of dollars in legal fees. A powerful demonstration of a paralegal's value to the law firm or corporation is made through the time reporting system. Bonuses and raises reflect not only reward for quality work product, but also the overall contribution to the firm's or corporation's bottom line.

MEETING YOUR MINIMUM REQUIREMENT

Most firms dictate a minimum billable requirement either on a yearly, monthly, or daily basis. The minimum is anywhere from 1,500 to 1,800 hours per year. Some firms stratify this requirement based on experience. Entry-level paralegals may be asked to contribute 1,500 billables whereas senior levels are asked to contribute 1,800. The theory is that it takes an entry level longer to complete the assignment and more write-off time is involved. Firms may also have different requirements according to practice special-ties. In some firms, corporate or probate paralegals are asked to bill less than litigation or real estate paralegals. The theory behind this practice is that corporate or probate paralegals have to work longer to bill fewer hours than litigation paralegals who do not have to switch client matters as frequently.

Some firms do not notify paralegals of the minimum requirement. Not only are these paralegals in the dark, but they also do not receive a sum-mary each month to tell them what has been accomplished. Paralegals have no idea whether they are meeting expectations. Firms that subscribe to the "mushroom theory" of employment practices (keep them in the dark—once in a while open the door and sprinkle with manure) are encouraging low productivity and confusing goals.

As a conscientious employee, pay special attention to the words "mini-mum," "suggested" or "recommended." Does your firm use this word as a guideline? Or is it really trying to say "must meet no less than?" Is the firm also trying to say that anyone meeting the minimum will be considered only an average worker? Is there a hidden message to excel beyond that which is required? If so, how many hours in excess of the minimum are con-sidered excellent? One hundred hours? Two hundred? Five hundred?

Do you know what is expected when you are told to bill x number of hours per year? If not, examine the following chart. Knowledge of the numbers translates into ability to budget time accordingly.

MEETING YOUR MINIMUM REQUIREMENT

Hours Requested: (calculated on 12 months, 52 weeks, 5 days)

Year	Monthly	Weekly	Daily
1,500	125	29	5.8
1,550	129.1	30	6
1,575	131.2	30.5	6.1
1,600	133.3	31	6.2
1,625	135.4	31.5	6.3
1,650	137.5	31.5	6.3
1,675	139.6	32.4	6.5
1,700	141.7	32.9	6.6
1,725	143.8	33.4	6.7
1,750	145.8	33.9	6.8
1,775	147.9	34.4	6.9
1,800	150	34.9	7
1,825	152	35.3	7.1
1,850	154.2	35.9	7.2
1,875	156.3	36.3	7.3
1,900	158.3	36.8	7.4
1,925	160.4	37.3	7.5
1,950	162.5	37.8	7.6
1,975	164.6	38.3	7.7
2,000	166.7	38.8	7.8

The chart lists hours that you are required to bill. It does not take into account vacation, personal days, holidays, ETO (employee time off), or other time off. If you are at a firm that requests 1,800 minimum billable hours, you are required to bill 7 hours per day. If you work an 8-hour day with 1 hour for lunch, *all* of your time at the office must then be billable. This means there is no time for breaks, chitchat, reading the paper, changing files, looking for lost items, or other extraneous activities that cannot be included when billing.

The chart is based on 4.3 weeks per month, which translates into 51.6 weeks per year. If you take a 2-week vacation, you will probably have to work overtime to meet the minimum requirement. Any firm requiring 1,800 hours automatically expects paralegals to work overtime.

If your firm's hours are from 9:00 to 4:00 with 1 hour for lunch, you have 6 billable hours during the day (with no overtime). If your firm requests more then 1,550 hours from you (6 billable hours per day), then you need to plan for overtime. If the firm expects you to exceed the minimum, plan accordingly.

UNDERBILLING

Former office manager, Diane Schroeder, has strong opinions about paralegals and the billing procedure. She has seen many billing wars in her 20+ years as a legal assistant and administrator. Formerly with Bronson, Bronson and McKennon and previously the litigation group administrative assistant for the Los Angeles branch of the 1,000+ attorney firm of Jones, Day, Reavis and Pogue, Schroeder offers this advice, "Paralegals are not billing partners, therefore, they should not make arbitrary decisions as to what to bill the client. Paralegals need to account for actual time worked. Deciding to write off time or cut the hours down exceeds a paralegal's authority."

Scott was a litigation paralegal who was assigned to a large bankruptcy litigation. He was seen working long hours and over the weekends. Yet when his monthly hours report was generated, he had only 100 billable hours. When questioned, Scott replied that because the client was in bankruptcy, it should not be billed too much because it was routine work.

Do not, under any circumstances, unless otherwise directed by the firm, account for only a portion of your time. Once you have made the decision to cut, you have caused two problems:

1. You appear as though you are not working.
2. The billing partner may assume that you did account for all of your time and, in an attempt to give the client a discount, slashes the time even further, causing the firm to lose profit.

Not receiving enough assignments is another cause for underbilling. "Go find the work," paralegals are constantly told. Yet, some paralegals feel slow periods are somehow understood and forgiven. According to Schroeder, this is the worst position a paralegal can take.

"The enire practice group would have to reflect low hours in order for me to assume that business was slow," she states. "In some large firms and corporations, the administrator knows paralegals only by numbers and names. They couldn't tell you if one paralegal was light on work. They judge according to numbers on the reports. The assumption is the paralegal did not work very hard during the month."

No matter how your paralegal program is structured, if you have a set number of hours to bill, the message from the firm is to *go and find the work.* Otherwise, you will have difficulty justifying your position. When reviewing time sheet reports at the end of the year, few will recall that for 2 months during spring, you had a "slow" period. The final, albeit unfair, judgment may be that you did not work hard enough.

DROPPING TIME AND PADDING TIME

You can lose billable time when you switch client matters. Ten minutes here and there add up. Three units a day, and you've lost half an hour. This is particularly difficult if you are a corporate, family law, or probate paralegal and work on many different client matters throughout the day. Many transactional paralegals must work a 9-hour day to get 7 hours billed. Use time-saving techniques such as setting up your day in advance, having all of your files organized, and utilizing strong secretarial support to help you.

Another way to drop or lose time is rounding down instead of up when billing. If, for example, you spent 26 minutes on a matter and are on a tenth of an hour system (bill for each 6 minutes), rounding down to .4 instead of up to .5 causes lost time. Make sure you are consistent with firm policy, however.

Padding time (accounting for more time than you actually worked) is unethical. Paralegals can be fired with cause for this practice. The only comment I have about padding time is *don't do it.* (Rounding up to the nearest tenth of an hour is not padding.)

TRAVEL TIME

Understand the firm or corporate billing policy when traveling. Ron was asked to travel to Atlanta from San Francisco. He billed the client for the entire travel time including the moment he was in the car from his home to the San Francisco airport, on the plane, and travel to his D.C. hotel. In the meantime, while on the 6-hour flight, Ron, who brought his laptop, worked diligently on another matter for a different client. He billed that client 6 hours. Since he flew after spending the day in the office, he also charged time for other matters. Ron ended up with 25 billed hours for the day. Needless to say, the administrator in the firm asked to see Ron upon his return.

Find out exactly how you are to bill for travel. Is flight time billable? If your firm has a branch office in a city you are traveling to, do they still bill the client for flight time? What is the policy? Do not pad your time or over-bill simply because you don't know policy. If each attorney in your firm has a different policy, go to the administrator and ask for a standardized policy for legal assistants.

UNDERSTANDING ECONOMICS
OF PARALEGAL TIME

Because you are vital to profitability, either in the fees billed or fees saved, it is necessary to understand the economics behind the billing procedure.

According to Bill MacMillen, former director of administration of the 100+ attorney firm of Lewis, D'Amato in Los Angeles, the best answer to "What makes a paralegal profitable?" is to compare paralegals with associates. Paralegals take up less space, use fewer services (including secretarial services), and thus have lower overhead responsibility. Firms need to realize just how profitable paralegals can be. They are usually billed out at a much higher percentage of base compensation than associates. The same number of billable hours are expected from paralegals as from associates. Add up all of these ingredients and you have a very profitable professional.

To simplify the economics of paralegal profitability, the Rule of Three has historically been used:

- Three times the paralegal salary equals amount of dollars the paralegal needs to bill to be profitable.
- One-third of the dollars equals salary.
- One-third of the dollars equals overhead.
- One-third of the dollars equals profit.

For example, Sue earns $40,000 per year:

$40,000 × 3 = $120,000 per year in billings
$40,000   = Salary
$40,000   = Overhead
$40,000   = Profit to the firm

Paralegal profitability is tied into the hourly fee. If Sue needs to bill $120,000 to be profitable, then simple arithmetic tells us that the minimum billable requirement dictates the lowest fee Sue can use for billing, or conversely, the hourly rate dictates the minimum billable requirement.

For example: $40,000 × 3 = $120,000 that must be billed

Minimum billable requirement set at 1,600:

$120,000 divided by 1,600 = $75.00 per hour

You can see how paralegals get placed in no-win situations when minimum billable requirements and billing rates do not mesh. Reluctance on behalf of the firm to increase billing rates when appropriate leads to problems in paralegal profitability. For example:

Sue at $40,000 × 3 = $120,000:
$120,000 divided by $60.00 per hour =
2,000 hours Sue needs to bill just
to reach profitability!

Some firms adhere to a formula of billing a paralegal at 150 percent of their base compensation and expect 1,600 to 1,800 billable hours. In such instances, after deducting 25 percent or 30 percent fringe benefit costs and whatever overheard is assigned, there is still a net income per paralegal of base compensation after coverage of that base.

Each firm has different overhead factors and in major metropolitan areas, particularly in Silicon Valley areas, the overhead factor may be significantly high. "A talented, well-compensated, well-managed group of paralegals," says MacMillen, "can be a firm's most profitable unit." Ask your administrator or CFO to explain the economics in detail. Understanding your profitability can take the mystery out of some of the firm's or corporation's expectations.

NONBILLABLE TIME, WRITE-OFFS, AND BAD DEBTS

Nonbillable Time—Frequently, paralegals are asked to perform assignments that are nonbillable. The firm feels these assignments ultimately benefit the firm or save dollars. Some firms have created three timekeeping numbers for billing:

- Client billing number: for all billable work
- Firm number: for administrative duties
- Client nonbillable number: for pro bono work or other work the firm has decided should not be billed to the client.

Unless there is a clear understanding about how much administrative or nonbillable time is allocated, you will have misunderstandings. Too much nonbillable time may render you unprofitable. If, however, the nonbillable time serves the firm directly, such as acting as the Custodian of Records, the firm may feel justified. Get a clear understanding of expectations. If you don't ask, you won't know.

Write-Offs—Although paralegals are often doing very different work than associates, the level of competency applicable to that particular work should be relatively the same as associates. Thus, the write-off percentage for paralegals should be relatively the same as the write-off percentage for all attorneys—based on firm history.

Some paralegals are unaware of how much time is written off by the billing partner. It is important to have this figure to know whether write-offs occur because of poor work product or excessive hours billed, or whether your time is used to negotiate fees with the client. There is nothing you can do if the latter occurs. However, if there are significant write-offs, you need to know the rationale in order to correct the situation.

Some firms have a pro rata policy. If a billing partner, for example, wants to write off 10 percent of the bill, she must cut from the partner, associate, *and* the paralegal. Cutting only from the bottom, that is, the paralegal, is the easiest method but also the most unfair.

Bad Debts—The firm may not always collect all its moneys due. You may never be aware of what percentage of your work is uncollectable; however, the administrator and partners may suddenly stop delegating certain clients to you.

The total amount of hours billed, minus write-offs, bad debts, and administrative or nonbillable time is the realization rate. Your realization rate is the final percentage rate telling the firm how much actual time it sees in dollars. Many firms withhold this information. It still remains a mystery as to why.

Summary

- Never decide on your own to underbill.
- Account for all of your time unless otherwise instructed.
- Understand paralegal profitability to understand employer's expectations.
- Know the limits of nonbillable time to remain profitable.
- Understand "minimum billable requirement" and allocate time accordingly.

Paralegal Career Guide Rule: If you don't fully understand your firm's or corporation's time reporting system or related expectations, find assistance immediately.

A WORD ABOUT APPEARANCES

There are probably few other professions where members arrive at a Saturday seminar dressed to the nines in conservative suits. Yet, many paralegals feel that the war to prove professionalism has yet to be won. It's rare to see attorney attendees wearing Brooks Brothers suits on Saturdays.

No matter how much we have eliminated the "isms"—racism, sexism, genderism—how you look still plays an important role in what conclusions people make about you. A term now in vogue is "looksism." This last bastion of prejudice, unfortunately, still runs rampant in many law firms and corporations.

Looksism is the act of stereotyping based on appearance. This practice has kept many from advancing up the career ladder. It is found over and over again in illustrations such as the following:

- An overweight person must be lazy.
- Obesity means lack of control.
- An older person with gray hair and wrinkles must not be very computer literate.
- People who don't dress well are not good managers.
- Blondes have more fun.
- If you are male, very tall, and particularly a person of color, you must have played basketball sometime in your life.
- A picture of a successful CEO or managing partner conjures up images of Denzel Washington or Glenn Close, but certainly not Drew Carey.
- And the all-time front-runner: The more attractive people are, the more successful they are and the easier time they have in life.

My favorite in the paralegal field relates to a friend of mine who, without a doubt, is gorgeous. This woman is tall, slender, dresses well, is smart, and successful. The most often heard description of her is frequently stated as a surprise, "and she's so nice!"

Appearances Are Impressions; Impressions Are Conclusions

The only way to fight looksism is through education. Right now, most people will tell you they absolutely do not participate in this practice. The reality is that most people are unaware that they do.

A few years ago, I was a guest speaker for attorneys and paralegals exiting the military. As part of the workshop, Nordstrom personal shoppers gave an eye-opening demonstration. The group was shown slides of a woman dressed in a straight skirt with coordinated sweater, inexpensive jewelry, wearing "comfy" shoes, and sporting a nondescript hairstyle. What, the group was asked, did this woman do for a living? The group didn't hesitate to suggest she was either a secretary or administrative assistant.

Next, the group viewed a slide of a young man wearing a tan suit, slicked back hair, brown shoes, white shirt, and nondescript tie. His occupation? "Definitely a salesperson or accounting clerk," the group concurred.

Two more well-dressed people flashed onto the screen. The woman wore a designer navy blue Armani-type suit, tasteful jewelry including pearls, and an upswept, neat, and well-cut hairstyle. The man wore a pinned-striped Brooks Brothers suit, red power tie, expensive looking shoes, and carried a fine leather briefcase. On the table beside him was the *Wall Street Journal*. Their occupations? "Without a doubt," the group concluded, "the woman is either a lawyer or CEO and the male is a stockbroker or CEO."

The Nordstrom consultants were quite pleased with themselves. We weren't looking at four different people; we were looking at one man and one woman. We had no idea we were viewing before and after pictures. Same people, different outfits and image—and different socioeconomic conclusions. Here was looksism using the most common stereotypical denominator. *What* you wear must be what you *are*.

Many articles and books addressing professional image actually avoid the real issue, and that is, while it is unfair to judge people by virtue of their clothing, conclusions *are* definitely made. Fortunately, we have been able to tackle and quash other prejudices. Unfortunately, it's going to take a lot of years of looksism education before the general public "gets it."

During those years, critical decisions about you are made by people in power. While some laws have emerged and cases have been won over discrimination involving obesity, mustaches on women, beards and long hair on men, and pantsuits for women in the workplace, few, if any, laws directly address professional appearance. Image consultants who insist that neat and clean with shoes shined and hair combed is the right image have apparently not competed in today's market.

It is not necessary to break the bank and spend excessive dollars on expensive clothing. It *is* important to dress within the unwritten style of the firm and to match the environment. Overdressed is as harmful as under, badly, or outrageously dressed. If, on the other hand, you have made a positive mark by "being different" and it works for you, don't change a thing.

CASUAL DAY

Casual day has brought about all sorts of interpretations of acceptability. Friday is casual day in my office. A few months ago, I looked around and thought for a second I had accidentally wandered onto the set of the *Rocky Horror Picture Show*. Employees were dressed in (no lie!) a bowling shirt; sweat pants; mules; tube tops; jeans with the knees and buttocks artistically torn out; a gray sweat outfit; and last but not at all shy about it, sandals with socks exposing someone's big toe. Hey, the socks were clean.

Trying to take action, I passively-aggressively sent out the "use and abuse of casual day" memo. I then received an e-mail from our San Francisco regional director (an attorney). "The best thing to do," he wrote, "is not to tell anyone *how* to dress. You must tell them to "use their best judgment." "Tom," I wrote back, "this *is* their best judgment."

Appearances don't stop at clothing. Don't forget to include accoutrements such as briefcase, portfolio, pen (that Goofy pen with the chewed-up eraser has just got to go), handbag, and laptop (outward condition and cleanliness of computer and case).

Your Office

The look of your office is also a statement. Without elaborating on right brain versus left brain organizational abilities (right brainers tend to stack documents and know exactly what's in each pile; left brainers file everything including lunch menus), bear in mind people draw quick conclusions based on what they see. *If they see it, it must be so:*

- If your desk or office is messy, then your work product must be messy.
- If your work product is messy, it must have mistakes.
- If there are mistakes in your work product, the content must be lacking.
- If the content is lacking, you can kiss that promotion goodbye.

CHAPTER 16

Getting Up Off the Sticky Floor

> The road to success is always under construction.
>
> Unknown

CREATING YOUR OWN SUCCESS

If there is any one hard-and-fast rule about career pathing, it is that to succeed we must set our sights on the next rung up the ladder. That's a pretty difficult rule for many paralegals to follow when titles designate tenure in the field (entry, intermediate, and senior). When no other rungs are offered, leaving the field seems to be the only option.

One thing is clear: In order to succeed by today's definition (money, status, recognition), take control of your career. And because job satisfaction plays such an important role in whether success continues (you may be successful but feel miserable), take steps to ensure your own happiness.

Rebecca, a successful litigation support manager in the Midwest, describes how she went along for many years guided by her career rather than doing the guiding.

"Whatever job I had," she says, "defined my career. I had little control over development. Each position determined what would happen to me. I had trouble being recognized as an expert, and moving ahead was impossible. Sure, I received healthy raises every year and the bonuses were great. But I didn't seem to be going anywhere."

Rebecca's experience was typical. While many firms have adopted a paralegal program, or at least a semblance of one, there is no guarantee of success, particularly if law firm professionals continue to harbor a very limited view of career possibilities.

Developing a Master Career Plan and Goals

Paralegals need master career plans. Too many paralegals believe upgrading and expanding their assignment is solely in the hands of the firm. It is almost by accident that some find their positions upgraded. If they work hard and produce quality work product, the firm is expected to promote them. Rather than follow their own master plan, they sit silently by, hoping to be noticed.

Other paralegals target appealing positions, such as trial expert, litigation support manager, and paralegal manager, but don't know how to take the steps to attain the position. They, too, hope that by working hard, the firm will notice and eventually respond.

Unfortunately, the firm or corporation cannot read your mind. Supervisors are not generally aware of inner desires and motivations unless you make them known. Alerting the firm to your advancement possibilities involves finesse, awareness of office politics, and motivation. But first, determine what you want.

Design your own advancement. You may want to advance on a vertical climb, even if you have to create that ladder. On the other hand, you may not wish to move up at all. Expanding horizontally by upgrading responsibilities outwardly is just fine.

Divide a blank piece of paper into two columns: present and future (1 year from now). On the left side of the paper jot down the current responsibilities. Now, on the right side, write down what you would like to be doing 1 year from now. What appeals to you? What assignments would you rather have? What position would you like? What would it take to get there? Do you need to take any classes? Gain recognition in a certain area of expertise? Change firms? Where will this lead? Where would you like to be in 2 years? Your strategy is the road you take to reach those goals.

Think through your career. Don't be afraid to include your fantasies. Having a flexible, well-thought-out plan will give direction to your career. You will be less at the mercy of the organization and more self-empowered.

Gaining Recognition Through PR

When you are ready, you may have to ask for advancement in a manner that is appealing to the firm and nonthreatening. Use good public relations within the firm to increase credibility and gain recognition as an expert.

Here are a few techniques:

1. *Writing the Proposal: Establishing Yourself as an Expert:* Writing a proposal, articulating a need and its solution, is an effective technique to show supervisors that you are either an expert in the area or have strong potential.

Your firm or corporation may need a new department or new equipment. Perhaps the firm needs its own in-house imaging and scanning system and you are familiar with the latest technology. Get a needs consensus from the appropriate attorneys. Get agreement that looking into new systems may solve some of the problems with workload. Draft a proposal that can help resolve some of those problems.

Don't step on anyone's toes. If the firm already has a litigation support manager, for example, don't develop your proposal. You'll commit a serious faux pas.

Your goal is to set yourself up as an expert. Make sure you do know the area, however! As the firm gravitates toward you as the expert, nothing is worse than having it find out you are long on proposals and short on knowledge.

2. *Take an Attorney to Lunch Program: Contacting the Conduit to the Power:* Paralegals often want to establish certain procedures, upgrade assignments, or establish a paralegal program but cannot seem to get the attention of the people who can make this happen.

Associates are wonderful conduits to law firm power. They generally advocate the paralegal programs, and are sufficiently open to hear you. They may not yet have the specific power to get you what you need, but they can usually get the partners' ear.

Taking associates to lunch is low stress. If your firm has an unspoken caste system that says attorneys simply don't eat with paralegals, breach it. Ask an attorney to lunch. You probably won't get turned down. If you do, don't personalize it. Just lay out your concerns and see if someone can help. Associates understand better than most that if the paralegal's job goes smoothly, their jobs are easier.

3. *The Power of the Written Word:* Establishing yourself as an expert can lead to recognition, advancement, and accomplishing goals. How do you go about it? One method is writing articles.

Start with local legal publications. Most paralegal newsletters are always looking for articles. Paralegal magazines such as *Legal Assistant Today* welcome articles submitted by readers. Other publications, such as *Law Office Computing,* may welcome a well-written article. Bar association magazines may be a little more fussy and want only articles written by attorneys. However, the editors have been known to accept articles hitting a timely topic. Even magazines from associations out of the legal field, such as accounting, insurance, health care, personnel, and computers, enjoy hearing from you.

E-zines, Internet magazines, have taken hold as a regular means of media communications. Writing for one of these magazines can be enjoyable. The magazines are always looking for content. They are much more open to accepting pitches for articles than traditional publications, and getting interviewed by an e-zine is not that difficult. Major traditional publications have e-zine versions; *Business Week, Newsweek, CNBC,* and *Time* are just a few of the publications online. Think about what might be timely or topical, and don't be afraid to pitch your article.

Let the firm know that you are gaining media recognition. Understand the firm's politics first, however (many firms require approval *before* an article is published). Be careful! Patting yourself on the back by sending the article to every attorney in the firm may be construed as self-serving and may backfire. There may be one person at a higher level, such as the administrator, with whom you can share your success. Generally that person will circulate the article with a note that the "firm" is getting recognition and PR. Great! You are now part of the team that helps make your firm or company a winner.

4. *Teaching:* If you can teach, paralegal schools are looking for you. Teaching is a great way to establish credibility as an authority in the field. Let your firm know. It is excellent PR for the firm. Benefit by getting first crack at the best entry-level paralegals without paying huge recruiting costs. Because you see the students in action and can recruit the best, the firm does not spend costly agency and advertising fees.

Ask one or two of the attorneys to be a guest speaker at your classes. Select a brief or pleading written by one of the firm's attorneys (eliminating all privileged information) and ask to use it as an example in class. Word will get around that you are promoting the firm and the paralegal program. Your class may tour the firm on an outing to see a "real" law firm or legal department. Firms generally respond positively because this is good promotion. The more credibility the firm has in the legal community, the higher caliber recruit it is able to attract.

5. *Give In-House Seminars:* Give an in-house seminar to other paralegals or even associates. Know the topic thoroughly and have impressive handouts. Ask a qualified person to review the handouts prior to the seminar.

You may also link up with another firm and hold joint seminars. Firms and corporations are always looking for a way to train staff at low cost. Thinking of targeting a position as a paralegal trainer? Here's an opportunity to write the proposal.

6. *Professional Organizations:* Holding an office or position in a professional organization strengthens credibility and recognition. In addition to making valuable contributions to the profession, your name gets recognized by other paralegals. Recognition helps when seeking another position or starting your own paralegal business. Firms generally support your efforts to promote the professional organization. The more positive image portrayed to the community, the better the firm looks.

7. *Start Your Own Organization:* Here's a fun way to gain recognition. Many professional organizations have sprung up to address new needs. Because the field is still new, all kinds of opportunities exist for professionals with a common bond to get together to promote the field.

When a group of us started the Legal Assistant Management Association (LAMA), eight of us from around the country formed the steering committee. We met by teleconference on a regular basis. We wanted to hold a conference to get the organization off the ground, but because we had no membership, we had no dues, therefore no money. So each of us asked our firms to put $400 into a pot to advance funds for a conference to start the organization. Today, the membership is thriving with over 600 members. Just as a side note, each person on the steering committee has met with phenomenal success in his or her career.

8. *Write the Newsletter:* Writing the newsletter for your firm or organization gives a distinct advantage—you have a pulse on what is happening. Here is a great opportunity to meet and work with many people on an entirely different basis from completing an assignment, establishing a more informal, casual rapport with attorneys and coworkers. The more they know you, like you, and experience your capabilities in other areas, the more likely you are to gain a good reputation and recognition as a leader.

9. *Write a Book:* Don't wait for someone to ask. Several legal publishers will accept an outline and, if the topic is timely, will want to publish it. Investigate the field and find out. Here is a great avenue for establishing credibility, expertise, and authority in the field.

Directing Your Own Career

Creating your own success can be fun. Sitting back and waiting for the firm or corporation to take notice is placing your career in the hands of another. Form an advisory committee with the sole purpose of building your career.

The committee gives you valuable insight from different perspectives. The advisory committee can consist of senior paralegals, managers, attorneys, paralegal entrepreneurs, administrators, and persons from outside the legal community. Meet with your committee regularly, either as a group or individually, for feedback on how you are doing. Acquaint them with your goal criteria and master career plan.

Target ancillary areas to help boost your career and gain recognition as an expert. Allow plenty of time for accomplishments and remain flexible in your plan. Creating your own success can become a major accomplishment in and of itself!

New Realities in the Legal Field

Historically, career progression was measured by a vertical move upwards. The move was rewarded through title, position of office, parking spot, better perks, and more money. In the early 1990s, this phenomenon was described as "upward mobility." Since Corporate America downsized, affecting the growth, profitability, and future of many firms, the yuppie euphemism is rarely heard. Upward mobility has been rare for many paralegals. This lack of mobility was, in part, due to the field's insistence on defining hierarchies through number of years in the field instead of expertise.

The new realities of today, however, have forced upward mobility almost to a standstill. This trend is witnessed in law firms through the new staff-attorney position—attorneys who remain with the firm but do not achieve partner status. Lifestyles, economics, and smaller gross margins and partner profits have contributed greatly to this change in hierarchical acceptance. It is no longer a source of shame for an attorney to pursue a career path different from those of colleagues.

Dr. Kate Ludeman in her book, *Earn What You're Worth*, says careers today are zigzagging. In order to successfully negotiate a career path, people must shift their paradigms. The old paradigm forced upward mobility. The new paradigm emphasizes lateral development and personal growth. The ability to view your career growth differently is essential to survival in today's market.

The new realities in the legal field promote teams and work groups instead of star performers. If you are used to receiving a lot of individual praise for your work, you may feel as though your performance is no longer valued. Instead of moving upward, paralegals can look forward to moving to more challenging teams.

Being specialized while having the ability to perform as a generalist is the future trend. *Cross-trained* is the current buzzword. If you are a real estate paralegal who can also perform general litigation duties, chances are you are more marketable than generalists or those in very narrow practice specialties, such as municipal bonds.

A specialist may be higher paid as long as the economy holds up for the specialty. In the early 1990s, many corporate paralegals who were generally higher paid than litigation paralegals suddenly found themselves out of a job altogether. The recession brought a near end to mergers and acquisitions. Corporate paralegals were out of work.

As the economy recovered, firms begged for the 2- to 4-year experienced corporate paralegal and were shocked to find out that few existed. Paralegal schools tried to enhance the market by adding more corporate programs, but it was still impossible to meet the demands of a recovering market. One firm in San Francisco was so desperate for experienced people that it advertised a $500 hiring bonus. The scuttlebutt among some naive paralegals was that this bonus was "insulting." Little did they know that hiring bonuses were commonly accepted by lateral associates and that these bonuses could be thousands of dollars.

The old tier system still exists in most firms. Included in this book is an example of the seniority system. However, in the new realities, some law firms have changed hiring criteria to more aptly fit the required skill set. Instead of bestowing paralegal status based on years in the field, firms are now assessing competency levels. Further, progressive hiring authorities credit paralegal experience conducive to *their* firms' needs rather than from past employers.

DEVELOPING A PARALEGAL PROGRAM

One wonders what would happen if there were no rules to break. Doubtless everyone would die of boredom.

Susan Howatch, British writer

The concept of a paralegal program was realized at least 15 years ago when firms finally accepted that paralegals were here to stay. Firms needed a process to motivate, reward, educate, and keep paralegals. Some felt calling this new group a "paralegal department" was too much like the clerical side of the firm. To pattern the system as closely as possible after the associates' career path, the more progressive firms leaned toward the term "program."

Success in developing a paralegal program depends on acceptance by attorneys. More accurately, unless commitment and action come from the top, the paralegal program has little or no chance to survive.

There is no program that is right for all firms and legal departments. Just as firms and corporate legal departments vary, so do paralegal programs. How to structure a paralegal program depends upon:

- Attitude in the firm toward paralegals
- Number of paralegals
- Ratio of paralegals to attorneys
- Practice specialty
- Level of sophistication of assignments
- Number of years the firm has employed paralegals
- Acceptance or insistence level of clients
- Billable rates
- Opportunity to advance
- Hiring criteria and recruiting methods
- Job descriptions
- Turnover rate
- Profit margin
- Incentives
- Placement of the program on the organizational chart
- Realization rule
- Cross-training
- Technology

Why have a program at all? It's really very simple. Paralegals, just as other professionals, need to know what employers want to meet expectations. It is unrealistic to assume any employee will meet and exceed invisible targets and goals. It's like trying to shoot a bullseye on a target you can't see.

Paralegal programs are also created to keep associates happy. If work is not delegated to the lowest competent level, eventually associates get bored, frustrated, and burned out and may quit.

In all fairness to paralegals and attorneys using them, work should be delegated to persons with the experience, skills, and education to accomplish the project. Having associates perform paralegal work makes as little sense as stranding paralegals without channels for finding answers needed in order to produce quality work product.

SETTING UP THE PROGRAM: FORMAL OR INFORMAL?

Your program can be a tiered system encompassing set standards for hiring and performance. Recruits enter the program with specific titles indicating levels of expertise such as entry, intermediate, and senior levels. Paralegals are given the opportunity to move up a career ladder with built-in rewards and recognition to acknowledge advancement. Or, a less formal program can be established consisting of specified criteria the paralegal is required to meet in order to expand responsibilities. Those criteria could be in the form of continuing education to stay up with the latest changes in law, attendance at certain meetings, required billable hours and completion of required assignments. No titles are given. The program presents a horizontal approach rather than a vertical climb upward.

The Tiered System

All other departments in a law firm provide upward mobility for their employees. Associates, clerical staff, computer operators, receptionists, file clerks, law clerks, and office managers are all given some sort of ladder. Why, then, would firms stop with legal assistants?

The tiered system is a message to the partnership for a legitimate and objectively applied system. How paralegals are moved through the system is a direct result of performance, not favoritism. To keep career people, a firm has to provide a career path that includes a title change. Titles signify a measure of success in today's business world. Even small firms need to provide those titles. In order to compete in today's market, a small firm needs to represent itself as having clout comparable to that of larger firms.

A comprehensive tiered system can have the following titled positions* (depending on practice specialty):

- Manager of paralegal services or paralegal administrator
- Paralegal manager (litigation) (corporate) (real estate)
- Litigation (or any specialty) support manager
- Case manager (sometimes listed below senior)
- Senior paralegal
- Intermediate paralegal
- Entry-level paralegal (some firms will call this position paralegal, then switch to legal assistant for all experienced positions above this level)
- Project assistant
- Document clerk or case clerk

(*Substitute legal assistant for paralegal if preferred.)

Each position has standards for recruiting, experience, education, and possibly tenure. The standards for a senior paralegal are shown below. A sample tiered-system chart for litigation paralegals is shown on page 203.

SENIOR PARALEGAL

Education:	B.A. or B.S. degree Certificate from ABA-approved school
Continuing Education:	Takes two approved continuing classes per year in specialty
Years of Experience:	Must have at least 6 years' experience
Specialty:	Must possess at least 4 years in a firm with related, designated practice specialty
Tenure with Firm:	Must have at least 6 months' tenure
Skills:	Draft documents, assist at trial, computer literate, must have supervisory and case management skills, ability to draft business letters and memos, some management and financial business background.
Billables:	Must consistently meet the minimum yearly requirement of 1,800 hours

The Paralegal Program for the New Realities

The paralegal program for the new realities designates status by specialty and actual experience rather than years of legal experience. A prime example is found in legal nurses. In some product liability firms, nurses have been hired on staff within the paralegal program to evaluate and summarize medical records, point out medical procedural errors, interpret medical terminology, and handle other legal/medical-related duties. These nurse-paralegals are usually hired and paid according to work history rather than years of paralegal experience. This subniche of the paralegal program has

SAMPLE: TIERED-SYSTEM CHART FOR LITIGATION PARALEGALS

Title	Education	Yrs. Exp.	Cont. Ed.	Skill Level
Senior	B.A./B.S. Certificate or comp. work experience	5+	2 classes	Management skills, drafts pleadings, attends trial, supervises others, legal research Billables: 1,800
Int. lev. 1 Paralegal	B.A./B.S. Certificate	3–5	2 classes	Drafting, research, some supervisory skills, fact. invest. Billables: 1,800
Int. lev. 2 Paralegal	B.A./B.S. Certificate	1–3	2 classes	Document org., simple drafting, case management, Shepardizing/ cite check, factual investigation Billables: 1,650
Entry	B.A./B.S. Certificate or 1 yr. exp. as Project Asst.	0–1	2 classes	Summarizing, indexing, doc. org. Billables: 1,500
Project assistant/ Case clerk	B.A./B.S.	0	1 class	Document org. & filing, doc. coding Billables: 1,500

become so strong in some parts of the country that an association for legal nurses has formed. Many contend they need their own program within the firm (see information organizations).

Other backgrounds bringing reward for expertise are the following:

- Information technology
- Banking
- Accounting
- Securities
- Entertainment
- Real estate (not necessarily the position of real estate broker, however)
- Intellectual property
- Immigration
- Trademark and copyright
- Patents
- Medical field: nurses, pharmacists, doctors, and lab technicians
- Foreign languages: Chinese, Mandarin, Japanese, Portugese, Spanish, French, and German

The new realities program places value on assignment progression. Those paralegals who now have the title of senior legal assistant may be in for a rude awakening if skill levels have not expanded. Some seniors have the title, status, and perks that go along with the position; however, they have been doing pretty much the same thing for the past few years. A frequent excuse heard is, "paralegals cap out at some point."

Sarah is a senior level paralegal with more than 10 years' experience. Her computer skills include WordPerfect 8.0, Word, Windows, and some light knowledge of spreadsheets. Her assignments include indexing documents, summarizing depositions, collating trial notebooks, preparing notices of deposition, and number stamping. A manager of the new realities program would not consider hiring Sarah as a senior level assistant. Even though Sarah interviews well, has a great professional attitude, and has excellent references, she may be offered a job as level III assistant, two steps below the senior or "expert" position, with less salary.

Cold? Perhaps. Fair? To the firm, maybe. However, in today's legal world, it's Sarah's responsibility to see that her assignments and skill level are regularly upgraded. Firms will not overpay for skill levels for which they cannot receive comparable bill rates. At this point, Sarah has two choices: correct her path to make herself more marketable, or stay where she is.

Titles other than those designated by years of experience are currently used. These include

- Senior legal assistant to managing partner
- Trial specialist
- Litigation support specialist
- Level I, II, III
- Immigration specialist
- Project manager

The new realities program acknowledges today's corporate climate and that downsizing has led to flatter organizations: removal of layers of management by downgrading or disposing of managers. The appeal behind this movement is that once the decision to downsize has been made, the salary of one senior level paralegal who does not exhibit senior level abilities can buy the services of several lower-echelon employees, resulting in a streamlined operation with fewer layers of management. Fewer approvals are necessary and things get done faster. The firm can be more responsive. Flattening causes disruption, low morale, even panic in the workplace, but in the end, it does have some distinct advantages.

The team concept now emerges. Employees can have a lot more autonomy because a manager's time is very limited. Here is a great opportunity to identify and capture the next level of assignment. The good news is that the team approach still allows growth from team to team. The bad news is that you may get lost in the shuffle as supervisors have less time to observe you.

In this type of program, the task of the team becomes the career goal. For example, you may be on the trial team for one of the largest toxic tort cases in history. Your career objective in the short term may be to work on the team gathering and preparing exhibits, locating witnesses, and gathering factual information. The next goal may be to prepare jury instructions, locate and interview expert witnesses, and prepare the first draft of responses. Attorneys today are not necessarily looking for paralegals who can move up in ranks. Instead, they seek out professionals who show potential to work on progressively difficult teams.

The vertical climb, in new realities, has been replaced with horizontal expansion. Clients are now acutely aware of the benefits of paralegals. They know which assignments should be performed by paralegals and at what level. Clients refuse to pay for anything more than necessary.

Anyone who masters the art of running a meeting competently and efficiently will most likely go further. It is during meetings that you will most likely be recognized. Many quality books are available on the subject of running a meeting.

Those Who Choose to Pass

Some firms have expressed no interest whatsoever in developing a paralegal program. Many of these firms, particularly the paralegals in these firms, feel much more comfortable practicing homeostasis—that is, everyone is categorized as equal, at the same level, and should advance together. Firms that practice homeostasis and then stratify by hiring paralegals at different experience levels may find it difficult to keep paralegals for any length of time. Firms cannot expect an entry-level paralegal to perform at the senior level nor at the same speed. Consequently, a senior paralegal performing at a level below her expertise will experience burnout and stress, the end result being turnover.

Tim, a senior-level litigation paralegal at a large international firm in Los Angeles, said that 11 paralegals in his firm do not want a paralegal program. Everyone is happy with the status quo. Upon closer examination of his program, we discovered that all paralegals in the department have similar education and average 6 years or more experience (Tim has 12), the attorneys are well-versed on paralegal use, and the average length of employment with the firm is 4 years. Because they do not stratify, there is less reason to formalize a program.

WHO GOVERNS THE PROGRAM?

Depending on the size of the firm, the program needs to be governed by a partner, associate, and paralegal, with financials overseen by the administrator. Some firms choose a committee that changes from year to year. Appointment to the committee of senior paralegals is deemed an honor. Some firms make a mistake of delegating overall supervision of the paralegal program to the youngest associates, who have their hands full trying to orient themselves. The newest associate hasn't yet had an opportunity to use paralegals, much less supervise them.

If the paralegal program is on the organization chart under overall supervision of the office manager or director of administration, your program is headed for trouble. Legal assistants must be supervised by an attorney. Unless the administrator is an attorney, work product cannot be supervised correctly. (However, in terms of supporting a paralegal program, you will probably find your best friend in the administrator.)

The paralegal program's place on the firm's organizational chart is directly under the associate position. Anything other than that categorizes the position as clerical.

DRAFTING JOB DESCRIPTIONS

Writing job descriptions is usually a fruitless, thankless task. When completed, they usually sit on a shelf somewhere collecting dust. Occasionally, a description may be brought out and shown off to the newest recruit.

But writing a job description can be a terrific opportunity to produce a nonconfrontational, educational tool to teach attorneys and legal assistants alike what you are doing, can do, and want to learn. Job descriptions are used to get a clear definition of what is strictly a paralegal function within the firm. The use of peer pressure will keep paralegal functions assigned to paralegals.

Remember, a law firm is different from a corporation in that it is governed by consensus through committees. Many legal departments are run the same way. Law firms create movement within the organization through group decision and peer pressure. If an associate wants to be thought of as a skilled and competent attorney, she certainly doesn't want her peers to think that she is performing paralegal work. If the firm supports the paralegal program, she won't be. The work will have filtered down to the correct level.

Getting the Firm to Participate

In an attempt to push the firm into action, some paralegals try distributing a "uses and abuses of paralegals" memo. The uses and abuses memo is distributed to every attorney in the firm with a list of what paralegals do and don't do. This is a direct confrontation and will get you nowhere.

Instead, first meet with appropriate supervising attorneys or committees. Ask them to participate in a job description exercise. Immediate benefits to the firm will be

- Educating attorneys about paralegal capabilities
- Defining and clarifying the paralegal position
- Positive economic realization by dropping assignments to the lowest competent level (which frees up associate time to be spent on more sophisticated assignments and saves client fees).

After securing approval from appropriate partners, meet with other paralegals to draft a memo to all attorneys or to attorneys in your practice section such as:

Memorandum

Date:
To:
From:
Re:

The Executive and Paralegal Steering Committees (or appropriate committees) request your input to establish firm consensus job descriptions of paralegals in this department. We have listed a proposed outline of assignments. Please take a moment to add, delete, or comment on the projects listed below. Your participation will help to keep paralegal and associate projects within the appropriate skill level. In order to meet deadlines on this project, please return this form no later than <u>Wednesday, June 1st.</u>

Include all assignments currently performed and all assignments you feel the firm should delegate to paralegals, even if this is not policy, and particularly if there has been controversy in doing so. Keep the memo in list form, as it is quicker to read and will invite more participation. If you have 25 attorneys in your firm and receive responses from 12, you are doing great! Do not expect all attorneys to participate.

When you receive responses, meet with your committee to redraft the memo. Send it back to attorneys with the following:

Memorandum

Date:
To:
From:
Re:

Thank you for your valuable input regarding paralegal job descriptions. The following is a consolidation of the firm's responses. If you have any changes to the description, please make them now. In order to meet our deadline, we need your response no later than <u>Thursday, June 15th.</u>

When finalizing the project, distribute job descriptions to attorneys, paralegals, secretaries, and office managers. Be sure it is in list form so that it becomes a working tool. All anyone needs to do to see if a project should be routed to a paralegal is to check the list.

WHAT ARE THE HIRING CRITIERIA?

There are two types of full-time paralegal employees: transitional and career. Transitional paralegals usually have graduated from college and are taking a year or two before entering law school or grad school. Their purpose is clear, their tenure with the firm is deemed short term, and turnover is encouraged. Firms that tend to hire transitional paralegals sometimes feel they are getting highly motivated people with superior academic backgrounds. Higher concentrations of transitional hiring are seen in major metropolitan cities, such as New York, Washington, D.C., and San Francisco.

Career paralegals, on the other hand, set out to enter and stay with the field. Educational requirements for career paralegals differ from region to region. Many firms, particularly major firms, require a B.A. or B.S. degree and a certificate. Some insist on a certificate from an ABA-approved school. Other firms will accept comparable work experience in lieu of a degree or a certificate or both.

Firms hiring only career paralegals tend to feel they are getting stability, dedication, and the full attention of these recruits. Los Angeles, Minneapolis, and Dallas firms lean heavily toward career paralegals. San Francisco and Chicago firms appear to hire both career and transitional professionals. Some of these firms also feel that, based on their strict hiring criteria (some only hire from the top schools; others may accept only the top 10 percent of the graduating class), they are getting the best and the brightest.

Other firms will set hiring criteria based on experience only and will look to find paralegals from comparable firms. They shy away from hiring entry-level paralegals primarily because they lack the person-power to train. These firms also feel they are getting the best. It's tough to argue who is getting what because the field seems to do well with people from all kinds of education and work experience.

Paralegal/Attorney Ratio

The ideal ratio of paralegals to attorneys is one paralegal for three attorneys. However, averages appear to be one to five. The maximum number of attorneys any one paralegal should be assigned to is five. In some firms you may find:

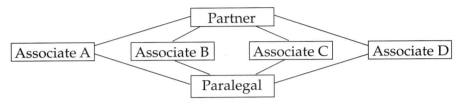

If you need more information regarding ratios, leveraging, and related economics, your firm may wish to contact a consultant, such as Bradford Hildebrandt and Associates (Houston), Altman Weil (San Francisco), or Price Waterhouse (Los Angeles, New York, Chicago).

THE PROGRAM IN ACTION

Orientation

Set up an orientation program for both new associates and paralegals. Teach new associates how to utilize paralegals from the moment they enter the door. Associates today have very different attitudes about paralegals than more senior partners. Because the field is new, anyone who has practiced law longer than 20 years probably will not have learned to use paralegals. New associates today expect paralegals to be part of the practice, the same as computers, secretaries, and billables.

Have a policy to educate new paralegals. One afternoon of showing the new recruit the photocopy center, bathroom, and library will do little to advance your program. The first week is the most crucial in setting the scene for the new employee.

Assign the new recruit to a "buddy" so that she has someone she can go to for every question. It's a very effective system. There's nothing new about it; it simply works.

Assigning Paralegals to Attorneys

Many debates have occurred over whether the approach to assigning paralegals to attorneys should be through a team or pool. Teams are assigned to certain attorneys and assignments are automatically received only within the team. A pool structure assigns projects according to case or client matters or as a new matter enters the firm. It really boils down to how your associate program is structured. The paralegal program should be as closely patterned after the associate program as possible. If associates are team-assigned to partners, then team-assign paralegals to associates/partners. If associates are selected for assignments on a pool basis, then the paralegal program should reflect this system.

Whichever system is right for your firm, it is generally more efficient to permanently assign paralegals to the same case or client matter throughout rather than assign projects on a piecemeal basis. Otherwise, background information learned by paralegals and associates becomes fragmented and no one person knows enough details about the case or matter. Too much time is wasted trying to bring new people up to speed on each new assignment.

Understanding Billing Rates for Advancement

Because you now have a program, you are entitled to stratify billing rates. A document clerk or project assistant can be billed at a lesser rate than an entry-level paralegal; a senior paralegal with expertise in a specialty can be billed at an associate rate. The administrator of the firm is the person to see regarding billing rates. Clients should appreciate the different rates for corresponding assignments.

Regarding paralegal advancement, the firm should not bestow only dollars as a reward. While monetary incentives are important and should not be overlooked, salary and bonus are private matters. *Outward* recognition of a job well done goes a long way in boosting self-esteem and motivating employees.

Some of the perks and recognition that firms and legal departments give individuals are:

- Better offices (even window offices when possible)
- Specific titles, such as corporate specialist, case manager, accounts administrator, senior paralegal
- Attendance at particular firm functions; although many firms exclude paralegals from attending certain social functions, including their senior paralegals is a recognition of status
- Expanded continuing education paid for by the firm
- Attendance at out-of-town seminars
- Better secretarial support; although all paralegals should have adequate support, some firms will give senior paralegals a secretary to share with an associate rather than a secretarial pool; others automatically structure this team.

KEEPING THE PROGRAM GOING AND UP-TO-DATE

Part of the structure of a paralegal program is regular meetings to keep avenues of communication open. If you are in a small firm with fewer than four paralegals, take the supervising attorney to lunch once a month and have an informal meeting. Exchange information, air concerns, and update each other on client matters. Don't wait for the attorney to set it up; you're liable to wait until Christmas. Take the initiative.

If your firm has from five to fifteen paralegals, set up a breakfast or luncheon meeting once a month in the firm's conference room. Ask attorneys to attend. Set up the agenda ahead of time through a memo. Ask an attorney to give a brief lecture to update paralegals on changes in the law or client matter. If a member of the firm has recently had a significant victory, ask her or him to talk about it and teach more about what your role can be in these kinds of matters. Use every opportunity to educate yourselves and attorneys in the firm. Ask the administrator to attend to teach more about the economics of your role in the firm. Invite the librarian to talk about research, the file room supervisor to give tips on retrieving client files quicker, and an educator from a local paralegal school with news about the field.

If you have more than 15 paralegals, divide the meetings by practice specialty, with one or two meeting together per year. Otherwise, the sheer size may be cumbersome. However, if your program works well by having everyone attend one meeting, then by all means do so.

Although rarely seen anymore, retreats are a great firm perk. Several firms have organized paralegal retreats for educational purposes as well as recognition of the position. Seminars, mock trials, and just plain fun are had at these retreats. The length of the retreat can be 1 day or 1 weekend. You may want to start out with a 1-day retreat to see how it goes and develop from there.

Continuing education is another important element of the paralegal program. It is necessary to include education requirements in the program so that paralegals are continuously updated in changes in the law. Although many firms have cut budget dollars for seminars and classes, a popular substitution is for one paralegal to attend a class then teach what was learned. This way, all benefit. In-house seminars taught by attorneys and paralegals are a great way to learn, and many firms do not hesitate to ask outside speakers. Title and escrow officers, insurance investigators, authors, judges, psychologists, accountants, computer experts, and clients are only a few in a long list of possible speakers. Another popular teaching method is video. Many firms videotape their own in-house seminars for teaching new recruits.

Finally, keep your program up-to-date through networking. Firms and corporations often share information about what works and what doesn't in their programs. While billing rates information will not be openly shared, most firms are happy to talk with you regarding structure. Gather information through your network about comparable programs, the latest in education and seminars, and the newest technology. Very importantly, your name recognition in the field is enhanced.

PARALEGAL INNER VIEW: JANET JIRAK— THAT'S IT FOR ME!

Name: Janet Jirak
Title: Paralegal
Specialty: Litigation/medical malpractice defense
Experience: 20 years
Education: A.A. degree from Indiana University/Purdue University at Indiana, Paralegal certificate from Southwest Paralegal Institute
Size of firm: 2 attorneys with a satellite office in Tucson
Job duties: Medical malpractice litigation defense. I am responsible for records gathering, abstracting depositions, keeping the insurance carriers updated on discovery issues, client interviews, and preparing witnesses. Also, general correspondence as it relates to records gathering; keeping in touch with different hospitals and organizations; working with attorneys; update trial notebooks; and reviewing boxes and boxes of documents. I have my own office but no secretary.
Prior experience: Lots of collection work. I was a paralegal in-house for a corporation in Houston, a drilling corporation that owned drilling rigs contracted out to various companies. Coordinated the meetings with local counsel all over the world such as Africa, South America, and Bermuda. I kept corporate books at the corporate level, reviewed contracts, and looked for liability language. I also coordinated with outside counsel on litigation and claims.

What software are you required to know?
   Word, Excel, Outlook.

What's your next adventure?
   I'm not sure. I'm moving to Tampa and I'm looking to get out of the paralegal profession. There's no further advancement opportunities for me. I'd like to get into risk management in a corporation or hospital. I'd

also like to get into a job where my legal experience could be beneficial to a corporation.

Where do you see the paralegal field headed?

I'm really out of touch with the industry. I don't know where it's going. It hasn't changed much from the time I started. I noticed finally they are starting to pay us better but that has a long way to go.

CHAPTER 17

You Call This *Networking????*

There's no such thing as accidental networking. Figure it out. Networking is a mission. When you're headed to a function to meet and greet people who can further your career, you have a strong sense of purpose. Even a chance meeting can provide a networking opportunity. Once you discover that new acquaintances have professional power, you instantaneously decide to make the meeting worthwhile. There's no real secret to it. Most people, myself included, hate to admit we network because then we reveal we're actually using the world's greatest career-building trick. Maybe we think it smacks of cheating. You know you do it, I know you do it, others know you do it, and you read that you're supposed to do it, but somehow you deny you're doing it. I mean, only the etiquettely-challenged would introduce themselves by saying, "Hi, I'm Jane. I'm here to network." *Yikes*.

Now, basically I'm shy. Oh, I know I give lots of seminars and speak in front of hundreds of people, but those one-on-ones are a killer. Chit-chat with strangers makes me nervous. I never know quite what to say. I solve the problem by avoiding it as much as I can. But following this prescription can lead to a very lonely life, not to mention dearth of clients. So, when I was invited to a book-signing party at a *very* exclusive old-money private club (which, to join, costs your entire savings account, requires a vote from the secret selection committee, and Daughters-of-the-American-Revolution background), I didn't know if I should go. I tried to rationalize. I'm CEO of a legal staffing business. Members of this selective club could be important clients and candidates. And, someone obviously thought I was worthy enough to grace the hallowed halls of haughtiness. Plus, maybe there would be a bonus: I'd meet Mr. Right. (Well, geez, even a little Mr. Potential wouldn't be so bad.) The downside? I didn't know anyone there so I would have no one to hide behind; and, I had purposely never gone there (lack of invite aside) because I didn't care for the idea of vote-you-in/leave-certain-people-out selective clubs. It went against my principles. Then there was another possible problem. For the past 50 years or so, the club was rumored to be anti-Semitic (not to mention what their attitude was toward other nonmajority types). I was quite certain my orthodox grandmother would turn over in her grave if she even thought I was considering putting one tiny toe in this establishment. And now I wanted to go in hopes of furthering my career? Was I nuts? When I ran this past people, they scoffed at me. "That 'problem' doesn't exist anymore. That was a long, long time ago. Really." Yeah, but in my mind how long ago was long ago? And did any of the people who had had that "problem" long ago belong to the club today? But the critical need to network and the idea of spending one more evening by myself watching reruns of "Law and Order" overruled my sensibilities. I made up my mind, boned up on my small talk, and headed to the chichi club with the iron barriers to entry.

I get all dressed up in my casual-but-elegant business suit, careful to make it black so people won't notice the slight weight problem. (Okay, okay, slightly more than slight) and jump into my . . . OKAAAY . . . OKAAAY . . . *really* more than slight (give a gal a break here) . . . car. I'm tooling down the road practicing my small talk: "How do you do? Nice-to-meet-you. Oh, I see, a lawyer? How interesting." And then one of those uncontrollable things that happens at precisely the wrong time happens. I start to perspire. I can't stop. I'm either very nervous or this is the longest hot flash in the history of menopause. Maybe my grandmother has gotten wind of what I'm doing. "Oh, God," I plead. "Not now." I turn on the air conditioner. I have one hand on the steering wheel as I fan cold air waves onto my face, which at this point, is dripping makeup and forming little brown polka-dots on my clean white collar. I'm panicked. I had forgotten to bring additional makeup and the secret I was in dire need of was not the secret to success. I reach the club, feeling a little like Phyllis Diller before her face lifts. Deciding to ignore my physical state, I take a deep breath, put a smile on my face, nod to the doorman and march right through the double mahogany doors, onto the marble inlaid floors, and past the authentic Biedermeyer furniture. I'm on a mission.

Confidence notwithstanding, the first few minutes after making your entrance can be disconcerting. Do I head for the bar? Do I find the hostess-with-the-mostest whom I've never met? Do I mosey on up to a group that is obviously engaged in appropriate chit-chat and chit-chat myself? A waiter with an elegant silver tray doesn't even ask, he just hands me a glass of wine. Good. Now I look the part. As I take a look around, I realize that the room is loaded with potential clients (gulp), but even my quick read on "How to Work a Room" hadn't prepared me for this crowd. The room is dripping with Armani and Versace. Poor Anne Klein. Her pantsuit seems out of sorts and I happen to be the one wearing her. Not quite brave enough to go say howdy and play networking, I go up to the table stacked high with the author's new books. I tell myself I'm doing the right first move. After all, this *is* a book signing party. Seeing a gentleman seated behind the table,

I automatically assume he is the author eagerly waiting to autograph purchases. I decide to help him out. "So Michael," I say confidently, (may as well get on first name basis immediately), "which was your favorite character?" The woman next to me sniffs and sighs, "This is Andre, dear, the cashier. The *au*-thor is over there with the *hos*-tess." Oh. Well, one faux pas isn't going to kill me. I stroll on over to the hostess and introduce myself. "Oh, yes," she says graciously and turns to the group. "What with the NBA playoffs tonight, I really had to scrape the bottom of the barrel to get people to come." The group laughs. I stand there with my glass of merlot frozen in my hand. I decide the comment wasn't aimed at me and she's probably just as nervous as I am. I ignore it and prepare to start my chit-chat with the group. The conversation was revolving around Mr. Harriweather's trip to Tuscany. I'm comfortable now. I've been to Europe. The conversation turns toward Paris. We're home now, baby! This stuff I know. I decide to chime in. "Paris," I sigh and sip my wine slowly. (I had learned three things in the 5 minutes I had been there: sniffing, sighing, and sipping slowly seemed to be important.) "When I took this American Express tour a few years ago . . . (What was that? A loud TSK, TSK to my right. The dyed-blonde with the 42 face lifts and fake pearl earrings is rolling her recently reconstructed eyes and shaking her head. Uh, oh. Obviously, no American Express trips here.) I change my direction. "Oh, I agree," I say. "The best thing about that whole disaster was pulling into Paris at dusk and seeing the gorgeous lights on the Eiffel Tower." Whew. That should score a few points. (Even if the trip was *not* a disaster but the best I'd ever had). But the group is looking at me funny. I realize I had started to sweat again and now my mascara seemed to have slipped off my eyelashes and settled into dark circles under my eyes. A couple of people actually take a step backwards. I really want to leave. But my guaranteed-to-fit-make-you-look-ten-pounds-thinner-panty-girdle was slowly rolling down my stomach. Obviously, a quick getaway wasn't about to happen.

The hostess-with-less-than-the-mostest chimes in. "You know, a nice Jewish girl like me has to be soooo careful when I travel to Europe . . ." she trails off. I wonder what *that's* all about. Why would she even bring up being Jewish? What point was she trying to make? Did she feel uncomfortable here? "Oh, speaking of *that*," says the ever-ebullient Mr. Harriweather with the affected English accent, "whenever I travel in Europe, I always claim I'm Canadian instead of American. You know, they don't hate Canadians there." Well, that much is true. There aren't enough of them. This was one of those situations where they built a whole country and no one came. But I remain quiet and sip my wine (slowly).

But Mr. Harriweather isn't finished. I wonder whether he knows that tweed jackets with leather patches on the elbows are not exactly *GQ* anymore.

"And my friend who travels with me claims he's Canadian too. And, guess what? Everyone buys it, and he's *Jewish!*" I spit my wine out all over what's left of the white on my blouse. He thinks his story is very funny. Now, I'm already having trouble reconciling the fact that I'm in this silly club to begin with, plus the fact that I'm preoccupied with how to shrink from the crowd because I can't seem to control this perspiration, coupled with the fact that my makeup that is supposed to be on my eyes is now smeared from ear to ear. I can't control my reaction. "*What?*" I blurt out incredulously. "Do you really think there are no Jews in Canada???" The room goes silent. I get the distinct feeling I have just stepped outside the guidelines of the handbook to good-taste networking. In any event, no matter what my personal feelings are, I've definitely gone beyond a faux pas.

At that moment a little bell tinkles. "Ah," says the hostess-with-the-mostest, "it's time for our author to begin his talk." Saved, I guess. But now I'm disturbed. What kind of people are these anyway? People head toward the row of seats. I sit down. I notice that no one sits next to me. In fact, I'm the only one in the entire row. Well, I say to myself, maybe I'm getting a little raunchy here what with all this sweating. I'm horribly self-conscious. The author talks. I listen. When the author concludes, the hostess/no mostest announces it's time for dinner. I get up. I do the only thing left available to me. I pretend I'm leaving briefly for the bathroom and without even thinking, I head right past the authentic Biedermeyer furniture, onto the inlaid marble floors, and right out the double mahogany doors to the parking lot. I realize that there may be some future explaining to do. *But on one thing I am certain: At no time will I ever again compromise my value system in order to further my career.*

Hopefully, no one has noticed I've left long before I'm supposed to. On the other hand, they're probably relieved after what went on and all. Unfortunately, the valet has lost my car. I wait what seems an eternity. Finally, he locates it and brings it up. As I'm about to make my getaway, I hear, "Yoo-hooo . . . yoo . . . hoo . . . oh, Ms. Esssss-trin!" Rats. Caught. It's Mrs. Macintosh, the head of the library committee, coming toward me waving one of those dang books. "You aren't leaving are you, dear?" Oh, Lordy, girl, get a grip. Of course I am. "Why, no," I say. "I'm just looking for something." Yeah. My front door. "Well, you've left your autographed copy of your book," she says in her sing-song voice. Great. A memento of the evening.

As I drive home, I realize that I made the right decision choosing to leave. As much as I wanted to meet new people and hit the networking circuit, this particular scene just wasn't for me. I found myself desperately trying not to be who I really was so I could fit in. What was I thinking? I didn't need to do that. Would I try networking again? Sure, But for now, I knew that networking doesn't work unless you feel comfortable, self-assured, and choose scenarios wisely. On that, I needed a little work. I decide that next time, I'll feel more confident and know what I'm getting into. As I drive up to my front door, I begin to feel safe again. I take off my wine and polka-dot spotted outfit, wash off what's left of my makeup, and flop down in my comfortable chair. I count my blessings as I switch on the TV. Wouldn't you know? I'm just in time for another rerun of "Law and Order."

CHAPTER 18

Paralegal Orientation Program for New Hires and Temps

"Let the good times roll."

(Song, 1946)

STARTING OUT RIGHT

Many law firms rest on their laurels when it comes to recruiting and retaining high-caliber employees. Arrogance, ego, and extremely high standards create an attitude that employees should be grateful to have jobs with a firm of such stature. Upon arrival, many new recruits are given the I-don't-really-have-time-for-this mini-tour: "We'll show you the bathroom, your office, and location of key personnel; gotta go." You figure out the rest.

Some firms and corporations have yet to discover the real reason that turnover is so high. These organizations with their heads buried in the sand attribute turnover and dissatisfaction to employee inability to meet their firms' high standards: "This is a tough place to work," people say as their chests puff out with pride. Well, sure—particularly when the first 6 months are wasted trying to figure out the system.

Few corporations and an even smaller number of law firms provide a structured orientation program for paralegals. More firms may have a formal program for associates; however, somehow paralegals fail to get included in the same process. Firms spend considerable recruiting dollars on ads, interviews, and agency fees yet drop the ball once the new paralegals arrive on their doorsteps.

Costs of hiring, orientation, and training of new employees along with corresponding nonbillable attorney and paralegal time range anywhere from $10,000 to $30,000 *per person,* depending on practice specialty and candidate availability. Paralegal orientation programs can reduce turnover and quickly position employees to generate revenue. The program can save a

221

firm thousands of dollars. Orientation programs should be implemented whether the firm has two paralegals or two hundred. Leaving employee orientation to chance stifles the probability of long-term employment and encourages substantial write-offs.

Orientation is just as important for temporary or part-time paralegals. A common firm philosophy is that because the paralegal (or case clerk, document coder, and so forth) is "only temporary," there is no need for formal orientation. This attitude often contributes to higher turnover and lower productivity.

Steps taken to reduce turnover improve client service, which in turn improves profit. Today's competitive legal environment requires formalized orientation programs to gain significant economic advantages. The objectives of a paralegal orientation program are to

1. Positively reinforce the decision to work with the firm

2. Provide a training vehicle

3. Reduce the learning curve

4. Increase the turn time when the paralegal becomes productive and profitable

5. Acquaint members of the firm with the new hire's abilities.

A planned orientation pays dividends because it results in fewer mistakes and a clear understanding of expectations. It is important to capture the paralegal's enthusiasm and leverage it for longer term. The result is improved client service, billings, and employee relations. A poorly planned or nonexistent orientation can quickly turn off a new employee and cause excessive dollars to be spent by starting the entire hiring process over.

If you are seeking avenues to redesign your job, you might consider establishing a formal paralegal orientation program. If your firm already has an orientation process, consider revamping it to meet the firm's current hiring trends. As always, you don't want to step on any toes, so be sure to get top management buy-in.

STRUCTURING AN ORIENTATION PROGRAM THAT WORKS

Imagine the new paralegal's anxiety on her first day. First impressions are conclusions, and law firms have a tendency to have long memories. No one is more aware of this than a new employee. Failure to experience inclusion in the workplace pushes people away. While some may never be able to pinpoint exactly what went wrong, we often hear, "I just didn't belong."

1. **Red carpet treatment.** Roll out the red carpet! Before the first workday starts, take the new recruit to breakfast or hold a coffee break to introduce him informally to coworkers. A social atmosphere often breaks the ice and reduces tension. Don't forget that sometimes employees are nervous about the new employee. Make sure that if you do plan a social event, employees are clear on the concept and include the newcomer in the conversations.

2. **Publicize the hiring decision.** I'll never forget my first trip down to Ft. Lauderdale to corporate headquarters. Posted on a sign in the front of the lobby was a warm welcome from the president and members of the organization. An announcement should be sent to all members of the firm or department with the new employee's bio. The newsletter is also a good way to extend a warm welcome.

3. **Control the new recruits' expectations through positive perspec-** **tives.** You are responsible for expectations developed through the recruiting process. If these expectations are overblown, expect to go back to the drawing board very quickly. New employees' senses are sharp. They soak up even the tiniest assurance that they have indeed made the right employment choice.

    Most likely, the new paralegal has interviewed extensively with other firms, particularly in candidate-driven markets. Selecting your firm may have been a difficult choice coupled with the emotional impact (whether happy or sad) of leaving her old firm. Here is the perfect time to reinforce the decision.

4. **Provide a structured training program** and start the new recruit off on the right foot. A well-planned program sets the stage. Starting a new paralegal off correctly gives proper direction, clear assignments, and necessary tools to do her job.

THE FIRST DAY

Orientation should be ongoing—whether 1 or 2 days, weeks, or months. Remember, it took you quite a while to find out the idiosyncrasies of the firm. Be patient.

Meet n' greet. A first day is as important to you and the firm as it is to the paralegal. Handing over the first-day orientation program to whomever may be available that day diminishes its importance. Schedule the first half hour with the person with whom the new recruit will mostly closely work. This person should welcome the recruit personally.

After the paralegal completes appropriate paperwork, such as insurance, I-9s, W-4s, and confidentiality and employee agreements, schedule a 15-minute meeting to personally welcome her to the firm. Avoid all interruptions such as phone calls and knocks on the door. Your message should be that this new person is an important hire.

Tour of the firm. Let others know in advance that the new recruit will be guided through the office. That way they can be sure to be around for an introduction. Include the entire building on your tour. There's no reason why new employees have to embarrass themselves by asking where to find the bathroom. (See the facilities tour checklist at the end of this chapter.)

Firm or company overview. Teach the history of the firm. Paralegals want to know the evolution of the firm/corporation; key clients and departments; years in existence; and the major players.

If your company has a mission statement, now is the time to present it. Review practice specialties, benchmark cases, distinguished personnel, ranking in the legal community (if any), commitment to the paralegal program, pro bono work, philosophy, and culture.

Have all necessary information ready for arrival. Be prepared to review each area. Be sure to include

1. Job description
2. Paralegal program information (if any)
3. Organization chart
4. In-house seminar information
5. Association dues information (if your firm reimburses for dues)
6. Seminar approval procedures
7. Billing requirements (if any)
8. Employee manual (or policy manual): If you don't have one, be sure to have ready information regarding:
   - Working hours
   - Overtime policy
   - Paydays
   - PDO (paid days off) or ETO (employee time off)
   - Travel policy
   - Insurance and other benefits, including 401k
   - Dress code/casual day

- Use of telephone, access code, and calling card
- Access code or password for computers
- Expense reimbursement policy
- Photocopying code and billing procedures
- Performance and salary review dates
- Rules of firm and building (even if you only have a few offices) including the parking arrangements or subway/bus/train stations

9. Keys or security card
10. Business cards (it's a positive sign if cards have already arrived)
11. Firm brochure, if available, or corporation's annual report or collateral material
12. Firm roster or list of necessary phone numbers
13. Sample time sheet filled out

14. Samples of regular monthly reports
15. E-mail and voice mail information
16. Sample time card, if any
17. Sexual harassment and discrimination policy
18. A list of nearby restaurants, cleaners, bookstores, office supply stores, gas stations, libraries, courthouses, and so forth
19. A list of firm-approved vendors
20. A client list (if approved by the executive committee)
21. Firm resume and newsletter
22. A copy of the firm's listing in *Martindale-Hubbell* or *Corporate* *Counsel* listing background information on attorneys
23. Any advertising, if the firm participates
24. Purchase orders and routing instructions
25. Firm branches or corporate subsidiaries and key players
26. Information regarding billing practices
27. Sample form letters, memos, correspondence, and form files with confidential information deleted
28. Firm Web site
29. Any other information necessary to learn about the firm.

Library training. Even though legal research beyond cite checking is off-limits to some paralegals, chances are they still need use of the library. While books and papers are fast disappearing into the paperless world, the new paralegal still needs to be shown where things are, access codes, online services, and where to go for help. Make sure an appointment is set with someone who can properly train. Even if your library is 10×10, your firm has a certain way of doing things that should be demonstrated to new people.

Computer training. Make sure someone is available at a specific time to acquaint the new paralegal on use of the firm's system. Be sure to include software packages necessary to this paralegal's position. Don't forget information regarding online services, e-mail, Internet, Web site, word processing, and so forth. Be sure to show the new hire where the printers are.

Time and billing training. If the paralegal has experience, chances are she is familiar with time and billing procedures. However, her experience may be with a different system. Take time to go over your firm's individual requirements.

Give the first assignment. Some firms make the mistake of assuming that assignments should commence on the second day. An assignment reinforces a sense of achievement and should be followed up later with words of encouragement. Everyone takes their best shot on their first day. Acknowledgment encourages the paralegal to continue to work at the same high level in future assignments.

Lunch. By now, the new paralegal may feel overwhelmed by the amount of information and by all the new faces. He's ready for a break and may have questions to ask in a more private setting. Taking the new paralegal to lunch on his first day is a time-honored tradition in many firms. It would be great to get as many attorneys involved as possible. It also wouldn't hurt anyone's morale if the firm paid.

Debriefing session. The wrap-up at the end of the day is as important as how it began, Review the first assignment and find out whether any red flags have gone up—by you or the new employee. Be sure the meeting ends on a positive, encouraging note.

THE MINI-ORIENTATION

Temporary paralegals, document coders, case clerks, assistants, preppers, and scanners also require an orientation even if abbreviated. Ramp-up time, productivity, and learning curves are all shortened through mini-orientations.

Because many of these people will be with you for only a short time and most likely were called because of a crisis-driven need, it is imperative to have a short, concise program that can be delivered to several employees at the same time. Some firms and legal vendors using temporary help schedule regular training and orientation sessions. Unless the temporary has attended these sessions, he cannot start the job.

Session #1: Review mini-package. Provide the temps with a shortened version of the new employee package. Be sure to include

1. Basic information regarding the case or client as approved by the billing attorney
2. Payroll paperwork if not hired through an agency
3. A temporary employee handbook, if possible
4. List of immediate supervisors
5. Firm policies involving handling of cash and securities, patent and trademark information, alcohol, drugs in the workplace, dress codes, driving of company vehicles
6. Time sheet information and completion instructions
7. Map of facilities pertaining to their work area only
8. Any required conflict-of-interest or confidentiality agreements.

Session #2: Mini-orientation. This skills training session includes processing information, case history, assignment information, computer training, and all other job assignment information. You may also wish to explain the organization's product or practice specialties. A face book with

Facilities Tour Checklist

_____	Office location	_____	Lobby and receptionist
_____	Colleagues	_____	Conference rooms
_____	Library	_____	Vending machines
_____	Supervisor's office	_____	Fire exits
_____	Word processing center	_____	Gym
_____	Service center	_____	Day care center
_____	War rooms	_____	Elevators/stairs
_____	Bathrooms	_____	Mailroom
_____	Supplies	_____	Training rooms
_____	Kitchen	_____	Imaging/scanning
_____	Printer locations	_____	HR department
_____	Photocopy machines	_____	Parking
_____	Fax machines	_____	Subway/bus/train
_____	File room	_____	Weekend entry
_____	Map of firm/company	_____	Newsstand
_____	MIS department	_____	Secretary
_____	Partner/supervisors' offices	_____	Cafeteria
_____	Other: _____	_____	Security

pictures of supervisors, relevant personnel, and phone extensions is also a good idea.

Execution of a good orientation program requires planning and follow-up. Most importantly, it requires buy-in from the firm's top management. Present the program to the executive committee or top partners or administrators. It's best to first sell them on the concept of the program. Then you have plenty of support as they eagerly await the details. Implementation and results are easier when executives are interested.

PARALEGAL INNER VIEW: SANDY STANDER—HELPING THE ELDERLY

Name: Sandy Stander
Title: Paralegal
Specialty: Elder & Disability Law/Probate and Estate Planning
Experience: 8 months in this field
Firm: Elder & Disability Law Firm, Overland Park, Kansas
Size of firm: 4 attorneys, 1 paralegal

Education: B.S. degree in Clothing and Textiles (1988) and a paralegal certificate from Johnson County Community College (1998)
Job duties: I draft estate planning documents (i.e., wills and trusts), handle probate and trust administration, and draft engagement letters and other correspondence to our clients. A typical day consists of preparing correspondence, drafting/proofreading documents, and occasionally making phone calls to clients or outside sources to get information.

What software do you need to know for this job?
    WordPerfect and Amicus Attorney (case management software).

What has been your most challenging assignment?
    When I first began this job, I was given the responsibility for all the probate files. No one else in the office had any experience handling probate. I had to figure out a lot of things on my own.

What's the most satisfying part of your job?
    No specific experience stands out but hearing clients tell me how much they appreciate the work we do and how we have eased their fears is very rewarding.

What are the education standards you think are necessary for paralegals?
    It is important for paralegals to have an education in paralegal studies to gain an understanding of the basics of law and to develop skills in legal writing and research.

What does your future hold for you?
    I plan to stay in elder law, and maybe get more involved in other issues that the elderly face, such as quality nursing home care and resident's rights.

Where do you think the paralegal profession is going?
    I think opportunities in the paralegal field will continue to expand but also become more competitive.

What would you change about the paralegal profession?
    I would not change anything except maybe the awareness in the legal community of properly utilizing paralegals. Generally, this is an ongoing issue.

And your advice to other paralegals would be . . . .
    Learn as much as you can and take opportunities available to you. You never know where it may lead!

CHAPTER 19

The Paralegal Manager

> I told the office manager that the firm could not continue to treat paralegals so haphazardly and expect top-drawer performance. It just wasn't going to happen. So she made me the paralegal manager.
>
> Former paralegal administrator

MANAGEMENT POTENTIAL

Becoming the paralegal manager is a top goal for many paralegals. But here's the catch: There are no schools and few, if any, seminars to prepare you for the role; no real on-the-job tutelage specific to the position exists; and many firms still have to be convinced they need the position. So how can you take an active role in snaring this prestigious and often lucrative management position?

If you are just starting out, go to a large firm and situate yourself within a hierarchy. Start moving into senior levels through case manager, group coordinator, assistant manager or litigation/corporate paralegal manager. If you are in a smaller firm and have the opportunity to create your own program, position yourself so that you have a clear shot at the top.

One of the biggest mistakes paralegals might make is to take a position at a small firm and automatically expect to leap into a top management position at a larger firm. Most paralegal managers have been promoted from within. If a firm does seek to hire from the outside, it tends to hire from a comparable firm. Therefore, when a large firm is evaluating paralegal manager candidates, it looks for work experience in similar form, with similar volume, number of paralegals and attorneys, clients, specialties, and education. Many of the problems you are asked to resolve are problems between the paralegal department and other arms of the firm.

Start thinking as if you were a financial manager. Paralegal managers today are held accountable for the profit and loss of the paralegal program. If the program does not earn profit for the firm, the paralegal manager is the one that is swept aside. Managers today are responsible for bottom-line profit for the firm. Many are asked to set and maintain their own budgets. Managers must understand the computer and accounting processes necessary for maintaining those budgets. Learn everything you can about spreadsheets, budgets, cost accounting, profit and loss, and how to hit the numbers you committed to in your budget.

The paralegal manager, in order to become invaluable to a firm, must understand the firm or corporation in its entirety. It is critical to understand how all of the various departments interface. You are the pivotal point, the visionary, the crisis manager, the nurturer. Each paralegal in your department becomes a revenue producer for whom you are responsible. Turnover, satisfactory work product, hiring excellent employees, training, and promoting the department to the firm and clients are all within your scope of responsibilities.

USING THE LEGAL ASSISTANT MANAGEMENT ASSOCIATION

The Legal Assistant Management Association (LAMA) was created in the early 1980s when a group of paralegal administrators (including this author) attended a seminar for managers given by the late, great Philadelphia Institute for Paralegal Training. It was evident to the attendees that similar problems and concerns mandated that they band together to formalize and advance their profession. The trend created by firms and corporations to promote a paralegal to manage other paralegals was well under way.

Today, LAMA boasts some 600 members across the country. Local chapters meet regularly. Once a year, usually in late October or early November, the organization holds its annual 3-day conference, attracting participants from all over the country. These savvy managers get together to share common problems, exchange information regarding trends, and expand their networks. Highly regarded speakers in the field teach the latest techniques in paralegal management. The conference is exhilarating, particularly for new managers who have not yet had the opportunity to obtain insights to comparable programs. In addition, LAMA also hosts regional conferences and publishes excellent materials and texts to assist you.

One of the most helpful information packages the organization puts together is a salary survey of paralegal managers, with detailed information regarding programs. This survey is produced every 2 years. It is an extensive survey covering firms and corporations around the nation.

If you are already a manager, whether your time is spent exclusively on administration or you are a "working supervisor" (some or all of your time is billable), LAMA is an invaluable source for you. Consider joining your local chapter. If there are no local chapters, contact the association for information on starting one. The annual conference is open to everyone. If you are an aspiring manager, you can gain valuable contacts by attending, plus you'll come away with a tremendous amount of new knowledge about your career.

GETTING THE PROMOTION

It's a myth that the paralegal who produces the highest quality work product will make the best manager. In order to manage, candidates for this position must possess general competencies, such as the abilities to

- Lead others
- Demonstrate authority
- Show a sense of belonging
- Ask for support
- Take reasonable risks
- Listen and respond appropriately
- Make decisions and take action
- Teach and coach
- Demonstrate good negotiating and persuasion skills
- Sell the program to others
- Sell yourself (explain how and why you are good at what you do)
- Position yourself for success.

Practical skills must include

- Expertise in a practice specialty
- Financial ability and understanding of law firm economics
- Understanding of the organization
- Knowledge of other practice specialties
- Demonstrated management and supervisory skills
- Background in personnel: hiring, training, and organizing teams of paralegals
- Effective oral and written communication skills
- Excellent follow-through
- Knowledge of the latest technology.

Getting promoted to paralegal manager is not simply a result of getting noticed by others. No matter how hard you work, how good you are, or how much you want the position, unless you reach out and claim it, you are liable to go unnoticed.

Preparing a Proposal

If your firm does not have an organized paralegal program, draft a proposal outlining a structure that would fit within the firm. Pattern the program closely after the associate program. Propose new positions, but do not propose specific names of persons to hold those positions. Let the firm do that. Your proposal should include:

1. *A needs analysis*—Identify the need and outline benefits to the firm including increased profitability and decrease in turnover

2. *An observation report*—Status of the current program, if any, or status of the state of the department

3. *Recommendations*—How to implement the program.

Interview attorneys and paralegals. Get feedback but do not identify any attorney or paralegal who may say derogatory things about the firm. Use the phrase, "one attorney states it may be helpful to the firm if . . ." Let all interviewees know that you are preparing a report and get permission to quote them. Keep the report on a positive note.

Include outlines of other successful paralegal programs, if possible. Network with LAMA members to find programs that are about the same size and practice specialty. Peer pressure works wonders in a law firm environment. Corporations also like to keep up with their competitors.

Many paralegal managers have relayed one common theme: No matter how high the management position, you are still in a subordinate position. You will not be able to tell the attorneys what to do; you are still at someone else's beck and call.

On the other hand, most paralegal managers express tremendous job satisfaction. They often have more autonomy and higher recognition than nonmanagement paralegals.

WRITING THE RESUME

If you are seeking a position as a manager outside of the firm, then you must draft a management-oriented resume. (See the sample resume following this section.) Include an "Objective" line, stating clearly that you are seeking a paralegal management position. Make sure the objective line fits with your goals. If you will take a group coordinator position or specialty position, then stating "Paralegal Manager or Administrator" may be too limiting. You may wish to state "Objective: Coordinator," which is somewhat vague but indicates manager.

In job description sections, be sure to highlight all management responsibilities you have in addition to describing paralegal assignments. Some phrases to use where appropriate are the following:

- Coordinated
- Coordinated team
- Coordinated project
- Supervised
- Supervised staff (do not mention numbers unless very large)
- Organized staff
- Recruited
- Delegated
- Interfaced with
- Prepared Request for Proposal
- Oversaw
- Evaluated
- Managed
- Structured
- Maintained
- Managed multimillion-dollar case
- Managed teams of _____
- Prepared performance evaluations
- Interviewed and selected vendors
- Counseled staff
- Assigned
- Administrative and policy duties
- Conducted orientations
- Drafted proposals
- Implemented policy
- Created
- Designed
- Prepared budget

The education section of the resume should reflect any paralegal management seminars and management and finance courses. Highlight all management, recruiting, and financial software packages.

Many times a paralegal manager position will not be advertised. These positions are found mainly through word of mouth and attorney or paralegal search firms. Administrators and managing partners are likely hiring authorities for these positions. Sending your resume to the administrator with a convincing letter may get a response, even though the firm may not be looking. The administrator may be convinced it is time for a change and therefore is a good contact for potential action.

Because this is a management position, the search can take longer than the search for a paralegal position. Plan on spending at least 3 to 6 months in the search. You may also want to consider other cities. Remember, only one person can lead the group, so there are fewer positions available. Don't get discouraged, and keep increasing your management and financial skills while searching.

SAMPLE: RESUME FOR PARALEGAL MANAGER CANDIDATE

NAME
ADDRESS
CITY, STATE AND ZIP CODE
PHONE NUMBERS
E-MAIL

OBJECTIVE: Supervisor Legal Assistant Management Position

RELEVANT EXPERIENCE

Management
- Delegated responsibilities to junior paralegals and case clerks, collaborating on daily priorities and maintaining smooth flow of work product.
- Designed computer system for major securities litigation.
- In charge of management of several large-scale cases. Organized systems for more effective use of personnel.

Supervision
- Successfully built a cooperative work team and promoted productive environment by:
  —delegating jobs in accordance with employees' skills and abilities;
  —treating employees with respect, maintaining a sense of humor;
  —welcoming constructive criticism and input on productivity improvement;
  —supporting morale by posting letters of appreciation from clients;
- Trained employees in how to deal with difficult clients and handle appropriate dispositions of cases.

Organization

*   Organized and improved filing system for litigation documents, saving time and increasing billable hours of employees.
*   Oversaw all facets of billing and recordkeeping for small law firm.

COMPUTER SKILLS

*   Proficient in Microsoft Word
*   Ability to train: Concordance, Summation, Case Central, Lotus and Lotus Notes

EMPLOYMENT HISTORY

1993-present	Litigation Paralegal	Smith & Smith Oakland, CA
1990-1993	Litigation Paralegal	O'Malley & Schwartz Los Angeles, CA

EDUCATION

Paralegal Certificate, Jones Academy, Attorney-Assistant Program, ABA-approved program, 1990
Bachelor of Arts Degree, English, UCLA, 1984.

SALARY

On the whole, paralegal managers are compensated pretty well in relation to the rest of the field. In New York, average salaries for managers at major firms are in the $75,000+ range. According to the most recent survey by LAMA, salaries across the country range from a low of $50,000 to a high of $100,000 plus bonus.

If you are seeking a management position, expect to increase your salary. Making a lateral salary move with upgraded responsibilities makes sense only if the position serves as a training ground. If you are looking to be promoted from within, asking for a salary that is 15 percent higher than the highest paid paralegal in the firm is not unreasonable.

Some firms will not give an increase in salary when you are promoted. Although this management practice is not designed to motivate, think twice before quitting in haste. See if you can get the title. That is the one tangible you can take if you do leave. Then use the title to catapult into the position and salary you really want.

CONCLUSION

The paralegal manager position is one position paralegals can count on to "put a star on their door." It is comparable to middle management in a corporation. The difference between this position and middle management, however, is that in order for the paralegal manager to move up, she or he has to take a position outside of the program. This can mean a lateral or upgraded position within the firm or corporation. Be open-minded, however. You are not betraying the field, the field has not betrayed you, and there is nothing wrong with moving onward. After all, even the president of General Motors tops out.

CHAPTER 20

Straight Talk from a Few of the Most Powerful Paralegal Administrators in the Country

It was involuntary. They sank my boat.

> John F. Kennedy. Reply when asked how he became a war hero,
> in Arthur M. Schlesinger, Jr.'s, *A Thousand Days* (1965)

REFINING THE PARALEGAL CAREER

Having interviewed, counseled, and given seminars to large numbers of paralegals over the years, I have found one pervasive theme: the continual push to keep improving. Repeatedly, I have heard the signals: requests to get more sophisticated assignments and creation of hierarchies, regulations, and certification. All were indicators of the desire for continuous refinement of the career.

To find the answer to "how do we continue to improve?," I needed to ask the question, "what do law firms want?" To research the answers, I invited two groups of topflight paralegal managers from some of the largest firms in the country to attend a roundtable discussion. I chose the manager position as a resource because managers know both sides of the fence: Their survival depends on their ability to understand both the paralegal and the attorney.

I wanted to be free to ask anything I could relating to the perception, use, and future of paralegals. I was fortunate to have a lively, informed, professional group of managers in both settings, one in San Francisco, the other at the annual LAMA conference in Houston, Texas. This national group brought varied backgrounds: Some were paralegals who worked hard to climb the ladder; one was not a paralegal, but had a master's degree in administration; and one was a name partner of a small firm, managing one of the largest paralegal programs in the country. These managers dauntlessly answered probing questions concerning the latest information paralegals need to advance in their careers. It was an opportunity to get the word out to paralegals from an insider's perspective. These veterans had the answers. Their very positions validated the unique talents and skills that qualified them to manage, supervise, train, recruit, and evaluate paralegals. They not only understood what it took to reach the top, but they could also touch it, smell it, feel it, and then turn around and give it back.

This was their opportunity to share it with you, and to their credit, they held nothing back. Here is what they had to say.

QUESTIONS AND ANSWERS

What are the most significant changes that are turning around the paralegal field?

The two biggest changes in the paralegal workplace can be found in (1) recruiting and (2) the paralegal's role in technology. Market conditions make it harder to find qualified candidates for the job. Many markets, such as Minneapolis, Washington, D.C., and Atlanta, are finding it tough to get 3–5 year experienced-level paralegals. These candidate-driven markets may have resulted from the recession or because people are less willing to leave firms. The transactional corporate paralegal is in demand almost everywhere. However, during economic downturns, corporate specialty jobs are hard to find.

Technology has changed the way paralegals do their jobs. Some firms are educating and pushing attorneys to use analysts and senior analysts in associate capacities. These job descriptions require that the paralegal train associates. Ideal candidates no longer know only word processing programs such as Word. They are expected to have excellent computer skills.

Database background and the ability to automate a case are required for more and more positions. Cases now require some level of automation regardless of whether the database has images linked to it. Paralegals need to understand objective and subjective coding.

A test to see whether paralegals have the ability is to ask them to describe how they use the information. What sometimes ends up missing is conceptual understanding. Some may have used databases but don't understand why the database was set up the way it was. This leads to ineffective use of the program. In general, it matters little which database engines paralegals have worked with, but rather that the paralegals understand what they are doing and can work effectively.

Some firms provide training programs on-site. Most entry-level paralegals have had a computer in college and understand word processing but have no idea about the litigation process. Other experienced-level paralegals have been with technologically challenged firms. However, when finally introduced to the new world, they make up quickly for lost time and opportunity.

Are there any unspoken or informal standardized educational requirements for entry- and experienced-level paralegals?

Across the board, many major firms required a B.A. or B.S. degree. The firms were split on the requirement of a paralegal certificate and particularly an ABA-approved certificate. Attitudes ranged from waiving the certificate for entry-level case clerk positions to mandating it as a hiring requirement. Some credit paralegal experience in lieu of the degree. The 2-year degree was not favored by this group.

Several firms hired J.D.s, primarily those who have the degree but who have not taken or passed the bar exam, and a few hired attorneys from other states working as paralegals. Attorneys in other firms expressed suspicion as to why this person would work as a paralegal; however, the attitude did not appear widespread.

Give us your real opinions of paralegal education programs for major firm candidates.

(Minefield! Minefield! Looking around at the tables, I was almost certain I heard hand grenades blowing up around me.)

The strongest consolidated message to schools was to give paralegals practical advice. Teach paralegals headed for major firms how to handle the unique workload. Paralegal schools, in this group opinion, did a great job of training for smaller or specialized firms. However, for many larger firms, the focus is different.

Paralegals in major firms are not expected to write briefs or conduct legal research. Although managers have tried for years to get the schools to listen, they don't feel they are being heard. Consequently, the importance of the certificate was de-emphasized in some of these firms. Some managers felt that a very glamorous image was placed on the profession by some educators, possibly to attract and validate the student's new career choice. Either that, or some educators had never worked in a major law firm.

What's your take on the voluntary certification movement? Is it really favorable in major firms? Will it sway hiring decisions?

A surprising, yet unanimous NO on this one. No consideration, extra credit, more dollars, or upgraded position will be offered. Why? Typical responses indicated certification added little value. The CLA or PACE designation was viewed as a personal achievement but one that did not benefit major firms. Any weight given at all recognizes some initiative and commitment to the profession to achieve it, but it wouldn't be a hiring requirement. On the other hand, it may help paralegals in smaller firms. It should be noted that none of the states requiring mandatory or voluntary designations at the time of the meetings were represented. (Following up on this question in another few years may render some interesting answers.)

Name the three top requirements essential to getting a job.

1. Technology skills: You must have either the experience or the ability.

2. Interpersonal skills: Attorneys recognize there is direct contact between the client and the paralegal. They must be confident that this person can communicate well.

3. Proven track record: How well you do in the workplace is critical for success. Law firms exist on substantiating and proving everything. They demand the same of their paralegals' work product. Proving yourself includes progression of skill level and additional education.

Name other important requirements.

Writing skills, academic achievements, and, a factor in the Midwest, longevity. Those firms and corporations in the West and the East did not weigh length of time with a firm as heavily (perhaps due to heavy downsizing).

Managers want intangible or life skills, such as the ability to be a problem solver, being flexible, and having a "can-do" attitude. Paralegals have to know how to present themselves, to supervise other people, and to work with a secretary.

Clients are actually asking for resumes or biographies on paralegals assigned to the case team. Marketing their paralegals to the clients is standard operating procedure in some firms.

The real picture now: temporary staffing—threat or boon to major firms?

Within the last year, one firm made a change to 100 percent temp-to-hire. This hiring method addresses some concerns with paralegals who interview well but perform poorly. A rapid growth mode with hiring emphasis at lower levels has driven this practice.

Paralegals seeking to find more sophisticated assignments are frequently advised to keep asking for them. What's the inside buzz on how to get those assignments?

Delegation of work to paralegals by lawyers is influenced by two factors: (1) quality of work produced by the paralegal and (2) attitude. Very little else is of concern to the delegator. In fact, the only thing a lawyer really wants to know is this: Can the paralegal get this job done right? Included in the phrase, "get this job done right" are all the other factors relating to quality and attitude: on-time, correct, cost-effective, ethical, efficient without alienating team members and clients, knows the next step, listens, and gives and executes instructions. Attitude reflects many characteristics. One is motivation; another is initiative.

How has ADR affected litigation paralegals?

Certain markets have seen the impact of ADR because, in some areas, there aren't as many of the huge lawsuits anymore. Trial is less of an option. Litigation departments in Canada have seen deep cuts due to ADR, according to Pat Hicks, former president of LAMA.

Should paralegals specialize or generalize?

A generalist background was appealing to these managers, perhaps as a preventative measure. Cited was the demise of real estate positions several years ago. Cross-training was emphasized as were subspecialties within the corporate area.

Where do we stand on billable hours? Are we observing the new "lifestyle" culture, or is that just wishful thinking?

The average number of billable hours ranged from 1,500 to 1,650 in this group. One firm required 1,800. Others set no minimum but did have a "hidden" acceptable target. A number (but not a quota) is determined as a standard for attorneys and paralegals.

Another measuring device is to benchmark average billed hours causing some to excel and others to fall short. While some firms don't advertise exactly *what* they expect, paralegals are supposed to determine whether they are keeping up through monthly or quarterly reports.

At the beginning of the year, some administrators ask paralegals about projects that might be charged to administrative time. At one firm, partners requested a paralegal to revamp a large filing system. The manager then credited the paralegal over 200 hours. Managers were clear, however, that someone who should but didn't have enough client hours may receive a warning.

How does task-based billing affect your firm or corporation?

The new billing trend does not appear to be widespread at this time. One manager said she had been waiting for it for 5 years. Even with task-based billing, time has to be tracked so the firm knows its costs. There was almost total agreement that task-based billing would not have a great effect on paralegals—that paralegals would still be expected to keep time, only a little bit differently. I'd like to ask this question also, in another 5 years.

Some firms accommodate and meet the client's need for task-based billings. But managers are confused as to how it will ever be possible to estimate the cost of a case, even with guidelines. In a few notable instances, firms were forced into task-based billing and found that alternative billing solutions actually leveraged work to the legal assistant department and took it away from associates.

One advantage to alternative billing is that a costly mistake does not occur when calculations are off due to low paralegal billing rates. However, the squeeze on associates may, in time, push those associates into the legal assistant ranks.

Client demands are forcing managers to prepare budgets, something unheard of a few years ago. Some clients have refused to pay for "lower level" case clerk tasks such as filing and database labeling. In an effort to fight back, some firms created a whole new position called document clerks not even in the paralegal department. These clerks are located in the records center and are assigned to major complex cases. They are then billed out at almost a breakeven or pass-through rate.

Other billing challenges are those clients who want a blended rate. Some return the bill to the firm with crossed-out items as a way of saying they won't pay.

Let's talk money.

Salaries appear to have stagnated in the past few years within this segment of the market. Cost-of-living increases of 3 to 4 percent are not uncommon. Although no one could point to survey data, salaries just don't seem to be moving up or down. This may be due in part to the economy and slight decreased demand for entry-level applicants.

One firm needed several 3- to 4-year people in the corporate area and received resumes from paralegals with 8 to 10 years experience. Unfortunately, the firm can't pay these people the money they may now be earning.

Experience so often is not fungible. Managers evaluate applicable substance level of work history. They may interview a paralegal with 10 to 15 years background that is equivalent to their firm's 7- or 8-year experience level.

Legal assistants must be responsible for developing their own careers. The days of entitlement have vanished. Understanding the correlation between salary and billing rates motivates growth. Price-sensitive clients know which skill level corresponds to billing rate and refuse to pay inflated rates for lower-level skills.

Bonuses, if any, may be based on merit consisting of a formula of billable hours, longevity, and a subjective evaluation of work product. Merit is interpreted as going beyond the job. Here's where the yardstick gets a little wobbly. Just exactly what is "going beyond the job?"

In some firms it means exceeding targeted hours; others claim high hours are not necessarily a positive sign. Value of work was assessed instead by using a formula comparing hours paid, amount of work, and cost per hour. Someone who worked a normal day and rendered profit to the bottom line was more highly valued than someone working overtime. Hardball questions, such as "is this person hoarding work and keeping it for himself?," implies, "is this person supplementing his income?"

Other bonus factors include contributions to the community, such as pro bono work and involvement in government or violence committees affecting the community. Interestingly, when asked why a paralegal should spend as much as 500 hours on pro bono work one manager answered, "better a legal assistant than a lawyer." So much for instilling values. In all fairness to the program, pro bono work is a morale booster as paralegals may receive very engrossing work and plenty of client contact. When managers assign a pro bono, the firm and paralegals recognize something special has been given. Crediting the hours as important billables; expecting paralegals to bill 1,800 hours per year *plus* pro bono work; and counting the hours as overtime were just a few of the policies followed.

Where do managers get their thrills?

"From my staff when they succeed. I love to watch them grow."

"Money is not a motivator. The thrill comes from the people."

"When a project receives a pat on the back. The firm looks to us to motivate other people. We have to be self-motivated. None of us have stayed involved with law firms this long by needing a lot of strokes. When we get it, it's appreciated, not expected."

Okay. You're all at the Annual Peter Awards for Professional Paralegals. As you accept your Pete, you are given one shot to tell all paralegals the ingredients they need to succeed. What would they be?

Have a realistic picture; accept things for what they are. It's a good career and a good environment. You put your own star on your door. Take responsibility for yourself and your career. Take pride in the profession. Learn people skills, interpersonal skills, and get the big picture. No one will hand you anything. In the end, it's all up to you.

KUDOS

My heartfelt thanks to the following managers who participated in the roundtable discussions. As always, kudos to fellow LAMA members and paralegal administrator colleagues for an insightful and honest look at the profession. Although some of these managers may have moved on, here is the group:

Debra Thompson—King & Spaulding, Atlanta, Georgia
    350 attorneys; 170 legal assistants and document clerks
Ann Dodds—Carrington, Coleman, Sloman & Blumenthal, Dallas, Texas
    100 lawyers and 25 legal assistants
Rebecca ("Becky") Bike—Vinson & Elkins, Houston, Texas
    500 lawyers; 175 legal assistants; 8 national and international offices
Paige Denton—Winston & Strawn, Chicago, Illinois
    350 lawyers; 50 legal assistants and trainees; 3 offices
Valorie Songer—Nelson, Mullins, Reilly & Scarborough, Columbia, South Carolina
    220 lawyers; 75 paralegals and project assistants; 5 offices
Lotus Wong—Assistant Manager, White & Case, New York, New York
    570 lawyers (300 in New York); approximately 135 legal assistants worldwide
Yvonne Nearing—Wilmer, Cutler & Pickering, Washington, D.C.
    235 lawyers; approximately 100 legal assistants and project assistants
Sharon Lonciani—Goodwin, Proctor & Hoar, Boston, Massachusetts
    300 attorneys; approximately 42 legal assistants
Lynne Kramer—Palmer & Dodge, Boston, Massachusetts
    170 attorneys; approximately 28 legal assistants
Peggy J. Giunta—Hale and Dorr, Boston, Massachusetts
    260 attorneys; approximately 70 legal assistants
Barbara Mundholm—Rosenman & Colin, New York City, New York
Debra Bellings—Pillsbury, Madison & Sutro, San Francisco, California
Rene Goldhammer—Orrick, Herrington, San Francisco, California
Holly McPherson—Crosby, Heafey, Roach & May, San Francisco, California
Muffy Mallory—Beveridge & Diamond, San Francisco, California
Brenda Moore—Littler, Mendelson, San Francisco, California
DeEtta Vincent—Thelen, Marrin, Johnson & Bridges, San Francisco, California
Joan Fink—Heller, Ehrman, White & McAuliffe, San Francisco, California

PARALEGAL INNER VIEW: CELIA ELWELL—
WORKING WITH GUN TOTIN' CLIENTS

Name: Celia C. Elwell, R.P.
Title: Legal Assistant II
Firm: Office of the Municipal Counselor for the City of Oklahoma City
Teaching: Adjunct Professor, University of Oklahoma, Department of Legal Assistant Education since 1986
Author: *Practical Legal Writing for Legal Assistants* Second Edition (West 1996) with Associate Dean Robert B. Smith, University of Oklahoma Law School; also writes articles for NFPA
Size of firm: 31 attorneys, 3 paralegals (includes Criminal Justice Division; Land Use Division, Litigation Division; Municipal Trust and Finance Division and Contract, Labor and Operations Division)
Years of experience: 15 years
Education: Paralegal certificate from University of Oklahoma, Department of Legal Assistant Education in 1986. ABA approved
Specialty: Litigation, appellate practice and procedure, and legal writing and research
Job duties: Each day's tasks are usually different, which is something I like about my job. I do all the things most litigation paralegals do, such as summarizing depositions; organizing, categorizing and indexing documents; drafting discovery, pleadings, correspondence, briefs, affidavits, and more; legal research in books and on Westlaw and the Internet; trial preparation; prepare for and attend depositions; and assist with strategy. I also spend my "spare" time researching the Internet looking for helpful legal sites. I meet with clients and witnesses.

What does a normal day look like?

If I am entrenched in a civil litigation case, then I'm researching, organizing documents, and meeting with attorneys. It's not unusual to be told at the last minute that I'm supposed to be at a meeting in the next 15 minutes with a client or witness. In short, there are no "normal" days. I work for all the attorneys in my office and I have a bad habit of not being able to say "no" when someone asks for help.

What has been your most satisfying experience?

Wow! Do I have to choose just one? Those come when I find the right legal authorities just in the nick of time. I have just the right document ready to hand to my attorney at trial when opposing counsel cannot find a particular document and I provide him with an extra copy I just happened to have, when all our hard work pays off when we win a trial, writing the brief that wins the motion, and just feeling like I've made a valuable contribution.

Any scary experiences you'd like to share?

I was going to trial with one of my attorneys to defend against an illegal arrest/detention claim made by a security guard. The man showed up at a hospital, wearing a gun, to take his children away from his ex-wife who was there for serious surgery. The original attorney, a friend of mine, had left our office for another position. I saw my friend shortly before trial and he warned me to be careful—the plaintiff had been ordered to go to numerous rage counseling sessions and was known to wear a gun at all times. It sure got my attention!

My most frightening experience was working with a secretary who had an extremely bad attitude and mood swings and carried a gun in her purse.

My most eye-opening experience was when we were defending a wrongful death case. The plaintiff had been driving the car and her mother was the passenger. She claimed that she never saw the stop sign because of high grass and weeds. She ran the stop sign and a pickup truck hit the passenger side of the car, killing the mother. The daughter was devastated and so was the rest of the family. We successfully defended the case and won at trial.

During the trial, I noticed that my attorney always greeted the family every day and treated them with the utmost respect. He expressed his sympathy for the family's loss and asked them to understand that he was doing his job but that didn't mean that he liked doing it in this particular case. In his examination of the daughter, he could have worked at drilling it in that the accident was all her fault. He didn't. He simply used the evidence to show how the accident occurred. He did his best not to make the daughter feel even more guilty than she already felt. Once we won the case, he again talked to the family to offer his condolences. As we left the courthouse, a younger attorney with us started whooping it up because we had won. My attorney told her to be quiet and that this was nothing to celebrate. He pointed across the lawn of the courthouse where the family was walking away with their arms around each other and reminded us that this truly was a tragedy which this family, especially the daughter, would live with for the rest of their lives.

Before this, most trial attorneys I had worked with always pulled out all the stops at trial to win the case and let the chips fall where they may. The opposing side was given no quarter. They were the enemy and they must be destroyed—it was as simple as that. This was my first experience in which the attorney trying the case did an excellent job of defending his client but with dignity and compassion for the other side. It made a huge impression on me.

What kinds of computer skills are necessary for your position?

I have a computer on my desk. I draft my own documents; my secretary makes revisions, copies, and envelopes. I need to know LEXIS and Westlaw and my self-taught knowledge of researching on the Internet has been invaluable. I'm required to know both WordPerfect and Word. Unfortunately, my office has a rather small budget for technology, so we have no software for summarizing depositions, no Palm Pilots—only one lap top for the entire office. We have Premise plus our law library for legal research. I would love to have an opportunity to learn and use more sophisticated technology.

What advice would you give your fellow paralegals?

That depends upon where they were in their career. If they were just entering the profession, I would advise them about picking a quality paralegal program and what to look for as far as curriculum, instructors, and credentials. I would tell them about the national paralegal organizations and the two national tests. I would emphasize ethics, integrity, and quality performance and work product.

For experienced paralegals, I would encourage them to look for ways to enhance their professionalism and to obtain career advancement. For those who feel unappreciated at their jobs, I usually advise them to get more involved in the local or a national paralegal organization, write articles, give seminars, teach classes, or write a paralegal textbook. Perhaps that person needs encouragement to muster the courage to sit for the CLA or PACE exam or just need a little nudge to get more involved in the profession. Everyone has their own talents and gifts.

What does the future hold for you?

I'm working on a massive Internet Research Guide for my own satisfaction and use. I hope to keep teaching paralegal classes until I drop.

It's interesting, but over the years, people have constantly told me about things I would never be able to do because I did not have a college degree. I was told that I would never be able to teach, publish, or be allowed to write briefs because I wasn't a lawyer. I wonder what other things I will do in my career that I should have never been able to do? I do not worry about what will happen next. I love being a paralegal.

What would you change about the paralegal profession?

I would like to see paralegals stop with the mine-is-better-than-yours mentality. You know, my paralegal school is better than yours, my degree/certificate/whatever is better than yours, my national test is better than yours, etc. My philosophy is that, if one of our fellow paralegals does something which enhances his or her professionalism or reflects in a positive way on that person regardless of what it is, we should all give that person a big pat on the back.

Is on-the-job-training sufficient?

No (as I run for cover), I do not think on-the-job training is sufficient. There are many invaluable things one learns on the job, many of which are not covered by what is taught in the classroom. However, I think paralegals receive the best education and training by graduating from a quality paralegal program and then receiving on-the-job training for approximately 6 months to a year. Also, when learning on the job, you are taught only what the attorney employer wants you to know. If legal research is not important to that employer, then you have no opportunity to learn about it. Not all attorneys know what paralegals are or what kind of tasks they should perform. How many attorneys do you know who know the definition for a paralegal, know what a paralegal can do, and know what a paralegal may not do? It appears that the days when someone could be trained as a paralegal on the job are coming to an end. With the greater emphasis on education, it will be more difficult for paralegals who learned on the job to meet the criteria set by state bars and legislatures and paralegal organizations.

What other pearls of wisdom do you have for us?

This profession is not for everyone. The work can be difficult. The people you work with can be difficult and have few, if any, personal communication skills (if you know what I mean). There are many deadlines that will be out of your control and will require long hours. You must be reliable, honest, ethical, and organized. People skills, plus oral and written skills are very important. You must be flexible and be able to handle—indeed thrive—on stress and deadlines. People who are not willing to make these kinds of commitments and will look to cut corners need to think about going into another profession. It's tough but a profession which also offers a great deal of satisfaction.

CHAPTER 21

Creating an Environment for Keeping Talent

Firms that do the best job of attracting and retaining good paralegals will most likely be the firms that have already shown strong commitment to innovative human resources strategies. Once, the average employee wanted only decent benefits such as medical insurance and an allowance for parking. Today, the average employee wants more—and above-average employees more still.

Even if you are a paralegal with no hiring authority, you may be in a situation to have input regarding your work environment. It's always helpful to know what the market is like both inside and out of the legal field. Anytime you can improve your situation, great! If not, and it seems to be a wise decision to change jobs, then what other employers are doing to retain employees is valuable information. It's always good to be aware of the kinds of opportunities and work environments that exist in the world of employment.

Perhaps your firm or organization already is providing personal laptops, great retirement plans, insurance for alternative medicine, or even pet insurance and dog walkers. These perks would have sounded absurd in the 1980s and even the 1990s. But the past boom in the economy caused things to change dramatically. Good candidates found themselves in a multioffer situation, and firms competed heavily to attract the best. Once the best arrived, nothing prevented aggressive headhunters or competitive firms from wining and dining these top candidates in the hope of persuading them to change positions. Combine this threat with overworked employees grinding billable hours in a sweatshop environment, and employees quickly realized that a jump to another firm probably wasn't a bad idea.

Balance of life and work adds to the wow factor of an employment package of a candidate or new hire, and employers are paying attention to the demand. While benefits might not be a dramatic employment-relationship maker or breaker, there has been increased attention paid to benefits packages by both employees and employers. Information is readily available on the Internet. Employees can visit almost any company's Web site to find out what benefits a competitive firm is offering.

Even if you are not in a position where you manage paralegals, you may be able to present your firm with information that can better serve your workplace. Be careful and don't squash any toes! However, a fact-finding mission which delivers the information in a nonconfrontational manner can position you as a knowledgeable human resources tool.

Employees still want the basics: good insurance (health, vision, dental, life); short-term and long-term disability coverage; and a pension plan and a 401(k). But given the media attention that many of the new economy start-ups are getting with emphasis on their seemingly wacky bring-your-pet-to-work-dress-any-old-way-no-titles-here work perks, old economy workers can't help but sit up and take notice. And let us not forget how quickly employees were to abandon ship at the slightest mention of stock options.

Employers, however, can't keep adding on benefits without worrying about rising costs—which is why you may see a budding theme in perks that don't cost money (such as casual Friday) and make a huge difference for employees.

Competition from dot-coms has forced all kinds of organizations to revisit their benefit plans. Technology has also influenced a candidate's choice of employment offers. No one who needs to be as heavily connected to the Internet or database management as paralegals should choose a firm that is trailing behind in technology. As paralegals become more familiar with customized service and research over the Internet, they'll expect and appreciate firms offering state-of-the-art equipment.

A poll of 660 working Americans conducted by the management search firm BridgeGate LLC, showed that benefits are more important to older workers: 30.1 percent of the 45 to 54 age bracket and 36.7 percent of those ages 55 to 64, as compared to 23.1 percent of all the respondents. Younger workers are more likely to be influenced by training opportunities (10.7 percent versus 4.7 percent for all respondents.)

Other factors influencing the change in benefits as a retention strategy include an aging workforce, dual income households, flexible work schedules, and difficult-to-deal-with HMOs. The lines today between work and home life are blurring, so employees need tools to help manage them more effectively. Employees having problems balancing work and home life are at more risk of turning over. There are Web sites available now that give employees discounts on anything from cars, insurance rates, sundry items, and more. They can get information about what their health insurance will cover. Organizations such as Hewlett-Packard, Metropolitan Life, Harris Bank, Novell, and other *Fortune* 500 companies are providing such services to employees in an effort to help them be more productive and satisfied. One site is *iClick.com* portal based in White Plains, New York.

Stock options are probably the sexiest benefit to hit the new millennium. The cost of options is probably also one of the most costly to employers. Many employees are being lured to jobs at Internet companies with stock options. The question is, are options really worth much?

The answer is not always. Stock options give you the right to buy your employer's stock at a set price after a given time period. By offering you options, companies reason they can count on your long-term loyalty because you typically can't make use of your options until about 3 years after you get them. But depending on the stock's price at the time, options may be worth a bundle or absolutely nothing at all.

Say you were hired by company XY in the year 2000 and awarded the option to buy 2,000 shares at $10 per share in 2003. That year rolls around and the stock has a market price of $15, meaning your options are now worth $10,000, or the difference between what you purchased them for and what you can sell them for now (you buy the 2,000 shares for $20,000, sell them for $30,000, and make a $10,000 profit). However, if the stock price falls below $10 in 2003, your options are worthless. Since you can't predict the market's swings, it's probably best not to count on options as your main source of salary. Think of them as a bonus instead.

The shake-up in the stock market may have caused stock options to be losing their appeal and has caused some people to reevaluate whether they will jump ship for a dot-com where it's not a sure thing. Russian roulette with careers is never a good idea.

Benefits can be a big influence in why a paralegal initially chooses one job over another, but there's solid evidence that benefits aren't a primary reason people stay. The quote by Tom Peters, "If your company is not enthusiastic, creative, and just plain fun, you're in trouble, serious trouble," is well-taken. A study by New York City-based management consultant Towers Perrin found the following four issues to be of prime importance for high-performing companies. These organizations:

- Provide a consistent and meaningful level of differentiation in pay for their top-performing employees
- Make performance a priority in their reward systems
- Believe that employees today want different things than past generations
- Communicate openly about pay and rewards and how those relate to strong individual performance.

The study showed that challenging work and work climate are the primary reasons that compel workers to stay with a company. Base pay is third on the list and benefits aren't in the equation at all. According to *Workforce* magazine (July 2000), "Managers control over 75 percent of the reasons why people leave the jobs." Those reasons include bad management practices, how people are treated on the job, communication, challenging and exciting work, continual opportunities to grow and learn, being recognized and rewarded for performance, having some control over their jobs and life, and knowing their work matters.

What is it that employees want? The *Baltimore Business Journal* reported a Saratoga Institute survey of more than 1,000 U.S. workers that asked employees to identify factors that would make them more likely to remain with their current employers. The top three responses are:

1. Training and mentoring
2. Earnings potential
3. Positive work relations.

Job security also ranked high. Only 27 percent said they were likely to stick with companies where their long-term employment prospects were weak. What makes a job attractive to these workers? Here are the top three responses:

1. Performance evaluations based on the employee's ability to develop improved methods of doing things
2. Goals mutually developed by supervisors and the employee
3. Job success based on the employee's responsibilities and accomplishments.

Employment Recruitment and Retention newsletter cites AT&T's tactic to retain "plateaued" employees. The company retains employees with a program called Resource Link. Designed to function as an in-house temporary service, Resource Link lets employees with diverse management, technical, or professional skills "sell" their abilities to different departments for short-term assignments. A similar program in your firm might help retain employees who would otherwise leave in search of new frontiers.

Flexible scheduling is another retention strategy that is promising results. It has helped overcome absenteeism by offering employees flexible work schedules. It is a small price to pay and reaps big rewards as some companies have found out.

At Xerox, one customer service center turned decisions about work schedules over to employees. With employee work teams in charge of scheduling, the company reports higher morale, better customer service, and a 30 percent reduction in absenteeism. At Johnson & Johnson, absenteeism among workers who made use of flexible work options and family leave policies averaged 50 percent less than for the workforce in general. And finally, at Aetna Insurance, retention of female employees following maternity leave rose from 77 percent to 88 percent when the company established a 6-month maternity leave policy and flexible return-to-work options.

Training is another powerful retention vehicle to keep employees motivated and enthusiastic. Lucent Technologies, for example, provides employees with 15 days of training each year. In addition, every worker designs his or her own "personal development plan" with the assistance of a coach from human resources. According to *Employment Recruitment & Retention* newsletter, the San Francisco-based Horn Group, a public relations firm, constantly bombards employees with training opportunities. The company offers employees cash that they can spend on any type of training they feel would help them do their jobs better. Employees use the "personal development fund" in a variety of ways: time management seminars, writing courses, and more. What a great way to retain paralegals! Think of how much more efficient, profitable, and up-to-date on the latest laws paralegals can be with regular training. If you give employees the chance to develop their skills within your firm, they'll be less likely to leave in search of better opportunities.

In *Success Secrets* by Mark McCormack, telling people, "You're doing a great job" isn't going to make them want to stay at your firm. It isn't specific enough. Praise can help the atmosphere but only if it is detailed and relevant. Here are McCormack's 9 praise-specific phrases that can get you started working better with your coworkers or managing your staff:

1. "You really made a difference by . . . ."
2. "I'm impressed with . . . ."
3. "You got my attention with . . . ."
4. "You're doing top quality work on . . . ."
5. "You're right on the mark with . . . ."
6. "One of the things I enjoy most about you is . . . ."
7. "We couldn't have done it without your . . . ."
8. "What an effective way to . . . ."
9. "You've made my day because of . . . ."

CHAPTER 22

Formal Evaluations

> We don't see things as they are, we see them as we are.
>
> Anais Nin, American writer (1903–1977)

WHEN ATTORNEYS EVALUATE PARALEGALS

Picture this. You are an attorney working with legal assistants. Up until this point you're a happy camper. Then, from nowhere, you are handed a form from an administrator and asked to evaluate and rate the legal assistants with whom you work. You've had a miserable day. Your client refused to show up at a deposition. The senior partner has been breathing down your neck for a brief she needed yesterday. You've billed 150 hours already and you're barely half into the month. You reach for the form.

Now picture this. You're the same attorney. You've had a terrific day. You won a motion for summary judgment. You received accolades from the senior partner on the Acme brief. You are personally responsible for a new client the firm has been courting for months. To celebrate you took the morning off and went swimming. You reach for the form.

Subjective? You bet. Human nature? Absolutely. Fair? Well, that's another story. So how do legal assistants know what attorneys *really* think? How is work product objectively evaluated? Why does one attorney think you're great and another thinks so-so?

Subjective Qualities

Ten skills most commonly evaluated when an attorney reviews your work product include the following:

1. *Teamwork:* Did the paralegal work in a harmonious manner with all of the players (attorneys, staff, vendors, supervisors, clients)?

2. *Ability to marshal information:* Did the paralegal gather pertinent information? Did she recognize important information above and beyond the original request? Did the paralegal present the information in a concise, organized manner?

3. *Knowledge of specialty:* Is the paralegal familiar with the specific assignments he can perform within his specialty? Can he suggest alternatives? Are the assignments performed consistent with the level of experience?

4. *Crafting practical solutions:* Did the paralegal solve problems practically, or did she miss the real issue?

5. *Workload management:* What is the paralegal's ability to juggle client matters and assignments? Is he on time with due dates?

6. *Judgment:* How does the paralegal handle day-to-day decisions? What is the outcome? Does the paralegal exercise independent thinking within the scope of her responsibilities? Does she know when to ask questions?

7. *Writing and analysis ability:* Are the paralegal's written assignments clear, concise, and accurate? Are they grammatically correct?

8. *Initiative:* Does the paralegal go the extra mile?

9. *Organizational skills:* Can anyone else locate the paralegal's assignments or documents at a moment's notice?

10. *Billable hours:* Does the paralegal meet or exceed the minimum billable requirement? Does the paralegal bill fairly to the client? How does the paralegal compare to others in the department?

Probably the 11th commandment in any attorney's mind is: Will this work product be compatible with my work product? Douglas Ditonto, attorney for Southern California Edison Corporation and previously supervisor of the business and property litigation paralegals, asks himself other questions. Is the paralegal eager and interested? Does she understand what's going on? If the assignment is beyond the paralegal's experience, does she speak up?

How can someone evaluate qualities that seem totally subjective, such as judgment? Ditonto asks if the paralegal focuses on the real issues. What is the paralegal's day-to-day decision-making ability? Does she think objectively? Judgment is made up of how well someone thinks independently, discerns information, and exercises discretion. Does she handle sensitive information correctly? Does she discern the true problems, events, and tactics?

Benjamin Seigel, of Buchalter, Nemer, Fields &Younger in Los Angeles and instructor for the paralegal program at the University of West Los Angeles, states: "I evaluate a paralegal based on how well the work product is thought out. I also look to see how well the paralegal worked with the lawyers." According to Seigel, attorneys have a tendency to compare the paralegal's performance with that of an associate. This can lead to big disappointment. "Once you start to expect attorney-level performance from a paralegal, you make a huge mistake. You can't expect a paralegal to do what a lawyer does." Attorneys and paralegals alike must remember that a paralegal does not have training equal to that of an attorney. According to Seigel, many attorneys upgrade assignments with a "sky's the limit" mentality. "Many attorneys expect the paralegal to progress as an attorney. For example, initially we give paralegals simple work such as summarizing documents and transcripts, drafting requests for production, interrogatories, and simple legal analysis. As we begin to receive great work product, we keep upgrading. At some point, it is possible to hit the areas where the paralegal is not trained (e.g., theory). Now our confidence level plunges downward because we get work product back that doesn't look like an associate's. The paralegal is held accountable."

Quantity and Quality of Work

One senior partner in a Los Angeles firm states: "Good billable time is an indication not only that the paralegal is working 'smart' but that [she has] become the right arm of the attorney and friend to the client. If I have to write off time because the work product is not up to par or the paralegal took too much time, I lose confidence in the paralegal. Often, it's not so much if the paralegal has the most hours, but whether those hours are good. I look to see if the paralegal's work product closely matches mine and when I combine their work product with my work, if it comes across as one consistent product."

According to Ditonto, quality of the work product should stand up. To point out to a paralegal how the assignment should be completed is fine, but having to review the basics influences his thinking as to whether he is receiving quality product. "Paralegals should be in the firm to solve and not create problems. . . . They are there to get things done," he stated. "Intuitiveness tells you a lot. It tells you if a person is fitting in with the group, which is very important for paralegals."

Appraisal Methods

In his book, *How to Do a Superior Performance Appraisal,* Dr. William Swan presents a convincing argument that a good performance appraisal depends on what you want it to do. No performance appraisal method is perfect; each one represents a compromise between strengths and limitations.

Common in law firms and in-house legal departments are the following methods:

1. Global essays and ratings. The evaluator is handed a form consisting of one question: "What is your overall evaluation of this individual's performance for the past year?" This evaluation depends on the evaluator's talent for literary composition. With respect to EEOC guidelines, global essay performance appraisals are legally indefensible because they are not easily shown to be job related. Accuracy and fairness remain questionable because the same standard cannot be applied throughout the firm; each manager has her own criteria for success.

2. Trait ratings. This commonly used performance appraisal is a list of personality traits like problem-solving ability, motivation, adaptability, and judgment. A number is assigned to each trait. One of the problems with this process is that most of the traits listed are very broad in definition, as is the rating criteria.

   According to Dr. Swan, trait-rating scales have trouble standing up in court because it is difficult to prove job relevance. This process makes a poor tool for employee development. Imagine a paralegal manager telling a senior paralegal, "you have to be more cheerful." The employee may think, "and . . . ?"

3. Organizational records. This appraisal is based on hard data, such as billable hours, production figures (for example, pages per hour summarized, documents coded or entered per hour), attendance, cost-effectiveness, and realization rate. Although this may be a highly objective and job-related measurement of performance, the downside is that individual contribution is eliminated.

4. Management by objectives. This goal-setting procedure or "work planning" performance review compares expected performance with actual performance. This method allows the paralegal to receive an objective and flexible appraisal. The system provides feedback along with planning for the next year's objectives. Flaws of this system lie in discounting contributions of an individual team member. The same standard cannot be applied to all employees with the same job title. It is, however, the best technique (according to Swan) for feedback, coaching, counseling, and improving of overall job performance.

5. Hybrid system. Combining the best features of goal-setting, trait-rating, and behavioral-based appraisals with an employee's self-evaluation is probably the most effective tool for law firms and legal departments. Performance objectives are set along with developmental objectives. Evaluators and employees build a productive and goal-oriented atmosphere.

What Other Attorneys Think of You Influences Overall Opinion

Evaluators overhear what other attorneys and coworkers think of you. Whether opinion is based on personality differences or is a valid criticism must be determined. Evaluators must look to their own experiences regarding your work product. If an attorney complains that your work is always late, is it because that attorney very rarely allows enough time for completion?

Reviews must demonstrate equality between players. Failure to speak up leads to more misunderstandings and further deterioration of positive opinions of both the employee and employer.

Diana Muscianisi, former paralegal administrator for the ten-attorney/five-paralegal firm of Crowe and Day in Los Angeles, reasons that many attorneys have a hard time confronting or giving suggestions to paralegals they manage. It is equally difficult for many attorneys to give praise. The paralegal winds up thinking either that he did a great job (because nothing was said to counter the notion), or that the work product was barely adequate because nothing at all was said.

It may be that even when attorneys are encouraged to "be honest" they hesitate to state their opinions fully. This avoidance pattern speaks to a strong desire by attorneys to be liked within the firm. "If you are not liked," explains Douglas Ditonto "it's difficult to get a paralegal to work for you. No one wants to be the kid on the block no one else will play with." One corporate attorney, who chose not to be identified, offered unsettling news: "There is fear in some corporations about putting a bad review in writing. If the paralegal is really terrible, the only way that an attorney can get the paralegal transferred is by writing a *good* review. No one wants a transferee who has screwed up in another department."

Lack of Authority

Many times the attorney who is evaluating your work product or preparing your review does not have the authority to

- Hire
- Fire
- Promote
- Set your salary increase or bonus
- Approve additional benefits, such as education, better office, title, and so forth.

The most the evaluating attorney can do is verbally give you significant praise for a job well done or complain to the supervisor if you do an inadequate job. A written or verbal review becomes the only tool by which an attorney most familiar with your work can have any impact on your evaluation.

STRATEGIES FOR A WINNING
PERFORMANCE REVIEW

Performance reviews, when given and received properly, are very effective communication and guidance tools. This is one time during the year that is specifically carved out for you and is an optimum time to position yourself for success.

Anxiety runs rampant in a firm or corporation around review time if managers are not careful to promote the review as a positive experience. "I try to prepare paralegals on my staff for the event," states Diana Muscianisi. "I am quite familiar with paranoia that hits a firm around review time if people are uncertain what is going to happen." Muscianisi, who spent most of her 10+ years as a paralegal and manager in one of the largest firms in the United States, sees to it that paralegals understand exactly what the process will entail. Muscianisi participates in a growing trend in law firms and legal departments to use the review process to the advantage of both the employer and employee.

Review Styles

There are three common stylistic approaches to a performance evaluation:

The perfunctory review. This review style is a quick "pat-on-the-back, this-is-your-increase, do-you-have-any-questions?" Generally, the reviewer does not want to deal with any problems and most likely does not understand the value of the review.

"I once worked with an attorney," Muscianisi relates, "who told me he didn't understand why we had to get any feedback from the employee. After all, he was the boss."

The coach approach. The reviewer who assumes the role of the coach is in a winning situation. Not only will this reviewer deliver the news in a style that is pleasant, but she is willing and expects to hear your thoughts. This reviewer will counsel, offer training, and provide necessary support. The review process becomes a springboard toward achieving further success.

The punitive review. This is a very harsh approach used when there is a serious performance problem. Rather than using the process to reward, something is held back, such as a raise or a promised promotion. You may be transferred to another department or asked to improve within a specified number of days when you will be re-reviewed.

Types of Reviews

There are two types of reviews: performance and salary. Most reviews occur only once per year. "The problem with reviewing performance on a yearly basis," syas Muscianisi, "is that it is not timely. Correcting an off-course pattern or waiting almost a full year to inform a paralegal that her writing skills are under par is harming both the firm and the employee."

Muscianisi recommends reviews twice per year. The first 6 months warrant a "performance only" review. This is the time to let you know how you are doing and plan for the second half of the year, when another performance review is given and salary increases are awarded. New recruits should be given an additional review after their first 90 days to allow both parties to determine whether there is a match.

Combining performance and salary increases in one sitting can be nerve-racking. Many people don't hear the reviewer because they think the real determining factor is in the bottom line. "Yes, but how much did I get?" runs through your mind. That is why many firms choose to have a two-part review. The performance section is given by an attorney and/or paralegal manager most familiar with the work. Salary reveiws should be given by the person actually determining the increase, usually the administrator and/or the paralegal manager. Sometimes the paralegal manager will have the administrator join in during the salary reveiw.

PREPARING FOR YOUR REVIEW

There are three topics covered in the review: your skills, your performance, and your objectives. The key is to come to the review armed with information in all three areas. You are not preparing to defend yourself; rather, you are substantiating your current position and sharing your goals. By doing so, you are taking steps to position yourself to move forward.

If you have prepared a master career plan, you already will have drafted a skills assessment and goal plan. If you haven't prepared your plan, now is the time to do so. For purposes of the review, structure a goal plan to fit with your current situation. For example, if your goal is to be a paralegal manager, what steps can you take in your current position to get closer to your goal? Are you a senior paralegal, but lacking strong supervisory experience? What steps can you take in the next 6 months toward your goal?

Can you supervise a team? A section? Put together a proposal? Select and supervise a project involving vendors?

To get proper perspective on your performance, you can prepare an accomplishment list by reviewing the Legal Assistant Assignment Request forms. If you are not using these, review your time sheets and calendars to track how you have done and what goals you have accomplished throughout the year. Reviewing this data may also provoke a few memories of projects that didn't go so well, so you won't be surprised if these surface in the review.

If you are due for a salary increase, find out ahead of time what percentage of increases the firm or corporation is expected to give. Do not arm yourself with information regarding the increases colleagues receive. Using this information weakens your position. Do, however, come prepared to answer questions such as "How can the firm improve its paralegal program?" or "Do you have any questions?"

DURING THE REVIEW: TECHNIQUES AND TRAPS

How to Handle Directives to Improve

Too often a reviewer gives a directive to improve only to have it fall flat on its face. Vague directives and responses have no merit. "Both of you need to be very specific," says Muscianisi, "because if you aren't, you're wasting time." Here is an example of a vague directive:

Reviewer:	We liked your work this year. The area we want to see improvement is in your organizational skills.
Marla:	OK. I'll try and get more organized.

How was Marla unorganized? Was it her office? Her work product? Her directions to her secretary? How was she expected to improve? Marla might have handled the directive this way.

Marla:	I would like to be more organized. Can you give me some specific examples of how I am unorganized so that I know how to improve?
Reviewer:	Yes. Here is a sample of the index to the research you did of all the products ACME Company produces. While the content was excellent, it would have been better if you had organized the index alphabetically by product name and region where it was produced.

If you receive a punitive review where a raise or promotion has been withheld until "improvement is seen," get very specific with the reviewer as to when this improvement is expected to happen. Does the firm want to see improvement within 30 days? 6 months? Find out. Ask the reviewer how your progress will be monitored. Can you structure progress reports? A vague directive to "see improvement in the future" does not help you. You must establish a time frame and a system to monitor your progress.

Almost all reviews pinpoint areas of improvement. Some evaluators call these "weaknesses," sending a negative message. No one person can possibly have all strengths. If you are told about improvements, find out how the firm will help you achieve this. "I once reviewed a paralegal whose writing skills were poor," says Muscianisi. "She asked if the firm would send her to a continuing education class. In addition, she arranged for a mentor, an attorney whose writing style she admired. She approached the attorney for help. Needless to say, I was very impressed with her attitude. Her next review was excellent."

Listen to the Successes

It's interesting about human nature. For all the good things said about us, we zero right in on the bad things. "When I am handed a stack of my reviews," claims Phill Signey, senior litigation paralegal, "I skim over all the pluses and my eye goes right to the negative remarks. Even if the negatives are only minor, and there's only one or two out of an entire stack, that's what I pay attention to."

According to Natasha Josefowitz, Ph.D., in *Paths to Power*, people learn more from successes than mistakes. That is why it is so important not to take achievements or successes for granted. It is the drive to be perfect that can cause you to undermine the very practices that make you a success. Listen when your reviewer talks about your accomplishments.

State Your Objectives

If the evaluation is drawing to a close and you haven't been asked about goals or objectives, don't hesitate to take a few moments to discuss this topic. Take out your goal plan and go over it with the reviewer. Be sure your objectives coincide with those of the firm; otherwise, you may receive a cold response. Your presentation should also include the benefit to the firm for helping achieve your objectives.

Now is the time to let the firm know your likes, dislikes, and needs. If you don't like sharing an office, now is the time to speak up. Work with the reviewer, not against. "How can we solve this problem?" is much more effective than "I want you to do something for me."

Avoid Emotional Responses

The review process is not the time to get emotional. If you find yourself angry or even in tears, ask to stop. Excuse yourself to get a drink of water. A good reviewer will interrupt the review and create an excuse to leave for a moment, giving you a chance to compose yourself. If that doesn't happen, tell the reviewer the truth, that you are upset by what you are hearing and would like to continue the review when you have calmed down. Don't belabor the process, however. If you are in the review arguing for an hour, it is unlikely the reviewer will want to continue this again on another day. Calm yourself. Anger and tears are not good negotiating techniques.

Some of us have delayed responses, particularly when we are angry. "If a paralegal comes to me a week after the review," says Muscianisi "and tells me she is angry with me about the evaluation I gave, my response is, it's too late. Talk to me during the review while I still have time to do something about it."

Thank the Reviewer

The reviewer usually puts in a good deal of work on your evaluation long before the two of you sit down. Be aware and let the reviewer know you appreciate the amount of time spent on the process. Help cement a good bond, as the reviewer can end up being a great ally.

A well-thought-out performance review will assist in the move onward and upward in your career. Presenting yourself as prepared, able to handle criticism, and ready for future challenges will earn respect from all involved.

NEGOTIATING FOR TOP SALARY INCREASES

Understanding Today's Salary Climate

It's surprising that a drastic recession creating massive layoffs, cutbacks, and downsizing failed to send a wake-up call to many paralegals. Those recently entering the field may be unaware that, previously, major firms across the country bestowed automatic yearly increases, anywhere from 7 to 15 percent, and awarded $1,500 to $20,000 yearly bonuses. Ah, yes, divine decadence. In many situations, tenure with the firm guaranteed job security. There were many "sacred cows" running around. Cost-of-living increases were "silent messages" from the firm: Beware, you're probably out the door.

Standard perks included continuing education, 100 percent paid parking or transportation allowance, 100 percent paid insurance benefits, and private offices. Cubicles were (and still are in many firms) considered demeaning, while window offices announced status. Some firms offered yearly paralegal retreats (which included well-known speakers), health club memberships, access to the firm's dining room, and inclusion in summer associate recruiting functions, such as parties and first-class concerts, theaters, and sporting events. When the biggest complaint by paralegals was noninclusion in summer associate parties, chances are that although paralegals worked hard, life was still pretty good.

The atmosphere was somewhat different for in-house legal departments and many smaller firms, but few worried about downsizing, layoffs, cutbacks, or losing a job when a case settled. Paralegals were more concerned with coping with difficult attorneys, maintaining quality work product, learning about computers (and arguing for one of their own), and getting ahead.

Billable hours expected in return were usually pretty high; in major metropolitan areas the minimum might be 1,800. Ironically, paralegals achieving the minimum were not necessarily considered stars. Simply put, they were "doing what they were supposed to do."

Today, divine decadence is no longer part and parcel of the law firm environment. Job security is a thing of the past, automatic salary increases no longer exist, and competition within the firm or corporate infrastructure is harsher. In order to get a raise, you must demonstrate more than longevity with the firm.

Negotiating in Today's Workplace

The arrival of TQM (Total Quality Management) brought with it a team concept. The theory behind creating teams is empowerment, which in turn emphasizes team building, group communication skills, and increased employee involvement. People who are empowered are thought to need less supervision, training, and praise as well as fewer managers.

Teams are sometimes referred to as pods, self-directed work teams, or modules. Within a team, a player must demonstrate that she is a cooperative member and a self-motivated leader, both in the same role. Confusion arises in acknowledging or recognizing individual contribution. Negotiating for yourself apart from the team can be tough.

Focus in the legal field has shifted sharply from promoting individual fulfillment to emphasizing bottom-line results. More and more employees are feeling less and less valued for what they do. The salary negotiating process is tougher than ever, as bottom-line results pressure employees to do more with less. Raises have most likely been determined at the beginning of the fiscal year, regardless of how you do during the year. Budgets are strictly adhered to and few exceptions can be made.

Getting a raise for yourself is a difficult task. Because many have identities tied directly to careers, asking for a salary that is comparable to our "worth" can become a conversation about self-worth. This kind of mixed-up thinking hinders us from artfully and unemotionally negotiating for our needs. We either reluctantly take whatever is handed out or come away feeling we bungled the job. The overall end result can be resentment, anxiety, and lowering of self-esteem.

Believe it or not, the negotiating process can be invigorating, exciting, and fun. Sitting at the negotiating table doesn't have to be a nerve-racking experience *if* you know what you are doing and what to expect. Remember, you are talking about market, competitive value, and dollars in exchange for skill level, and *not* self-worth. By keeping this a business transaction, not an emotional issue, you will get closer to obtaining your final goal.

Who are the Players?

Before walking into the meeting to discuss your salary increase, understand that reviewers are in the dominant position. They are in possession of the missing piece of information—they already know the amount of your increase. While this gives them an "upper hand," it's merely temporary. As we go through the negotiating strategy process, you will see how to be in a position of strength rather than defenselessness.

Start by assessing the background of the negotiators. Attorneys have at least 3 years of negotiating skill training in law school. Unfortunately, I am unaware of any comparable programs for paralegals. Administrators or paralegal managers have undergone the negotiating process so many times during hiring season or year-end that they have equally sharp skills. The strategy is not to outmaneuver your "opponent" but rather to bring about a mutually beneficial conclusion where both parties are satisfied.

Find out ahead of time exactly what the negotiator's limits of authority are. You are about to entrust your livable wage to her. Does she have full, limited, or no authority? Is this person really only the messenger, or the person who actually calculated your increase? This bit of information is vital to your strategy to calculate just how far you can effectively take negotiations, or whether you need to enlist this person's help in a meeting with the ultimate authority.

Your Prenegotiating Research

Research the market. Use your unique fact-finding skills by reviewing as many paralegal salary surveys as possible. It is particularly important to find out what surveys are used by the firm. It will do no good to put merit into the local paralegal association survey if the only survey the firm views with credibility is that of the ALA (Association of Legal Administrators). Use of a national survey can sometimes backfire if you are in a region or city that pays more than other parts of the country. Lower salary input brings averages down. For example, Los Angeles is one of the highest paying cities for paralegals. Using national information brings the averages down, whereas local surveys keep those salaries up. Many firms don't like surveys compiled by paralegals. They prefer data supplied by the supervisor. Therefore, surveys such as ALA (Association of Legal Administrators) and LAMA (Legal Assistant Managers Association) have become very popular.

Ranges. Unless you are with a corporation that sets down specific grades equal to a specific salary, you will fall within a range. Firms intent on keeping good employees find that their paralegals fall within the upper 10 to 25 percentile.

Percentage of increases. Find out what percentage of overall increases the firm intends to give for the year. Some firms have a more liberal policy than others, and those firms will announce, either formally or informally, that the increases will be between x and x percent.

Corporations generally announce information prior to budget preparation. Each firm or corporation is unique. Some pretend not to let percentage of increases become public information, yet somehow "the grapevine" (not always the most reliable source) is chockful of information.

Another source to ignore is how much colleagues received. It's really not information you are entitled to, and whether this person is undermarket, has extenuating circumstances, or is coloring the truth is not your business. If you are a senior-level paralegal receiving top salary, the firm may have decided to cap your salary. We will discuss how to deal with this particular situation in a moment.

Practice tip. If the firm has decided to give, for example, raises between 4 and 6 percent, don't expect to receive 7 or 8 percent because your work was superior this year. Most firms and corporations will try to stay within budgetary restraints.

History of assignments for the year. Your prenegotiation research should include a history of assignments for the year.

You will be in a stronger negotiating position knowing your accomplishments, who said great things, and how your level of assignments improved over the year.

Know your billables. Know whether your minimum billable hourly requirements were met (if in a corporation, make sure to meet required hours). If this is a criterion to determining amount of the raise, know ahead of time whether you have met or surpassed requirements.

Find out your percentage of write-offs. In some firms, this is information you are entitled to; in others it's a well-kept secret. Don't violate firm policy. However, if judged on this criterion, know about it to improve your situation, if necessary. Are write-offs a result of fee negotiation between partner and client, or a result of bad work product? Don't wait until the negotiating process to find out whether you have met tangible criteria. It'll be too late to strategize.

Calculating Your Acceptable Increase Range

By conducting prenegotiating research, you will have a pretty good idea what to expect. Decide what your acceptable range of increase will be. Say, for example, you are currently earning $36,000 per year. After completing your prenegotiating research, you determine that current market value for your position is $38,000 to $40,000. The firm will give raises this year between 3 and 7 percent. Your firm's billable requirement is 1,800 hours per year and your total is 1,900. Your percentage of write-off time is minimal, and your history of assignments demonstrates an increase in responsiblities (you were the case manager on *Doe*). Attorney Smith was more than satisfied with your work; however, Attorney Jones was upset with several summaries. Overall, it was a pretty good year.

A quick calculation shows that a 7 percent raise brings $2,520 more per year, for a total income of $38,520 per year. Your natural reaction is to want the full 7 percent. However, a reality check says that your billables did not far exceed the minimum and there were some concerns over portions of your work. You decide that your range of acceptability (what you will comfortably settle for) is between 5 and 7 percent. Do not lock yourself into one number. A range allows flexibility.

Now, with prenegotiation work completed, you are ready to sit at the table. Be sure to bring all documentation to the meeting. It's better to walk in with more information than actually needed.

Remember the power of the written word, particularly in a law firm. People generally believe what they have read. Recently, there was an article in a local newspaper about a woman who was struck by a car as she crossed the street. A week later, the paper ran another article stating that it had misidentified the woman. In the meantime, the woman phoned her brother to let him know that she was alive and well and not harmed at all. "But I read it in the paper," claimed the brother. Because it is written, it must be so, even in a law firm where the very nature of the litigation department is to dissect or question the written word. Policy manuals, procedures, and job descriptions are carefully drafted. The fact that most of them sit on a shelf for 5 years until the firm decides on new procedures or job descriptions is irrelevant. The firm may want to bring out their written word (budget, surveys, and reviews), and you will immediately be able to counter with your written word.

At the Negotiating Table

Whatever brought you to the table (review time, discovering you were below market, a midyear increase for additional duties, leaving but a raise could make you stay, promoted but received no increase), culminates with the one-on-one meeting. The difference between negotiating for a raise and negotiating for salary on a new job is that in this case, the "opponent" will most likely state the figures first, putting you in an advantageous position. You can (1) happily accept, (2) use a total counter approach (using your prenegotiation research), or (3) use a limited counter approach.

Use a total counter approach when you are uncomfortable with everything you have just heard from your opponent. For example, you have determined that the acceptable range of increase is 5 to 7 percent and you are handed a 4 percent increase. Don't get insulted. You know immediately what kind of work you have ahead.

Use a limited counter approach when what you have just heard from your opponent is partially acceptable. For example, you just learned that you will receive 4 percent, which you decide to accept provided other necessary needs are met. Because you were case manager this year, there are other tools you will need for your position. You accept the 4 percent and negotiate for the tools.

At the outset of either approach, realize that whatever salary or perks the firm decides to bestow upon you must be met with a realized benefit to the firm in doing so. Train yourself to present a benefit to the firm for each request. Assuming that the firm will automatically know what the benefit to the firm is undermines your position. They may have to have it spelled out—in which case be prepared.

Negotiating Through Job Redesign

The evaluation process is fashioned to point out areas of strength and improvement (some firms still insist on calling these "weaknesses"). In this business climate, how well you perform your duties does not always render a significant raise or promotion. Some companies have adopted the attitude, "that's why we pay you—to do a good job."

As dysfunctional and unmotivating as this sounds, businesses will do just about anything these days to avoid rising overhead. Since corporate clients have revolted against excessive legal fees, raising paralegal billing rates to accommodate salary increases is not always the best way to retain clients.

What can you do? The budget game is an odd game at best. Interestingly enough, most firms and corporations can skirt around budgets through a "budget deviation." This justification can be accomplished through a new position or redesigning the job you have.

Redesigning your job involves homework and a plan. If you are having performance problems for any reason, now is the time to clean up your act. If it is your pattern to turn in assignments late or with errors (no matter how small), take steps toward correction. Otherwise, you will not be able to sell management on a job redesign.

One very effective technique is to focus on strengths you can turn into opportunities leading to a better job within the firm. For example, in Jim's yearly salary review, he requested a salary increase that went well over the cap of 9 percent maximum (for stellar performance). While he had performed well, there wasn't too much his supervisor could do to get Jim a higher increase. Jim's strengths were managing other paralegals and excelling in recruiting and staffing. He countered by redesigning his job to capitalize on his management techniques. The firm no longer had a paralegal manager full-time and was most likely not willing to recreate the position. Jim's homework showed that at least 15 percent of an associate's time was spent traveling to a suburban office to supervise, manage, and recruit paralegals. Jim redesigned his position to reduce the associate's time to 5 percent. Jim would pick up the other 10 percent, thus causing the firm to benefit through increased associated billing dollars.

Further, Jim's computer and training expertise enabled him to redesign his position to include instructing new hires, eliminating expensive outside consultants. Had Jim resigned his position as a full-time manager, chances are he would have been turned down. Reasons for rejection—the firm's reluctance to hire a nonrevenue-generating administrator, and Jim had no full-time experience as a manager.

The important lesson here is Jim created an opportunity to rise within the organization *and* get more money. Redesigning his present position to play up his strengths resulted in opportunities stretching beyond his current job description. This allowed the firm's administrator to approve a raise that went beyond rewarding good past performance. Now the firm had a new position and could expand beyond the allotted budgetary restraints.

Go for the Gold: Negotiating for Other Perks

There are other forms of compensation besides salary. These perks are the equivalent of dollars in your pocket. Let's say Sue wanted an 8 percent increase, which totals out to $2,880, but she is able to get only 7 percent ($2,520). She immediately negotiates a CEB course for herself worth $300. Her total compensation package increases by $2,820. She's happy and the firm is happy, a mutually beneficial negotiation.

So, what can I negotiate? How do I get the firm or corporation to agree? Here are a few suggestions together with benefits to the firm.

- **Title**—Get an official title. You may have to make one up. This is worth its weight in silver: You can take it when you leave and use it to springboard your career. *Benefit to the firm:* Through a title, you can raise my billable rate because I now become an expert in this field. You can also win more client confidence by presenting a specialty paralegal on their matters.

- **Continuing education**—Increasing knowledge in your field can increase the level of job assignments and responsibilities. *Benefit to the firm:* This investment will bring more expertise to the firm. We will be able to delegate a broader range of assignments downward from the associate. This frees up associates for a higher level of assignment, thus increasing billables and decreasing turnover in both associates and paralegals for lack of stimulation and overload of repetitious work.

- **Salary bonus**—Not to be confused with year-end, Christmas, or merit bonus, the salary bonus is a great counter when the firm gives the maximum salary increase and you are still far apart. It is a one-time bonus given in addition to the yearly or monthly increase. When the firm says, "This is all we are allowed to give according to the budget" (that written word again), respond with, "I appreciate all of the work that has gone into calculating my increase. However, we are still $1,000 away from where I should be in the marketplace. Let me propose a one-time salary bonus." *Benefit to the firm:* Amortized over one year, it is a minuscule amount of dollars that they can probably pull from a different part of the budget.

- **Better office**—*Benefit to the firm:* I will be closer to attorneys I work with, making it more efficient for them to use my skills.

- **Time off for teaching a class**—*Benefit to the firm:* Here is great PR about our paralegal program. I will also spot those entry-level paralegals we may want to recruit for our own firm, saving agency fees, newspaper ads, and other related recruiting expenses.

- **Cross-training**—*Benefit to the firm:* You can use my skills in other areas of the firm. As our corporate (probate, etc.) work decreases or has its peaks and valleys, you can still use my expertise in other areas. My billables won't suffer and I will maintain profitability.
- **Association dues**—*Benefit to the firm:* An inexpensive way to acknowledge professionalism.
- **Your own or shared secretary**—*Benefit to the firm:* As I enter a more senior status position, I am capable of putting out more work. A secretarial pool situation does not allow the firm to fully maximize my output.
- **Firm credit card**—Touchy area, this one. *Benefit to the firm:* Because I am usually at my credit limit on my own credit cards, by using a firm credit card for traveling expenses, I will not be prohibited from fully doing my job.
- **All expense paid trip to out-of-town seminar**—What a great learning experience for you! *Benefit to the firm:* I will be able to inform the firm on the latest policies discussed at the seminar.

If the Firm Caps Your Salary

Admittedly, this is a tough situation. Generally, capping is done at the senior levels and is a result of the firm's inability to raise paralegal billing rates. Now is the time to negotiate a management level position, if you are not already in one. If you are, now is the time to boost yourself one step higher, even if none exists. The salary bonus is a good strategy. You may also be able to negotiate a stronger merit bonus.

It's possible that you won't have favorable marketplace data, so you will need to conduct an independent survey to find out what other senior paralegals with upgraded titles are making. Enlist the help of your supervisor, who can more readily obtain information. There has been discussion between managers as to whether the informal survey is legal or legitimate. If you are at all in question, bounce it off one of the firm's attorneys. Some firms have no qualms at all. Don't be afraid to sound out other areas of the country. Adjust the salary according to your marketplace. Remember that a specialty within almost any practice area can help justify an increase beyond what the firm may want to give.

John was a senior litigation paralegal with more than 8 years' experience in a midsized firm in San Francisco. He was earning $43,000 per year. The firm felt his performance was superb but the full 8 percent raise would bring him $1,640 over the $45,000 cap the firm could offer paralegals. The firm did not want to lose John, nor was John particularly interested in leaving. Since John had demonstrated talent in litigation support software, he was able to successfully negotiate a title—litigation support advisor (not quite manager, but getting closer); a course at the local university worth $400; a one-time bonus of $750; and an upgraded, faster computer. He positioned himself to springboard right into the area in which he was most interested. The firm was satisfied because it was getting a more valuable employee without compromising its boundaries.

NEGOTIATING SALARY FOR A NEW POSITION

Almost everything we have talked about so far can be used to negotiate salary for a new position. However, there are some additions and adjustments.

Instead of the one-time salary bonus, you may be able to negotiate a hiring bonus. This technique, used primarily to bring in lateral associates, is also a good technique for senior- or management-level paralegals. For example, Julie was a litigation support manager seeking a lateral move. Her salary at her present firm was $43,000. The new firm was not willing to offer more than $41,500. Julie was able to make the move for $41,500 plus a $1,500 hiring bonus. Her risk was in betting that the following year her raise would take her beyond the $43,000 mark. It may not take her as far as her previous firm would have, but she positioned herself for advancement in the new firm, not easily done in the old firm.

When you have done your homework and are comfortable with your acceptable range, never announce to your potential employer that you are "looking for between $36,000 and $38,000." Playing your hand gives the potential employer permission to offer you $36,000, and possibly less. I can't tell you how many paralegals I have heard complain that they couldn't believe their ears when the offer came in for the lower amount. This is a business transaction. No firm or corporation is going to give you top dollar out of the goodness of its heart or because you're a nice person. Ask for exactly what you want. Give yourself an acceptable range, but ask for the top dollar.

Present Salary versus New Salary

The salary question usually comes in two varieties. "What kind of salary are you looking for?" is *not* permission to name your dream salary. ("I'd love to see $85,000" is not quite the answer if you're currently making $30,000.) Either in place of or right after the "looking for" question will be, "And how much are you currently earning?" This is the crucial spot in your negotiating process. It's best to talk in terms of total compensation package (your salary plus your year-end bonus and any overtime that you were paid last year). You will have to break it down for the interviewer, but the goal is to meet or surpass your current salary. Don't include benefits such as parking, medical insurance, and so forth. Be careful on the overtime issue. If you are moving from a firm or corporation that pays overtime to a firm that doesn't, you're likely to take an unwanted cut if you don't negotiate carefully.

If you are looking for a princely bump up, you're going to have to justify it. The best thing to do is to answer each question and pause. "I am looking for $40,000." Stop. Wait for a question. Don't justify this yet. "My total compensation package is $35,000." Stop. Wait for a reaction. What will immediately go through the interviewer's mind is: What makes this person worth $5,000 more to this firm than where she is currently employed? "My present firm, while I am not eager to leave (always make yourself a little hard to get), is not able to pay market value for me at this time," or "My skill level has surpassed the salary I am currently earning. I have worked very hard the past year(s) to upgrade my skill level to _____ which could fit in nicely with your firm's current needs."

If you are leaving too much on the table, leave the door open to be rereviewed in 3 to 6 months. If you are negotiating for a new job and didn't get quite what was expected, ask to have a salary review in 90 days. Some firms have the attitude that you are an unproven commodity. A 90-day salary review (*not* performance, which can mean no increase) can be negotiated. Be sure you get the rereview or salary review in writing. Three months down the line it will be difficult for the reviewer to recall exactly what was said, or it's even possible that the same person will not be in that position.

What You Can't Use as Negotiating Tools

Stick to job skills and duties. Don't waste your time trying to justify more salary by using the following tactics:

- I have to drive farther.
- The hours are different.
- I have 1 hour for lunch at my old firm but only 45 minutes here.
- I have a better office where I am now.
- I'm going to get a raise in 6 months at my present job (stick to what is, not what might be).
- I have to pay the babysitter more.
- It costs more to park here.

- I will have to wear a suit; my old firm is less formal.
- Sue got a 10 percent increase.

I once sent a candidate from Los Angeles to interview with a firm in Orange County. The candidate wanted more money because she would have to drive an hour to work. The administrator was less than sympathetic. Her drive from Pasadena was an hour and a half. Needless to say, the candidate did not get the job.

EFFECTIVE NEGOTIATING TECHNIQUES

How you portray yourself in the negotiating session has an overall effect on your success. If you appear nervous, angry, emotional, upset, hostile, insulted, ready to do battle, or negative in any way, your chances of succeeding can decrease.

If, on the other hand, you portray a positive, confident, easygoing professional (even if you are extremely nervous), the other party will probably mirror you. In order to effect a smooth session, here are some phrases you might use (put into your own words) when you've hit a snag:

- "Let me give you a different perspective on that."
- "However" (never "but," which is too negative).
- "I understand how you feel." Empathy is a great tool.
- "I understand how you have reached that conclusion. However, let me present a different interpretation of the data."
- "I need your help."
- "An alternative solution might be . . . ."
- "According to market . . . ."

If you hear the famous line, "If we do that for you, we have to do it for everyone," suggest an alternative. For example, "I realize if you send me to a continuing education class, you'll have to send everyone. An alternative solution is to send me and upon my return, I will hold a training session for all paralegals. That way, everyone gets trained."

If you hear, "It's not in the budget," respond with "Here's a way we can make it happen." Including the other party in a team approach is always effective.

Don't Use Ultimatums

All I can say about ultimatums is, don't issue them. They aren't effective. An ultimatum, such as "If I don't get this raise, I'm leaving," may cause you to leave. You are put in an adversarial position. This tough spot in the middle of a law firm whose reputation rests on how well it handles adversaries is not a pretty picture.

A decision to leave should be based on many factors. If you did not come away in a better position, wait at least a month to mull things over. Make an intelligent, informed decision about leaving. Above all, don't walk into the negotiating session with an "all or nothing" attitude. You'll be defeated easily.

Establishing Commitment and Deadlines

One of the most common techniques salespeople learn is to get a commitment from the buyer. The same technique works in a law firm. "If I understand correctly," you say, "you'd like to see every paralegal in this firm receive discovery training." "Yes, definitely," says the firm. "Great. An alternative solution would be . . . ."

According to Herb Cohen, author of *You Can Negotiate Anything,* conclusions to the negotiations will occur as close to the deadline as possible. Therefore, in order to make this an event that concludes within a realistic time frame, establish a deadline for resolution. If you are negotiating for a position, find out when a decision will most likely be made. If they are deciding between you and one other candidate, inform them that you would appreciate knowing by a certain date, as you have other offers to consider. If you are negotiating for a raise and the firm needs to think it over, ask how soon they can get back to you. If they say "next week," get a day. Otherwise, you can get bumped because of other priorities.

In order for things to move, get involved with the process. Only you can take your career and make it what you want. The negotiating process is a perfect opportunity to help shape that career.

PARALEGAL INNER VIEW: SIGRID LAYNE— FIGHTING THE UNIONS

Name: Sigrid Layne
Title: Paralegal
Firm: National Right to Work Legal Defense Foundation, Springfield, VA
Number of attorneys/paralegals: 10 attorneys, 4 paralegals
Experience: 7+ years
Education: B.S. degree/Administration of Criminal Justice, University of North Carolina Chapel Hill; Paralegal Certificate from the Institute for Paralegal Training, an ABA-approved school in Philadelphia

Job duties: My main job is to answer e-mails to the foundation from people asking for legal help. We have a Web site and people hear about us. I go through the e-mails and decide whether we can help them. The foundation provides legal assistance to people who feel they are being coerced into being a union member. We only assist people who feel like their employer is telling them they have to be a union member to keep their jobs. We deal a lot with strikes—much like the one the actors are having in California, regarding commercials. We're not against unions. We only protect those who might get fired it they have to cross the picket line to support their families, or victims of violence. I refer clients to attorneys on staff. If I can't, I have a database that I recommend like the NLRB or EEOC. I know just about everything on the Internet.

I conduct research. Attorneys will give me an issue and I will come up with some cases using Westlaw or LEXIS. If they give me a topic, I may have to search a lot of sites. For example, one of the attorneys wanted me to find the first date of a case in any newspaper. I had to search extensively. I work a lot of hours. Sometimes I could be here until 6 or 7 at night. One of the perks I have, though, is that my firm pays for my education.

I also work for an attorney where we do the Massachusetts teacher's case. This is a situation where the teachers belong to a union and object to paying fees. I work on those from beginning to end. They're being told, "If you don't pay your money, we'll fire you."

Another attorney I was working with was assigned to a case in Michigan. We all went to Lansing and did the research for 2 weeks. It was a lot of fun. We worked 12-hour days but afterwards, we went to Canada or Detroit. I had never flown before.

This sounds like an awesome responsibility. What do you like best about the job?

To me, it's always doing the research and I find what they want. I didn't go to law school because I like behind the scenes. I like finishing tasks. I like libraries and research. I found one issue for an attorney in an hour. That's what it's all about.

Does this job pay well?

People want to know how much money I make. It's not about the money. It's about the gratification of the job. It's about what you do.

Where would you like this job to take you?

I think I'll always be a paralegal. I don't think I'll burn out. I want to be a manager and teach entry-level paralegals the ins-and-outs of the field. It's hot now and we need paralegals and managers who train people just coming into the field. I don't think I'm using anything I learned in paralegal school except research skills. Everything is hands-on experience.

Where's this career going, can you tell us?

I have seen on the Internet that paralegals think we should be certified. I only agree to the extent that not anybody can call themselves a paralegal. You must have work experience or education. I hope eventually it will be a recognized field as the job duties become more defined. I'd like to see less secretarial duties, more travel, more trial and research responsibilities so attorneys respect you for what you do.

CHAPTER 23

How Partners Get Paid Those Big Bucks

Have you ever wondered how partners get paid? Usually, paralegals are aware that partners split the profits at the end of the year and get by for 11 months on some kind of lowered salary or partner draw. Other than that, most of the mechanics as to how the pie is divvied up remains a mystery. Why is it important that paralegals have this insider information? The more you understand the economics of your industry, the better grasp you will have on what it is you need to do to get ahead. If you worked as a buyer in retail, you would have to understand how much a dress cost wholesale in order to know how much to mark it up and how much profit the store would receive. The more you participate in generating that profit, the better chance you'll have to advance within the company. The more you understand about profit, the better you'll react when certain decisions in the firm are made.

All too often, paralegals and other nonattorney members of the firm do not have a realistic picture of what profitability looks like. When raise time comes around, and certain requests for increases are deemed out of reach, employees sometimes rationalize that the request was denied and therefore unfair because, after all, "the partners are the ones making the big bucks around here" (off my hard work is the often implied complaint). How those big bucks are made no one is quite sure, but at least it feels better to put the blame on greed rather than on practicality.

In the September 2000 issue of *Partner's Report,* Joel Rose, consultant to law firms, discussed partnership compensation plans. Following is what he had to say.

A DIGEST OF SELECTED PARTNERSHIP DISTRIBUTION PLANS

Percentages. The most frequently used system involves percentages determined at the beginning of each year, backed by statistics for each attorney that show billable and consequential nonbillable time, billings, collections, aging of accounts receivable, amounts of write-offs and write-downs of un-billed time, disbursements, and write-ups of bills.

For example, a firm of three partners may determine that each will share in the net profit by allocating 45 percent, 30 percent, and 25 percent, respectively. The gross fees collected total $650,000; with overhead at 42 percent; the net profit to be distributed is $377,000. At the end of the year, the first partner, with a 45 percent allocation, receives $269,650; the second, with 30 percent, receives $113,100; and the third, with 25 percent, receives $94,250. The percentages, as recommended by a firm's committee, may be final or subject to approval by the firm's management.

As firms increase in size, problems arise. First, it may become burdensome to calculate each partner's percentage share. A second difficulty inherent in using a percentage system is that the total of percentage points must equal 100. If a partner wants to receive a greater percentage, one or more partners must relinquish a corresponding share.

Units-of-participation distribution plan. This system allows the partners to achieve the same allocation results as a percentage plan without having to contend with the 100 percent ceiling. Under a units plan, partners are assigned units in accordance with their contributions and other factors. The firm places no limit on the total number of units that may be assigned.

For instance, in the firm of AB&C, A may have 40 units, B may have 35 units, and C may have 25 units. A will receive 40/100ths of net profit, B will receive 35/100ths, and C will receive 25/100ths. The following year, the allocations to B and C are increased: A receives 40 units; B, 40 units; and C, 30 units. A and B each receive 40/100ths of the firm's net profit; C receives 30/100ths. Although A's proportionate share of income decreases in the second year in relation to B and C, A has not had to "give up" any units.

Percentages or units of participation with a reserve ranging from 5 percent to 10 percent of net profit plan. This plan is based on the year's performance. The reserve is allocated to individual partners based upon their perceived contribution to the firm, determined either under a formula or subjectively.

For example, a firm has a net profit of $377,000 and 10 percent reserve. The distributable profit to be allocated, according to straight percentage, would be $339,300—that is, $377,000 minus $37,700. The reserve, $37,700, is allocated to deserving partners subjectively, based on their contribution to the previous year's performance. Factors that a committee may consider in determining how to allocate the reserve may include hours worked, fees collected, consequential nonbillable hours devoted, business origination, profitability as the result of billings and collections, administrative skills, and the like. After analyzing the partner's respective contributions, the committee may determine that one partner should receive 50 percent of the reserve, or $18,850, for having originated substantial fees. A second partner receives 35 percent of the reserve, or $13,195, for having managed a large case and collecting substantial fees. A third partner receives 15 percent or $5,655 for having developed an in-house specialty and managing the associates' career-development program.

Variable of percentages or units approach. This approach establishes a variable of percentages or units based upon seniority, reputation, past performance, and anticipated performance, with the balance or profits divided equally. Each partner receives a variable draw.

For example, A receives $120,000; B, $150,000; and C, $95,000—determined according to the preceding factors. At the end of the year, the balance of the net profit to be distributed amounts of $57,000. This is divided equally so that each partner receives a bonus of $19,000.

Some firms establish standard draws among all partners or among classes of partners, paying variable bonuses according to each partner's contribution. For example, at the beginning of the year, all partners or classes of partners may receive a standard draw of $95,000. At yearend, the committee allocates variable bonuses based upon partner's contributions to the firm.[1]

Because the environment is changing for law firms, changes in partnership compensation affects you, as a paralegal. Revamping anyone's pay structure affects firm's revenues, structure, competition, client loyalty, valuation, and more. It affects your compensation package now and in the future. When firm revenues drop, even a small percentage, painful and sometimes adverse reactions by the firm occur. These reactions can take the form of decreased staff bonuses, salary, perks, and more. The more money the firm earns, the fewer problems it generally has—on the surface, at least. Flaws in partner compensation plans tend to stay beneath the surface as long as there is a lot of money coming in the door—but watch out if income drops!

Paralegals generally have little or no access to information regarding how well the firm is doing. Frankly, most firms feel it is not information that needs to be shared with staff. However, a well-run firm reflects a much higher morale which is important to your overall job satisfaction. Those firms that maintain fiscal responsibility by channeling revenue back into the business are operating correctly. Partners who pay every penny of profits to themselves and head to the bank for working capital are not managing their firms properly.

---

[1]Reprinted with permission from Joel A. Rose, Joel A. Rose & Associates, Inc., Cherry Hill, New Jersey; 800-381-1645; www.joelarose.com.

PARALEGAL INNER VIEW: SPENCER COSPER—
PARALEGAL TURNS VENDOR

Name: Spencer Cosper
Company: CaseCentral, Washington, D.C.
Title: Sales Executive
Years of experience: 1 year at CaseCentral; 11 years at Litigation Systems, a regional scanning bureau; also owned Cypress Technologies, Inc. in Baton Rouge, Louisiana.
Job history: Our largest client was Baker and McKinzie. I cut my teeth with them. I was working as the assistant to the General Counsel of a *Fortune* 500 company that went bankrupt. It was the third largest electrical contractor in the United States. They were bonded by Aetna and represented by Baker & MacKinzie. While I was on this case, in walk two partners (I had no grasp of the magnitude of their reputation) and they offer me a position to come work for them reviewing tens of thousands of claims. Therein began an enjoyable life-altering experience and entry into the paralegal profession. I dove into that and was eventually offered a position as construction litigation expert.

I came to the business as a paralegal consultant and saw the need for a litigation technician. My wife and I started our firm to offer scanning and coding to B&M. I was assured if you build it, they will come. We took on other firms as a result. This was somewhat in the infancy of scanning days back in the early to mid 1990s when scanning was a new concept. When I sold the company, it was a concept as opposed to now where it is a commodity. After selling the business, we came to D.C. when Litigation Systems, Inc. acquired us. My wife is still a project manager there. I was in San Francisco on a large case as I was a sales rep for LSI. I took one look at what they were doing with their browser-based ASP model and told my wife, "I have seen the future," and wanted to go to work for them. Six months later, they offered me a job. I came from digging through boxes to a sales executive.

Job duties: My responsibilities are finding and obtaining and generating new revenue opportunities on the east coast. Through traditional means, which includes networking and leveraging existing client relationships, we're well known. We spend half of our time responding to inquiries about us. We have a repository solution for large cases. Beyond that, it's typical sales approach that anyone in the legal market is challenged with—which means picking up the phone and calling. The source is any number of information pieces including directories, AmLaw 100 list, etc.

Application Service Providers is a phrase widely embraced. We provide an application and like to think of ourselves as ASP+. You have a big case that involves a number of parties with lots of different sites, geographies, diverse parties in different locations and because our application takes place on the Internet, it is browser-based. If you have access to the Internet, you can access our site and do, in effect, with the browser what you do with your client server that sits in your office. Anyone can access with passwords and take advantage of a common database. They can access secure sites—but not anyone can log in. It is an extremely secure environment.

What's the biggest challenge of this job?

I think right now, the biggest challenge is continuing to differentiate ourselves from the increasing crowded space in ASP. There is an explosion in legal ASP. The challenge we have is to try to make sure we are accurately perceived by the market in how we are different. I am routinely amazed when I am out in the market.

How's the money?

You can make good money in the legal arena. I like working with the people. You shouldn't be in sales if you are not a people person.

What's your next step?

I really like what I'm doing. This is an exciting place to be right now. We're on the cutting edge of technology in a constantly evolving market. Scanning and coding isn't anything like this. We are constantly being challenged by the needs of our clients for new and better things to do. Who can say what the limits of the Internet are?

Predict the future for us.

As the Internet becomes more and more commonplace and high bandwidth becomes more available, everything is going to be moving toward the Internet. The whole idea of loading into a browser is there. We have attorneys and paralegals who are not carrying around their laptops anymore. Because I can go to any computer at any location and I can log on to a Web site from that computer, I have everything I need from there. You don't have to carry a laptop. It is changing the paradigm of the way people will take care of their cases and manage documents.

There cannot be enough said about embracing Web-based technology. I believe that is the direction everything will go. Being aware of all of these changes and being comfortable in the way law is practiced is clearly not only beneficial but, frankly, bulletproofing comes to mind. If you want to be at the top of your job, you must embrace and work with this technology because it will become standard. People don't call up and say whether we're going to scan and code. That's a given. They're now saying, "let's turn to an ASP."

CHAPTER 24

Toxic Bosses

> Go ahead. Make my day.
>
> Clint Eastwood in *Dirty Harry,* 1971

EMOTIONAL ABUSE

The first edition of the *Paralegal Career Guide* included a section entitled, "Dealing with Difficult Attorneys." Along with hundreds of other career authors, I categorized workplace behavioral problems into tidy little boxes, classified by cutesy labels, such as "the whiner," "the screamer," "the mixed-message sender," and offered up Dear Abby-like suggestions to effectively cope with the offender.

Since that time I have had the good fortune to "go to the top of the mountain" by personally experiencing toxic bosses. I say good fortune because, as paralyzed as I was, the revelation was emblazoned in my memory forever, becoming the most valuable lesson of my career:

No one has to tolerate emotional abuse.

The great silent secret of the American workplace is that emotional abuse is a far more pervasive problem than sexual, age, or race discrimination. While activists, politicians, and litigants crowd the airwaves decrying incidents of harassment or wrongful termination, no one to my knowledge wants to look openly at chronic emotional abuse and the terrible toll it routinely takes. Emotional abuse can run rampant in the workplace, and particularly in law firms. Who among us has not experienced verbal lashings from a ranting attorney, raging administrator, vindictive colleague, or even the firm's best client?

This is not the occasional flare-up or venting of emotions. Emotional abuse is routine verbal battering by a firm member or client causing a chaotic environment, state of flux, animosity, or anxiety in employees. This behavior is usually tolerated by management for those who hold positions perceived as "important." Rarely is this behavior tolerated from someone who has no strong political standing in the firm.

Rainmakers and firm "stars" labeled "difficult to work with" are either excused from unacceptable behavior or given slaps on the wrist when the offense is committed. Without proper education of what encompasses emotional abuse, the entire firm can then participate in the cover-up. No firm willingly admits to emotionally abusing employees. However, in my opinion, a few actions illustrate how a firm can enable an abuser:

1. Moves the abuser to an office out of the mainstream (taking no real steps to correct the problem)
2. Tells employees "that's just the way John always behaves"
3. Explains constant turnover of workmates such as secretaries with "he's hard to work for," or worse, "she's just very demanding" (touching here on the gender issue)
4. Constantly checks the offender's mood to determine the kind of day coworkers can expect
5. Tolerates an atmosphere under which employees live in constant fear of losing their jobs
6. Tolerates a client who constantly yells or hangs up the phone on employees while constantly threatening to remove the account
7. Not realizing the impact of a constant and repetitious threat to employees that "if they don't do (blank) they will lose their jobs"
8. Tolerates constant and continuous "scolding."

The following examples illustrate typical circuitous support of the abuser:

1. A partner is told that he should not have yelled at an associate in the hallways. He should have done so in his office.
2. The administrator silently comforts upset employees in the hope that the partners will talk to the offender.
3. Hard-to-believe behavior by attorney A is tolerated because she brings "important clients" to the firm and is a heavy revenue generator. Someone in the mailroom, however, is fired for similar behavior.
4. The firm has "talks" with the abuser yet is convinced the problem "isn't that bad," while employees at a lower level swear otherwise; the firm describes the emotional abuser as "abrupt and sometimes rude."
5. The abuser is deemed a "sacred cow," important to management because she holds a magic key: she's the only one in the firm the client likes or the only one who knows the computer system. She may be the only person who can, in turn, manage a "difficult" attorney. This person, in effect, holds the firm hostage.
6. The phrase "politically incorrect" is used to downplay the behavior.
7. Employees hesitate to answer the phone, dread listening to voice mail, or do not promptly return calls from "him."

The cycle of abuse stemming from attorneys, according to *California Lawyer* magazine, begins when law professors verbally batter their students, turning out "mean-spirited attorneys who browbeat their opponents and mistreat clients." This article could have added "and tyrannize their staff and colleagues." One paperback, titled *29 Reasons Not to Go to Law School* (Nolo Press, 1982), illustrates what happens to people before and after school: "Before law school, a human being has compassion, intelligence, ego, love and mirth. After law school, most of those qualities have disappeared and now the lawyer has ambition, ego, compulsive inclination and a competitive nature."

Some paralegals acquiesce to screaming, harsh criticism, or continual threats of job loss. To not endure it can be construed as a weakness: "You've got to be tough to work here." (It's better not to risk your job by addressing the abuse.)

One employee talked about a temporary job she held for 2 years. The litigation supervisor was described by superiors as having a "brusque management style." The temporary had another story: "One day," she said, "So-and-so was in a bad mood because a federal investigation was causing everyone in the office distress. He told me I was fired and sent me home. A couple of hours later he called and asked what I was doing home. We never knew from day to day what would happen next."

Employees are taught to "take the heat" and, in doing so, receive positive feedback: "You're the only one who can handle Screaming Mimi." So repetitive and constant are the incidents in some offices that it becomes almost impossible to distinguish between letting off steam and abusive behavior.

Avoiding or denying abusive behavior reinforces its pattern and promotes tolerance of unacceptable behavior. Occasionally, a higher-up will mediate or consult with these troublemakers, but the general tendency is to create solutions that fail to address the real causes. Rarely is the offending behavior made the focus or the abuser forced to change. Employees participate in the conspiracy by refusing to speak up.

"Stress is the number one injury in the workplace," says Dr. Jerome Franklin, a noted Beverly Hills psychiatrist. "Because an arm or leg isn't broken, companies may not realize the harsh impact on the employee," he says. "Stress is sometimes looked at as a lessor injury, if an injury at all. Insurance payments have been severely cut in this day and age. People are reporting physical injuries instead of emotional. Physical therapy is substituted for psycho-therapy."

THE SOLUTION

Emotional abuse is so common in the workplace, particularly in fields where egos clash (such as law), that most of us don't recognize when it happens. Sometimes we believe because we may have erred we deserved to be yelled at or called names—it was our fault: "Tom was in one of his moods and yelling so loudly, I'm sure everyone down the hall heard it. He called me 'stupid' again for missing the deadline. I'm just going to have to do better." It may be true that you have a performance problem. However, you *do not* have to endure constant verbal abuse, even if it does come from a higher-up. Most likely, you would not accept the same behavior from a colleague of equal standing. It's astounding that because an authority figure does it, it's accepted.

What can you do? Ad hoc solutions include reporting all incidents to your supervisors; telling the abuser that you will not accept the behavior and leave the room if it continues; and keeping a diary of the incidents. You might request a transfer to another department. Unless the abuser violates a written policy between the employee and employer, though, the only remedy at this point may be to quit, and you may need to consult an attorney.

Utlimately, emotional abuse is a management problem and must be addressed by firm leadership in a large context. As a member of the firm, you have an obligation to yourself and your coworkers to stop the abuse. Real solutions to this costly behavior are systemic. They involve:

1. Overt and consistent recognition by management
2. Breaking the silence that surrounds such incidents to promote open airing of employee concerns
3. Creating a firmwide policy not to accept abuse under any circumstances
4. Opening communication channels to give sustained life to the new nontoleration policy.

Paralegals, along with all employees, must be trained to identify unacceptable behavior and taught how to deal with it. Only through policies, education, and follow-through will this last bastion of abusiveness in the workplace be wiped out.

In firms where abusive behavior is prohibited, employee morale tends to soar. Turnover is low and more quality work gets accomplished. The greatest fear behind fighting workplace emotional abuse is that you will lose your job—a very real possibility. Ask yourself two very hard questions:

1. Will this situation change?
2. Is staying in this unending scene worth risking my emotional health?

If the answer is no to both number one and two, you are on the right track. You may want to get advice from appropriate supervisors or human resource personnel.

If the answer is no to number one but yes to number two, walk very carefully (you may be in no condition to run) to the nearest therapist and get yourself a reality check. You may be worse off than you think.

Eight Ways Firms Can Prevent Emotional Abuse

Ida Abbott, a management consultant based in California and previously a partner in a major San Francisco firm, believes strongly that preventing and addressing abusive behavior in the workplace is the firm's responsibility. If you believe that you or someone in your firm is being emotionally abused, seek out an administrator, human resource executive, partner, or senior level associate who has the power to help.

Abbott's eight steps to prevention are the following:

1. Establish a firm policy that explicitly and unequivocally states that all attorneys and employees are expected to treat each other with courtesy and respect and that abusive behavior will not be accepted. Make it clear that the firm will take complaints seriously and will take appropriate disciplinary action against anyone who engages in such behavior.

2. Teach attorneys and staff what constitutes acceptable and unacceptable behavior.

3. Design a complaint resolution system in which designated people act as advisors, intermediaries, and investigators. (Incorporate the system into the existing grievance procedure or sexual harassment claim process, or make it new and separate.) The system should include:
   - A focus on behavior and conciliation; not blame or punishment
   - Procedures that are simple, quick, and flexible
   - Notice to clients of the firm's policy
   - A means to ensure confidentiality if the employee requests it.

4. Include input from both attorneys and nonattorney employees in the system design process.

5. Carefully select and train the people who will hear and respond to complaints.

6. Design a comprehensive plan for publicizing, explaining, and encouraging people to use the system.

7. Consistently, promptly, and fairly enforce the policy.

8. Establish a method for soliciting feedback from users to continuously improve the system.

Calming Upset Clients and Coworkers When the Volcano Is About to Blow

Rule Number 1: Never take it personally. It may be true that you may have made a shaky judgment call or mistake in an assignment. Although accepting constructive criticism is part of the job, you are entitled to receive the message professionally.

Rule Number 2: Listen for the facts—don't mix in emotions. Be patient. The person who is upset may have difficulty articulating the core of the matter.

Rule Number 3: You cannot control someone else's behavior. You can, however, change your behavior to help keep from escalating the incident.

Rule Number 4: Understand four basic needs of someone who is upset:

1. To be understood
2. To save face
3. To feel important
4. To get comfort.

Rule Number 5: Use skillful listening and feedback techniques to get to the real problem. Adopt a concerned body posture, tone of voice, and facial expression. Never sound condescending:

1. Look the person in the eye
2. Stop talking and remain calm
3. Concentrate on what this person is trying to say
4. Signal that you are listening and concerned: "If I understand correctly, what you are saying is . . . ."

Rule Number 6: Acknowledge the emotion neutrally:

1. I can see that you are upset by this discussion.
2. I understand your reaction.
3. I can understand how you would be upset.

Rule Number 7: If an apology is in order but you have strong feelings against it, try to compromise using neutral statements:

1. I am sorry that happened to you.
2. I am sorry you are so dissatisfied with my assignment results. Please tell me specifically what wasn't right so I can correct it.
3. Of course, you can *always* say you're sorry.

Rule Number 8: If trouble occurs reaching an agreement, make comments directed toward finding a solution:

1. What is the next step?
2. What do you think is a fair way to settle this?

3. What will make you happy?

Rule Number 9: Don't let emotions escalate the scene:

1. Call for a time-out
2. Excuse yourself professionally and politely say: "I need to discuss how

we can best solve this. I'll just be a moment"; or, "I'd like to get my supervisor's opinion on this."

Rule Number 10: Never get into a situation in which an enraged person threatens you or becomes violent. Always rely on your instincts if things seem to be getting out of hand. Learn nonverbal communications: clenched fists, agitated tone, tense body posture, red face. Look for evidence of drugs or alcohol.

If you sense a potentially violent or threatening situation, leave immediately and call someone such as a supervisor or security officer. Above all, do not feel silly about calling the police if you need to. It's better to risk feeling stupid than end up in a hospital.

Never accuse anyone of being drunk or on drugs. This puts you and your firm in a liable situation. Handle the situation through normal human resource channels.

PARALEGAL INNER VIEW: NOAH WORTMAN— ATTORNEYS RELY ON THIS PARALEGAL

Name: Noah Wortman
Title: Paralegal
Specialty: Plaintiff Class Actions—Shareholders and derivative shareholders actions
Years of experience: 5 years
Education: B.A. Political Science from Columbia and B.A. in Bible Studies
Firm: Morris and Morris, Wilmington, Delaware
Firm size: 4 attorneys, 3 associates, 1 paralegal
Job duties: In this securities related firm, one of my responsibilities is to read the *NY Times* and the *Wall Street Journal* and other periodicals,

combing them for case-related articles. My job is to find out what is going on with the company. Why would stock prices drop? I have a routine I go through and I basically live on the Internet. The first thing I do is to look at the PR archives, LEXIS and pull stories for the last month. I see if other firms have filed anything yet. I review the stock run and corporate profile off of the Dow Jones Interactive. What's been going on with that company to cause a drop in price? I look at the SEC filings, 10Ks and 10Qs. Was there insider trading? Than I report back to the attorney.

I will also pick things out if I see something in the news and bring it to the attorney. I always take the initiative. I got my training basically in college when I worked here during the summer. It was trial by fire. I have my own office but no secretary.

Prior history: I started working in New York for a major law firm. I didn't care for it. I was in charge of 10 cases with two senior attorneys. The attorneys treated us badly. I still plan to go to law school. Initially, I fell into this job. I'm 25 years old and I grew up on computers. The attorneys tap me and keep me involved in their computer systems. I have created coding sheets and I supervise one of the other secretaries.

What is your biggest challenge about this particular job?

Right now, I am working on a brief with a partner. I proof it and put together the volumes of appendices and make sure the formatting is correct. A challenge is to take something that is nonexistent that is going to be submitted to Federal Court. I need to keep everything coordinated at the same time juggling.

What do you like best about this job?

Everything that I do, they seem to take seriously. The attorneys value my opinions and judgments. If I say this seems like a viable case or not, they take that seriously. They do not believe that because you are a paralegal, your knowledge isn't worth anything. I'm treated like an associate.

Where do you think the paralegal profession is headed?

I'm not 100 percent sure. I read an article about a year or two ago that says the paralegal field is hot. If the person clicks, it's worth the investment for the firm. In my experience, not all paralegals are treated the way I am at this firm. It would be fantastic if they were. I know that's not the way in the rest of the world which causes a fair amount of dissension in the field. I agree with a lot of people in saying that I don't think the majority of attorneys know what to do with paralegals.

How's the money?

Could be better, it's hard to tell. It's relative to the market you're in particularly in terms of what first-year associates do. I can get overtime which is fantastic but at the same time, I'm lumped in with the support staff which I don't like.

To whom do you report?

I report to the office manager for administrative issues, and for assignments, I go to the attorneys who are extremely accessible.

Do you belong to any paralegal associations?

I belong to the Delaware Paralegal Association and just joined the LAT (*Legal Assistant Today*) forum to connect. I haven't felt connected to other paralegals. I'm connected with the firm, though.

What would you like to do next?

I'd like to go to law school but I'm staying put for the time being.

CHAPTER 25

Positive Career Changes

> When one door closes another door opens, but we often look so long and so regret-fully upon the closed door, that we do not see the ones which open for us.
>
> Alexander Graham Bell

REASONS FOR CHANGING POSITIONS

There are seven basic reasons for changing positions:

1. Salary
2. Location of position
3. Lack of recognition
4. Personality conflict

5. Stress and burnout
6. Downsized or laid off
7. Fired

Paralegals change for all seven reasons plus one:

8. No further growth potential/lack of promotion.

According to Mark Gorkin, M.S.W., noted author, speaker and leading authority in the areas of stress and humor: "Most other careers see people changing positions due to one of the seven reasons listed above. Paralegals have another incentive to leave—lack of promotion—and generally exhibit at least three reasons to leave for an extended period of time before the actual decision is made."

One explanation as to why some of us hang in there at all costs can be found in Dr. Brian DesRoches' book, *Your Boss Is Not Your Mother:*

> Once you are aware of the tendency to bring your family's emotional patterns to the office, you see it everywhere.
>
>   Your company may actually encourage these behaviors. Most organizations do. Five conditions exist in almost every workplace that foster these old, unproductive ways of thinking and acting—and keep them in place. [They are]:
>
> 1.   The workplace is a breeding ground for stress.
> 2.   In the workplace, emotional desires are often thwarted.
> 3.   The expression of feelings has no place at work.
> 4.   The invisible world is a fact of corporate life (i.e., you can't talk about it, or what really goes on inside your organization is actually different than what appears to the outside world).
> 5.   In the corporate pinball game, everyone bounces off everyone else.

For some paralegals, there is tremendous fear of facing a job change, even at the risk of staying unhappy on the job. Old patterns are comfort zones. At least they know what they have. Other paralegals aren't quite sure *why* they are leaving, only that "it's an awful place to work."

Dr. DesRoches points out that in every workplace, three desires remain dominant:

1.   To feel *included* and *recognized*   3.   To feel *accepted* and *liked* by others.
2.   To feel *competent* and in *control* of our jobs

In order to cope with uneasy emotions, such as frustration, anger, hurt, disappointment, rejection, or shame, we often gravitate unconsciously toward the tactics our families used to deal with uncomfortable relationships.

When Do Most Changes Occur?

For many paralegals, changing positions rarely occurs when one adventure comes to a close and it is time to begin another. Rather, something momentous needs to happen to push that paralegal out the door. Downsizing is only one threat to the position. The job search becomes frantic, anxiety ridden, and fraught with certain deadlines, often initiated by the paralegal. For example, "I want to find a new position after the bonus but before review time."

Hiring seasons are generally cyclical: June and October are peak periods when firms tend to increase staff: October 15 through January 15 is the slowest hiring period at law firms; February 1 through the end of March is the season with the most available positions in a firm due to normal attrition. Corporations have their seasons according to their industry, but generally experience slow recruiting around the holiday-New Year time.

From October 15 through January 15, many paralegals thinking of leaving will stay with a firm, no matter how miserable they are, in order to get the annual or Christmas bonus. Then, ironically, not wanting to appear ungrateful, they politely wait to give notice until at least 2 or 3 weeks after receiving the bonus.

Some paralegals wait to see what their salary increase is, then leave when they are disappointed. Leaving becomes a direct reaction to an action taken by the firm, rather than a proactive position taken by the paralegal.

During the slow recruiting season in law firms, from the end of October to January, some paralegals suffering from "bonus anxiety" consult placement agencies until the raise or bonus is given. Then, depending on the action of the firm, the paralegal either puts the job search into play or holds off until the next big crisis. Thus, a pattern develops. We are happy only until it isn't good anymore, then we are forced to leave. We wait until something happens to motivate us to make a change rather than planning the change well in advance.

It's okay to change positions. On average, paralegals change positions about every 2 years. The trick is to change positions because you are the captain of your career rather than a slave to your job. Changing positions needs to be well-thought-out and a proactive activity. Reasons for leaving a position should include the following:

- You have a better opportunity to meet your goal plan.
- There is no longer any forward movement.
- Your needs have changed.
- The position no longer meets your criteria for success. According to Dr. Adele Scheele in *Skills for Success* (Ballantine), success is "culturally defined as: money, power, status;" and "personally as: job satisfaction, peace of mind, challenge, involvement."

The impetus behind leaving a position is to define your career, rather than your career defining you.

It's Okay to Leave Because of the Money

Although it is okay to leave your job because of an unhappy situation, it is not the preferable way to command your career. Let's take the salary issue, for example. Don, an intermediate litigation paralegal working for a midsized firm, wanted to leave his position because the money was too low.

His salary was slightly under market, and he had been with the firm for a year and a half. After negotiating with the firm, he was unable to successfully obtain the necessary increase. I asked Don a few questions:

> Q: "Was the salary acceptable when you took the position and signed on with the firm?"
> Don: "Of course, or I wouldn't have taken the job."
> Q: "What changed that?"
> Don: "Well, I just feel that I'm underpaid for what I do. Further evidence of that is the paralegal salary surveys which show I'm slightly under market."
> Q: " Why was it okay a year ago?"
> Don: "I guess I was at a different level of expertise then. I'm doing more advanced assignments now. I'm considered the computer expert in litigation support. I guess you could say I've changed my game plan."

What Don had discovered was not so much that he wanted more money (to which he was entitled) but that his strategy and career plan had changed. Because of his actions (becoming a technology expert), Don was entitled to be rewarded for that expertise. If Don had taken time to proactively plot that strategy, he would have discovered eventually he might be at odds with the firm. He would have been able to plan accordingly, instead of impulsively deciding he wasn't paid what he was worth. The issue was not whether the firm would recognize (with dollars) Don's growth, but rather had Don chosen a firm that could not keep up with his fast track?

It's also okay to leave because of location, lack of recognition, conflict, stress, or lack of promotion. However, take the necessary steps to command your career. There's no time like the present to start.

DECIDING TO CHANGE POSITIONS

The following is a list of thought-provoking questions. There are no right or wrong answers. The questions are designed to discover whether leaving is for the right reasons or because of an incident that, given some time, will either blow over or correct itself. Write down the answers and review them. Is a pattern developing? Do all indications point to changing positions due to proactive career development? This doesn't mean you can't or shouldn't leave! However, awareness of what is really happening can empower you to take action.

51 Questions to Ask Yourself About Leaving Your Job: A Reality Check

1. Why do I want to leave my job? (Name a specific reason, person, situation.)

2. Am I leaving over what I think I might get as a salary increase?

3. Am I leaving over what I think I might get as a bonus?

4. Will disappointment be so great that the only way I can cope is to leave?

5. Will I be embarrassed to stay here?

6. Have I conducted appropriate research: reviewed salary surveys, compared the firm's history of raises, found out ahead of time what percent of increase can be expected?

7. Am I paid under market? Can I successfully negotiate to bring my salary up to or over market?

8. Do I enjoy my colleagues?

9. Do I enjoy the support staff?

10. Do I enjoy my supervisors?

11. Do I enjoy the attorneys?

12. Which people do I enjoy the most? (Name names and positions.)

13. Which people do I enjoy the least? (Name names and positions.)

14. Is my reason for leaving really focused on the behavior of one person or a group? If so, who?

15. Is a transfer out of the department possible?

16. Do I enjoy my work? (Overall.)

17. Which aspect of my work do I enjoy most?

18. Which aspect of my work do I enjoy least?

19. In which aspect of my work do I feel most competent?

20. In which aspect of my work do I feel least competent?

21. Is most of the work I perform in areas I feel least competent?

22. Am I in over my head?

23. Am I performing repetitious work with no new stimulation?

24. Have I done anything about providing stimulation? Am I waiting on an outside source (for example, the firm, supervisor, attorney) to provide that stimulation?

25. Am I not meeting someone else's expectations (attorney, supervisor, colleague, spouse, friend, mentor)?

26. Has the firm changed since I started?

27. Have I changed since I started?

28. Have we gone in the same or different directions?

29. What is my physical working environment?

30. What is my vision of how that physical working environment should look? Is it realistic? Am I angry because I don't have it?

31. Am I working too much overtime?

32. Have I paced myself? Have I said no at the appropriate times? Have I looked for alternatives or a team approach?

33. Is the firm's billable hour expectation realistic? Is it realistic for me?

34. Do I like working this hard? Am I working hard enough?

35. Do I really want to go to law school? Grad school? Do I fantasize that I am in another career?

36. Am I searching for a better paralegal job as an alternative to law school, grad school, or fantasy career?

37. What is *my* definition of job satisfaction?

38. Is that what I'm getting?

39. Has anyone told me recently that I did a great job?

40. Would it be nice to hear (or hear it more often)?

41. Does this position meet my goal criteria?

42. Will it ever?

43. Did something happen recently (an event, a situation with an attorney, colleague, supervisor, a review) that prompted my dissatisfaction? Was it the straw that broke the camel's back?

44. Can I get where I want to go from here?

45. Am I clear on where that is?

46. Am I left out of good assignments, colleague support, socializing with attorneys, making friends at work?

47. Have my colleagues advanced while I have not?

48. If so, is there a logical explanation? Would someone else believe that?

49. Do I have the halo effect? Can I live up to that image?

50. Is there someone at this firm that I can talk to who would be happy to help me? Does she have the right power to do so?

51. If I got everything or part of what I wanted on my list, would I still leave?

MAKING THE CHANGE

If you have decided to change positions, let me be the first to congratulate you! This is not an easy task, and it needs careful strategy and planning. Let's talk about some practicalities of the job search. You may have heard these before, but if you haven't been in the job market for a while or haven't always picked just the right position, you may want to review the basics.

How long will it take to find a job?

The length of your job search depends on certain factors:

- Time of year you are looking
- Current trends in the marketplace
- Your practice specialty and its marketability
- What's hot
- Level of expertise: Entry-level paralegals right out of school and senior-level paralegals usually take longer. Legal secretaries just breaking into the paralegal market may also take a little longer.
- Salary requirements.

The average job search length for a paralegal presently employed is anywhere from 6 weeks to 6 months, or more in some cases. This includes time to send out the resume, arrange for interviews, second interviews, offers, and giving notice.

How much notice should I give?

Do not give notice until you have an offer in hand. Professional courtesy is usually a minimum of 2 weeks to a maximum of 30 days, depending on your involvement with the firm. Any more than 30 days is too much. The firm views you as a "short timer," in limbo. The firm will want to move on with business at hand: finding and training a replacement.

What if I am unemployed?

You are in a more strategic and desirable position if presently employed. However, if it happens that you are unemployed, don't panic. Investigate a temporary agency to tide you over.

What if I give notice and get fired?

While this doesn't happen very often in the legal field, it does happen, particularly in corporations with high turnover. Sometimes corporations and law firms feel if you are joining the competition, the firm may be better off if you leave right away. If this occurs, try and get the new firm to move up the start date, but it isn't always necessary to tell them what happened.

While I'm job searching, who, at the present firm, should I tell I'm leaving?

Hopefully, no one. However, practically speaking, reference checks may make that impossible. There may be one attorney or supervisor you can take into confidence, but the best bet is to say nothing to anyone and ask the new firm to check references after an offer has been extended. People cannot be expected to keep your secret.

How do I arrange for interviews while I'm still working?

Use your personal days, lunch hours, or comp time or develop a root canal. Try not to abuse the system or your present firm will catch on immediately that you are job hunting. Do not expect, however, that potential firms will welcome you at 7:00 A.M. or after 6:00 P.M. Interviewers have personal lives also and are most likely interviewing more than one candidate. They want to interview during regular business hours. Try not to schedule more than one or two interviews per week, if that many.

What about using a placement agency?

In recent years, paralegal placement agencies have sprung up around the country. These agencies are sometimes owned or managed by paralegals who are familiar with various practice specialties, administrators, job descriptions, and firms. In my opinion, they may be particularly helpful because they can speak your language. Unfortunately they don't exist in every city or even in every state as of this writing. Therefore, if you do choose to use an agency, make sure it meets some or all of the following guidelines:

- Specializes in the legal field
- Recruiters handling you are former paralegals or have worked in a law firm or corporate legal department
- Has a good reputation and is used by firms or corporations with whom you are seeking employment
- Does not attempt to talk you out of what you are looking for and into an entirely different position to fill their job orders (for example, a legal secretary who wants to become a paralegal is convinced to stay in the legal secretarial field because the recruiter can place her/him faster).

It isn't necessary to pay a fee to the agency. Most agencies today are employer-retained (the employer pays the fee). There are executive search agencies that require fees from the candidate, but, as of this writing, I am unfamiliar with any that specialize in the paralegal field.

What if I have been in my present position for more than 10 years? Does this help or hinder me?

The dichotomy of this situation is that on the one hand, law firms and legal departments are looking for stability in an employee. On the other hand, some employers view a candidate who has stayed in one position "too long" as not much of a risk taker and "not easy to train" in new procedures. You are going to have to find an employer who fits in with your way of thinking.

Is there such a thing as being in the market too long?

Yes, definitely. Keep careful records about when and where you sent your resume and interviewed. Nothing is worse than the prospective employer running across your resume three, four, and five times. The impression is that (1) you can't seem to get a job, and (2) there must be something wrong. If you are using an agency, find out where your resume has been sent and mark it on a tracking form.

If you are in a small community and have been looking for more than 6 months, you might hold off the search and begin again in another few months. Conduct a thorough investigation as to why you haven't landed that job yet.

What about training my replacement?

Professionally speaking, do what you can do without leaving the firm in the lurch. However, whether you want to acknowledge it or not, firms expect some turnover and can deal with your replacement. You are not expected to put off the start date with your new employer because a replacement hasn't been found. Document the file, write up status reports, and have status meetings with attorneys and staff on your caseload. Make every effort to leave in an organized and thoughtful manner. Don't burn any bridges; it's too small a community.

What if I've job-hopped a little?

Each interviewer's measure of job-hopping varies somewhat, although the rule of thumb is 1 year or less at each position. Some interviewers consider a succession of jobs for 18 months or less to be job-hopping. A prospective employer will interpret bouncing around as an indication of what might happen if they hired you. Look at your pattern and correct the flight path. Eliminate jobs held for 6 months or less from your resume. If asked, however, whether you worked during that period, answer truthfully.

THE NEW POSITION: DESIGNING YOUR NEW JOB

It's an interesting phenomenon about change and experiences. So often, we know we want to change positions, but we're uncertain what that change should be. Our experiences, however, tell us exactly what we *don't* want. We come away from a position with a list of what the new position won't be.

- "I will never again work for a large firm."
- "I will never again work for a solo practitioner."
- "I will not summarize any more depositions."
- "I will not do any client intake interviews."

Pretty soon we sound like a Girl or Boy Scout reciting our credo of "thou shalt nots." Certain about what we *don't* want, we haven't the faintest idea what we *do* want. Starting the job search is like deciding to go "shopping" on a Saturday afternoon: not looking for anything in particular, except that when we see it, we'll know it. When approaching a job search in this manner, it's no wonder there are many returns and exchanges.

Designing your new job is not a complicated matter. It is really an inventory of likes, dislikes, vision, motivation, and capabilities. What can become complex is how the new position fits into your overall goal criterion: Where do I want to be in my career? The following section can assist in your job design. Take a hard look at the types of responsibilities you have now and write your current job description as *you* see it, not necessarily as how your present firm describes it. Be honest in your competency assessment and how you like doing these assignments. Because you are extremely competent in one area does not necessarily mean you enjoy it or vice versa. A sample job skills list is given. Remember, though, because of the versatility and diversity of paralegal job descriptions (no two seem to be alike!), create your own, according to your present situation.

How to Use the Job Design Chart

Following this section is a blank job design chart. Use this chart to find out what duties and tasks you love to do and which you do best. We're often in jobs performing duties we are skilled at but dislike intensely. This leads to job dissatisfaction and burnout.

First, list skills, using what you are presently doing in your current position, past performance, and what you might like to do in the future. (A sample job skills list for intermediate-level litigation paralegal follows the job design chart.) On the left-hand side of the chart, rate skill level, according to your evaluation. Then, following the listings on the top of the page, place that skill under enjoyment level when using that skill.

The chart demonstrates skill and assignments to focus on when looking for your next position. Skills listed in the lower right-hand box, particularly under "Extremely Competent/Strongly Dislike," are burnout skills. Watch out!

Deciding on Your New Position

After conducting an analysis of the new position, prepare a new job design including areas in which to compromise. (A new job design form follows.) If you decide you really do not enjoy a small firm environment and are looking for a large firm, would you consider a large legal department of a corporation? Many paralegals decide they wish to work for a corporation only after coming out of a law firm environment. If you are one of those paralegals, would you consider a law firm if it had all other criteria desired? Say, for example, the primary reason for moving to a corporation is that you want to move up the corporate ladder. However, would you consider a firm that had a career path and promoted into other areas of expertise?

Keep all options open. Have an idea what the new position looks like and how it assists in your goal plan. Know areas of compromise. These areas

JOB DESIGN CHART

	Totally Enjoy	Enjoy Very Much	Like	Prefer Not to Do	Strongly Dislike
Little or No Skill					
Competent					
Extremely Competent					

SAMPLE: JOB SKILLS LIST FOR A LITIGATION PARALEGAL— INTERMEDIATE LEVEL

Supervise—Oversee, direct staff
Trial preparation—Code documents
Trial preparation—Index documents
Trial preparation—Summarize depositions
Trial preparation—Prepare indices
Trial preparation—Organize documents
Trial preparation—Prepare jury instructions
Trial preparation—Prepare witness lists
Trial preparation—Prepare exhibits
Trial preparation—Prepare exhibit lists
Writing skills—Draft motions
Writing skills—Draft pleadings
Writing skills—Draft memos
Writing skills—Prepare speeches
Writing skills—Draft articles
Computer skills—Input documents
Computer skills—Code documents
Computer skills—Search and retrieval
Computer skills—Organize documents
Computer skills—Manage databases
Computer skills—Create special databases
Teaching skills—Train entry-level paralegals and case clerks
Teaching skills—Train new recruits
Teaching skills—Conduct seminars
Teaching skills—Teach new software programs
Legal research—Shepardize
Legal research—Cite check
Legal research—Conduct factual research
Legal research—Use LEXIS/Westlaw
Legal research—Pull case law
Interfacing—Work with attorneys
Interfacing—Work with paralegals
Interfacing—Work with support staff
Interfacing—Work with vendors
Interfacing—Work on team
Interfacing—Work independently
Interfacing—Work one-on-one with attorney
Factual investigation—Supervise asset searches
Factual investigation—Witness interviews

Factual investigation—Conduct research
Pretrial—Conduct document productions
Pretrial—Coordinate document productions
Pretrial—Prepare lists of documents
Pretrial—Travel to document productions

FORM: NEW JOB DESIGN

Assignment Level:
My new position should include the following assignments:

	Must Have	Would Like	Can Compromise	No Compromise
1. _____				
2. _____				
3. _____				
4. _____				
5. _____				

Location:
My new position should be located in any of the following areas:

1. _____
2. _____
3. _____

Working Conditions:

1. _____
2. _____
3. _____

Overtime:

1. _____
2. _____
3. _____

Environment:
My new position should have the following environment:

1. _____
2. _____
3. _____

Career Path:

1. _____
2. _____
3. _____

Salary:

1. _____
2. _____
3. _____

Bonus:

1. _____
2. _____
3. _____

Continuing Education:

1. _____
2. _____

Industry:

1. _____
2. _____
3. _____

Client Contact:

1._____
2._____

Perks:

1. _____
2. _____
3. _____

Supervision:

1. _____
2. _____

Law Firm versus Corporation:

1. _____
2. _____

allow for flexibility in areas you probably haven't even thought of or explored. But also know areas in which you absolutely will not compromise. Don't ignore what you already know to be true.

PARALEGAL INNER VIEW: CINDY LANGAN— BIG FIRM, BIG TECHNOLOGY

Name: Cindy Langan
Firm: Miller, Canfield, Paddock and Stone, Detroit, Michigan
Number of attorneys: 150 attorneys with 8 offices in Michigan with a total number of attorneys at 250; we are the largest firm in Michigan
Specialty: The firm specializes in public finance, labor, e-commerce, litigation, and more
Title: Legal Technology Manager
Years of experience: 10 years
Education: B.A. in Business Administration; working toward an MBA in Technology Management at the University of Phoenix

Job Duties: My day-to-day responsibilities vary. I do long-term planning and education to encourage attorneys to use technology. I design and implement databases on Summation and Access. I convert client data so paralegals and attorneys can use it. You don't really have to know something about a program to run the program. All of what I do is behind the scenes. We did a major rollout last year, so everyone had to learn everything new. They're just getting to the point where they don't have to think about litigation support. You match up the computer with what they do. They're now using technology on everyday cases, not just the big, fat cases. If I had a dime for everyone who said, "I don't have any big cases," I'd be rich. Being a legal assistant, I can show them how to do it.

How did you make this career transition?

I made the transition by developing a knowledge independently. My father is a computer nerd. I became the legal assistant who was the computer guru and was the one who knew everything. My resume was legal assistant, but I had the specialty. The firm hired me because of those skills. I transitioned in it part-time, then full time.

Where does someone at the top go?

I don't know. I'm very happy here. I bill time when appropriate. There's no position above me here I could shoot for. I work for the Director of Information Systems and I'm very happy because I need technology to succeed. I can also help people out in the field. My clients are the attorneys. I run my business like I consult.

Where is the career going?

I would like to say more and more law firms would have more people like me on staff, but I'm not cost-neutral. At some point, I may be. I rarely see lawyers invest like they should. Your budget should triple every year. It's not something you can invest in once every 3 years. I hope more attorneys will see the value in it. I'm not sure they will. Just because technology makes you more efficient doesn't mean people are going to use it.

CHAPTER 26

Career Questions and Answers: "Ask the Expert"

Throughout my own career, I have been privileged to have been asked by well-known publications for my opinion on trends and events taking place in today's workplace—all of which apply to the careers of paralegals. This chapter presents a few of those interviews.

ON RE-ENTRY TO THE WORKPLACE:

BusinessWeek Online sought answers for its Work & Family column. They ask an interesting question regarding re-entry into the workplace:

BW: What should a job seeker do when, after spending several years as a stay-at-home mom, she's not being taken seriously during job interviews? She's got relevant work in the industry, but interviewers seem to want to focus on her absence for several years and on the fact that her original background, more than a decade ago, was in teaching.

CE: Employers can be so short-sighted, and, frankly, closed-minded by making generalizations. Do they think that as you reach in your briefcase for a copy of your resume that a teething ring will fall out? It's up to you to demonstrate that the interlude at home had absolutely no adverse effect on your ability to do this job!

First of all, if the candidate has made it into the interview by using a resume, booking the appointment herself, or using a staffing company that has pitched her successfully, she's doing something right. No employer calls a candidate for an interview unless they have some interest. The problem appears to be in how the candidate is "closing" the sale. Being absent from the workplace for several years is only an objection to the sale, which you can overcome.

The trick is to get the interviewer off the absence and on to your relevant skills. In reality, there are laws that protect the stay-at-home parent. Employers, technically, can only ask, "Did you work during this period," calling for a yes or no answer. However, go tell that to someone with whom you want a job! What the candidate needs to do is to answer the question of why were you not working during these years by saying, "If, what you are asking is, are my skills up-to-date?, the answer is yes." Then elaborate by talking about what you have done to keep those skills up, i.e., taken classes, practiced on the computer at home, read relevant materials, written articles, etc. Even being responsible for the household budget, PTA meetings, and coaching the kids' soccer team count.

You must illustrate for the employer how those skills tie in with the job—as most have no imagination and cannot draw the parallel. You might say something like, "My leadership skills are demonstrated by my position as chairperson of the PTA where I was responsible for organizing the meetings, balancing the budget, and coordinating fund-raising events." Then, tie those skills in further with your past history: "I obtained those skills when I was a teacher where I was responsible for . . . ." Talk about the skills needed in teaching: organization, leadership, evaluation and assessment, planning, working with difficult personalities, enthusiasm, working within a budget, patience, continuing education. Just because the last job was 10 years ago does not mean the skills have disappeared. Concentrate on the "soft skills" such as effective communication skills, interaction with people, willingness to learn, etc. Employers have the "what have you done lately" mentality. Meet that mentality head-on by giving examples of your skills.

Walk into the interview prepared. Research the company ahead of time and be sure to let the interviewer know you know something about the job and the company. You can get on the Internet, ask your staffing agency, or get an annual report. Employers are impressed with candidates who can answer the question, "What do you know about our company?" or "Why do you want to work here?" You might answer by saying, "This is precisely the kind of company in which I would like to re-enter the workplace. I read where the company recently . . . ." Stay off subjects such as benefits and vacation for now.

You might also negotiate for a "trial" period. Suggest starting as a temporary worker so the employer can have a time frame in which to evaluate your skills before making a full-time offer. You might suggest starting the position at a slightly lower salary with a performance/salary review in 3 months. Look the employer straight in the eye and acknowledge their concerns. Say something like, "I understand how you feel. If I were in your shoes, I might have the same concerns. However, here is how we can both arrive at a mutually beneficial employment relationship." Employers want to be put at ease that their hiring decision is the right one.

Do not underestimate the power of dressing for success. Make certain that you have on the right power suit, hairstyle, and even your glasses are up-to-date. Look successful. People tend to make up their minds about what you can do in the first few minutes of the interview, and that assessment is made in part from your appearance.

As the interview is drawing to a close, reiterate your skills. Tell them why you are qualified for the position and how enthusiastic you are about the possibility of working for this company. Enthusiasm is a great trait. Close on a positive note such as, "I know that my skills and desire will demonstrate that I can do this job. When will you be making a decision? If you need me to return for another interview or provide you with samples of my work, just let me know."

Thank the interviewer for his/her time and be sure to follow up immediately with a business letter that, once again, reiterates your skills, enthusiasm for the job, and why you would be a good fit.

ON JOB-SHARING:

CNBC.com wanted to know:

CNBC: Tell us about job-sharing and how it affects today's workplace. How did job-sharing come about?

CE: Job-sharing is a result of tremendous publicity about the "Mommy Track" a few years ago. Not wanting to be left out of a vertical climb up the career ladder, job-sharing was first designed as a vehicle for women desiring to keep one foot in the workplace and the other as an "at-home" mom. In the past couple of years, the extremely tight candidate market has forced employers to seriously consider job-sharing as a means to filling otherwise vacant positions.

CNBC: For what kinds of positions does it work best?

CE: Job sharing works best for those positions requiring routine and repetitious tasks, for those where information is readily available, and for those where the personal imprint of a worker is not necessary or completion of a project is not based upon one person's knowledge. The range of positions varies widely. Some of those positions could be paralegal, secretary, manager of hourly workers, bank tellers, stock broker, help desk, word processor, records manager, or administrative assistants. Some of the more professional positions may be certain lawyers, accountants, even doctors and dentists.

CNBC: What are the advantages for an employer?

CE: An employer may be able to fill a hard-to-fill specialty position more readily. The employer cuts costs by reducing overtime costs (one person is unlikely to work more than 40 hours in 1 week). The employer also gets the advantage of two points of view and sets of talent for the price of one.

CNBC: What are the advantages for an employee?

CE: Job-sharing is really more advantageous for the employee. A working parent can spend more time with family; a student more time studying. Burnout is apt to be less likely. The position allows the professional employee wishing to work part-time to stay on track for promotion or partnership by being seen and "remembered."

CNBC: Are there certain personalities/mindsets better suited for job-sharing?

CE: Those personalities requiring less "star" recognition are best suited for job-sharing. A job-sharer may not get all the credit for a project and therefore should be a person who isn't seeking stardom. The true "team player" is essential here. A person who needs less start-up time and less supervision should do well as does a person who needs less explanation of assignments. Someone who can pick up right where the other left off. Also, a person who is good at mimicking style. For example, in many job-sharing situations, the end product must appear as though it were prepared by one person—perhaps the writing styles must be the same or the product or project must be seamless. A person who is detail oriented is a must as it is important that when the change-off occurs, things do not slip into the cracks. Good communication skills, both written and verbal, are imperative so that the job-sharers can understand where and what to pick up, along with the ability to ask the right questions.

CNBC: Is job-sharing just for women or are men jumping in?

CE: We see mostly women in a job-sharing situation. However, job-sharing is not gender discriminatory. It is for any employee who needs to work part-time and finds work in a full-time position. So far, however, while I do not have a survey from which to quote, it appears that women outnumber the men.

CNBC: Can you tell us about people who have job shared?

CE: One paralegal I know job-shared for over 4 years for an in-house legal department. She job-shared with one other paralegal while attending school for her master's degree in psychology and then while completing her internship. She and her job-sharer worked on a high-profile, complex litigation case which demanded people who understood the case and were able to contribute individually and as a team. She has now left the paralegal field and has a highly successful psychotherapy practice.

CNBC: Can you give some advice to a job-sharer or manager of job-sharers?

CE: 1. Learn to emulate your co-worker's style. Anticipate that employers will hold you responsible for your co-worker's productivity and work quality. They may not necessarily know which person was responsible for various parts of an assignment and they might not care. They just want the job done right.

2. Employers: Learn the value of communication with your job-sharing employees. Set up a reporting system so that you are in the loop. Don't expect things to be flawless if there is no system that accommodates for clear communication. This system might include e-mail, voice mail, weekly reports, regular meetings, a daily work sheet, a liaison, or a checklist.

3. Employers and employees: If one of the job-sharers is not carrying his or her weight, it is important to rectify the situation immediately. Otherwise, there is a domino effect: Everything can come tumbling down, and quickly.

CNBC: How do you get a job-sharing position?

CE: While many employees love the idea of job-sharing, it seems to be the least likely choice for employers because of the intricacies of setting it up. As this tight candidate market gets even tougher, it may get more popular. But that is only if employers are given the suggestion and made aware of steps to make it work. It may not occur to most employers to utilize this effective technique for getting the job done. It is up to employees to suggest it and to sell the idea to potential employers.

ASSOCIATE SALARIES SOAR

Frontier magazine in Chicago asked the following questions.

FM: How has the substantial increase in associate salaries affected law firms? The obvious: Is a three-figure salary reasonable for a fresh law school graduate with very little legal experience?

CE: The salary issue speaks to market value rather than legal experience. When demand goes up and supply goes down, as in any industry, the price goes up. It has very little to do with what's reasonable or fair. The competition for the top 10 percent of the top 10 law schools is fierce, compounded with a nationwide candidate shortage. Anytime unemployment goes down (lower than 4 percent), there are usually more jobs than qualified candidates. Let's look at it this way: How much were firms losing by not being able to attract top candidates? They needed to decide: Should they lower their hiring standards or should they compete more fiercely? Frankly, I doubt the first firms to move to three figures anticipated as many major firms would follow as quickly as they did. The legal industry is not known for responding quickly. The first few firms to reach three figures spoke to the first priority on most candidates' list: money. In that regard, the firm with the most money won. It was a highly competitive move. Are they worth the price? Only if clients agree to pay the increased hourly billable rate. That remains to be seen.

FM: Can we assume that incoming first-years' workload will increase as a result of the increase? Will they be expected to do more—increase billable hours, get more clients, stay longer at the office (no social life), etc.?

CE: *AREYOUSERIOUS????* All kidding aside, I think if you check with many of the firms you will find the minimum billable (or "suggested" hours) has gone up. If they haven't, I assure you, there is an unspoken agreement that associates with fewer hours are headed for extinction with the firm. I think you will see some associates performing lower levels of assignments in an effort to bolster billables. On the other hand, you may see some firms requiring associates to delegate downward and perform a higher level of assignment than previously in order to justify the new rates.

FM: Do you predict turnover with first-years due to the salary increase? (The reasons may range from the partners' expectation for harder workers, longer hours, etc.)

CE: Yes. We have worked with over 2,500 candidates and over 2,000 clients. In the past 2 years, we have seen a significant increase in associates who will change positions only if it is to an in-house position. The reasoning is less stress, fewer hours, less competition, stock options, and no billables. Interestingly, with candidates from major firms, it is only after stress, quality of life, and billables do we hear career path, quality of work, or change in specialty as a reason for leaving their present position. I always tell my staff that most of our clients and candidates do not come to us because they're feeling good. They come because they're in some kind of job crisis. Up until this Spring, the desire to move to dot-coms was hot, hot, hot. In some instances, we saw associates quit major firm positions to take a fraction of what they were getting.

FM: If the salary has hit at least $125K, can we expect future increases, and, if so, by how much?

CE: It has even been reported that a few Silicon Valley firms have offered as high as $155,000 for first-years, but my guess is that firms will level off for a while. Increased salaries eventually will mean an increase in fees. The push back from clients on increased fees remains to be seen over a period of time. This is reminiscent of the early nineties when, starting with insurance companies, clients revolted over excessive fees. Giants in the industry toppled. I doubt anyone who survived wants to go through that again.

FM: Will support staff (secretaries, paralegal, operators, etc.) be affected by the increase in terms of fewer promotions or fewer or no raises?

CE: Paralegals have already been affected. Some firms have raised the minimum billable ("suggested") hours. A few firms have increased salaries for paralegals. I suspect that some firms will have to reinstate merit bonuses depending on profitability rather than bonuses based on billables. Remember, most paralegals and secretaries have no real vertical climb up a career ladder. They are not going to make partner. Promotions are apt to be horizontal (increased responsibilities, change in title, etc.). Firms are in a pickle here because retention strategies are an issue. While I don't have a survey from which to quote, it has been our experience that the average length of employment for paralegals and secretaries appears to be 2 to 3 years.

FM: Why do you think firms are increasing the salaries? Is it an ongoing war on salaries to compete for the best talent or is the underlying reason to drive the competitors out of business? How will they make up for fewer profits and how much will potential clients tolerate? Will potential clients seek out smaller, less expensive firms?

CE: Competiton for the best and the brightest in a tight candidate market is the primary reason firms increased salaries. The firms' biggest marketing tools are talent and reputation. Some firms believe that lowering hiring standards is not an option. If the firm does not have a strategic plan and thinks that raising salaries will drive competitors out of business, it had better have a CYA plan for itself. Current statistics are that the top 100 firms have approximately 50,000 attorneys. Given that there are about a million attorneys in the United States, clients are going somewhere and know they have other options. Smaller firms are more entrepreneurial, can react quicker, and keep their overhead down.

FM: How will the increase affect partners who get profits? (It seems kind of ridiculous for firms to increase salaries this high for first-years who are basically dodging legal malpractice during the first year.) Will this mean that newly admitted lawyers (fresh grads) can charge clients $300 to $400 per hour, and are such fees reasonable?

CE: It has long been the theory that first-years are not profitable for the first 18 months of employment. Conversely, clients have become very savvy and no longer want to train attorneys on their dime. Many have demanded that paralegals perform a variety of the first-years' assignments. Some firms appear to be hiring fewer first-years and fewer laterals—increasing current staff billables, cutting bonuses, making sure that most secretaries are assigned to three attorneys (or two attorneys and a paralegal). There are firms pushing their technology departments as profit centers; some are said to call some legal secretaries "legal assistants" or "legal executives" and bill for certain duties. More and more partners are required to be "rainmakers." In Silicon Valley, more firms are taking stock in start-ups. There are all kinds of techniques for raising profits and absorbing first-year increases. While I am not privy to executive committee meetings, I cannot imagine that partners will agree to take cuts in profit sharing for very long. They will look to more cost-efficient methods to run the firm.

FM: Will there be resentment on the part of more senior staff and a surge of egos versus the incompetents?

CE: Incompetents rarely last long in a major firm anyway. However, I think that less ramp-up time for first-years will be allowed. Resentment? There is always resentment anytime any employee comes in at a higher salary than incumbents. Some of this is the entitlement theory: I have been here for x years and am entitled to higher pay for my longevity and loyalty to the firm. This sustainer theory emanates from when we were children in school: All you had to do was show up, do your homework, and you were automatically promoted into the next grade. This is what has been the pay practices for associates in law firms for years. Two-year associates are paid $x to $x, 3-years, $x to $x. Two 3-years are billed $X. I believe that the lockstep pay scheme for laterals will eventually go by the wayside and firms will look more to the achiever salary structure: Pay-for-performance will take over. Billing rates according to expertise rather than years in the field will emerge.

FM: The obvious: How will this affect current and future job seekers looking for jobs in large firms? Do you think that firms will cut back on on-campus interviews and other recruiting measures? Will this make the competition for firm jobs more competitive and harder to get in? Will the only chance a fresh grad will have to get in is through connections or when firms lose their current associates?

CE: With most firms on an even playing field (with the exception of a few who are paying even more than the going rate), firms no longer can hold highest dollars as their ace in the hole. Hiring bonuses, perks, partnership tracks, guaranteed year-end bonuses, practice specialty, and technology all play a part in a candidate's decision to choose a firm. A lot depends on the economy. Right now, candidates have the upper hand. Anytime the economy is great, candidates are the dominating party. Any downturns and firms have the upper hand. I don't think that firms will cut back on recruiting on campus but I do think they will take more advantage of current technology for recruiting, i.e., videoconferencing interviews. Firms have to prepare themselves for the change in culture and the X & Y generations—the 15-second-sound-byte generations. These students have been brought up witnessing Baby Boomer parents change jobs frequently, downsized, laid off, change professions. Baby Boomers had it differently: Their parents took a job and stayed 10, 20, or 30 years. Generations X & Y don't expect to stay forever in any one law firm. Many may even expect to change professions. Firms need to adjust hiring practices, retention strategies, training, and expectations to accommodate these generations. I would not be surprised, under current conditions, if firms open up their hiring standards somewhat and increase training programs.

FM: Do you predict that associates benefiting from the increase will stand less of a chance of becoming partners?

CE: Yes, I think overall, despite what the intentions of the firm may be, the economic reality is that fewer partnerships will be possible.

FM: Will this mean that newly admitted lawyers (fresh grads) can charge clients $300 to $400 per hour, and are such fees reasonable?

CE: Of course, on the face of things, $300 to $400 per hour for a 26-year-old kid right out of school with no experience can seem outrageous. On the other hand, let's look at what salaries and services cost in the legal field. Take Los Angeles, for example. Legal secretaries in major firms are getting anywhere from the low $50s to $60,000 per year, plus overtime, overhead, and bonus. They are not revenue producers. Does it make sense then, to pay twice as much for an academic wizard who is an income-generating producer? Many top paralegals are billed at $125 per hour, some even at $150 and $175. Clients apparently pay those rates. Given those fees, is it reasonable then, for a firm to ask $300 or more for a first-year Yale, Harvard, Stanford grad with top grades who is under strict supervision of a more senior associate? And, let's look at the billing procedure. As aware as clients are, how many of them really question the bill in terms of how many years' experience each attorney has? Law firm bills are not sent to clients stating: Jones, first year associate, 2 months experience @ $250 per hour. They simply say, Jones @ $250 per hour and list the amount of hours and services rendered. If the client is satisfied with the services, it is unlikely to ask about the billing attorney's years of experience. So, say the bill is for a senior associate and a first year. The bill reads Smith @ $450 per hour; Jones @ $300 per hour. On that basis, if the client is happy with the results, it looks like the client is getting a good deal using Jones. Let's be clear, though. If rates skyrocket and clients pay, there's no issue. It's relative to the "if they don't ask (years of experience), we won't tell" policy.

QUICK SUCCESS TIPS

Pearson Publications, a well-known publisher of paralegal texts, asked the following question.

PP: Can you give our readers (paralegal students and working paralegals) a few tips on what they need to succeed in this career?

CE: Sure!

1. Employers are looking for highly educated paralegals these days. The more education you get, the better. Prefer degrees and/or certificates.

2. Do not underestimate the power of technology. Almost every open position requires knowledge of technology and as many computer programs as you can master. It's more than word processing these days. Employers want you to know spread sheets, database management programs, desktop publishing, calendaring and docketing, timekeeping, and litigation support programs.

3. Learn your way around the Internet. It's critical. Part of a paralegal's job is factual investigation. Who better than a paralegal to find information on the Internet? There are jobs out there now that require paralegals to maneuver around the Net.

4. Learn what's hot. Right now corporate transactional (securities transactions, mergers and acquisitions) is very hot. Ditto for intellectual property! Remember, in a bad economy, specialties like corporate or real estate take a nose dive. Good economies bring them back.

5. Understand the dynamics behind business. The more you know about the inner workings of business transactions, the more you are worth to employers.

6. Employers today complain that paralegals can't write. By writing, they mean business memos and letters. They particularly like paralegals who can draft pleadings, but, trust us, solid grammar skills and coherent sentences win every time.

7. If you are an "older" student, do not take the attitude that employers want "younger" students. The average age of paralegal is between 36 and 38. This is a second and even third career for most. We know of one man who took an article to an interview which talked about how "older" students are more patient, bring more expertise, have longer attention spans, and may have a stronger work ethic than today's Generations X and Y.

8. Before you interview with any firm, find out everything you can before you get there. Nothing impresses an employer more than to find out you've done your homework about the firm and really want to be there because you're so impressed with its track record.

9. Right now, we are experiencing a candidate tight market which means that there are more jobs than candidates. Employers, however, still take the top students first. Learn everything you can in class and visit some law firms and in-house legal departments to get first-hand knowledge of what it's like.

10. If your school has an internship program, try very hard to participate. Employers generally choose students who have gone through the internship program over students who haven't.

WHAT TO EXPECT IF YOU RELOCATE FOR CAREER PURPOSES

Achieve **magazine:** Do professionals often not go into a relocation with their eyes open? In other words, what do they often fail to check out in advance with respect to moving expenses, cost of living changes, school systems, attractions, etc.?

CE: Many professionals, when offered a position in a new location, see only the razzle and dazzle of the offer. Since work takes up two-thirds of our lives, the focus is on if and how the new job can be done. Then the fantasy takes place: We fall victim to "how it's going to be" syndrome. No one really knows. However, relocatees can have an easier time of it if they do their homework. Top on the list of things people fail to realize: actual cost of moving (not all costs are figured in—usually only the movers are calculated); change in cost of living when it's higher (no one gripes if it's lower); effect of weather conditions (particularly if moving from a warmer climate to a colder one); status of neighborhood (many professionals are uncertain of where the new community "fits in"); actual driving/commute time to the new office (people forget about what traffic conditions are in rush hour). However, few people neglect checking out school systems. It's one of the top items on the list.

What you might do is to get on to any one of the major staffing firm's Web sites. Most of them have a relocation subsite that can tell you what it costs to live in the new community. You can enter the salary you are earning now and find out what those dollars translate to in the new community. For example, if you are earning $100,000 in Los Angeles, this may mean $125,000 in Troy, Michigan.

You should also get on a Realtor's site such as *realtor.com* and find out what housing is like. Bear in mind that you need to know what the neighborhoods are like first. One of the biggest mistakes relocatees make is not spending enough time in the new location before the move. They are unprepared for what hits them. A weekend looking over the new city while the company is courting you is not enough. Perhaps you can commute for a few months prior to moving or go spend a vacation there with the intent on viewing it as the locals do. Remember, if you do scout it out quickly, that does not represent how the new location will be year-long.

AM: Is it possible that—given the unexpected expenses—that a $10k raise to move may not be much of a raise at all?

CE: It's very possible! Consider the hidden expenses: additional clothing; possible additional transportation (another car perhaps); deductibles on insurance, temporary housing; possibly new or additional furniture or appliances; deposits on phones, rent, gas, cable, electric, water, etc.; time until first paycheck and start date; spouse possibly is unemployed; new membership fees for whatever; first visit expenses such as doctor, dentist; perhaps additional taxes (moving from a state with no state tax to one that has it, for example); insurance costs; and more.

AM: Are employees starting to successfully negotiate the cost of a move with a new or current employer? If so, how does one do this diplomatically but effectively?

CE: This is one of the tightest candidate markets ever. Employers, therefore, are more willing than in previous years to pay for additional perks and expenses. If an employer expects you to pick up and move, negotiations for reimbursement or advances on the move should be acted upon immediately. An employee might say, "I understand that my total compensation package is $XX. How much does the company reimburse for moving expenses?" When you get the answer, you might respond, "Will that be paid in advance or as a reimbursement?" In other words, you are not assuming that moving expenses are up to you. Frankly, there is nothing diplomatic about it. If an employer expects you to move, they should not be shocked when the question arises.

AM: What are the key factors that every professional must consider before agreeing to a relocation?

CE: Moving to a new location goes beyond job satisfaction. What impact does the move have on the family? How isolated might you end up? Are you the kind of person that can make new friends? Does change upset you? What are the sacrifices? What are the rewards? Does the upside outweigh the downside? On the career side: Do you really have to move for this kind of opportunity? Would it be better if you did? What is the opportunity for a career path if you make this move? Will the move take you in the direction you want your career to go? And, how easy is it to go home again (if necessary)?

CHAPTER 27

Reaching Out: The Joys of Writing and Teaching
Stacey Hunt

After you have put enough years into your profession, you will have amassed a good deal of knowledge and experience, and many beginning paralegals would benefit greatly from the wealth of information you have to offer. As we all know, there are a lot of things to learn about being paralegals that we don't get in our formal schooling. New ways you have created of maintaining case data, preparing for trial, or working with support staff would be greatly appreciated by newcomers to the field. Besides the joy of sharing your knowledge with others and having a creative outlet, teaching and writing can become a lucrative side business with which you can supplement your regular salary.

PICK UP A KEYBOARD AND DO IT!

The budding paralegal writer has many advantages. First of all, most of us were taught writing skills as part of the program from which we graduated, and we have plenty of practice writing on the job. Second, every law firm, and every paralegal within the law firm, has a unique approach to solving a problem or tackling a project. That puts each of us in a situation where we have knowledge and a perspective that other people probably don't have. Finally, there is a plethora of legal (and legal support) publications out there just dying for material to fill their columns. Although most of these won't pay for your efforts, they do provide a great training ground, create an opportunity for you to develop a readership, and allow you to build a portfolio for future use.

Choose Your Audience

Your first step in writing an article is to decide who you want to write an article for. Other paralegals is an obvious choice, but there are other possibilities. Local bar associations and legal newspapers, whose readership is composed of attorneys, may welcome articles from paralegals on such topics as the best ways for attorneys to use their paralegals in a particular practice area, how to hire and work with a freelance paralegal, or how paralegals are using the Internet to do legal and factual research. The legal support professions, such as process servers and court reporters, often have their own organizations and newsletters. Because it's usually the paralegals these people interface with in the law office, they appreciate receiving articles dealing with the best way to provide their services to the firm. Legal secretaries also have their own associations. There is some crossover in paralegal and legal secretary duties, so their association newsletters may be willing to print your articles.

Choose Your Topic

As with your audience, there is a variety of types of information you may want to share. Most publications are looking for "how-to" articles, useful tips with practical applications in the law office. This is your forum for sharing your ideas, for example, on how to organize trial exhibits, how to handle a sensitive interview in a family law matter, the best way to summarize medical records, or tips on writing informative and accurate time sheets. Some journals want a little more heady material, such as editorials. If you like to get on a soapbox, you can write articles about the glass ceiling for paralegals in law offices or why paralegal salaries should not be tied to associate salaries. The third type of article that can be written is more general and career-oriented, such as advice on how to switch specialties, time management, or how to start a mentoring program for your local paralegal school.

Choose Your Publication

When you are first stretching your wings, it is best to start with small, local publications. These would include the newsletter for a paralegal school or the journals put out by the local paralegal association or bar groups. These publications are usually hungry for material and don't have a lot of hoops to jump through to get published as long as your article is of good quality.

You may want to call the editor of your target publication to find out any requirements, such as minimum or maximum number of words and what the deadline is for submission. Some publishers will ask that you release your copyright to the magazine. This means that your article becomes their property and if you want to reprint it in another publication, you will have to obtain permission. If you are not sure of the tone or style to take, it is helpful to obtain a few issues of the newsletter to see the types of articles they print and whether the writing is of a high level and scholarly or more simple and direct.

If you are not sure what you want to write about, or just need some practice, you can call the local paralegal association and see if they need people to help with the newsletter. Often, volunteers are needed to write reports of the membership meetings or board meetings so that people who were unable to attend can find out what happened. If you have recently been to an interesting educational seminar, offer to write a synopsis of what you learned.

Although the local rags seem small, they can lead to bigger things. Newsletters are often circulated among larger publications that look for ideas, leads for stories, or new authors. I wrote an article for my local association newsletter which ended up in the hands of a writer for the *Los Angeles Daily Journal,* one of the largest legal publications in California. The writer called me and asked me to write an editorial which was spotted by Chere Estrin—who offered me a contract to write a book. These things really happen!

After you have gained some experience with the small publications and have sharpened your craft, you may want to turn your attention to the journals published by the two national paralegal associations. Because both of these journals are published by nonprofit organizations, you will not be paid for your submissions.

The National Association of Legal Assistants publishes *Facts & Findings: The Journal for Legal Assistants.* Published quarterly, the journal features articles about substantive legal area, court rules, and recent developments in the paralegal profession. NALA publishes editorial guidelines on its Web site, *www.nala.org,* which gives prospective writers some guidance as to the size of the article, the different types of articles accepted (some of which are categorized in "departments," such as technology, education, and ethics), and how the article is to be submitted (single/double-spaced, hard copy, on a disk or by e-mail).

Marge Dover, Executive Director of NALA, says articles are solicited from working paralegals as well as from professional writers. "We consider the journal as part of the continuing education we offer to our members," says Marge, "so we prefer articles that are educational as opposed to news."

Facts & Findings normally publishes articles that appeal to a national audience, although it will consider articles about something very unique or special in a particular state. According to Marge, all submitted articles are verified for accuracy.

The National Federation of Paralegal Associations publishes the *National Paralegal Reporter.* The magazine is bimonthly and includes in-depth features, how-to articles, and legal updates on such issues as case law, legislation, and education. Each issue is devoted to particular practice themes which are scheduled far in advance. Hopeful authors can contact *editor@ paralegals.org* to learn what practice themes are scheduled for each issue. While the magazine does not actively solicit articles from nonmembers, NFPA is always open to interesting topics that will benefit its readers. The "Features" section of the magazine offers the best opportunity for writers to be published. Topics in this section cross practice lines and should be of interest to readers regardless of their fields. Sample topics include violence in the workplace, computer forensics, grandparental rights, and using research skills in a genealogy hobby.

NFPA does not publish editorial guidelines but does accept proposals for articles. Proposals should be sent to *editor@paralegals.org* up to a year ahead of time because slots for articles fill in quickly. The editors suggest that authors stand a better chance of having their articles accepted if they study recently published issues, which are posted on the association's Web site at *www.paralegals.org.* If you do not have access to the Internet, NFPA can be reached at P.O. Box 33108, Kansas City, Missouri 64114, 816-941-4000.

The only independent national magazine devoted to the paralegal profession is *Legal Assistant Today. LAT* is owned by James Publishing, which also publishes *Law Office Computing* and a series of practice books for paralegals. Besides employing professional writers, *LAT* welcomes submissions of news stories, photographs, and articles from working paralegals, and will pay anywhere from $100 to several hundred dollars depending on the type and size of the material. If you are extremely knowledgeable in your field you may obtain a coveted columnist slot. Feature articles are accepted on assignment only, so before you go to the effort to write out the entire article, send a query letter to see if the magazine will be interested.

According to Rod Hughes, editor and publisher of *Legal Assistant Today,* the strongest areas of demand for articles from the magazine's readers are substantive how-to articles and personality profiles. "The how-to's should generally be designed to offer not only the beginner, but also the seasoned paralegal, inside tips and advice on how to be more accurate, efficient, and successful in their daily tasks. The personality profiles usually offer our readers a look at how their profession makes an impact, and show how paralegals often find themselves at the center of an incredibly diverse and exciting legal atmosphere."

Offering a tip of his own, Rod suggests that new writers familiarize themselves with the editorial guidelines before contacting the magazine with an inquiry. "It will give you an 'in' with the editorial staff if, on first contact, you can demonstrate an understanding of the magazine's procedures. This, along with strong writing skills and adherence to editorial deadlines, will almost always lead to future assignments."

SO YOU WANT TO SEE YOUR NAME ON AMAZON.COM

Okay, writing feature articles has now whetted your appetite to author an entire book. Most of the books written about paralegals and what they do are written by paralegals just like you. The only difference is *they* had the joy of sitting up at their computers into the wee hours of the morning while you slept. If you are willing to make a huge commitment of time and energy, and your family is willing to let you do this, writing a book can be a very satisfying outlet for your knowledge and artistic skills.

SO YOU WANT TO BE A TEACHER!

There comes a time when the thought crosses our minds that it would be fun to get in front of a class and impart wisdom and knowledge to a room full of hungry and eager minds. After all, movies like *Stand and Deliver* and *Mr. Holland's Opus* are very inspiring and give the concept of education such a noble and romantic air. Is teaching for you? And if so, how can you get a shot at a classroom?

Do a Self-Assessment

Before you start knocking on the door of the local college, it is wise to have a good long talk with yourself to find out whether you have what it takes to be a first-rate teacher. Students in paralegal studies programs work hard for their certificates, and they expect and deserve the best possible instruction. You wouldn't want to waste their time. Go through this list of questions and think honestly about how you would answer each of them.

1. Will I be able to make the necessary time commitment? A well-thought-out course is not just about class time. A lot of behind-the-scenes work goes into preparation, including outlining your lectures, finding and copying handout materials, reading the textbook ahead of the students, preparing tests and homework assignments and grading them, working with struggling students, and completing the paperwork required by the teaching institution. Not only that, but you must also be willing to constantly update your material, year after year, to keep it fresh and current. Most paralegal instructors are also full-time paralegals, and we all know what kinds of hours that entails. You need to decide whether, along with work and your other commitments, you will have enough hours in the day to properly prepare for and conduct your class.

2. Do I have enough energy to not only keep myself motivated, but to excite others? Most paralegal courses are taught at night, and you will not be the only one who will be coming to class after a hard day of work. Most paralegal students are working adults who are going back to school to learn a second career. In order to keep both yourself and them awake for an evening class, you are going to have to be not only informative, but entertaining as well. Your self-assessment should include determining whether you have the energy and stamina to excite students about the material you will be teaching and infuse them with enthusiasm about the profession.

3. Am I good at public speaking? Unless you are comfortable in front of an audience, you will not have the necessary self-confidence to run a classroom.

4. How well do I know the subject matter I plan to teach? Things don't always go according to your lesson plan. As a teacher, you must be ready for all sorts of unexpected questions from your students, and the only way to do this is to be totally familiar with and very experienced in the area of law you will be teaching. To add to the difficulty, paralegal students are usually mature individuals who are very serious about their newly chosen career. They are a tough audience and will call your bluff if they think you are hedging on answers to their questions. (The upside of this is that their positive attitude about learning is refreshing.)

5. Will I insist on the best from my students? Will I have the courage to give an "F" if it's deserved? We all remember how difficult it was to receive less than good grades when we were in school and how much fun it was to complain about the tough teachers who gave us too much homework. But we also knew, deep down inside, that we learned more from those tough teachers. You must ask yourself whether you can put aside your very human desire to be liked and do what it takes

to get your students to give you their best work. The last thing they need is a pushover.

6. What is my attitude toward the paralegal profession? And toward attorneys? Your students are excited about this career. Are you? Do you still maintain your enthusiasm about your profession? It will be up to you to fire up your students to be the best they can be. You will not be able to do this if you have personal ambivalence about the way the profession is headed, or if you are dissatisfied with how attorneys treat paralegals on the job. Students will quickly pick up on any negative attitudes you may harbor.

If you do not have any teaching experience, there are some things you can do to hone your skills before applying for a position. Check with your local paralegal association to see if they need speakers for their membership meetings or educational seminars. This will give you a chance to put together an hour or two's worth of lecture material, prepare some handouts, and get in front of an audience to speak. And since these engagements are usually voluntary, no one can fire you if you blow it the first time! With feedback and honest self-assessment, you will be able to learn a lot from doing a small seminar.

Other ways to get some practice include offering to guest lecture in a friend or former instructor's class or volunteering for the local paralegal school's tutoring program, if one is available. The last suggestion has an added benefit: It will introduce you to the school administration and give you a chance to impress them.

Landing a Teaching Position

Your first step in locating a teaching job is to find out whether the paralegal schools in your area hire paralegals to teach,* and, if so, what credentials are required. This may vary depending on the type of institution you are trying to hire into. If the program is taught out of a community college or private school, only an associate's degree may be needed. If it is part of a 4-year college or university, a bachelor's or graduate degree could be necessary. Some schools will waive degree requirements if the paralegal has enough years of experience in the field. Unofficial "credentials" schools look for in their teachers include some form of certification, such as the

---

*Amazing as it may seem, not all programs allow paralegals to teach, preferring the services of practicing attorneys.

Certified Legal Assistant designation given by the National Association of Legal Assistants, and membership in a paralegal association.

Following your initial research, the next step is to get to know some of the teachers in the program or the program administrator. If you are attempting to obtain a teaching job at your alma mater, this will be simple—you will probably already know many of these people. If the school is new to you, however, there are other ways to meet the movers and shakers. First of all, program coordinators and directors usually like to stay involved in their local legal communities and are probably members of your paralegal association. If you are also a member, you can meet and get to know them at the membership meetings or by working on a committee together.

Another way schools stay connected to the community is through advisory committees. The purpose of these committees is to obtain feedback on ways to improve the curriculum and to get suggestions for marketing the program and for the placement of graduates. Your paralegal program may have such a committee, and practicing attorneys, paralegals, educators, judges, and members of the public are invited to join. If you can land a spot on an advisory committee, you will make some important connections.

Another important task is to obtain a copy of the course catalog and educate yourself about the program and who the instructors are. Program directors often tap their existing instructors for suggestions on whom to hire to fill vacancies, so it is a good idea to get to know some of them. Usually, they will be practicing paralegals and attorneys in the area, whom you may have already had contact with through your work or by belonging to the local bar or paralegal associations. Familiarizing yourself with the program will give you ideas about which courses to teach, should openings come up. It will also show you holes in the program which you may be able to fill with your special talents. For example, suppose you are very good at managing large databases of documents and running the litigation support software to accomplish this. Upon reviewing the catalog for your local paralegal program you notice that no one is teaching this material. You could contact the program coordinator and pitch the idea that law firms require their paralegals to be computer literate and that more technology-oriented classes should be added to the curriculum. Who knows? You may find yourself teaching a brand new class!

I Got the Job. Now What Do I Do?

After congratulating yourself on joining the academic world, it's time to settle down and prepare for your class. Your first step will be to create a syllabus. A syllabus is a list of the topics you will be covering in your class and what your goals will be. You will list the required textbooks and any other materials the students will be responsible for. The syllabus should also contain a policy section where you set forth your rules for conducting the class. For example, you can outline your procedures for the submission of late homework (if any) or the giving of makeup exams. Will you allow extra credit? How can your students contact you if they have any questions? Spell out your policy on cheating. It is best to give such information to the students in writing so they cannot complain later that they didn't know the rules.

If you are teaching a course that has been taught before, the school may be able to provide you with an existing syllabus. If not, or if you are trying to design a new course, an excellent resource is the American Association for Paralegal Education (AAfPE). AAfPE sells sample course syllabi in a variety of areas and also offers guidance on appropriate teaching facilities, faculty and program director qualifications, marketing and promotion, student services, and model curricula. You can contact AAfPE at 2965 Flowers Road S, Suite 105, Atlanta, Georgia 30341, 770-452-9877, or on the Internet at *www.aafpe.org.*

Your next step is to choose what textbook you will use. The school will either have an established textbook for your class that it wants you to continue using, or else it will provide you with a list of possible books and allow you to pick your own. Most publishers will send review copies so that you can make a good choice, so don't hesitate to ask for one.

Review the potential textbook carefully, beginning with the table of contents. Make sure the book covers the topics you list on your syllabus. Skim the chapters to make sure they are well written and organized. Few books are perfect, but if you can find one close enough, you will have the option of supplementing it with handouts of your own.

Another thing to consider when choosing a text is its value to the students. Select a reasonably-priced volume which will be a good resource for the students long after they leave your class. Check the school's curriculum to see if some of the topics in your class overlap with another. For example, you may be teaching a legal writing class and someone else is teaching a legal research class. Try to work with the other instructor to choose one book that the students can use in both classes.

Once you select your textbook, you are ready to formulate your lesson plan. This is more difficult than it sounds. You must create a well-paced, systematic schedule for the teaching of the material. For example, you can't lecture about material in the book if you haven't assigned it to be read yet. You can't schedule a test until all the homework on the test material has been graded and returned. It isn't fair to the students to have a large homework project due the same day as a test is scheduled because they won't have enough time to study. You have to decide such things as how many tests you are going to give, what type of homework you will assign, whether you want the students to work in groups or alone, and whether you are going to give pop quizzes. You don't want to overburden the students with work (and yourself in grading that work), but if you give too little, you won't be able to properly assess their progress.

The best way to approach this task is to draft a proposed schedule for teaching the course. First of all, find out how many weeks are available in the teaching period, taking into account any holidays which may reduce the number of class nights. Then create a chart with the number of weeks going down in rows in the left column. Across the chart are columns for (1) the topics you will be lecturing on, (2) what handouts you will be giving, (3) what reading assignments will be given, and (4) what homework will be assigned. Create your schedule by filling in the chart. For example, the first night's lecture can be taken up with introductions, getting to know the students, covering the syllabus, and an overview of the class. Your handout that night will be the syllabus. Their reading assignment that night will be chapters one and two of the text. The homework assignment column will be blank because you wouldn't do that to them on their first night would you? The second week your lecture will cover the material that was in chapters one and two. Your handouts will be homework assignment number one, together with some helpful forms. The homework assignment will be due in 2 weeks. Besides the homework, you also ask them to read chapter three in the text. Make sure you indicate in week four of your chart that the homework assignment is due, so that you don't accidentally assign something else on week three that is due at the same time. Continue filling out the schedule until you cover the whole teaching period. You will probably need to juggle assignments somewhat to make things fit. Seeing the whole semester or quarter laid out will give you an idea of whether you are assigning too much or too little work. You may need to adjust things as you go (especially your first time teaching the class) if the students get behind or bored, but you will come across as very organized if you have a "road map" like this to follow.

As you are preparing your lesson plan, think of creative ways you can use to get the information across to the students. While lecturing is the obvious choice, it can be lethally boring for a 3-hour night class. Find videos to use to supplement your lectures. Demonstrate something on the computer or bring in a guest speaker. Have the students work on group projects to heighten their interest. In a discovery and trial preparation class taught by one of the authors, the students were divided into plaintiffs and defendants groups. The students had to serve each other with different types of discovery requests and then respond to the ones they were served with. An instructor in the same program who taught the litigation class brought in a court reporter friend and conducted an entire deposition so the students could see how it worked.

As a practicing paralegal, you are in a unique position to make the learning "real" for your students. You can give them examples of how you used the tools you are teaching them in your own work. This will make the knowledge much more meaningful and less abstract for the students.

A Possible Career Change?

Some of the paralegals who began teaching in their local programs enjoyed it so much, they took full-time teaching positions at the school when openings arose. These positions lead to other things, including being offered the position of program director.

Legal software vendors are often looking for people to help train users of the programs. If you have both a legal background and teaching experience, you could work your way into this type of position. You'll never know until you try!

PARALEGAL INNER VIEW: TAMARA HALLEN— TRADEMARK PROSECUTION DOESN'T MEAN A CRIMINAL ACTION

Name: Tamara Hallen
Corporation: Allergan, Irvine, California
Title: Associate Trademark Paralegal
Years of experience: 8 years in patents; 2 years in trademarks
Specialty: Intellectual property/trademarks
Number of attorneys and paralegals: 9 attorneys, 9 paralegals
Education: B.S. degree in marketing; Paralegal degree and certificate
Job duties: I deal mainly with foreign trademark prosecution (about 75 percent of my time) which entails filing, prosecution, and maintenance of trademarks worldwide. I handle 77 countries and deal with approximately 50 foreign attorneys. After filing an application (I have filed 243 applications so far this year, 450 department total), we deal with objections from the various trademark offices and have to present arguments and evidence proving why registration for our mark should be granted. We also negotiate letters of consent and use agreements with

competitors who own conflicting marks. Many documents (powers of attorney, letters of consent, agreements, etc.) need to be legalized which requires dealing with the secretary of state and various consulates. Beyond this, we (three paralegals make up our trademark department), share the operational requirements for the department which include docketing all incoming mail, maintenance of the database that tracks the activity and status of approximately 10,500 trademarks, processing foreign attorney invoices, assisting corporate personnel with trademark related questions, and notarizations (I've done 139 this year).

Additionally, we have weekly one-on-ones with our supervisor advising her of the status of our docket (our docket sheet is printed each week showing us all that is due within the next 2 months) and our intended activities for the week.

What do you find exciting about your job?
I find it challenging to deal with the foreign attorneys. In most cases, we have to provide them with arguments and evidence to present to their trademark examiners. This requires research to determine arguments that have been successful in other countries as well as evidence or registrations and use worldwide. This is complicated by the fact that each country has its own laws and what works in one [country] does not necessarily work in another.

I guess you have to know quite a few software programs.
In this job I'm using the PC as well as Mac; Word, WordPerfect, Microsoft Outlook, Excel, PowerPoint, FileMaker Pro, Worldmark Plus, E-mark.

How do you keep up on the latest changes in your field?
Publications, seminars, etc.

What makes you feel great about your job?
Successfully achieving registration due to arguments resulting from my own research.

So your biggest challenge would be . . .
Presenting convincing arguments and evidence.

What's the demand for your specialty?
I think it is growing. Intellectual property is purported to be the largest growing field in law. The Internet has a lot to do with this.

Is the money good?
Yes, I think so. Allergan pays higher than the salary surveys that I have seen.

What would you change about the field if you could?

I don't have any comments as to proposed changes. I am, however, very pleased with the passage of AB 1761 [California] defining the paralegal profession.

And your pearls of wisdom for other paralegals?

If you are young, maybe you should consider law school. As an attorney, you will be paid much more for the same kind of work.

CHAPTER 28

Legal Secretaries Seeking Paralegal Positions

The most logical response to hearing that a legal secretary wishes to enter the paralegal field is that the secretary will probably have little or no problem making the transition. And that's true to some extent. Making the actual transition can be a breeze. It's getting in the door that can cause the anxiety. Getting an employer to accept you in a field that bridges support to the attorney staff may cause you unexpected anxiety.

The degree of ease entering the paralegal field from legal secretary can vary according to the region of the country, years of experience, practice specialty, and educational background.

HANDLING EDUCATIONAL REQUIREMENTS

Because there are few standardized educational requirements to become a paralegal and because educational preferences vary widely across the country, you probably have just as much of a shot at becoming a paralegal as anyone else. However, chances are your skills and educational background may be scrutinized more closely than a person entering from a different industry.

Most major firms now require a B.A. or B.S. degree for paralegal positions. Some firms waive that requirement in lieu of experience. While many of the firms welcome legal secretarial experience with open arms, others will not consider it in exchange for the degree. Whatever the reason for this prejudice, be it caste system or lack of understanding of exactly what you do, you may encounter this attitude when seeking a paralegal position. Smaller firms and solo practitioners can be less rigid. Larger firms that pattern their paralegal programs closely after the associate program might be less likely to waive the criteria. It's up to you to educate these firms about your potential. Hammer home the advantages of hiring you instead of an entry-level paralegal. Legal secretaries possess much more knowledge and understanding of legal terminology and court procedures than most people entering the paralegal field.

If you have a B.A. or B.S. degree, you are in a strong negotiating position. If you do not have a paralegal certificate, now may be the time to get one, with or without the degree. If you need to attend school while working full-time, there are schools with night programs. Be very careful when selecting a paralegal school. Offering a night program is not the only criterion to select that program. Find out the following:

- Does the school have a successful placement office? If so, what percent of each graduating class is placed in firms and corporations? What is the average length of the job search? What firms hire their graduates? (Get names.)
- Will they give you the names of graduates to contact for references? Ask the alumni for names of other graduates that the school didn't give you, and call them.
- What is the school's success rate for placing paralegals with legal secretarial background? Can you contact these graduates as well?

Additionally, do your homework about the firms and legal departments in your city. First, target several firms and corporations where you would like to work. Call the paralegal hiring authority to find out:

- From what schools does the firm prefer to hire? Many firms have no particular hiring criteria at all, but you may find that the school you want to attend is not considered by the firms you want.
- Does the firm hire paralegals with legal secretarial background? Many firms will refuse to answer. However, ask whether there are any paralegals with legal secretarial background you can talk to in order to gather background information about the paralegal field in general.
- Ask about the hiring criteria. You will get an idea as to how to crack open that door.
- Does the firm promote from within?
- Do most of the firms in your region require the certificate to be from an ABA-approved school?

If you live in a region of the country where there are no nearby paralegal schools or you are already doing paralegal work without the title, a good avenue for you may be the National Association of Legal Assistants (NALA) certification program (CLA). The certification is widely accepted in some regions but virtually ignored in others. Unfortunately, many employers inundated with paralegal schools are either reluctant to recognize the certification or are unfamiliar with the distinction. Many have schools they prefer right next door. The NALA certification is awarded upon completion of a 2-day exam. Attendance is required at certain seminars and courses. Part of the exam calls on knowledge obtained on the job. Contact the organization and find out how many NALA certificates have been awarded in your region in the past 5 years. Ask the firm whether it recognizes the certification. Get names and phone numbers of NALA-certified paralegals and find out how the certification helped their careers.

It seems easier for legal secretaries to enter the paralegal field in certain specialties such as personal injury, workers' compensation, probate, family law, immigration, and some areas of litigation. Any practice dominated by repetitive forms appears to welcome legal secretaries without B.A.s and certificates more than areas of law where you will have to draft original documents.

EDUCATING EMPLOYERS ABOUT SKILLS AND ABILITIES

The perceived difference in the employer's mind between you and the paralegal will be that presumably the attorney tells you exactly what she wants you to do, how to fill out a form, and what words to use. The paralegal is supposed to be able to draft simple, original documents. (However, most secretaries are more familiar with court filings, proper forms, dates, and certain procedures than many paralegals.)

Let's talk about drafting for just a moment. Many secretaries will say, "Wait a minute, I do some drafting." Be very careful. Filling out a form or composing a letter does not constitute drafting documents. The employer wants to know whether you have performed original drafting assignments, such as gathering all of the information, assimilating it, and then writing *from your own thought process* as opposed to transcribing someone else's thoughts or notes (an example may be drafting answers to interrogatories). If you have actually drafted, great! That is the kind of information to impart to the employer.

Negotiating Your Salary

Why is it so important to educate the employer about your capabilities and types of assignments you have performed? Because if you are a legal secretary with several years of experience and want to enter the paralegal field, some employers will expect you to take a cut in salary.

Starting salaries across the country for entry-level paralegals are anywhere from $23,000 to $34,000 per year, depending on region. Some firms do not pay overtime for a paralegal but will for a secretary. If you are presently earning less than this amount, obviously, you should get an increase when you enter the field. However, because the current shortage of legal secretaries has pushed the salary level upward, many secretaries are earning very healthy salaries, some as much as $70,000. The differences between the salary of paralegals and secretaries is that the secretary is considered overhead, not income generating, while the paralegal is billed to the client. The rate of salary is captured by at least 3 times. The theory is while paralegals start out earning less money, because they are billable there is no cap on salary. Unfortunately, this theory does not hold true (paralegal salaries do level off). In many firms, paralegals are eligible for a bonus based on merit and/or billable hours while the secretaries at the same firm are eligible for a bonus of only 1 or 2 weeks' salary.

Pat, a former legal secretary who is now a successful corporate paralegal, analyzed a cut in salary to become a paralegal this way: "If you were taking a train from New York to San Francisco and decided to stop off in Minneapolis for awhile, would you get on the train and go back to New York in order to get to San Francisco? Or would you get on the train and continue on?"

If you decide to become a paralegal after spending significant time as a legal secretary, would you go all the way back to the beginning and start over again? Or would you continue on in your career in the legal field?

Benefits to the Firm in Hiring You

When the salary question finally emerges in the interview, use the negotiating techniques previously discussed. Here are a few additional answers to use when selling yourself to the firm:

- I am already familiar with this practice specialty. The firm will spend fewer dollars training me.
- I work well under deadlines.
- I am familiar with the culture of a law firm and its environment.
- My computer skills are more sophisticated and law oriented than the average entry-level paralegal from another field.
- I know how to work well with difficult attorneys.
- I know my way around the courthouse, secretary of state's office, administrative agencies, and so forth.
- I can deal with legal vendors, and I know who the best are in this community.
- I know how to handle the law firm clients, particularly when they are under stress.

- I have the strong organizational skills necessary for a paralegal position. If I didn't have these skills, I wouldn't have survived as a legal secretary.
- I am used to working with volumes of paper.
- I am familiar with the legal terminology a paralegal needs to know.
- I already understand the Master Calendar and docketing system.

Writing Your Resume

Part of the reason some secretaries encounter difficulties when seeking a paralegal position is that their resume emphasizes clerical skills rather than the skills necessary to become a paralegal. Skills and abilities to emphasize when drafting your resume for a paralegal are:

- Organizational skills
- People skills
- Knowledge of legal terminology
- Any projects you have supervised
- Any staff you have supervised
- Computer expertise—paralegals are expected to know word processing packages and to be familiar with databases. If your computer expertise extends to other software and hardware knowledge, be sure to emphasize this under a special section entitled "computer skills."
- Foreign languages
- Degrees, certificates, or seminars you have attended (law related)
- Accounting ability, if any
- Areas of law you know
- Familiarity with court systems
- Docketing knowledge
- Recruiting skills

Do Not:

- List how fast you type
- List all of the clerical machines you use, for example, 10 key adding machines by touch
- List your day-to-day clerical duties, for example, answered phones, opened mail, reviewed calendar, made travel arrangements, set appointments. Keep the resume slanted toward the professional rather than the clerical side. Employers do not need to be reminded of clerical

skills—it's understood that you have them. Further, those are not the skills that will impress your potential employer.

Do:

- Use the objective or goal line at the top of the resume. Be very specific about your intent to enter the paralegal field.
- Follow the guidelines regarding interviewing and dressing for success.
- List your progression as a secretary. For example, if you started as a word processor and became a secretary to the managing partner, demonstrate the growth pattern in your resume.

A sample resume follows at the end of this chapter.

Getting Promoted Within Your Firm

If you enjoy your firm but would rather be a legal assistant, try to get yourself promoted within the firm. Tackle a few paralegal assignments, with the approval of the supervising attorney and get feedback. Ask an attorney to help. If that attorney isn't interested, find another attorney who is. Many times, other paralegals will rally to your support; so will the office manager or the director of administration. Find a paralegal who will act as your mentor and can show you how to complete certain assignments. Make sure the appropriate powers-that-be are aware of your talents.

If you can't seem to be placed in the paralegal program and are performing paralegal assignments (according to the law firm's job descriptions), see if you can at least get a title, even if part of it is "legal secretary." If you do have a split title, use legal secretary last (for example, "paralegal/legal secretary") on your resume. However, make sure you get an official designation from the firm. Titles can be checked along with references.

SAMPLE: FUNCTIONAL LEGAL SECRETARY RESUME

NAME
ADDRESS
CITY, STATE, ZIP
PHONE NUMBERS
E-MAIL ADDRESS

PROFESSIONAL EXPERIENCE

Legal Procedures:

- Composed simple contracts, declarations, court forms, pleadings
- Maintained docket system
- Researched company, state, and federal agencies' rules and procedures
- Prepared settlement demands and supportive documents
- Assisted in document productions
- Prepared deposition summaries
- Communicated with clients and insurance adjusters regarding claims

Administrative:

- Prepared office procedures guide
- Acted as liaison between staff and management
- Scheduled witnesses for depositions
- Calculated monthly firm expenses for fee applications
- Designed directory systems for access to pleadings, agreements
- Recruited and interviewed junior secretaries

Computer Skills:

- Expert in Word
- Experienced on the Internet
- Familiar with LEXIS and Westlaw
- Experienced in PowerPoint and Excel

WORK HISTORY

November 1998–Present: Jones and Smith
Legal Secretary to Managing Partner

March 1993–November 1998: Smith and Day
Legal Secretary to Litigation Partner and two Associates

EDUCATION

Associate of Arts Degree, Business Administration
College of the Pacific, San Francisco, California, 1997

PARALEGAL INNER VIEW: LUCI HOOVER—
HOW ONE LEGAL SECRETARY MADE IT

Name: Luci Hoover
Firm: Hinshaw & Culbertson; Rockford, Illinois
Title: Paralegal
Number of attorneys and paralegals: 25 attorneys, 3 paralegals (two full-time and one part-time)
Hinshaw & Culbertson has a total of 21 offices, mostly in Illinois but some in Wisconsin, Georgia, Florida, Minnesota, Indiana, Missouri, and California
Education: I have worked in the law field as a secretary and later functioning as a paralegal since 1964. I have only had my paralegal certificate since 1993. I have a B.A. from Concordia University in Mequon, Wisconsin, in Business Management and Communications. I graduated magna cum laude. I have a paralegal certificate from Roosevelt University in Chicago and I graduated with honors.
Job duties: I work primarily in the areas of real estate (usually handling applications for real estate tax exemptions for religious, charitable, and municipalities, corporate maintenance and litigation). As far as any "specialty," I probably have the most expertise in real estate exemption work.

What does a paralegal do at Hinshaw & Culbertson?

My typical day is anything but typical! While the corporate and real estate work can be planned and scheduled, I also work on special projects with various attorneys in the litigation field. I enjoy the research and problem-solving tasks and generally dealing personally with clients. The nice thing about the firm is that they allow me to work on my own, knowing that I am responsible for getting the job done. While I can't sign the documents which need to be filed, I am responsible for organizing and preparing everything needed as well as drafting the individual documents and affidavits required, particularly in the area of real estate exemptions. I also accompany the attorney if we need to appear at a local Board of Review hearing.

I do enjoy the unusual and am always up for a challenge. I love the opportunity to learn more about new areas and increase what I know.

What was the toughest assignment you've tackled?

I can really think of two and they are both very different from one another. The first was the compiling and preparation of an application for real estate tax exemption for a retirement/nursing home. Another firm had already prepared and filed this application but it was denied by the Illinois Department of Revenue. It took many months of reviewing documents, blueprints, computing square footage for the various areas, and putting it all together before we could get it filed. I was very pleased that our application packet was accepted and we were able to obtain tax relief the client was hoping to receive.

The second most challenging (not necessarily that it was less challenging) was my involvement with our school district's desegregation suit. While the lawsuit had been ongoing for many years, we were petitioning the court to give the control of the schools back to the school district. The amount of discovery that was generated was enormous! Because there was so much discovery being exchanged, I established a system of not only Bates stamping each page, but keeping everything updated on an index which referenced each document.

Once discovery was complete, we began preparation for the trial. We were required to present our exhibit binders to opposing counsel and the court prior to the start of trial. I was actually working on this case with a paralegal from the Washington, D.C. firm which was cocounsel. Our complete exhibit binders totaled 17—each being 3 inches. We subsequently added another two or three binders with additional documents. The day before each witness was to be put on the stand, we were required to submit copies of the individual binder for that witness to opposing counsel. It meant a lot of late nights getting everything organized so the attorneys could hit the deck running the next day. It was very interesting to be a part of that team.

The case went for 15 days but it was spread over 2 months. It was a good experience and really gave me an opportunity to put my organizational skills to work.

Where did you work prior to this firm?

I worked 9 years for an attorney who worked primarily in family law. Every day dealt with emergencies because of the fact that to each client, this was the most important case because it affected their life. Working in family law can be very stressful mostly because there are not the types of cases where you can plan out ahead what you will need to do and actually have it happen that way.

What's your take on computer skills?

I am very thankful that I was a secretary for many years. It is imperative that a paralegal type and be computer literate with the programs we use. I do believe that in today's society, with everyone being able to type, paralegals and often attorneys, are responsible for their own work product. I prefer to do my own typing because I can type faster than the time it would take me to dictate something, review it after it is typed, and sign it.

What do you have to say to future paralegals?

If you can't type accurately (not necessarily that you have to be fast) and if you can't put a sentence together correctly, go back to school and work on it. The one thing that I have found is that the attorney needs to be able to put his/her trust in you. If you prepare something and whether it is for your signature or the attorney's, it needs to be neat and correct. If they lose their trust in your work, you may find that you don't have a job for long.

What's in store for you?

I teach part-time in a paralegal program at the local business college. I enjoy very much what I do with Hinshaw & Culbertson and I enjoy teaching. Both are very rewarding. I would like to continue doing what I do until I retire. I would then like to work part-time, on my schedule, and continue to do what I currently do! I am also looking at getting a master's degree in paralegal studies. If I do that, however, it is for me. I am not doing it to advance in a different direction.

Can you suggest any changes for the profession?

I don't want to change the profession, but I would like to see students get more hands-on experience within their classes. The education received from books is great, but when you can put it to practical use, you are worth your weight in gold.

What's your take on education for paralegals?

I definitely believe in education, however, I also believe that on-the-job training is important. We need to crawl before we can walk. Learning from the beginning what is expected of a paralegal and being able to take specific classes in each area is important. Sometimes when training on the job, you only get bits and pieces of knowledge but you never get the chance to go in-depth with the training. It's sort of like putting a Band-Aid on something as opposed to fixing it. I don't discount on-the-job training, but I think that the best paralegals get both on-the-job training and a formal education. It's important to continue your education after you have graduated. I strongly believe that when you stop learning you stop living! The best paralegals I have seen are the ones who attend seminars, read books, and search the Internet for answers. They are the ones who network with other paralegals and share their expertise.

CHAPTER 29

Creating a Business

> . . . and the trouble is, if you don't risk anything, you risk even more.
>
> Erica Jong, American writer, b. 1941

What paralegals in their right minds would want to risk security, stable income, pension plans, benefits, bonuses, plush surroundings, automatic increases in salary, and a guaranteed parking place to open their own businesses? Probably paralegals who no longer want to be someone *else's* retirement.

Opening up your own business in the legal field can create opportunities you once only dreamt of. For many paralegals, it takes away built-in caps on income. It also offers challenge, excitement, success, recognition, imagination, innovation, and risk.

CHARACTERISTICS OF THE ENTREPRENEUR

There are probably very few people who, at one time or another, haven't thought fleetingly of opening up the perfect business that would solve all their problems. However, the difference between the dreamers and the doers is the range of risk we are willing to take. Entrepreneurs are not necessarily people who throw all caution to the wind. Rather, the successful entrepreneur will take a calculated risk, judging the anticipated outcome, weighing carefully the upside and downside. While many entrepreneurs share similar characteristics and traits, there seems to be no one formula that can determine whether you will be successful in your venture. However, here are some similar characteristics and traits of entrepreneurs:

- The entrepreneurs' primary motivation is they no longer want to work for anyone else. In corporations, employees figure out that employers earn at least 25 to 30 percent more than employees. In law firms, paralegals reason that the more hours they personally bill, the more bottom-line profit for the firm, the larger the *partner's* piece of the pie.

- Entrepreneurs are driven by an idea and the success of the idea, not the money. The money becomes a by-product of the success.
- Entrepreneurs are well organized. Even if they do not appear to be outwardly organized, entrepreneurs have their own system, such as a list of notes of things to do, a reminder pad, a stack of papers (don't touch that pile, I know every piece of paper in it!). Entrepreneurs think in organized layers.
- Entrepreneurs are not always the greatest in financial matters or accounting procedures. They are generally full of ideas, concepts, and vision and hate to get bogged down in what they consider minutia.

  Many learn accounting procedures only after they have started their businesses. When speaking to accountants, they want to know only the bottom line and whether they're in good shape. How they got to the bottom line causes them to glaze over.

- Entrepreneurs are generally high-energy people without a 9:00 to 5:00 mentality. They forget to look at the clock.
- Entrepreneurs have exceptionally strong marketing skills.
- Entrepreneurs think, act, and react quickly. Many times their attitudes are "right or wrong, make the decision, then act on it."
- Entrepreneurs have no problem generating work. This is an important criterion for paralegals considering opening up their own businesses. Because the profession is a "helping" occupation, paralegals evolve from an environment where assignments originate from a separate source, the attorney.

  While many paralegals, certainly senior paralegals, know what the next step may be, there are few opportunities to initiate the work flow.

- Entrepreneurs are most commonly the oldest child in the family. According to Joseph Mancusco, author of *How to Start, Finance and Manage Your Own Business* (Prentice Hall), entrepreneurs tend to be the oldest child 60 percent of the time.
- The issue of education among entrepreneurs has always been divided. According to Mancusco, studies in the 1950s and 1960s showed many entrepreneurs, such as Edwin Land, Polaroid's founder, who dropped out of college. More recently, we have the story of William Gates, founder of Microsoft, who also dropped out of Harvard when he was 20 years old. Although no studies currently exist on the educational background of paralegal entrepreneurs, it appears that backgrounds are as diverse as educational requirements.

- Entrepreneurs have the attitude of the optimist, "to believe that with the right amount of time and the right amount of money, you can do anything." This can be a very difficult concept for any one emerging from negative reinforcement. Some law firms have the attitude that you are only as good as your last time sheet. If this has happened to you, do what you need to do to surround yourself with positive thinkers.
- Entrepreneurs have the ability and the need to compete. They are stimulated by the chase.

WHAT KIND OF BUSINESS?

It seems as though every month there is a new business opening up in the legal community. Some succeed, some fail immediately, and others make a slow but gradual climb upward, gaining recognition through good products and services and word-of-mouth public relations. If you have an idea and have spotted a need, nurture it, research it, and see if you can make it fly in the community. The following are companies (some paralegal-owned) that you might consider if you are looking to open and establish your own business:

Seminar company. The need for continuing education continues. Certain states, such as California, have passed requirements (MCLE) mandating that attorneys receive a certain amount of continuing education per year. If licensing or educational requirements pass for paralegals, the need for seminars increases.

Software technology company. The need appears endless in an industry which really only recently got on the computer bandwagon.

Corporate services. Several paralegals have opened highly successful businesses to prepare and file corporate documents, reserve names, conduct litigation searches, retrieve documents, and research county, state, and federal records. These companies also incorporate companies and file UCCs.

Litigation support software programs. Technology is changing extremely rapidly. What worked yesterday is out-of-date tomorrow.

Fax filing agency. Faxes court documents to be filed and retrieved.

Photocopying services. Even though firms are getting more sophisticated service centers, the need to send documents to a vendor to be copied exists, as does on-site photocopying.

Scanning and imaging. The biggest and latest massive movement in the legal field.

Asset search company. Attorneys generally have to go outside of the firm for this service, which includes skiptracing, background reports, location assets, and financial reports.

Translating service. A great assistance for personal injury, international law, workers' compensation, trade law, and other practice specialties.

Court reporting. Okay, so it's getting out of the paralegal realm, but it's related!

Paralegal school. There are approximately 700 paralegal schools in the country today. Perhaps there is an area in your state that could use this school. Some areas are more concentrated than others.

Litigation support company. Provides document indexing, coding, database design, retrieval systems, training, repository, and imaging and scanning operations.

Placement firm. Provides recruiting and full-time placement services of legal staff for law firms and corporations.

Timekeeping and billing software. There is always a need for new software for time and billing, conflict of interest, trust accounting, billing and calendar systems.

Temporary placement services. The need for temporary paralegals varies from state to state and can go up or down depending on the economic climate.

Courier or messenger services. Perhaps you have heard many law firms or corporations in your city complaining about the need for such a service.

Medical records summarizing. A highly skilled arena that may be of interest for those of you with a combined background in the legal and medical fields.

Event planning. Attended many firm functions that you know you could have thrown together better? Perhaps your skill in this area can be combined with your knowledge of how the firms want to see their parties, functions, and picnics succeed.

Secretarial service. With the shortage of legal secretaries pronounced across the entire country, perhaps you can use your supervisory skills and provide a service for typing, word processing, and so forth in your offices, particularly for smaller firms.

Arbitration and mediation services. Can you find an attorney who would be interested in joining you in starting this type of service? Be sure to research whether nonattorneys can run this type of service in your state. If not, perhaps you can find attorneys to start the company who will hire you to manage it.

Forensic technology. The technology involved in creating computer-generated animations for trial.

Exhibit preparation. Several paralegal-owned companies have evolved to prepare demonstrative evidence for trial and deposition. If you have an artistic background, you may find this a creative way to tie in your many talents. These companies prepare time lines, graphs, charts, diagrams, medical illustrations, photo enlargements, models, and more.

Expert witness. Was your former career in a field you could now tie in with your legal expertise? Were you a nurse? Engineer? Human resource expert? In construction? Environment? Accounting? Health care? Insurance? Agriculture?

Lien/foreclosure service. Prepare lien defaults and foreclosures for attorneys.

Computer consultants. Use your computer expertise to train in software programs, develop macros, install systems, and review software for clients.

Genealogical investigations. Heir location and missing persons service.

Travel service for law firms and legal departments. This service is highly specialized. As a paralegal, you understand the need for finding hotels near the courtroom. You may also provide other services such as locating court reporters, photocopying services, secretarial services, and conference rooms for traveling attorneys, paralegals, and professional staff. You certainly would understand their needs for stress-free vacations!

PARALEGAL INNER VIEW: KIM NOWSAD— NETWORKING DOESN'T MEAN WE'LL DO LUNCH

Name: Kim D. Nowsad
Company: Litigation & Technology Consultants, LLC, Detroit, Michigan
Title: Litigation/Network Consultant; primarily acting as a litigation support consultant with network experience; I am also an authorized Summation reseller.
Years of experience: 18 years
Number of attorneys/paralegals: None
Education: B.S. in Finance from the University of Detroit 1984
MSF from Walsh College 1991
Job duties: I am currently involved in several database projects ranging from a possible class action on gas and oil leases, environmental issues, patent infringement, and employment law. It is my responsibility to assist the attorneys and legal assistant/paralegals with the management of the case from the standpoint of document management.

What's one of your most challenging assignments?

Designing and coordinating the building of a database of approximately 100,000 pages of exhibits with 1 month before trial.

Where do you get your kicks in this job?

Seeing a case that I worked on from the very beginning finally get resolved. A legal assistant/paralegal in larger firms rarely has the opportunity to work on a case from beginning to close.

Be honest. What was the scariest/most frightening/eye-opening experience for you?

Realizing that there are so many cases with hundreds of thousands of documents and depositions and finding out that there wasn't any type of document management in place.

What kinds of computer skills does a computer expert need?

I have to keep current on both network technology as well as constantly using the databases. I like to see everyone exposed to at least Windows 98. Most of the newer applications will not be supported on Windows 95. They should have at least some experience working in a network environment (not with the network itself). They should have an opportunity to see the server room and meet the IS/IT staff. This would give them a better understanding of how technologically advanced their system is and that they can also rely on their staff for support.

What does a successful professional such as yourself have to say to paralegals looking for that climb up the ladder?

Don't be afraid to ask questions or be creative. My personal philosophy is that there is no such thing as a dumb question. If you don't know the answer or can't understand something, it is unlikely that you will produce the product that you are expected to. Sometimes ideas that you have may generate new ways of looking at a problem. Also, keep up on available software. I'm not saying to review every product on the market . . . just know that some software vendor may have a product that can assist you. There are many products on the market. Lastly, join a litigation support group. They are inexpensive and your firm may even pay for membership. A group can always give you advice on various issues and technology.

Waving your magic wand and changing the profession, you come up with—

I think that attorneys who use their legal assistant/paralegals to create lists or indexes are losing out on one of the best resources they have available. I have seen multiple lists/indexes of practically the same documents that are created over and over. Use a database and learn how to generate reports from existing data. The legal assistant/paralegal can provide immense assistance in document review and summaries instead of creating lists.

Do you think it is important for paralegals to have an education in paralegal studies or is on-the-job training sufficient?

I think both are equally important, but I believe that hands-on with a knowledgeable attorney who is willing to take the extra time would provide the best combination.

What's in store for the future for you?

I have moved from being a paralegal to owning my own company that provides litigation support consulting and also sells litigation support software. While it will take awhile to become fully self-sufficient, the rewards of being my own boss far outweigh the hours.

And, O wise one, tell us about the future of the profession.

I see the profession moving along at a fast pace that may, unfortunately, leave several people behind. It has always been a changing profession. However, as cases get larger and more document-intense, the need for a technology-versed legal assistant/paralegal will also increase.

CHAPTER 30

Trial: The Brass Ring
Stacey Hunt

A career goal of many civil litigation and criminal specialty paralegals is to second chair at trial, preferably a major trial. What is it like assisting at trial? Just how do you go about getting that coveted spot? And will you be able to handle the stress? Because stressful it is. Yet with that stress comes the thrill of seeing all your hard work on a case come to fruition. Every pleading, every piece of discovery, all the information from witnesses you helped track down—it all comes into play. And you are there to see it happen first-hand. It is the difference between sitting on the bench watching the game and being out on the field playing. Here are some tips to get yourself out onto that playing field.

CHARACTERISTICS OF A GOOD TRIAL PARALEGAL

Trial paralegals share many of the same traits as all good paralegals. They must be observant, excellent problem solvers, detail-oriented, organized, and know their case files inside and out. The one main difference is that trial paralegals must be able to perform these tasks with split-second timing, under the scrutiny of judge, jury, and opposing counsel, and without the opportunity to make even a single mistake. They must be able to think on their feet, stay alert for long hours, be flexible, and, if the trial takes place out of town, be able to quickly ascertain the lay of the land. They have to be good at reading people—recognizing when jurors are becoming bored or confused or a judge is getting impatient. Last and most importantly, trial paralegals must have an almost telepathic link with their attorneys. The best trial paralegal knows what the attorney needs before he even realizes he needs it, recognizing when he is concentrating and not disturb him, and protect him from anxious clients who want to get a word in.

HOW TO GET YOUR BOSS TO TAKE YOU TO TRIAL

Things are quite different today from when Perry Mason practiced law. With a witness or two and a couple of files, the fictional TV lawyer was able to put the whole case to bed within an hour. But today's cases are increasingly complex, multifaceted, and challenging. Paper evidence has evolved into demonstrative evidence, which can take the form of anything from mounted blow-ups (exhibits) to high-tech, multimedia presentations. The dollars at stake can be enormous, and the client deserves the best representation possible. Any attorney will tell you that trying a case alone is a difficult prospect today, especially if a jury is involved. In addition to taking notes, keeping the exhibits organized, questioning witnesses, and planning strategy on the fly, the trial attorney must also maintain a rapport with the jury, watch for signs of tedium or annoyance, keep focused, and be ready with impeachment materials when there is a sudden turn of events. On a major case, all of this is not humanly possible for just one person, thus creating all sorts of opportunities for a clever, ambitious paralegal.

Before asking to second chair at trial, you must first do a little groundwork. Start small by asking to accompany the attorney to a few hearings. This will give you important courtroom experience, however brief. See if your boss will allow you to attend and help with depositions. You will get a chance to observe how examination is conducted and how witnesses respond to questions. You will also gain necessary experience working with exhibits in a less stressful environment than the courtroom. Following the hearing, share your observations with the attorney so that she can see how observant you are and can get used to relying on your suggestions.

Once you feel you are ready, ask to help with a small trial. Hopefully, the attorney will grant your request, but sometimes you may need to overcome apparent initial hesitation. Attorneys might turn down your request to second chair at trial for a couple of reasons. They might prefer to take an associate with them for training purposes, or the client cannot afford to pay for both of you to attend the trial. They might need someone back at the office to "mind the store." There are ways to counter all of these arguments and convince the attorney to consider your practical request.

It is true that watching a trial attorney at work in the courtroom is excellent education for up-and-coming associates. However, this may not be the best choice, either for the client or the trial attorney. In reality, the associate probably does not know the file nearly as well as the paralegal does. During the workup of a case, associates are usually more involved in taking some of the depositions, conducting legal research, and writing motions. Once the case is ready for trial, those skills are no longer in play. Necessary at this stage is someone who has summarized all the depositions and knows what they say; is familiar with every exhibit and knows how to put her hands on them in seconds; and who can work with the courtroom clerk and bailiff to arrange for last-minute transcripts and equipment. This professional is an expert with the computer equipment and software that was used to organize the case and with the audio/video equipment that will display the information to judge and jury. She has established a relationship with the witnesses, experts, investigators, and other individuals who will either be involved in the trial or who will make it run smoothly . . . in other words, the paralegal who has been assigned to that case from day one. The associate may simply not be familiar enough with all aspects of the case to make an efficient trial assistant. Like it or not, the attorney's legal training can sometimes work to his disadvantage when working with a jury. He loses that "lay person" perspective, and gets lost in the legal jockeying. A paralegal, while having a great deal of legal knowledge, can still see things from a lay person's point of view and can help keep the attorney connected with the jury.

An associate may not always be the best choice because her billable rate is almost certainly higher than yours, creating a greater expense for the client. As we well know, clients are not particularly fond of paying for an associate's learning curve. If you are denied a second chair position because the attorney is taking an associate, here are a few suggestions to (diplomatically and cautiously!) make:

1. "It would be less expensive for me to assist. How about if the associate attends the trial, but to observe and suggest?"

2. "I am the person on the team most familiar with the documents and computer program. Perhaps the associate and I could both assist and we could split up the duties."

3. "The legal issues in this case are so complicated, I might be able to help you come up with ways to better explain things in lay person's terms to the jurors so that they can understand."

If the reason the attorney gives for not allowing you to second chair is that it is not in the client's budget, here are some counterarguments:

1. "Would you say that my assistance has made you more efficient during the rest of the case? Trial is no exception."

2. "I believe knowing how my work product is used during the trial would be of enormous educational benefit to me. Would you be willing to write off my time at trial as a learning experience?"

3. "The federal courts and courts in some states allow for the recovery of paralegal fees by the prevailing party. If we win, perhaps the other side will have to pay for my time.

Finally, if the attorney wants you to stay behind so that you can take care of problems that come up at the office, suggest that it might be better for an associate to stay behind, since you would be unable to give legal advice or make any major judgment calls in the absence of an attorney.

Often there is a simple reason why the attorney is not taking you to trial—he simply has always done it by himself and sees no reason to change now. If you can get such an attorney to try utilizing your assistance just once, it may change his mind forever. Be persistent. Prove yourself during the workup of the case. Explain to the attorney how important a career challenge it is for you and that the case may be better served by your participation in the trial.

THE TRIAL EXPERIENCE—WHAT TO EXPECT AND HOW TO SURVIVE IT

The trial experience is a true roller-coaster event. It is full of incredible highs, like watching your witness blow the other side out of the water with her testimony. It is also filled with enormous lows, such as when the court rules that you cannot bring in certain evidence crucial to your case. The hours are long, the work sometimes tedious, tempers can get short, and you can forget your personal and social life for the duration of the trial. But the experience is addicting and the tension exhilarating. That's why courtroom dramas, both in the movies and on television, are so popular. People's reputations, freedom, financial well-being, and even lives are at stake. Your presence at the trial can and will make a difference.

Getting ready*

In some jurisdictions, a judge will have been assigned to your case from the beginning and you will know who will be presiding at the trial. You may already have had contact with that judge's courtroom personnel (e.g., clerk, court reporter, bailiff) from prior motions or other proceedings. If not, you should telephone the clerk and bailiff and introduce yourself. Let them know that you are the paralegal to attorney so-and-so, who will be trying the case such-and-such, which is scheduled to go forward in their courtroom next week. Ask whether the judge has any special rules, likes, or dislikes

---

*There are many good books, trade journal articles, and continuing education courses on trial preparation itself, containing advice on preparing trial notebooks, creating demonstrative evidence, organizing exhibits, subpoenaing witnesses, etc. That is not within the scope of this chapter and we assume that you already possess much of that knowledge, and many of those skills.

which you should know about. If you are going to have special equipment in the courtroom or have any special needs, check with the bailiff. It is his job to help you with these types of matters and he will appreciate not having any unusual requests sprung on him the first day of trial.

If you do not know ahead of time who your trial judge will be, you will have to save your introductions and questions for the first day of trial, when you receive your courtroom assignment.

If you do know to which department your trial has been assigned, make an effort to stop by before the trial to do some reconnaissance of the courtroom. Note the location of counsel table and where it sits in relation to the jury box and bench. This will help you decide on the best size and placement of any blow-ups or other demonstrative evidence. If you will be using laptop computers, overhead projectors, tape players, or other electrical equipment, note the location of the closest power outlets (sometimes located in the floor beneath the counsel tables). You can then make decisions about whether extension cords will be necessary.

Sure you've prepared the attorney's trial boxes and notebooks, but don't forget about some things *you* might need. Take your own binder with things in it such as a list of witnesses' telephone numbers, the phone number of your process server in the event an emergency subpoena must be served, and some blank subpoenas. If you will be trying a case out of town, you may want to take a list of good research Web sites in case you have to do any legal or factual research on the fly. Locate the closest law library and all-night copy center. You might want to throw in some change for parking meters or telephone calls. If you have a cell phone, make sure the battery is charged up, and bring an extra battery or charger. Those little "traveling offices" that can be found at stationery stores can be very helpful. They are zippered pouches that contain miniaturized staplers, staple removers, tape, paper clips, rulers, pens, and pencils, among other things. You will also want a large supply of legal pads for notetaking, and you may even want your own copies of the trial exhibit list and witness list, a list of the files you are bringing with you, a laptop computer with blank disks, the database from the case, if any, and anything else you might find useful. It is a good idea to throw in a few blank firm checks for unexpected expenses, such as daily transcripts from the court reporter.

Courtroom Decorum

It goes without saying that you will be dressing and behaving at your absolute best in the courtroom. Judges, even younger ones, are still fairly old fashioned, conservative people, who demand and expect your respect, so make your mother proud! Choose conservative, dark-colored suits and dresses to wear. Shoes should be pumps for women and polished leather shoes for men. No article of clothing should be cut too low or too high. Wear tasteful, low-key jewelry, much as you would wear to a job interview (see chapter 24).

When the judge enters the courtroom, the bailiff will announce her arrival. Some judges still expect everyone in the room to stand as they take or leave the bench, so be prepared. Otherwise, the bailiff will be instructed to announce something along the lines of, "Remain seated and come to order." That is your cue that you don't need to stand. For the most part, paralegals will be able to perform their functions without attracting much attention from the bench. However, if the judge does talk to you for some reason, perhaps to ask a question about an exhibit, you should always address the judge as "Your Honor."

Because the jurors, if any, will be watching and judging you as well as the attorney and client, you must always present yourself professionally and warmly to them. Maintain eye contact as much as possible and smile pleasantly. It is customary to stand whenever the jurors enter or leave the courtroom. Never, *ever* speak directly to a juror, whether it be in the restroom, hallway, or anywhere else. Opposing counsel may be looking for an excuse to declare a mistrial and may accuse you of anything from discussing the case to being friendly in order to sway that juror's decision. Even if you were only discussing the weather, the appearance of a breach of ethics could sink the trial. You may smile and nod if recognized, but if the juror begins a conversation, politely remind him or her that, due to court rules, it is improper for the two of you to speak. If a situation like this occurs, be sure to immediately tell the attorney what happened.

Courtrooms are generally set up with two counsel tables. The standard protocol used to be that the counsel table closest to the jury box was reserved for the defendant and his counsel and the table farthest from the box was for plaintiff and her counsel. However, many judges now have their own preference on where the parties sit. Sometimes signs are posted indicating which table is assigned to whom. If not, check with the court clerk or bailiff and, depending upon whom you represent, you should proceed to and begin setting up at the proper table. There are usually two or three chairs at each counsel table, one for the attorney, one for you, and possibly one for the client if he chooses to sit with you. Some clients prefer to stay in the audience seating area, and, sometimes, depending on the client's temperament, the attorney may prefer that the client not sit at counsel table. Try to keep the papers, binders, boxes, and other materials in your area neat and tidy. Not only are you less likely to misplace something, but it will present an air of organization and professionalism to the judge and jury.

If you need to say something to your attorney while court is in session, do so in low tones, but do not whisper. Another option is to write a note to the attorney and pass it over for her review, but keep this to a minimum as some judges find it as distracting as your fifth grade teacher did.

Practice a pleasant form of poker face. It is poor form to look bored or annoyed when a hostile witness is testifying, or to sigh or make distracting noises. If something happens to panic you, such as a misplaced file or exhibit, you must never outwardly show it. Simply deal with the problem quickly and quietly. If it's something you can't soon handle, let your attorney know and she may ask for a short recess. If a decision or verdict is in your favor, don't gloat or make any outward sign of celebration. If it is not in your favor, keep your disappointment to yourself.

Pitchers of water and paper cups are usually kept at the bailiff's desk, and you are usually welcome to help yourself during the course of the trial. It is best not to fill your cup to the brim, just in case the cup gets tipped over at counsel table. The less water, the fewer soaked files!

If you value your life, you will remember to turn off your cell phone and/or pager when you enter the courtroom. Some judges shrug off a ringing cell phone in the middle of trial, but most are not so forgiving. Consequences run the gamut from a tongue-lashing to permanent confiscation of the offending phone.

Helping with Jury Selection

One of the most difficult and critical parts of a trial is the selection of a jury. Volumes of materials have been written on techniques for choosing the best jurors for your case. If the stakes are high, attorneys can hire experts, such as psychologists, to help create a model of the perfect juror. Investigators can be hired to do background checks on each of the potential jurors. Any scrap of information can be helpful—everything from occupation to political affiliation to the bumper stickers on the person's car. Paralegals may be involved in working with these experts before the trial.

Unless you have unusual skills or training in this area, most of the jury selection work will be done by the attorney. Sometimes you may be asked your opinion of or your gut reaction to a potential juror. Most of your time will be spent taking notes of the answers given by the potential jurors to the various voir dire questions being asked by either the judge or attorney. If you can take down the pertinent information, it will allow the attorney a better opportunity to read the jurors' body language, maintain eye contact, and begin building a relationship with the jury.

Another useful task you can take on during the jury selection process is to keep track of the remaining number of peremptory challenges for each side. In a jury trial, each side in the case is allowed to bump a certain number of jurors without cause. This can become a very tricky poker game as each party maneuvers to keep in the jury box the people that seem sympathetic to his side, while excusing those that aren't. Attorneys have to be careful that they don't use up all their limited number of challenges on moderately indifferent jurors only to find none left to use when a really hostile person is selected from the panel. For similarly strategic reasons, they have to know how many challenges the other side still has remaining. A good paralegal can keep track of how many challenges each side has exercised.

Once the jury is finally impaneled, the paralegal can help the attorney learn their names, maintain warm and friendly eye contact with them, and observe their body language for signs of boredom, irritation, or lack of comprehension.

Notetaking

Another useful function the paralegal can serve during the trial is taking accurate notes of the testimony, the judge's rulings on any oral motions that come up during the trial, important deadlines imposed by the judge for submission of jury instructions or other items, and any follow-up work that comes up based on events that occur during the trial each day.

The notes can be kept on blank binder paper that is prepunched and inserted into a notebook, or it can be kept on multiple volumes of legal pads. When making notes, write the date at the top of the first page and indicate in your notes whether it is the morning or afternoon session. This will make it easier to get back into your notes at a later date to find something that happened on, for instance, Thursday afternoon. Indicate the name of the witness on the stand and whether the examination is direct, cross, redirect, or recross. If an exhibit is introduced with that witness make a note of the exhibit number. If a witness makes a particularly important admission or says something else singularly important while testifying, place a star or other marker in the margin of your notes. Later, when the attorney is preparing for her closing argument, you can collect all of these important points for her to weave into her presentation.

Keeping Your Eyes and Ears Open

Another very important task for the paralegal is to be a second set of eyes and ears for the attorney. You must learn the art of taking notes while still watching and listening to the judge, jury, witness, opposing counsel, and your attorney. You should be very aware at all times of what the witness is saying and in what direction the testimony is headed so that you can anticipate any possible needs. Following are some examples of this type of awareness.

- If the attorney is questioning the witness about Exhibit 10, but the witness mentions something in Exhibit 4, pull Exhibit 4 out and have it ready to hand to the attorney in case he wants to question the witness about it.
- A hostile witness begins saying something that you know contradicts what she previously said on that topic. Quickly find the offending passage in the deposition transcript or interrogatory answer and hand it to the attorney for follow-up.
- If the attorney is coming down hard on a hostile witness and you notice the jury is starting to sympathize with that witness, pass the attorney a note (or use some other prearranged signal) warning him to lighten up. Similarly, remind the attorney if he has forgotten to pursue a line of questioning or introduce an exhibit with a particular witness.
- If some ideas come into your head for further questioning or good cross-examination questions, note them down and hand them to the attorney.

Dozens of opportunities to be of assistance will present themselves to you if you are vigilant and think quickly. Don't wait to be asked. Volunteer!

Evidence Management

One of the paralegal's most critical functions is the care of the exhibits, deposition transcripts, demonstrative evidence, and other important items, the presence of which (or lack thereof!) will often make or break your case.

In this day and age, exhibits are usually premarked before the trial. The parties have likely exchanged lists of exhibits and each party will know what the other's exhibits are going to be. This will allow you to prepare handy charts ahead of time such as the one in the following example:

Exhibit No.	Description	Introduced	Admitted	Denied

One chart can be filled in with the plaintiff's exhibits and another with the defendant's. Leave spaces at the end to write in unexpected exhibits, as they seem to always come up during even the most well-planned trials.

You will need to make up several sets of exhibits, including a set of originals, one set for you to refer to, and one to give to opposing counsel. Often the judge wants her own set of exhibits; this is one of those things you will want to check on beforehand with the clerk.

During the course of the trial, exhibits will constantly be grabbed and used with a witness, and then cast aside. At each break, it is a good idea to locate all the exhibits and put them back in order on the counsel table. Also during the break, it is important to go through the list of introduced exhibits with the attorney and make sure that he has moved all of them into evidence. Compare your list with the courtroom clerk to make sure her list of exhibits, numbers, and what has been admitted into evidence matches yours. Get the next batch of exhibits ready that are going to be introduced.

If you are using blow-ups, charts, or other forms of demonstrative evidence, keep them out of the way until they are needed. You will need to check with the bailiff ahead of time to see whether the courtroom is equipped with an easel upon which to display the blow-ups. Otherwise, plan on bringing your own. The attorney may like to have some sort of pointer or laser pen available to bring certain items on the chart or blow-up to the judge and jury's attention.

Another valuable task a paralegal can perform is to be ready with impeachment evidence. This is done while a witness who is hostile to your side is on the stand. The witness may, out of the blue, say something that completely contradicts a position he took during prior discovery, that is, in a deposition or an interrogatory answer. A paralegal familiar with the file and with carefully organized documents can put his hands on the contradictory material in a matter of minutes. If you are using a laptop computer at trial, the deposition transcripts can be loaded into litigation support programs upon which a word search can be performed for key testimony. Exhibit lists and discovery responses can be typed into word processing programs or scanned and used in the same way.

It is important to remember the "30-second rule." In a trial, a judge or jury watching and waiting for an attorney to find a piece of impeachment material or other item will become distracted and lose interest after 30 seconds. Although this doesn't seem like a long time, sit and watch a clock with a second hand for 30 seconds. Believe us, it can seem like hours in a silent courtroom, with all eyes on you! Top-notch trial paralegals have their files highly organized, know where everything is, and have the tools ready to make or beat that 30-second rule.

Working with Equipment

Today's sophisticated trial presentations sometimes call for the use of computers with projection equipment attached. These display on a large viewing screen what is actually being shown on the computer screen (ELMO systems). Using bar coding, CD ROMs, and other devices, the trial team can show the judge and jury such things as excerpts from videotaped depositions, documents that have been scanned into the computer, slide presentations, and other multimedia displays. Simpler cases can still make use of overhead projectors to display documentary evidence and TV/VCR combinations to show videos of actual events (such as in the Rodney King beating trial) or created "day-in-the-life" videos. Sometimes the evidence is in the form of audiotapes, ranging from taped 911 calls to recordings of corporate board meetings.

It often falls upon the paralegal to not only arrange for the presence of the necessary equipment in the courtroom, but to be able to operate it as well. Paralegals can make themselves even more invaluable by learning the software programs that are used to display multimedia presentations, such as Summation Blaze, Concordance, PowerPoint, Doculex, or Trial Director. If you are not the most computer-literate person in the world, don't panic. If the production is extremely complicated or out of your league, there are experts who can be hired to provide the necessary equipment, set it up in the courtroom, and operate it for the trial team.

If you feel that equipment wrangling is something you are comfortable with and can handle, whatever you do, make sure you test it before it is actually used. This testing is a two-step process. First, set all of the equipment up in the privacy and comfort of your own office and learn how to work it inside and out. The second step involves setting up the equipment in the courtroom before it is actually needed and testing it again. Make sure your plugs will reach the electrical outlets. If audio equipment is involved, such as a tape deck or television monitor, make sure the sound can be heard throughout the courtroom. Often the sound quality from the built-in speakers in this type of equipment is so tinny, it will not project adequately. It may be necessary for you to plug in an auxiliary speaker to boost the quality. Make certain to place the monitors, screen, or other display equipment where it can be seen by the attorneys, judge, and jury. This may involve using multiple monitors—one for the judge, one for the witness box, and a large one that can be viewed by the jurors and all counsel. If extensive cabling is required, your technician may require several hours to set up the equipment and cover all of the cables. Once the courtroom is set up with your equipment, turn on the computers, the monitors, and the other devices, and make sure they are functioning properly and that the software is loaded and running.

If you plan to use a real-time connection for a live feed for testimony, contact the court reporter at least 2 weeks in advance to verify that her system will be compatible with your software and exactly who will be responsible for providing the connecting cables.

Taking these steps to coordinate the equipment and technology ahead of time will help ensure that your courtroom presentation goes smoothly.

Trial Ain't Nine to Five!

Believe us, you will never work so hard as while you are in trial. Most judges begin their days at 8:30 or 9:00 A.M. and take a short break mid-morning to give the court reporter and jury a rest. Lunch breaks are usually from noon until 1:30. There is another short break in the afternoon, and the day is over around 4:30 or 5:00 P.M. Don't think you will be getting a rest at those breaks. During those times, you will be planning further strategy, explaining events to the client, calling witnesses on the telephone to tell them it's time for them to head to the courtroom, gathering the next batch of exhibits, making copies of something you've forgotten, setting up equipment, and checking in with the office to see if any fires back there need to be put out. And forget right now any ideas that your day will be over at 5:00! Evenings are often taken up by re-reading deposition transcripts of the witnesses who will be testifying the next day, outlining questions, doing legal research on an unexpected issue that came up, picking up expert witnesses at the airport, reviewing your notes of that days' proceedings, and further discussing strategy. Sometimes you may have to create a new piece of demonstrative evidence. Or you may have to fix a broken piece of equipment. There is absolutely no way you can anticipate every problem that might occur. You simply must use your best problem-solving skills and make things happen. Remember, *this is war!*

Paralegals have been asked to do a lot of strange things during the course of a trial. We spoke to several experienced trial paralegals who related their favorite war stories.

Connie Scorza, CLA, CAS
Andre, Morris & Buttery
San Luis Obispo, California

When I worked for a criminal defense lawyer in Kalispell, Montana, we encountered a situation in a murder trial we were defending where a prison informant was offering damaging testimony about our client. We heard this man was unpopular in the prison and several inmates offered to come forward to discredit the "stool pigeon's" credibility. However, we worried about the impression on the jury if the inmates testified dressed in their prison jumpsuits. I was recruited to become the firm's haberdasher. Armed with notepad and measuring tape, I went to the prison and measured each of our witnesses for new clothing. I quickly became a very popular person, as it had been years since many of those men had worn any "outside" clothing. Anyway, my shopping complete, I enjoyed watching each of our witnesses take the stand against the "stool pigeon." Unfortunately, our client was found guilty. The jury reported that while the jailhouse testimony was amusing, they discounted it all.

Tita Brewster, CLA
Freelance Paralegal
Las Cruces, New Mexico

While working for Ropers, Majeski, Bentley & Kohn in Redwood City, I was involved in a large trial in the federal courthouse in Los Angeles. We had a large suite in a hotel, which we turned into our war room. My boss was very good at losing important papers, so each night before trial, I made sure I personally packed up everything we would need for the next day. One day as he was preparing to put our expert witness on the stand, he realized he had misplaced all of his notes outlining the questions he was going to ask. We tore everything apart looking for them, and I knew I had seen them in the box the night before. Finally I asked him to think about everywhere he had been that day and he suddenly realized he might have left them in the men's room. There was no way the judge was going to allow a recess, so I had to knock and enter the men's room in the courthouse and search it stall by stall until I found the notes. Yes, the men's room was occupied, but there was nothing I could do but apologize and press on. It was a real "Ally McBeal" experience.

Marcy Jankovich, CLAS
Jackson County Prosecutor's Office
Jackson, Michigan

In my work for the Prosecutor's Office, I have had many strange circumstances arise. The most unusual had to be when we were trying an inmate who was HIV positive and in the last stages of full-blown AIDS for assault with intent to do great bodily harm. Since the inmate was known to be a "spitter" it fell upon me to secure him in a way that would allow him to see and hear the proceedings, but would keep everyone else in the courtroom safe from him. I created a "Hannibal Lector" type device out of a medical face mask over a hockey goalie's mask, which covered his face, but prevented him from spitting.

Moon Lim Canon
United States District Court, Northern District of Oklahoma
Tulsa, Oklahoma

During a 4-day trial while working for an insurance defense firm in Oklahoma City, I was recruited to serve a subpoena on an employee of a car manufacturing plant. I stood in the pouring rain outside the plant from 6:00 A.M. to 8:00 A.M. asking each person who came up to the door if he was the witness in question. By the time I got him served, went with him to his supervisor, and waited for him to be excused from work, I was soaking wet all the way through my suit and down to my high heels. My hair was plastered to my scalp and my makeup had run down my face in giant rivulets. However, my instructions were to bring the witness directly to court, so off we went. We entered the courtroom and I led the witness through the gallery to the swinging doors between the gallery and the bar. I held the swinging door open for him and then as I turned to pass through, I released the door too quickly and it slapped me on soaked bottom, making a soggy sound which might as well be a clap of thunder. My shoes squeaked with each step I took as I walked the witness up to the stand and then returned to my place at counsel table. I sat in my chair with a wet "squelch" and it felt as though everyone in the courtroom was staring at me. How I got through the rest of that day I'll never know. All I can clearly remember is shivering in the cold courtroom and watching my fingernails turn blue. By the way, we won that case and the client sent me a dozen red roses after the trial. I also got a nice bonus that year that paid for a new suit and some raingear.

As you can see from these experiences, a trial paralegal must be ready for ANYTHING! But as with any work that is very demanding, the rewards can be as great as well. Go ahead—grab for the brass ring!

PARALEGAL INNER VIEW: BRENDA RADFORD— THE LARGEST JUDGMENT IN THE HISTORY OF PERSONAL INJURY

Name: Brenda Radford
Firm: Bode and Beckman, Washington, D.C.
Title: Paralegal

Number of attorneys and paralegals: 8 attorneys, 2 paralegals
Specialty: Civil litigation
Education: 2 years college; paralegal certificate from Lamson Business School, Tucson
Years of experience: 7 years
Job duties: I handle all litigation for personal injury concerning medical malpractice. I answer discovery; gather documents for discovery; attend trial; prepare trial notebooks; locate witnesses; interview witnesses and clients; and request medical records. I also prepare settlement statements and distribute checks. I have my own office.

Tell us about a case you walked away from feeling great job satisfaction.

It was a wrongful death case. An informant, a kid, was killed. Our client's son, an ex-druggie, went to the police and told them something he had heard in this row house. They talked him into going back into the row house and getting more information for a search warrant. He wasn't watched. He wasn't let into the row house. There was a raid the night before. Walking back, some gang members tried to rob him and ended up killing him. His mother became our client. This was the biggest case I ever worked on. It received tremendous media attention and was very challenging. We won a $98 million judgment—the biggest judgment ever awarded for this kind of case. It was great!

What's your biggest challenge?

Each case brings on something different. Sometimes research is a challenge as far as trying to locate information that is not readily available.

What's your next career step?

I'm waiting to see. I'd like to get into paralegal personnel. Litigation is so intense.

Give us your prediction of the paralegal profession.

The profession is getting stronger. The challenge is in educating more attorneys and people in how to use us. It's different from support staff. The field has lots of growth potential.

CHAPTER 31

A Quiet Revolution

Good old Watson! You are the one fixed point in a changing age.

Sir Arthur Conan Doyle, 1859–1930

TECHNOLOGY, THE CHANGE-AGENT
FOR THE LAW FIRM

When Marilyn Haaker went to work as a paralegal straight out of the UCLA Attorney Assistant Training program 20 years ago, her tools were red pens, an IBM Selectric Typewriter, index cards, a manual Bates numbering-stamping machine, the *Bluebook,* a hand held dictating machine, and lots of cardboard boxes.

My, my—how things have changed. Today Haaker spends most of her time on the computer performing her job. Her tools are a PC, color printer, fax, e-mail, cell phone, hand-held computer, beeper, voice-activated computer, imaging and scanning equipment, voice mail, laptop, and videoconferencing equipment. "The legal field had no choice but to catch up with Corporate America," Haaker says.

Technology has finally caught the attention of most lawyers and paralegals in the last decade, slightly slower than the rest of the workplace. And with blinding speed computers and other technological gadgets have profoundly changed where and how paralegals work. As a result, law firms are forced to change the way they are organized. Paralegals are forced to adjust the way they think about their careers and how to manage them.

Gone are the days of the so-called law firm contract, when bright-eyed new grads who worked hard and remained loyal to the firm or corporation could count on partnership or senior paralegal status. Management guru Peter F. Drucker in his book, *Managing in a Time of Great Change,* says: "The stepladder is gone and there's not even the implied structure of an industry's rope ladder. It's more like vines, you bring your own machete."

Drucker also believes that in 10 years companies will outsource all work that does not career-ladder up to senior management.

In many firms, vertical ascents to partnership have been supplanted by lateral moves. This phenomenon is evident in the staff attorney who can move into partner status but never attain equity partnership. It's further evidenced in the paralegal community with senior paralegals and paralegal managers who manage large programs yet are still expected to bill time. The days of entitlement have vanished.

Increasingly, prospective employers ask candidates not for a list of job duties but for descriptions of how they have used technology in creative ways to benefit the bottom line.

The era of the paternalistic firm who shepherded protégés through the hierarchy is over—probably for good. Waves of layoffs in corporations and law firms continue. This trend has spawned a fast-growing class of contract and temporary workers, entrepreneurs, and independent consultants. These and other paralegals are finding that they must direct their own careers, and in order to do so, technological skills are mandatory.

THE DIAMOND THEORY

The traditional pyramid structure of the law firm, thick at the bottom with new associates and narrow at the top with partners, has been replaced by what Fred Bartlit, one of the country's top litigators, refers to as the diamond structure. The diamond is thick in the middle with experienced lawyers and other revenue-generating producers and thin on support staff and management.

At the heart of the changes are three factors:

1. After 20 years of exponential expansion in the number of attorneys, there is a substantial glut that will continue throughout the next generation.

2. Corporations, reeling from a 20-year escalation in legal costs, finally are taking steps to reduce legal expenditures.

3. Technology has changed the way that firms do business. It has forced firms to become more efficient, impacting the billable hour concept. The more efficient the firm becomes, the fewer hours it has to bill, the more it hustles for clients.

These changes suggest that demand will increase for legal professionals at the high- and low-skill ends of the training scale (experienced lawyers and paralegals, and entry-level document coders and clerks). But there will be far less demand for younger associates and generally trained paralegals and far less opportunity for them to gain the experience necessary to enhance their employability. "There are probably two to three times as many lawyers working in litigation as are needed," Bartlit said in the 1995 *Polk Report*.

In the new realities, the diamond structure forces legal professionals in the middle to change not only through specialization, as in the old days, but by developing an array of technological and people-oriented skills. In this environment, successful law firms will be the ones that deliver the best results, in the most cost-effective fashion. Bartlit, formerly with the Chicago firm of Kirkland and Ellis, has created the firm Bartlit, Beck, Herman, Palenchar & Scott. The firm is experimenting with replacing the traditional hourly fee-for-service billing arrangement with performance-based fee arrangements. Even though Bartlit, Beck is a defense firm, the firm structures its fees around results. The firm earns one fee for a "loss," another for a "win."

By eliminating the incentive to bill more hours, the firm has redefined the optimum configuration of its staff. In the pyramid structure, associates are the heart of the law firm profitability because they are billed at high hourly rates, paid at lower hourly rates, and encouraged to bill as many hours as possible in their quest for partnership, whether or not the work is important to the success of the case. Although this structure heightens profitability, it also means that law firms spend years training young associates, only to send them to other firms when they fail to make partner. A similar concept is found in those firms and corporations that pattern their paralegal programs to mimic associate programs.

By contrast, Bartlit, Beck is structured like a diamond—with few associates at the bottom, a heavy concentration in the middle, and a small number of senior litigators at the top. The experienced trial lawyers do the bulk of the work, and because they are result-oriented, rather than time-oriented, they tend to do work necessary for the win. The firm hires only a handful of associates each year. They are trained to try cases efficiently and are groomed to remain with the firm.

Although other firms have not restructured so dramatically, many already hire fewer associates. And today's associates understand that their chances of making partner are far lower than they once were. Paralegals, on the other hand, understand that certain lawyer tasks must be delegated to the lowest competent level; therefore, chances of the level of assignment upgrading are greater.

Paralegals need to prepare through classes and on-the-job training for the onslaught of sophisticated assignments. Without technology, chances for getting or keeping a position diminish. The following are a few suggestions for making your career work in the new realities:

1. Learn the computer. This means you need to know more than Word or other word processing programs. Spreadsheets, database management programs, and desktop publishing are only a few of the coming requirements.

2. Get a home computer. Explore the Internet. Learn through handling your personal finances electronically.

3. Take control of your career and learn as many skills on the job as possible. Someone will always want to show you how. If your corporation or firm offers computer training in a different department, ask to be included.

4. Enroll in computer classes at the local community college or paralegal school.

5. Don't forget interpersonal skills. Technical proficiency isn't enough for today's paralegal. The emphasis in the workplace today is on teams. Learn how to be a good team player.

6. Let technology work for you. Don't stand at a fax machine when you can send faxes directly from your office with a PC equipped with a modem.

Technology has become a critical component of employability at every level of legal professional. While this emphasis on specific skills has made the selection process more time-consuming, it has also meant that firms are more likely to hire permanently professionals with those skills when they find them.

CHAPTER 32

Surfing the Net

CONNECTING NEED WITH TALENT

I just love it every time firms get caught with their pants down. They literally hand paralegals a brand new role to play in the workplace! The best advice I have ever received on how to build success is very simple: "Create a need, then fill it."

Firms have unwittingly created a position for expert information gatherers/factual researchers to act as the splice in the skill gap. Rarely has a more perfect opportunity to redesign your job or make a career move presented itself.

What does the position look like? Firms need an expert who can train lawyers, employees, and new recruits in online services and research. They must be shown the most cost-efficient way to use this technology. Remember, one of the primary purposes of online services is to save time and money. Those unfamiliar with online services will waste precious dollars.

Guidelines, manuals, and vendor lists need to be created and published within the firm. Research is necessary to find out about specific services, who is using them, and how they apply to the firm's practice.

Last but not least, research on the Internet has to evolve into a job duty that has been delegated. We may see a designated Internet research specialist responsible for search and retrieval of information. Establishing a new job is a critical strategy for positioning yourself within the firm.

Action Items

Review benefits and skills designing a job such as Internet specialist/researcher:

1. As the designer and implementer, you can mold the job to take advantage of your skills. Envision yourself as a pioneer in this specialty, much like some of the litigation support managers today who were pioneers in this field, many now earning six figures. Picture yourself cofounding a new association such as an Internet Legal Specialist Association (ILSA). (Don't overlook this key strategy. The careers of the eight steering

committee members of LAMA—including the author—have been helped tremendously by the continued support of the organization.)

Paralegals, are you thinking ahead? You can take this job almost anywhere, even out of the legal field if that's your goal.

2. A distinct advantage: Paralegals are already trained. The paralegal position was developed to save costs, generate revenue, and save attorneys time and clients fees. You are trained, experienced, and focused on providing alternative low-cost solutions for the law firm.

Firms, are you there? Staring right at you is the best possible candidate profile for a revenue-producing, cost-saving position and a great way to empower employees.

3. You're three-quarters of the way there. As a paralegal, you have most likely gained valuable experience as an information gatherer, fact finder, researcher, technoliterate, manager/supervisor, trainer. Some of your characteristics include detail oriented, team player, diligent, and focused. You probably handle stress very well. Your accomplishments include a demonstrated track record for continuously upgrading assignments. Sure sounds like an Internet specialist/researcher.

Review new and innovative technology and processes and determine the potential impact for your firm, clients, and career. Don't wait for explosions such as the one that Internet has thrown at us. By staying alert, focused, practical, and innovative, staying ahead of the game becomes a cinch.

CREATING A PARALEGAL INTERNET SPECIALIST POSITION

Previously we talked about redesigning your job as part of your tactical plan for higher salary or better position within the firm or legal department. One of our goals may be to move yourself up or over on the invisible paralegal career ladder. Creating a position as a paralegal Internet specialist or researcher is one avenue to explore. Here is an outline of a five-step plan that can propel you into a cutting edge career.

A Five-Step Plan

Step I. Determine your "buyer" of the Internet specialist position. Who would use this service? Who will recognize the need and reap the benefits from a designated Internet specialist? Determine the size and scope of your target audience, which will consist of two categories: those who need training, and those who need research assistance. Look for:

1. Training candidates:
    - Any member of the firm exhibiting warning signs of technophobia. The technophobic employee cannot expect to hang on to the disease and succeed in today's law firm. All the resistance in the world can melt when technophobes have someone they trust.
    - Members expressing a desire to learn more but have "no time" available.

2. Research assistant candidates:
    - Almost everyone needs help now and then. Determine the actual level of comprehension of those who claim proficiency in online services. Use the same technique for determining computer proficiency: "How familiar are you with the computer?" Answer: "Very familiar. I know WordPerfect 5.1 and DOS."
    - Those who have only a vague concept of the importance of the Internet and evolutionizing technology. Some have plunged into the waters while others have delicately tested their big toes. Those who rate less than an A or B+ in knowledge of information technology will benefit from a law firm specific Internet specialist.

Step II. Management buy-in. You will need buy-in from upper echelons or you will not move anyone to action. Go to the person with the highest authority who will listen to your ideas.

Warning: all firms and legal departments (of any size) have their own unique structure, hierarchy, and office politics. Make sure that you don't crunch any toes in your bid for a new or expanded position.

If you can't go directly to the person or committee who can sign off on this position, choose the next ranking authority figure who is open and approachable. This is your "helpmate" to sell the concept to management.

Have a general idea of cost savings and potential ways to increase revenues through use of the Internet. Don't sell too hard. Right now, you are dealing only with planting the seed.

Stick to reasoning and rationale that coincides with the firm's needs. Using entitlement as a persuader is probably not a good idea. Statements such as "I need something more to do," or "I have worked hard and deserve a promotion" are self-serving. You must convince the firm that expanding your role into a specialty position benefits the firm. Rationale to overcome objections include the following:

1. Use the analogy of the law librarian and library user: The ability to maneuver around the library does not mean you have the expertise of the librarian.

2. Failure to properly prepare for major changes in the delivery of legal services can escalate firm overhead at a time when the low-cost provider prevails.

3. As a paralegal, you can supply the necessary talent (demonstrate skills, traits, characteristics, and accomplishments). Here is an extraordinary opportunity for the firm to send a positive message to employees. Increased employee morale goes a long way.

4. Few firms and in-house departments have anyone trained as an authority on the information super-highway. Some employees have taken a seminar or two and spent lots of time on their own surfing the Web in a catch-as-catch-can attempt to learn. There are no designated hitters to save the firm time and money. Until now.

5. Lacking dedicated specialists, the chance to capture fully cost savings and increased revenues on the Internet diminishes.

Next, prepare the plan:

1. Research how firms such as yours have put the Internet to work; illustrate the benefits, and do not assume readers of your plan will draw natural conclusions—the field is too new.

2. Research actual costs of using the Internet. Be sure to anticipate number of users, increased use as more people get on line, increase use of computers, number of dormant computers, and various services you will need. Be very realistic; do not underestimate. You will always be the hero if you complete a project for less cost than originally budgeted. However, I know of no one who is applauded for going over budget.

3. Prepare cost comparisons to illustrate how much money the firm could save (be honest!) if they had an in-house Internet specialist such as yourself. Compare your time, hourly rate versus outside seminars, trainers, classes off-site, downtime of revenue-generating producers while waiting for training, outside consultants, and downtime while trying to find someone to answer questions.

4. Research the implications for the current year and beyond. How much business, how many clients, and what portion of market share will the firm or corporation lose unless it incorporates proper use and education of this tool? Keep coming back to the dollars.

5. Track emerging trends: How is the Internet revolutionizing the legal field?

6. Research the new challenges posed for law firms.

7. Write a plan that makes sense for your firm's culture and is easy to execute. Readers struggling with highly technical and unfamiliar terminology will not find your report exciting, so keep the language in lay terms. You now need firm buy-in so you have "buyers" to support the plan. You can't create a new position if there's no perceived need for what's coming up.

Step III. Access and use the Internet.

1. Evaluate costs of hardware and software requirements for getting connected.

2. Evaluate service providers to get the best firm fit.

3. Understand and flush out cost-containment issues from the administrative and financial perspectives; take all "hidden costs" into consideration.

4. Take courses to expand your expertise; evaluate each one for applicability to the firm. Recommend it, always through proper channels.

5. Research the how-to's of marketing on the Internet. Law firms have finally embraced the advertising concept. They now take the view that the Internet is an adjunct to necessary marketing.

6. Research and prepare guidelines for acceptable and unacceptable business and legal uses of the Internet. What are the restrictions on use? Work with your office manager, supervising attorney, human resource director, MIS director, or appropriate supervisors/colleagues to get buy-in. Don't expect to drop a plan ready for execution on their desk without prior communication. You may think you've taken the initiative; they make think you've invaded their territory.

7. Teach members of the firm the lingo of the Internet.

8. Find out how to access cost-saving research, data, graphics, software, and other legal and business resources through the Internet. Compare service providers.

Step IV. Ready, set, surf.

1. Perform legal research, factual research, and informational studies on the Internet.

2. Locate expert witnesses; review employee benefits; gather data for clients, cases, and attorneys on businesses, trends, competition, cases, and demographics; assist attorneys in establishing guidelines for clients.

3. Learn how to access information for regulatory-compliance issues.

4. Learn how to access government and state agencies, legislation, and financial and market information.

5. Join newsgroups pertinent to your specialty.

6. Expand into marketing: Get your firm involved in building its image online through reports, newsletters, home page, and other cost-effective, business-building vehicles.

7. Determine which employees should be online. Initiate guidelines and restrictions of Internet use to legal and business applications.

Step V. Making your move into management or specialty position.

1. Analyze the real costs, now that you are up and running.

2. Analyze productivity. Is too much time spent in the "chat" rooms? How much faster is it to use the Internet? Have billable hours increased? Is more substantive work accomplished?

3. Refine the plan and make improvements. Set up guidelines, disciplinary measures, and additional costs of inappropriate use.

4. Promote the use through PR, inhouse training, articles, and war stories. Get buy-in from executive committees or top management. Filter training and support mechanisms among the firm's partners, associates, paralegals, and support staff.

5. Review and research resources of practice specialty importance.

6. Set up beginner, refresher, and new online services information training on a routine and regular basis. Market the seminar carefully to stir up interest. Make the training session fun, not mandatory. Doom and gloom have already been used to motivate people to learn new things (the train is leaving, don't get left behind). Empower people to attend. If your firm culture includes a warm sense of humor, take advantage of it. An example:

Sample Memo #1 to the Firm

The first Monday of every month at 12:00, advanced Internet training is held in the conference room. We are honored that John Jones (managing partner) has bravely elected to throw off the shackles of bondage to the law firm of the past. He would have written this invitation himself; however, he is a little busy now exercising fingers. Memorialize this inaugural event with an instant photograph of you together with our managing partner. A wonderful souvenir for your family.

Sample Memo #1 accomplishes the following:

- Announces you have top management buy-in and commitment (John Jones, managing partner). Employees want to follow the leaders.
- Acknowledges this step isn't easy ("bravely elected").
- Hints at the message choosing to stay uninformed may keep you behind the rest of the firm ("throw off shackles of bondage to the past").
- Makes it easy and fun, not a threatening, confrontational atmosphere dealing with your weaknesses or skill gap ("instant photograph"; "wonderful souvenir").

Sample Memo #2 to the Firm

The second Monday of every month a 57-minute new online services demonstration is held in the south team room. Lunch is provided. (Vegetarians, junk-food junkies, those carb monitoring or fat intake measuring, and cholesterolly challenged mortals are encouraged to attend.)

Learn more about our secret weapon to drive the competitor crazy. It's the year of Acme Industries! Come hungry and ready to learn.

Sample Memo #2 accomplishes the following:

- The session is quick and under control allowing you to manage your time productively.
- Food is always a draw. No one has an excuse not to attend.
- Corporations, more than law firms, get the adrenaline pumping when a challenge against the competitor is introduced. It's the thrill of the hunt. Many law firms will downplay the idea (old-regime thinking— "it's so tasteless"). Although the "conquer the competitor" atmosphere has been less pervasive in legal departments and firms, current pressure to capture new clients and marketplaces and realization that new clients equal more bottom-line dollars are changing this old-fashioned attitude.
- A message is delivered that employees at all levels are part of the team.

Now, if your strategy is to seek official recognition *after* the plan is in place and you have proven yourself, lay stake to the claim and strategize when best to make a move for more dollars.

CHAPTER 33

Litigation Support: Systems, Software, Services You'll Need to Know

> General Failure Reading Drive C.
>
> Chilling message found on your PC

AN OVERVIEW

Dear Readers:

Litigation Support has been around for more than 20 years now. Some of you remember indexing documents on 3×5 cards; dictating file names from thousands of boxes; debating with your firm whether you should computerize the documents at all; and sending everything to word processing.

Because litigation support expertise is so widely varied, from entry-level document analyst and coder to highly technical professionals, it was almost impossible to choose a topic that didn't insult some level of expertise. Therefore, because this book is about choosing and directing your paralegal career, this chapter is directed toward those who are either entering litigation or have no knowledge about litigation support. The topic itself is another book.

For those readers who have mastered the art of choosing the right software, know the lingo, and know plenty about litigation support, please go directly to the next chapter. For those of you who are considering a change or seeking to expand, this chapter gives you a cursory overview of systems, software, and services that make up today's litigation support arena.

Thanks. I'll catch up to you in the next chapter.

Sincerely,
The Author

The Reign of the Resistance

It took more than a swift bolt of lightning for law firms to finally realize that clients meant business when mandating: Keep legal fees down. Known to be sluggish, this time almost to the point of self-destruction, the legal machine delayed response to the information technology age. Startled to discover automation is required to keep costs down, the field scrambled, much like a puppy on linoleum—a lot of motion going nowhere.

Consumer awareness and the urgency of competitive pressure drove the explosion toward technology. Firms, pushed to provide high-quality work at lower prices, sought immediate action to maintain profitability. Fierce competition today continues to force lawyers toward new technology to deliver better and faster results.

More than one consultant has uttered the pronouncement that the field is speeding toward another pivotal change. More than one consultant has declared that the field, in fact, has been in the throes of change for the past 10 years. You must remember above all else: Whatever you read today can change tomorrow (including this chapter!).

Case Management

Sandra G. Schley, Ph.D., in the article "Communications Come of Age" (*Law Technology Product News*, March 1996), quotes Eric Haas of Price WaterhouseCoopers:

> Clients' concerns about legal costs have led to a rising demand for case management. A major impetus behind case management has been the desire of legal services users to understand, contain and control their legal fees, and subservient to that, the service they are buying. With case management, law firms are better able to manage their projects. For example, they can compare projects to budgets and make a mid-course correction regarding a matter.
>
> Equipment is powerful, competition strong and attorneys finally open to the concept to justify a surge of interest in case management. There are two keys: A Windows environment making it possible for software to be more intuitive and affordable hardware.

Schley cites three central benefits applying to all practices: improved project management, improved budgeting, and improved access to information. According to Schley, the biggest benefit of case management, particularly for corporate legal departments, is control that allows management of outside bills, tracking case activities, and coordinating efforts of in-house attorneys across one or more locations. Additionally, it helps manage people. Here is a significantly improved approach to determine work-load volumes and assignments. Case management gives attorneys and paralegals ability to leverage past work product.

Just Say Know

What do you need to know to know litigation support? According to Ron Sharpe, author for *Law Technology Product News*, function, structure, and relationship of information in law firms are "interwoven in complex and dynamic configurations. The same item of information may serve multiple functions, manifest different physical and logical structures, and assume various relationships over time with other information in the environment." For example, client/matter information may include contact management, case or matter management, word processing, document management, timekeeping, and accounting.

Litigation support generally applies to preparation and delivery of the litigation discovery process, normally for the management and retrieval of volumes of documents for the fact-finding process, depositions, document productions, trial, ADR, response to requests, and so forth. The nature of the work—process and procedure—invites a new career path for interested legal assistants. Just as the field was emerging some 25 or 30 years ago, with little definition, no designated career path, and few regulations, so goes the emergence of the litigation support career today. Already, a minihierachy has evolved.

Certainly not news is the coveted position, litigation support manager. Responsible for managing technology and personnel, these professionals can earn excellent salaries. For more information on the career, contact the Litigation Support Managers Association.

For novices, the areas you need to learn are systems, software, and services. Take courses at your local paralegal school, university, or community college; call any of the software vendors and find out about training; sign up at your firm when any software or hardware training sessions are offered; and read, read, read. Learn the secrets of all good management consultants: Look toward the firm's needs rather than at various products and services.

(Products, organizations, or services mentioned here do not imply endorsement or recommendation and are referenced for teaching purposes only. We apologize in advance to any company not on the list and invite you to write us for the next *PCG* edition. Those chosen were done so randomly.)

It's fair to assume that between the time the *Paralegal Career Guide* has gone to print and the time you are reading this, some changes have occurred.

SYSTEMS, SOFTWARE, AND SERVICES GUIDE

Electronic Evidence: The Latest Career Path

If you're baffled as to where to take your career, take heart. A new horizon for paralegals may be found in the world of electronic evidence. In litigation, the relevant data has to be produced to the other side. Up until about 10 years ago, the production was in paper. Law firms would engage in huge, costly document productions. The more advanced groups would scan and code and build databases. Electronic device discovery goes straight to the electronic data on your computer to retrieve backup tapes, e-mail data on desktops, documents and searches that information. Databases are built so that attorneys can now select documents online.

Electronic Evidence Discovery, Inc., based in Seattle, is one company that has captured this niche market. "Electronic evidence is going to overtake paper discovery," says Chuck Kellner, Vice President Eastern Region. "Almost all paper out there now has been created by a computer and that data still exists and can be processed much more easily than boxes and boxes."

No more boxes? Whatever will paralegals do? "Convince your law firms," Kellner says. "Usually the disks and tapes are left over until the end of a paper project when an attorney decides it's an emergency. The next project of the paralegal should remind the attorney that the electronic evidence selection should be assessed and, under the Discovery Rules, dealt with as a likely contingency that it will have to be produced."

According to Kellner, dealing with electronic evidence among the top 2000 law firms is commonplace. Plaintiff firms are more aggressive in using it in complex litigation cases. In large corporations, it is more often the rule than the exception. Among smaller firms, there is an awareness to the point of identifying when there is a need to recover deleted data but not so much looking at electronic evidence as a substitute for paper.

"At EED," Kellner says, "we produced six million pages in 10 weeks of less. The data came from several locations on two continents. Some of the most gratifying work now is in not making the forest weak and devising purely electronic solutions to a lot of the discovery and review problems without converting paper. It's faster and it's cheaper."

Kellner's position as Vice President is constantly being defined. His responsibilities include managing projects for large case litigation and merger and acquisition second requests. Consulting to corporate law and IT departments, he advises techniques to reduce the litigation risk of electronic data. Speaking to clients, developing specs for projects, learning about stored data, pricing, proposals, negotiations, selling, and supervising the operation of the projection are only a few of his day-to-day responsibilities.

Kellner's biggest challenge professionally, along with his greatest job sat-isfaction, is working with senior counsel in large corporations and talking with them about the risks inherent in years and years of stored backup tapes and e-mails. Kellner, a former attorney, consults with in-house coun-sel regarding the basis of requests in litigation and managing through the identification and acquisition of those data stores. He represents the com-pany in providing risk management measures for the future.

How can a paralegal carve out a new career in this emerging technology? Paralegals work with clients on a project on a day-to-day basis. "Learning about both the content of the files as well as the technology used to create the files and the search and the review systems is a good way to start," Kell-ner claims. "The best thing to know are things used day-to-day in a law de-partment: e-mail systems, what is a mail box, server, where does all the data live on the desktop, server, backup tapes. If you were asked to find some-thing, how would you go about it? Learn as much about technology as you can. Work as closely as you can as you sift and review those documents. There's a career path forming in law firms, law departments, and tradi-tional coding vendors. Now's the time to take advantage of it."

Litigation Support Terminology and Products

ASP. An ASP is an *application service provider,* a vendor that offers soft-ware over the Internet for rental on a pay-as-you-go basis. Instead of in-stalling and maintaining software on the desktop or corporate network, the ASP customer accesses applications from the ASP's server using special software or a standard browser. The market for these "apps-on-tap" is expected to grow to at least $2 billion by 2003, according to the *Harvard Management Update* (July 2000). For more information on ASPs, visit *www. aspconsortium.com* or *www.aspnews.com*.

Bar coding systems. Bar coding technology is used to catalog and index documents. Part of an off-line Bates stamping program, it is a means of qual-ity control in the scanning process. The process eliminates the possibility of pages being overlooked or scanned twice because it reads the bar code on each page and halts production if the bar codes are not in sequence.

Calendar and docket scheduling. Provides a method of tracking dates and deadlines. Systems are available for firmwide application or tailored to specific needs of internal departments. The system can be designed to prompt days, weeks, or months in advance. Some systems include a mod-ule to prioritize work according to deadlines. Often, a calendar and dock-eting system is implemented to the firm's e-mail.

Case management software. Provides overall management of files by client, matter, docket, firm, budget chronology, invoice A/R, and dates. Includes software specifically for in-house legal departments; may provide tracking of outside counsel invoices, monitor check requests, track specialties and business unit bill-backs; may provide document management and a research library.

Completely integrated systems used in legal departments or throughout include detailed calendar, e-mail, phone messaging, scanning, general ledger accounting, and automatic time and billing entries; automatic diarying, indexing and calendaring of pleadings and deadlines; conflict checking; statutes of limitations checking.

CD-ROM. Provides information such as legal directories (Martindale-Hubbell); Parkers Directory; personal injury verdicts and settlements (instant access to cases); legal information including primary state and federal statutes; case law full-text search; and in-depth legal analysis, practice guides, and legal forms. CD-ROM is also used as a storage medium for document imaging.

Court document retrieval and process services. Provide resources for nationwide public searches, retrieval, and filing services; UCC searches, corporate, and real property records.

Demonstrative evidence companies. Provide photography, video, and trial exhibits; anatomical models, deposition video services; x-medical illustrations; and presentations for arbitration, mediation, and other forms of ADR. Also available are multimedia presentations incorporating animation, live video, documents, and, graphics. Presentation systems can include laser disk with bar code, laptop presentation, overheads, slides, and more.

Deposition and transcript management software. Discovery Products and Summation are two in a host of software packages that will search multiple transactions simultaneously for names, key words, and phrases. Deposition exhibits can be cataloged and cross-referenced to witnesses. Portions of testimony can be copied and/or integrated with other documents or other databases.

Document management systems and software. Systems are designed to manage volumes of documents. Documents are typically managed using relational databases allowing the design of various fields to be tailored to specific needs on a case-by-case basis. Information is abstracted from documents and sorted in a database. Searches are performed in the database to locate documents possessing information required. Dates, names, companies, key words, and subject matter are commonly used fields. Certain document management systems have the ability to be integrated with a deposition and transcript management system and/or an imaging storage and retrieval system.

Document processing companies. Provide image scanning, document coding, database design, microfilming, repositories, and image retrieval systems; also document assembler merging and assembling client/case data into document templates

DSVD. Voice-over data or digital simultaneous voice and date capability. It permits two individuals, connected by a single phone line, to carry on a conversation while their PCs exchange data. In business, two long-distance parties could discuss changes in a document while sharing the program on screen. In the real world, it means two adolescents trash talking while bashing each other in the latest gore-and-score video game.

Expert witnesses. Know where to find them through the Net, agencies, recommendations, and trade journals. Learn how to search for cases where a particular expert was involved or for an expert who specializes in a particular field. Look for expert witness search agencies. Develop personal and/or firmwide expert databases.

Groupware applications. Networked applications are designed to facilitate electronic connectivity and collaboration within and among law firms and their clients. Lotus Notes is the granddaddy of this groupware trilogy. Groupware software is designed to facilitate the creation, management, and distribution of the disparate data types and documents. Groupware enables firms to expand the use of computers and networks beyond glorified typewriters and e-mail to encompass online discussion forums, electronic publishing, and automated and intelligent routing of information and documents.

Imaging and conversion service bureaus. Provide a complete range of automated litigation support services: image scanning, document coding, database design, microfilming, document repositories, image retrieval systems; project management, high-volume scanning; OCR/processing (often overlap with document processing companies).

Imaging Systems. Image management systems can link with deposition and document management software. Eliminate the need for pulling and re-filing of documents by enabling images to be viewed on the computer monitor. Imaging systems are also great for archiving and storing documents.

Information retrieval products. Full-text search products that can read and index ASCII, Word-Perfect, or Word files.

Concordance for Windows is an "industrial strength" text retrieval program; allows the user to gain access to names, phrases, depositions, documents, and reports. Can search by word, phrases or combination. Retrieved records are displayed with all search words highlighted.

Information retrieval services. Provide in-depth information on business, government, education, leisure communities, and more.

Intranet. Private networks that use Internet technology: a method for lawyers and clients to work together on transactions and litigation. Most deals and lawsuits have a home page—a place where lawyers can share information with clients or with adversaries. Lawyers from around the world are able to negotiate and mark up documents together using Intranet software specifically designed for these purposes.

Jury research companies and consultants. Provide services and products for mock trials; juror questionnaires for jury selection; surveys and posttrial interviews. (Many belong to the American Society of Trial Consultants.)

Legal directories. Provide a marketing tool and information: biographical profiles of lawyers, law firms, judges, online newsletters, regulatory alerts, firm descriptions, press releases, practice group descriptions, and more. (*West's Legal Directory™, Martindale-Hubbell*)

Legal online network. Provides clipping service, e-mail, legal forums, and click service to Westlaw, LEXIS libraries, legal directories, employment services, and more.

Legal research companies. Provide online legal research. Researchers comprise partner, associate, and law clerk levels, Supreme Court clerks, and experts.

LEXIS-Nexis office. LEXIS-Nexis Office software, a Windows environment on research and information needs. Can save research results in Folio VIEWS Infobases.

Litigation copying. Novices only: for those just entering the field (experienced paralegals know this area all too well), litigation photocopying is a paralegal's answer to her worst document production. These photocopying vendors specialize in litigation copying, and they understand confidentiality, security, and other issues that apply to the legal field. Know vendors you can trust to get the job done quickly and cost-efficiently. Vendors offer services such as on-site copying, scanning, velobinding, document labeling, and more.

Litigation support consultants. Provide a full range of consulting services, such as information systems planning, evaluation of technology alternatives, project management, platform selection, network planning, telecommunications, hardware and software configuration, document management and system design and implementation.

Litigation support service companies. Provide comprehensive, coordinated solutions for total litigation management. Services include discovery, support services, consulting, imaging, coding, OCR, photocopying, repository creation and management, database design, electronic courtroom trial support, law office systems integration creation and conversion, and image search, review, and retrieval systems.

Multimedia trial consulting. Court trial presentations, optical imaging, jury consulting; can integrate imaged documents, graphics, animated video and videotaped depositions.

Online research. Provides current information and access to public records, federal and state law, attorney general opinions, bill and regulation tracking, comprehensive collections of leading practice guides, information on jury verdicts, primary and secondary sources, research, and more. (Westlaw; LEXIS)

Realtime litigation support software. Provides computerized, online instant transcripts of proceedings; search, annotation, and reporting; issue coding, notes, reports. Can offer features including ability to receive real-time translation from court reporters and text searching to synchronized digitized video stores on CD-ROM (such as LiveNote).

Remote site imaging. Provides equipment and personnel to almost any site including businesses, warehouses, and document storage facilities.

Security devices companies. Provide equipment (such as card printers and ID cards) for offices who want to limit access to specified areas. Used for highly sensitive cases.

Systems integration services. Provide network planning, installation, training and support; internal PC networks, LANs, WANs, Internet business services, fire walls.

Technical shows. Various legal technology shows and conferences are held around the country. A few are the following:

1. LegalTech; usually three to four shows per year in New York, Los Angeles, Chicago, or Washington, D.C.; has over 100 leading hardware and software manufacturers; attended by over 3,500 lawyers, MIS directors, litigation support experts, legal administrators (212-877-5619)

2. ABA TechShow: sponsored by the American Bar Association; annual show.

3. Law Journal Seminars-Press seminars; computer law, online issues, software, outsourcing, multimedia, software licensing, and software development and distribution; doing business online; integration and telecommunications. Law Journal Seminars-Press, 345 Park Avenue South, New York, NY 10010. (800-888-8300). E-mail to: seminars @ljextra.com. Web site: *www.legalseminanrs.com.*

Technology consultants. Consultants providing independent consulting to law firms and legal departments including strategic technology planning; network and desktop infrastructure; process reengineering.

Temporary staffing providers. Agencies provide temporary project support, such as attorneys, paralegals, document coders, preppers and scanners, case clerks, legal secretaries, temporary administrators, and support staff. Temporary staffing is also referred to as flex-staffing, part-timers, supplemental staffing, project support, and contract workers.

Timekeepers and billing systems. Software for law office calendar, tickler, and case management systems. Can link programs for billing right from calendar. Billing software can integrate with general ledger, accounts payable, trust, and calendaring systems.

Trial notebook software. For laptops or PCs to organize, search, analyze, and annotate (such as Litigators Notebook).

Voice recognition. Comprehension of vocal commands and for speech-to-text dictation.

PARALEGAL INNER VIEW: MARY MARVIN— DON'T OVERLOOK LITIGATION SUPPORT

Name: Mary Marvin
Firm: Robins, Kaplan, Miller & Ciresi, LLP; Minneapolis, Minnesota
Number of attorneys/paralegals: 200+ attorneys, over 300 support staff in 7 offices
Years of experience: 7 years as litigation/case support manager; 7 years as paralegal
Education: B.S. in Education from UW-Stout, Menomonie, Wisconsin
Prior work history: I taught high school for 5 years, then interviewed with the law firm and was offered a paralegal clerk position. I moved into the paralegal role in 3 months. I received a lot of on-the-job training and took classes but didn't obtain a paralegal certificate.
Job duties: I don't really have a typical day. I like to interact with people the best. When I first became the Litigation/Case Support Manager, our two main functions were supervising temporary employees on coding projects, and prepping and loading ASCII files of transcripts into our full-text searching software. It has evolved greatly in the past 7 years and we are now doing much more with imaging, OCRing, and electronic discovery.

When I first became manager, we also did litigation support graphics. This evolved into an in-house graphics department that I manage. We have two designers that do marketing and litigation support graphics.

A couple of years ago, the firm decided it needed a Web site and I became the liaison with the vendors for the Web site. I am still a member of our Web site development team and continue to be the liaison with the developer. My responsibilities now include litigation support, the Web site, and graphics.

I really enjoy my job and look forward to coming to work each day. Because of my changing role, we created a new position of Litigation/Case Support Coordinator. This position handles the work flow in the department, including arranging for the temporary employees that we use on our in-house coding projects. We do the majority of our coding in-house.

We market the litigation support services to the attorneys which is a challenge because they are so caught up in everything else. Our imaging is on the forefront as is accessing our databases and images via a Web repository.

How did you land a position of Litigation Support Manager from that of paralegal?

I was a paralegal for 7 years. I was doing a lot of traveling and I had a baby which made traveling more difficult. There was a manager opening in the litigation support department. I didn't know as much as I needed to about litigation support, but the attorneys and paralegals encouraged me to pursue the position because of my background as a litigation paralegal. When I got the position, the staff was open-minded as to how the department could integrate better into the litigation teams. We reorganized the department together.

How's the pay?

I'm satisfied.

What does your crystal ball say about where this profession is headed?

Good question. Now, more than ever, with what vendors have to offer and the way technology is changing, we can't turn a blind eye as to what's outside our in-house department.

CHAPTER 34

Just Do It

Life is what happens when you are making other plans. . . .

Betty Talmadge

CLOSING COMMENTS

Thanks for coming this far with me. I have no magic words of advice, no special potions to dispense, and no brain trust to call up to ensure you success in your paralegal career. I will admit that a very, very small part is luck, but, for the most part, we, as individuals, are responsible for what happens to us.

In closing, I have written an open letter to attorneys and supervisors of paralegals. In our quest for career development, it is always necessary to get commitment from top management. Otherwise, you can beat the drums as loudly as you'd like, but no one will come running.

You may wish to use this letter to help get support for further career development. I have addressed only one aspect, training, the foundation for launching success. You may wish to rewrite this letter as a memo; use it to supplement paralegal use information; or just read it, and know that striving for achievement is best accomplished through a great coach. But first, you've got to get one.

The paralegal profession has made monumental strides in a very short time. It's due to dedicated, hardworking, caring individuals such as yourself who take the time to investigate new ways of doing things. Some suggestions may work for you, others may not, and still others simply need a little tweaking to make them fit into your plan properly. Always remember that nothing is ever in concrete. It is only through change that we will continue to evolve.

Happy career pathing. I wish you outrageous success.

OPEN LETTER TO ATTORNEYS AND SUPERVISORS
OF PARALEGALS

Dear Colleagues:

The paralegal who is submitting this letter has probably just finished reading the third edition of the *Paralegal Career Guide*. The reader just absorbed a wealth of information regarding shaping and improving paralegal job skills. I discussed how paralegals can receive better assignments and cost-effective training and how they can improve their communication skills in the workplace. Hence, the purpose of this letter.

To begin with, I would like to introduce myself. My background in major firms led me to hold positions as senior executive in a billion-dollar company, president of an international division of a leading legal services corporation, and successful entrepreneur. My 15 years' experience in the legal field has allowed me to experience unprecedented changes in the legal workplace and has given me the ability to spot healthy or unsound career trends. I have had the good fortune to have eight career books published.

My observations and experiences with attorneys and paralegals have assisted me in writing this book. I ask that you take only a few moments to review some suggestions that may dramatically contribute to your continued efforts to meet increased client demands for delivery of quality low-cost legal services.

Paralegals have become a key component today in delivering lower-cost services, saving attorneys time and money, and maintaining good client relations. An associate entering practice today expects to work with paralegals, just as senior attorneys expected to work with legal secretaries. In 35 short years, paralegals have made their mark. They're here to stay.

Given the clear advantage paralegals bring to your practice, my strong advice is to learn to work *with* the paralegal position, not *against* it. This group of highly intelligent, motivated individuals needs your help to give the firm or department better service and higher-quality work product. While you and your colleagues may be pretty certain that you are using paralegals with the best intentions, paralegals may have a very different opinion. You may be unaware of your firm's unwitting participation in hampering paralegal growth in your firm.

We have strongly emphasized to paralegals that the thoroughfare to job success is up to them, that career development is solely their responsibility. By putting them in the career driver's seat, we ask that you help navigate the road:

1. Whether or not you like it, accountability for paralegal performance lies with you, as the ultimate authority and paralegal supervisor. It is your responsibility to see that your client receives the highest-quality service

possible. To make that happen, it is necessary to see that all parts of the delivery system are in top shape and working order. In order to achieve results, training is required.

2. Training is a two-tiered approach: Paralegals need skill training, and you may need training on how to train or what to delegate. Both of you have an idea of what skill training is necessary. The problem may be that each of you may have differing opinions as to level and scope. For example, you may feel that the paralegal needs to improve writing skill as it pertains to business correspondence; the paralegal may not realize you are referring to polishing and concentrates instead on drafting. Communications must be open, friendly, and direct. You are, after all, the employer, and whether we want to acknowledge it, along with hierarchies come perceived boundaries. Paralegals are not mind readers, and they cannot imitate what they haven't already experienced.

3. After identifying development areas, find out how long it may take a first- or second-year associate to complete a similar assignment. Plan time, usually no longer than an hour, to visually and thoroughly explain execution of the new assignment. Allow a few more hours beyond the associate time estimate for completion. Charge the client or matter only the time the associate would have billed, and charge the balance of time to administration or training. The client has received supervised work product at lower fees; you have saved the associate time enabling her to perform work at a higher level; a paralegal is trained, who, on the next assignment, most likely will bill less time. All it took was a little of your time, albeit precious.

4. Be cognizant of the wide range of expertise paralegals bring into the field. Having only a few years of legal experience does not dismiss the value they may bring as highly trained experts in business, industry, science, or the arts. Use these wide experiences in your practice areas.

5. When communicating instructions, bear in mind generational differences. Baby Boomers and Generation Xers have met head-on in the workplace. They are significantly different in how they hear, interpret, and process information.

As a supervisor of paralegals, you need to learn how to make maximum use of their skills. While we are asking paralegals to assume responsibility for their own careers, they may not know how to bridge the gap from wanting to learn to what and how to learn. Don't hold it against them. Find out instead.

Ask paralegals about other skill areas. Listen to what they tell you about the cost benefits of intertwining these areas with your practice. Find out where they need training. While costs are certainly an issue in this downsized, information technoliterate workplace, I have given them several suggestions for cost-efficient training.

Thank you for taking this time to invest in your organization's paralegals. It's highly unlikely that you will regret the added value your participation brings in opening up paralegal opportunities. Effective training will cut the learning curve, decrease write-offs, bring up billing rates, and cause more dollars to drop to the bottom line.

If you have any questions, please be sure to ask paralegals. They know how and where to find the answers.

Sincerely,

Chere B. Estrin
CEO
The Estrin Organization

Helpful Periodicals, Books, and Guides

> What really knocks me out is a book that, when you're all done reading it, you wish the author that wrote it was a terrific friend of yours and you could call him up on the phone whenever you felt like it.
>
> J.D. Salinger, *Catcher in the Rye* (1951)

Via Subscription, Software, Online Services, or the Good Ol' Bookstore

These periodicals and guides are listed for information purposes only; all may have subscription rates or purchase costs. This is only a partial list because it would require an entire book to list everything! There are many, many resources. While every effort was made to make sure this list was accurate, things change quickly, particularly in the computer world. Therefore, we cannot guarantee the accuracy of the information. For those wishing to submit additions for the next edition, please contact the publisher.

ABA Journal: Monthly informative national magazine put out by the American Bar Association, Chicago, IL. *www.abanet.org.*

ACCA Docket: The Journal of the American Corporate Counsel Association (ACCA). Readers are members of ACCA. Applicable articles for in-house lawyers include practice information, strategic planning issues, human resources, various survey data, and handling outside counsel. Bimonthly publication. Subscription for nonmembers: 202-296-4522; 1225 Connecticut Avenue, NW, Washington, DC 20036.

American Lawyer: A slick, well-read, essential human interest monthly magazine targeted to major firm lawyers, in-house counsel, and legal professionals. 212-973-2800.

American Society of Corporate Secretaries, Inc.: For those experienced paralegals in corporate law, a bump up to corporate secretary in a corporation is a natural career path. The 1995 salary survey conducted by the ASCS showed salaries between $60,000 and $120,000 per year. While 60 percent of those surveyed were attorneys, the remaining 40 percent are nonlawyers. Contact the association at 521 Fifth Avenue, New York, NY 10175, or call 212-681-2000.

American Staffing Association: This is the association to which most staffing agencies in the U.S. belong; it can assist you in locating a full-time or temporary staffing organization that specializes in legal placement. Located in Alexandria, VA, the association can be reached at 703-549-6287.

Association of Legal Administrators: Publishes a monthly journal and newsletter in alternating months and an annual directory for members only along with a comprehensive salary survey. ALA, 175 East Hawthorn Parkway, Vernon Hills, IL 60061, 847-816-1212.

Barrister: Publicaton of the American Bar Association, Young Lawyers Division, 750 North Lake Shore Drive, Chicago, IL 60611.

Business WeekOnline: Find out what's going on with your corporate clients. *www.businessweek.com.*

The California Lawyer: Widely read magazine targeted to California lawyers. 415-252-0500; 1390 Market St., San Francisco, CA 94102.

CCM: The *American Lawyer*'s bimonthly corporate magazine. 212-973-2800; 600 Third Avenue, New York, NY 10016

CFO & Controller Alert: A fast-read resource to help financial professionals boost case flow, control expenses, manage their resources effectively, and stay in compliance with ever-changing regulations. Good for paralegals who want to know more about managing costs and profitability. Subscription service: 800-220-5000.

Chronicle of Higher Education: A weekly publication to serve more than 440,000 college and university professionals.

CLE Group: Log on to the Internet for audio-based continuing legal education (CLE) delivered in "realtime." CLE Group of Menlo Park, California, has launched CLE.NET, a web site dedicated to providing CLE-accredited audio programs on a variety of topics.

CNBC.com: Get the latest daily news online.

Corporate Legal Times: A monthly publication targeted to corporate in-house legal departments. Subscription: 312-654-3500; 3 East Huron St., Chicago, IL 60611; available online from LEXIS-NEXIS and Westlaw.

The Daily Journal: A daily newspaper with San Francisco, Los Angeles, and Seattle versions. Subscriptions: 915 E. First St., Los Angeles, CA 90012.

Directory of Corporate Counsel: This legal directory is similar to *Martindale-Hubbell's* corporate law department section. Published by Harcourt, Brace Jovanovich, it lists attorneys who are in-house counsel for various corporations.

Directory of Legal Employers: A list of more than 1,000 private, government, and not-for-profit legal employers released annually by the National Association for Law Placement. Available in most law school career services offices or from the publisher: Harcourt Brace 800-787-8717.

The Docket: A bimonthly magazine by the National Association of Legal Secretaries with up-to-date substantive information, human interest stories, profiles, and war stories. Subscriptions for nonmembers: 918-493-3540; 2250 E. 73rd Street, Tulsa, OK 74136.

The Electronic Bluebook: A guide to legal citation form, *The Bluebook: A Uniform System of Citation* published by the Harvard Law Review Association, is now available as software from Technology Training Associates.

Encyclopedia of Associations: More than 23,000 associations in the United States listed in 17 categories, including trade, commercial and business, legal, government, public administration, military, and education. Excellent resource for those paralegals seeking alternative careers. Available through Gale Research.

Everything You Need to Know About Being a Legal Assistant: A collection of informative and humorous career advice articles written by this author. Delmar Publishers: 800-347-7707.

Facts and Findings: A journal for legal assistants featuring authorities in the field, current information in continuing legal education, and a forum for the latest paralegal news. Published by NALA (National Association for Legal Assistants): 918-587-6828; 1516 South Boston, Tulsa, OK 74119.

Guerilla Marketing Online: Part of a continuing series of marketing books by Jay Conrad Levinson who writes with co-authors, this time with Charles Rubin (Houghton Mifflin, 1995). Most of the Guerilla Marketing books are written in a fast-read style. Read the suggestions keeping an eye toward tweaking for the legal environment. You may want to think in terms of your present position, how to sell yourself for a new position, or learn how to market a legal vendor opportunity you are seeking.

Guide for Legal Assistant Education Programs: A tool for selecting a legal assistant education program published by the Standing Committee on Legal Assistants, the paralegal approval process committee of the American Bar Association. The Guide includes information concerning a legal assistant career, educational program listings, and a list of current ABA publications that address legal assistant issues. Currently, there are approximately 200 ABA-approved schools throughout the country. In total, there are approximately 800 paralegal institutions. Staff Director, ABA Standing Committee, 750 N. Lake Shore Dr., Chicago, IL 60611.

Internet Groups—Seven Great Newsletters by the ABA

- Leadership & Management Directions
- Network 2d
- Litigation Applications
- Word Progress
- Unix/group Newsletter
- Lawyering Skills Bulletin
- Counselor's Computer & Management Report

Published by the American Bar Association: 312-988-5619; 750 N. Lake Shore Drive, Chicago, IL 60611. *www.abanet.org.*

The Internet Lawyer: The *Internet Lawyer* is a monthly newsletter focusing on the practical use of the Internet by lawyers and paralegals. The site also features full text of selected articles from the monthly TIL newsletter, a selection of search engines for research, a "Cool Site for Lawyers" collection, and free sample copies of TIL.

Law and Legal Information Directory: Descriptions and contact information for more than 30,000 law-related institutions, services, and facilities including bar associations, court systems, law schools, legal periodicals, public defender offices, and more. Available through Gale Research.

Law Office Management & Administration Report: An informational, monthly newsletter (LOMAR) targeted to managing partners' law firm administrators. Topics include compensation issues, research tools, conferences, software packages for law firms, and marketing tips. Subscription: IOMA, 29 West 35th Street, New York, NY 10001-2299; Fax: 212-564-0465; LOMAR Business Directory on the World Wide Web at *www.ioma.com/ioma*.

Law Office Computing: A monthly publication that helps put the power of computers in the palm of your hand. Case management, litigation support, time and billing, word processing, online research, excellent articles. 800-394-2626; James Publishing, P.O. Box 25202, Santa Ana, CA 92799.

Law and Politics: Trendy, outspoken, humorous, monthly magazine about Minnesota lawyers. 612-335-8088; 527 Marquette Avenue, Minneapolis, MN 55402; e-mail: lawnpol@aol.com.

Law Practice Management: A bimonthly publication addressing management, personnel, marketing, technology, lawyer-client relations, and administrative issues. Published by the Law Practice Management Section of the American Bar Association: 312-988-6115.

Law Technology Product News: The latest information technology news and other Internet legal news, online technology, multimedia creation, licensing and distribution, and new software. 212-696-1875, or visit online at *www.ljx.com/ltpn*.

Legal Assistant Management Association: Publishes a quarterly newsletter containing valuable information about paralegal management issues. Available to nonmembers. LAMA, 2965 Flowers Road South, Atlanta, GA 30341. *www.lamanet.org*.

Legal Assistant Today Magazine: A must-read for every paralegal. Published bimonthly, this glossy magazine presents timely topics, how-to advice, information technology, salary surveys, success stories, substantive information, and, of course, this author's career advice column. Discounts for paralegal students. James Publishing: 714-755-5450, Costa Mesa, CA.

Legal Management: The Journal of the Association of Legal Administrators. Published bimonthly. Membership in ALA entitles members to receive the magazine. Subscriptions are also available to qualified members of the legal profession who request it. 847-816-1212; P.O. Box 1186, Skokie, IL 60076-8186.

The Legal Times: A Washington, D.C. weekly legal newspaper. *www.legaltimes.com.*

LEXIS Counsel Connect: The online service connecting law firms and corporate legal departments worldwide. 800-955-5291; 600 Third Avenue, New York, NY 10016; *www.cconect@reach.com.*

Manager's Legal Bulletin: This twice-monthly bulletin offers expert advice on how to avoid "red flags," practical action tips, promotion decisions, termination procedures, and real-life examples for managers in all industries. 1-800-879-2441.

Metropolitan Corporate Counsel: Articles written by law firm attorneys directed toward in-house general counsel. Monthly publication. Subscription: 908-654-4840; 1180 Wychwood Road, Mountainside, NJ 07092.

Million Dollar Directory: Published by Dun and Bradstreet, this publication lists substantial corporations throughout the United States. Great for job leads.

Moody's Industrial Manual: A listing of about 3,000 publicly traded companies. Moody's Investor Service, 99 Church Street, New York, NY 10007, 212-533-0300.

National Association for Law Placement: An organization of legal employers and bar associations engaged in the recruitment and placement of lawyers. Where lawyers are hired, so shall paralegals follow. 1666 Connecticut Avenue Suite 325, Washington, DC 20009, 202-667-1666.

National Law Journal: National weekly tabloid-style newspaper with darn good journalism. 800-274-2893; 345 Park Avenue, New York, NY 10010.

New York Law Journal: New York's weekly also available on CD-ROM. 212-545-6089. *www.NY.com.*

Paralegal Compensation and Benefits Report: Published annually by NFPA (National Federation of Paralegal Associations, Inc.), this salary survey presents data gathered from more than 1,400 paralegals located throughout the United States. Includes salaries, benefits, vacations and sick leave, insurance coverage, bonuses, profit sharing, levels of education, and billable rate information. A 30-page report. NFPA: 816-941-4000; *www.info@paralegals.org.*

The Paralegal Educator: The newsletter for AAfPE (American Association for Paralegal Education). Brief, informative information targeted to paralegal educators. 2965 Flowers Rd. So., #105, Atlanta, GA 30314, 770-452-9877.

Paralegal Reporter: Quarterly publication by NFPA (National Federation of Paralegal Associations) regarding association news, articles, paralegal updates, and reference materials. 816-941-4000; P.O. Box 33108, Kansas City, MO 64114-0108.

Performance Appraisals: The Ongoing Legal Nightmare: Updates for employee evaluation programs, including what you can and cannot say during a performance appraisal, forms, and documents. Alexander Hamilton Institute: 1-800-879-2441.

Personnel Journal: The Human Resources Director's monthly publication full of articles on the latest updates in employment trends, hiring, and laws.

The San Francisco Recorder: Northern California daily legal newspaper. 415-749-5400.

Standard and Poor's Corporate Records: Boasting the top corporations in the country, this directory is full of valuable information including tidbits on the legal department.

Thomas Register of American Manufacturers: A 12-volume directory that lists almost all U.S. manufacturers, both privately held and publicly traded. Thomas Publishing Co., 1 Pennsylvania Plaza, New York, NY 10119, 212-695-0500.

Vault.com: An online resource with a legal section filled with valuable information, job leads, newsletters and more. *www.vaultreport.com.*

Wall Street Journal: One of the best resources for corporate information along with great job-hunting articles and right-on-point articles about staffing trends. *Wall Street Journal,* 200 Liberty Street, New York, NY 10281, 212-461-2000.

West's Legal Directory: The legal directory for the Information Age, the Internet, Westlaw, CD-ROM, Quicklaw. Internet access via CompuServe, Delphi, America Online, Prodigy, and *Law Journal EXTRA!.* 800-455-4565, or e-mail to: *wldinfo@research.westlaw.com.*

What Color is Your Parachute?: A practical, perennial manual for job-hunters and career changers by Richard Nelson Bolles, revised yearly (Ten Speed Press). Great tips that apply to any field. Available in many bookstores.

Workforce: Monthly magazine for human resource management, this publication offers excellent articles regarding training techniques, HR decisions, business ethics, organizational development, legal trends, and staff development. Good resource for paralegals with management responsibilities. Published by the Society for Human Resource Management: 703-548-3440; 606 North Washington St., Alexandria, VA 22314.

Vegetarian Times: Well, we *should* say *something* about staying healthy. Subscription: 800-829-3340.

Yellow Books: A series of 14 directories of law firms, corporations, news media, associations, not-for-profit organizations, financial organizations, and federal, state, and other entities. These handy directories tell you who's who in management of leading corporations, law firms, and other entities you may need to research. Leadership Directories, 104 Fifth Avenue, New York, NY 10011, 212-627-4140.

Online Resources

One of your primary duties as a paralegal is to be able to quickly put your hands on information that will enable you to more efficiently assist attorneys. This may mean selection of an online vendor. You may be seeking support for an Internet repository, time and billing software, research assistance, preparation of documents, Web hosting, full-text searches, electronic data for discovery, exhibit organization, case management, or searching for an ASP (application service provider).

If it is up to you to either select or recommend a service provider, be sure you get references, and not just the ones provided by the vendor. Reach deep into your network and get the scuttlebutt. Bear in mind that one firm's experience may not be another's so check out enough references to get a wide range of opinions. Online forums such as the litigation support managers daily one-list (*www.onelist.com*) is one way of soliciting opinions from across the country. Just a few of the questions you'll want to ask should be about:

- performance
- quality assurance
- easy access to information
- downtime
- trained staff
- reputation
- cost-efficiency
- ability to honor estimates
- understanding of what needs to be done
- ability to deliver on time
- accuracy
- methodology
- former clients
- potential conflict of interest
- customer service
- availability of technicians

- length of time in business
- financial stability
- location (if a factor)
- crisis-management ability
- training capabilities
- hidden costs
- performance at trial (if necessary)
- compatibility with your firm
- overall knowledge of their specialty.

Here are just a few sites selected at random that were available at press time.* These sites may offer services, products, hardware, software or on-line/offline services. Not much is free, though!

http://4.21.247.201
ABA Law Practice Today, sponsored by the ABA Law Practice Management section. The LPM section is the ABA's largest publisher of books; sponsor of its annual TECHSHOW; and home to *Law Practice Management* magazine and *Law Practice Quarterly* newsletter. Sign up for the section's free, monthly e-mail newsletter, *LawPractice.news.*

A

adr.org
The American Arbitration Association with information about mediation, arbitration, and other forms of alternative dispute resolution.

abanet.org/genpractice
ABA's General Practice, Solo and Small Firm section. Much of the content comes from the pages of the section's magazine, *GP Solo.* Also at the site are selected articles from the section newsletter, *Solo.*

abanet.org/lpm
A Webzine sponsored by the Law Practice Management section of the American Bar Association covering all aspects of the business of practicing law.

acca.com
The American Corporate Counsel Association for in-house counsel. Offers information on membership, job bank, and articles.

---

*These sites were selected at random and do not reflect endorsement by either the author or publisher. Adapted in part from *Law Technology News* August, 2000; *Legal Assistant Today* magazine; *Legal Management* magazine.

Access.gpo.gov

Provides documents from the General Accounting Office; the Office of Management and Budget; and other Federal agencies.

Accutrac.com

A software program for records management, marketing, conflicts, contact management and workflow.

acs-dbs.com

Featuring ATRIS™+; strategic consulting; knowledge management; Web design/development; systems integration; conversions and migrations; document management; and outsourcing. Company is based in Horsham, Pennsylvania.

alanet.org

The Association of Legal Administrators, the online headquarters of the international organization of law firm managers. The site is divided between public areas and those for members only. Contains many of the most practical features, including current industry news, document-delivery and reference services, and a database of ALA members available for peer consulting. For nonmembers the greatest appeal of the site may be in its *Job Bank* and *Management Gateway,* a collection of links to legal and management resources on the Web.

Amtelsystemscorp.com

A direct line system allowing users to relay and receive silent messages in confidentiality. Alerts customers to incoming calls when they're on the line with someone else.

altmanweil.com

One of the better known legal consulting firms offering a site full of articles on management and related topics including law department and law firm management, alternative billing, technology, marketing, strategic planning, economic and financial management, human resources and organizational psychology. There is a store to purchase surveys, newsletters, and other products.

amicusattorney.com

Integrated software system that tracks all information, people, schedules, communications, documents, time sheets and more on each of your files. For firms up to 200 users.

antitrustinstitute.org

American Antitrust Institute

asaint.com/legal

Offers Visual**One**, a Knowledge Base Management System that links the law firm's front- and back-office operations—from initial client contact to courtroom to controller. Includes relationships and matter management; scheduling and docketing management; marketing projects and mail list management; advanced conflict avoidance.

theattorneystore.com

A "shopping mall" for legal products such as office supplies; books and forms; furniture and equipment; stock trades and research; computer center; software; Web services; insurance; and more.

B

Bid4Assests.com

An online marketplace for buying and selling high-value, distressed assets from financial, government and bankruptcy sources.

Blumberg.com

Bankruptcy software for chapter 7, 11 & 13, including official forms for bankruptcy.

Bowne.com

A full-service information management company offering business outsourcing, consulting, facilities and technology management services including word processing, litigation support, document imaging, database management, reprographics, distributed print, Help Desk and *JFS Litigator's Notebook*®.

C

Casecentral.com

San Francisco-based company with case management center allows users to track documents during discovery and other phases of the litigation. Software for imaging functions, version controls, and users' ability to annotate and redact documents. Provides Internet case management services including high-volume batch printing, electronic data analysis and database management.

Casesoft.com

Offers TimeMap, a chronological visual that can be used during hearings and trials. The product can be used to explore time-based relationships between key case events with simple-to-use text boxes and charts.

CaseStream.com

Casestream® Litigation Intelligence™ notifies you automatically of new cases involving your clients. Find out judge's previous orders, litigation history of the adverse party, and positions taken previously by opposing counsel.

Ceb.ucop.edu/

California Continuing Education of the Bar: CLE courses for attorneys.

Cle.lawinfo.com/cle.html

Continuing Legal Education Online: CLE courses for attorneys.

clientpamphlets.com

A site in alliance with Blumberg Excelsior, a company that sells legal forms and software. Offers information for lawyers who want to expand their marketing but avoid the cost of creating a pamphlet of their own.

clswin.com

A Microsoft Solutions Provider integrating applications and centralizing key information. Provides time and billing; case management; accounting applications; and productivity tools. Based in Minneapolis.

Compulaw.com

A legal calendaring software program to schedule dates with attorneys; edited, jurisdiction-specific rule sets that include state and federal litigation, bankruptcy, intellectual property and more. A Los Angeles-based company.

Computerpackages.com

A patent and trademark docketing system. Offers on-site training and phone support for 1 full year. Provides an open system utilizing the full version of Microsoft Access database software.

Consumerworld.org

Want to know what's the best product? Or who's a good service provider? This site has a list of lemon cars and a list of consumer agencies and organizations.

Copyforce.com

An independent referral network of litigation copying, imaging, and coding firms in the world with service available in over 120 cities worldwide.

CorporateLegalTimes.com

Corporate Legal Times: a tabloid-sized monthly magazine that covers in-house legal departments issues, trends, and news.

Corpexnet.com

A site to order corporate kits, stock certificates, corporate or notary seals, and publications. Promises next day guarantee on orders received by noon.

CourtEXPRESS.com

A legal ASP eAttorney.com service which includes information services on the eAttorney site. Users can obtain docket sheets, cases and party status reports, run criminal searches, and get case information from the U.S. Supreme Court as well as from various district, bankruptcy and appellate courts.

Courtlink.com

This site merged with CourtLink Inc. of Bellevue, Washington, and offers real-time Internet access to more than 700 federal, state, and local court systems and provides an alternative to the existing dial-up Windows-based program. Helps users track cases, search multiple court records simultaneously (by name or case number), sort results, and order documents.

Ctadvantage.com

CT Corporation: offers multiple corporate qualification filings state-by-state. Corporate Filing Manager has interface and intelligent prompts to complete a corporate filing.

D

datacert.com

An application service provider (ASP) that offers secure, e-commerce-enabling services to businesses of any size. Offers e-billing and data reconciliation.

Dataflight.com/V7

A litigation support product featuring Concordance and Dataflight software services to capture, index, store and retrieve data. Information management, deposition, summarizing, and repository services.

decisionquest.com

DecisionQuest: experienced trial, visual and strategic communications consultants specializing in juries.

Deponet.com

A booking service for local and out-of-town service scheduling depositions, videography, and process services, and interpreting and translating services in the United States.

Divorce@blumberg.com
For New York uncontested divorce.

dsl.compuhelp.com
Provides Rhythms DSL at speeds up to 7mbps. Provides integration services for law firms and in-house legal departments. Based in New York City.

E

eAttorney.com
Integrated suite of Web-based applications storing all relevant case information together which is available through a single point of access. Includes document management, time keeping/billing, and contact management.

e-collaborate.com
A 24/7 Web-based service that brings teams together online for secure document distribution and collaboration from first draft to final proof sign-off. A Merrill Corporation company.

eLawCentral.com
One-stop destination for wired legal professionals on the Web. Sites that will help you get things done.

Elite.com
Featuring Timesolv™ a Web-based time and billing service to track and bill time and expenses online or off-line.

Ettorneys.com
Law firms' clients can provide ratings for their attorneys and other attorneys and judges can also participate. Individuals searching for an attorney "have a valuable advantage by viewing the ratings collected by the National Attorney Rating Service."

F

Findlaw.com
A comprehensive site providing links to books, case law summaries, legal forms, secure document service, articles, video, audiotapes, Web sites, organizations, training courses, vendors and software. It also provides directories of marketing consultants, information on CLE programs and more.

Fiosinc.com
Provides litigators a solution surrounding the acquisition, conversion, management, analysis, and distribution of electronic data associated with

the litigation discovery process. Assists with discovery planning and coordination, and retrieves discoverable electronic evidence. Based in Portland, Oregon.

G

genesysna.com

Genesys Conferencing offers products and services including TeleMeeting™, a reservation-free audio conferencing service 24/7; operator-assisted conferencing; e-conferencing via audio streaming; video Web streaming; interactive presentations; and VideoWeb Meeting/Reservations service. Genesys also offers videoconferencing.

gsionline.com

LIVEDGAR™, Global Securities Information, Inc.'s comprehensive research platform is a transaction research tool to find answers to M&A precedent research. Find concise summaries of each deal; download income statements; search preferences for transaction data reporting.

Guru.com

A site targeting freelance professionals (marketers, lawyers, artists, designers, engineers, and more) offering a free job-matching service where users can browse through a contract job directory.

H

hildebrandt.com

Hildebrandt: one of the more well-known consulting firms to law firms and in-house legal departments.

hornbook.com

The online version of a quarterly periodical focusing on malpractice avoidance, firm management, and professional liability.

I

ibanet.org

The International Bar Association. Offers information on membership, newsletter, and annual conferences.

ibm.com/smallbusiness/legal/wc-law120

A Web service provider offering WebConnections for Lawyers, a Web appliance, e-mail for everyone at the firm's name; 24 × 7 × human support and firewall security. Also offers CourtLink and JusticeLink online research and filing services.

I-dep.com

An online live deposition service providing full video and two-way audio, real-time court reporter transcript, and private messaging to any laptop or desktop PC. The template lets you see and hear the witness being deposed, read the transcript, and even ask questions. Objections can be made with the click of a button.

IdNames.com

From Network Solutions®—a domain name management provider with a full range of services that search, register, maintain and secure your Internet identity in over 192 countries.

incspot.com

Tools for corporate filings, UCC searches, and filing prep. Online ordering and reporting.

ioma.com

The Institute of Management & Administration providing legal business resources. Publishes management newsletters including *Partner's Report; Law Office Management & Administration Report; Controlling Law Firm Costs; Compensation & Benefits for Law Offices;* and *IOMA's Pay for Performance Report.* Offers business directory.

ipcenter.bna.com

Launched by BNA Inc., The Intellectual Property Professional Information Center is an exclusive resource Web site for daily news on intellectual property laws and trends as well as a full range of other resources regarding IP law.

IPWW.com

A resource for court decisions, international treaties, newest copyright laws, and emerging trends all in areas of intellectual property law with commentary from prominent intellectual property attorneys. By subscription.

interserve.com

An international process service providing official and unofficial service in any country "from Afghanistan to Zimbabwe."

J

jamespublishing.com

An independent law book publisher. Also publishes *Legal Assistant Today* magazine and *Law Office Computing.*

judicata.com

A litigation support system available at case driven cost. Gives control to capture, store, search, and share information produced in litigation. Web-based high speed, worldwide access to multiple data collections that are scalable to hundreds of millions of pages in size. A division of Trion Technologies based in Arlington, Virginia.

Juris.com

A time and billing, management reporting, trust accounting, accounts payable, check writing, firm accounting, financial reporting, drill-down inquiry, ad hoc reporting, conflict search software.

JurisDictionUSA.net

A Web-based legal service bringing a single-source, 24-hour tool accessible from anywhere. Includes case management, calendar, time entry and billing, encrypted e-mail, document repository, law library, daily updates, and free CLE.2.

jurisearch.com

Unlimited online access to California Supreme Court and Courts of Appeal Cases; California Rules of Court; Local Rules; Fair Employment and Housing Commission Cases; daily opinion summaries and decisions of California Supreme Court and Courts of Appeal; U.S. Supreme Court and 9th Circuit cases filed.

K

Kaplancollege.com

Online courses and programs in paralegal studies taught by attorneys.

Knowledge4m.SRA.com

An SRA International site offering knowledge management; intranets/extranets; information assurance; document management; remote access; network design and implementation; and systems integration. Six offices: Atlanta, Boston, Chicago, Fairfax, New York, Washington, D.C.

L

lfmi.com

The Law Marketing Portal offers information on legal marketing featuring a wide-ranging library with articles by marketing experts. Its job bank lists openings for marketing professionals and a resource directory collects member recommendations for the best forms, consultants, photographers, restaurants, meeting places, and more.

lakewoodconferences.com

Free online newsletters, "Online Learning News" and eLearning including 200+ workshops and hands-on learning labs.

Law.com

Includes The Litigation Practice Center offering litigation resources, including papers from experts and scholars; course book excerpts; and practice-specific links. Covers procedural and evidentiary issues such as law and motion, alternative dispute resolution, attorney's fees, insurance, antitrust, unfair competition, product liability, and securities. Offers a weekly e-mail subscription service.

LawCommerce.com

An electronic marketplace offering technology communications services for the legal industry. Members are able to use aggregated buying power to reduce costs on purchases on everything from legal software to temporary staffing to computers.

Lawgic.com

Document drafting software technology combining legal research, issue analysis, and drafting into one streamlined process in the areas of family law, estate planning, employment law or corporate law.

Lawline.com

Online law-related media programming. The site has a new online audio program: *Crimes on the Internet* which discusses such issues as expectation of privacy in the workplace and the repercussions on the employer of employee misuse of e-mail privileges.

lawmarketing.com

A law marketing portal that is a one-stop destination to find out how to promote your law firm effectively. Designed for marketing directors and administrators, the site includes a free searchable collection of marketing advice, legal marketing tools, technology, news reports on marketing seminars, job openings nationwide, and upcoming marketing events. Visitors can also join the LawMarketing Listserv which was started in 1996 and has grown to more than 1,200 members.

Lawofficecomputing.com

Law Office Computing online offering free software reviews compliments of *Law Office Computing* magazine. Product LOCator, an online database of legal software reviews, offers the legal community a quick and easy way to get opinions on law office technology. Access over 300 independent reviews via the full-text search engine.

Lawoffice.com

A FirmSite® from West Legal Directory® offers a comprehensive Internet marketing solution constructing site only for the legal profession. Maintains your site, making changes as needed and provides monthly usage reports.

Lawtechnews.com

Law Technology News Web site offering a free 1-year subscription (at press time). Provides information on the latest technological advances from evidence presentation and legal research tools to software and Internet upgrades.

Lawtech.hotresponse.com

A response service provided by *Law Technology News* for information about products or services. Also offers *"Second Opinions,"* a column by independent consultants and lawyers. A few of the products and services discussed are Novell; Worldox; iManage; Time Matters; GroupWise 5.5; Lotus Notes; Corel; WordPerfect; Microsoft Word; Microsoft SQL; Microsoft Exchange; and Microsoft Outlook.

lawyerexpress.com

A free site providing resources for lawyers doing research and communications with colleagues and clients.

legalassistanttoday.com

A bi-monthly magazine specifically for legal assistants/paralegals. Offers LAT-Forum, an online e-mail listserv where members of the profession can come together to discuss issues and receive valuable information.

Legaldocs.com

Useful, Mac-friendly legal forms.

Legaledge.com

A Web-based service to track all aspects of matters and cases including people, docket events, notes, and documents from just about anywhere. Offers a user-friendly Web browser interface and Ask Away℠ a time-saving tool to ask questions in plain English, such as how many new cases were opened this year? How much did the last case settle for? and more.

Legalex.com

Rules-based case management software that allows the rules of the court in which a case is filed to drive management of that case. It keeps tabs on who did what, when, tracks settlement negotiations with opposing parties, and manages case documents. ProLaw Software empowers Legalex SQL 8.0. Gives users information on who's working on the cases, does conflicts checking, indexes word processing documents, assembles documents based on the case's requirements, and more.

legalseminars.com
A division of law.com in San Francisco: CLE courses.

legalspreadsheets.com
The Lawyer's Guide to Spreadsheets, a companion to the book of the same name by John Treddenick, a partner in Colorado's Holland & Hart, former editor of the ABA's *Law Practice Management* magazine.

legintent.com
Legislative Intent Service researching the legislative history of any state's statutes; constitutional amendments; initiatives; regulations of state agencies, rules of court; local ordinances; federal laws and regulations.

lexisOne.com
Free case law, legal forms, and information for small-firm attorneys.

lexis.com
A legal research service including LEXIS® Search Advisor, Case Summaries and Core Concepts and *Shepards®* Citations Service.

Lexis.com/shepards
Shepard's® Citations.

loislaw.com
Offers primary law coverage and legal research via the Internet for all 50 states, the District of Columbia, and 18 federal law libraries.

M

Mediconnect.net
Retrieves and scans records for users via online order form. It then digitizes the records before sending them to the user's Abacus Law's document management system where it creates an archive to store and track the records.

MerrillDirect.com
An Internet based service for the development and preparation of financial documents by corporations, law firms, investment banks, and accounting firms. Online users can choose from secure, self-serve modules for EDGAR conversion and filing when you need word processing backup. A Merrill Corporation company.

Merrillntext.com
A 24/7 Web-based foreign language translation service that uses secure Web-based distribution of documents to clients worldwide.

Mygalaxy.com
Galaxy, a vertical Internet directory launched this site to help Web surfers personalize and retrieve customized stock quotes, business news, weather, and more. Also offers free e-mail.

N

Nals.org
The association of legal professionals—formerly the association for legal secretaries. Site offers membership and conference dates.

NameProtect.com
A monitoring service designed to help companies protect their brands nationwide. The service provides monthly alerts of potentially conflicting trademark and domain name activity from relevant sources worldwide.

Nationalcorp.com
Nationwide Registered Agent, corporate and secured transactions (UCC) services based in New York City.

Needleslaw.com
Customizable case management software specializing in case management for the personal injury attorney.

Netlds.com
Lexis® document services offering UCC-related lien searching and filing; corporate searching and filing; registered agent services; motor vehicle titling and registration; mortgage assignment searching and filing.

Niku.com/solutions/4legal.html
An intranet/extranets solution which provides an Internet-based platform for collaborating with clients and outside counsel. Provides a flexible hub that affords users secure access to case repositories, discussions, and calendars. Enables clients to exchange and manage documents in a secure environment; conduct secure private conferences; and automate calendaring and scheduling.

NowDocs!.com
Enables customers to print, bind, and ship documents located on casecentral.com to any of NowDocs.com's 14 same-day delivery facilities nationwide or internationally.

O

Oknb.uscourts.gov/Court%20Information.htm

The Northern District of Oklahoma Bankruptcy Court has a Web service to get information and view documents from pending cases.

Olympus.com/digital

Olympus America, Digital & Imaging Systems Group provides an easy-to-use digital voice recorder for legal dictation with a recording capacity of more than 150 minutes and allows downloading voice files to a PC. Includes IBM ViaVoice Millennium speech recognition software.

P

PalmOS.com

A Web site that offers information about the Palm operation system. It includes information about new products and services based on the Palm operating system, events, and more.

parasec.com

A California-based corporate filing, UCC and document retrieval service with nationwide capabilities.

paralegals.org

The National Federation of Paralegal Associations. Offers articles, information on membership, and more.

PCLaw.com

An integrated time-billing and accounting system including trust accounting; general ledger and financial statements; accounts receivable; bank reconciliation; conflict checking; management reports; and more.

peertopeer.org

Sponsored by LawNet Inc., an organization of technology users in the legal industry made up largely of MIS directors, controllers, administrators, and attorneys with an interest in technology. It publishes a quarterly newsletter as well as various white papers on topics such as litigation support and MIS hiring and retention. It offers an annual conference attended by more than 1,200 members.

Pitneybowes.com/pbms

Provides law firms with technology and professional expertise to manage, control, distribute, archive, and retrieve document work loads. Delivers full range of advanced mail, reprographics, digital printing, facsimile records, and imaging, as well as case, administrative, and litigation management and secured Internet delivery solutions.

pli.edu/public/webprograms.htm
The Practicing Law Institute: training programs, CLE, bookstore, and more.

privacycouncil.com
An online resource for business and consumers dealing with global privacy issues. The site's main pages and navigation tools have been translated from German and Spanish. The site offers a library on privacy on the Internet. Japanese and French translations will be available soon.

ProLaw.com
Offers ProLawPortal, an integrated software that provides authorized users controlled access to the entire law firm via the Internet. Case, contact, and document management as well as billing and accounting in one solution.

Q

QuickSift.com
An online service providing summarized precedents from an entire agreement, definition, or section with one simultaneous search from internal sources, EDGAR, or both.

R

RealLegal.com (purchased by law.com)
An application service provider to allow for Web-based automation of daily operations including electronic transcript signatures, transcript repository management, RealTime deposition transcription, and other services. e-transcript binder™ allows you to connect directly to your court reporter and view transcripts live. RealTime allows testimony in a deposition or trial setting to be instantly relayed to an attorney's computer for review and note-taking while it is being reported by the court reporter.

Redgorilla.com
Wireless online expense entry, Web access from any Internet-connected computer. Sells a subscription service called the Gorilla Go-Pack, a wireless connection to the Web, via a WAP (Wireless Application Protocol)-enabled device like a smart cell phone. WAP devices strip out the graphics and other computing intensive parts of Web pages so that you can see a Web page on your PDA or cellular phone readout.

Researchersfyi.com

A litigation support service based in Tucson, Arizona. The site offers a link to its parent company and online e-mail access to sales representatives.

S

SerengetiUS.com

Serengeti: A union of leading legal software and services from case management to e-invoicing, time and billing, videoconferencing, document construction, business intelligence, secure messaging, and more.

Srisoftusa.com

SriSoft Corp. is an offshore data-conversion company that can turn a firm's hard copy data into an electronic file on CD-ROM. Staff can then use that CD to upload data onto office computers of intranet sites or retain it as a secure backup file. Company is located in Englewood, Colorado, and is a division of SriSoft Corporation Pvt. Ltd. with headquarters in Bangalore, India. Offers data conversion, catalog conversion, CAD/GIS solutions and as-built modeling and drawing development from its U.S. office.

stilegal.com/ltpn.html

Legal-specific billing system which allows users to customize and launch client-related functions they use most often.

Summation.com

Online/off-line software, and iBlaze an online/off-line litigation support solution that concurrently accesses multiple document repositories online. Download key information onto your notebook as a minirepository then use it off line.

Surety.com and realLegal.com

Incorporates Surety.com's Digital Notary Service into realLegal.com's Electronic Transcript Signature Service for e-transcript.

T

taxbase.tax.org

For tax professionals: access to daily tax news and analysis at the federal, state and international levels plus a complete tax research library. Access to the full texts of the Code, regulations, court opinions, and thousands of other U.S. and foreign documents.

www.tax.org

Offers free services and information from Tax Analysts Inc.

TechLawinc.com

A litigation support vendor for document processing applications, including scanning and data conversion; coding and OCR; electronic discovery services; and image-based database building.

TheinsuranceXchange.com

Information on business insurance. The site includes directors' and officers' liability insurance for the health care industry and offers property and casualty insurance.

timeslips.com

An award-winning time and billing software featuring custom bill formatting, links to other business software programs, and a Web interface.

tracers.com

An asset discovery and skip tracing (locating services) company. Also offers document retrieval from courts or other repositories nationwide.

Trademark.com

An online search service integrating the federal and state trademark databases with a comprehensive collection of common law files. Search product names, business names, slogans, designs, and more.

trademarkinfo.com

A trademark and copyright service (not connected with the federal government).

Trialpro.com

Software for trial exhibit organization, preparation, and presentation. Includes Post Production Time-stamp program to synchronize digitized deposition video with the corresponding transcript text; bar code printing for indexed access to exhibits; and comprehensive real-time annotation tools.

U

ur-law.com

A 24/7 Web-based access to stacks of documents via a secure browser connection to the Web. From Merrill Corporation.

V

voycabulary.com

Here is a resource for business writing containing lookup features in English (dictionary and thesaurus), medical, acronym, Spanish, German, French, Japanese, Dutch, Swedish, Portuguese, Russian, Hungarian, and Welsh.

W

Westlaw.com

Customized legal research including "Westnews" for news and business information. Features Dow Jones Interactive® to find news and background information about virtually any person, company, or issue.

Wirelessverticals.com

Mobile TimeBilling by Wireless Verticals. Software to enter client time and expense information from a Palm PDA to a Blackberry to a smart cell phone. Then that device dials the law firm computer network and sends its info into the database. Wireless Vertical also promises Windows Pocket PC connectivity soon.

Worldox.com

A document manager to search, view, download, and upload files.

Y

youdictate.com

A Cyber Secretaries voice-to-document service which is then e-mailed to any location worldwide all in about an hour. Dictate from anywhere, day and night.

Staffing Agency Web Sites*

Staffing agencies can be indispensable, particularly if you are not certain what firm is just right for you. The good ones have inside information on current positions. But searching on the Internet is different. Landing on a site does not mean the information is current, and, if you are using a job board, you might miss the human touch. Strictly speaking, job boards are not interactive and rarely offer real live folks who can tell you the inside scoop on the position you seek. But staffing agencies are different, and in a time where good candidates are difficult to find, the good ones will contact you faster than you can leave your computer to answer your phone. Be sure you know, though, when you are applying to a staffing agency rather than registering on a job board where you are usually in direct contact with the employer.

Following is a random sampling of just a few of the job boards and legal staffing registrations. Who really knows how many career sites exist? It's hard to say. The *Los Angeles Times* claims 10,000. *The Weddle Report* (a newsletter for recruiters about the latest on the Internet) claims as many as 40,000.

The American Lawyer's listing of staffing companies jumped from 13 to 691 in 20 years. These days, some legal recruiters are franchisers with branch offices across the country. Others are multilevel international organizations; some are publicly held corporations. Most have e-mail and many have Web sites and affiliations with other recruiters around the world. As the legal recruiting industry has matured, a professional organization has

---

*Chosen at random. Does not indicate endorsements. Any staffing company wishing to be included, please contact publisher for next edition of PCG.

grown up around it. Many recruiters are members of The National Association of Legal Search Consultants. There is a growing trend for employers to ask that NALSC's code of ethics be included in contracts. And, NALSC recently created an individual membership category for temp and staffing firms if those firms are also in the business of full-time attorney placement.

Be advised that some of the staffing or search engines may handle only attorneys. Don't let that deter you! You never know when they might need paralegals.

California

The Estrin Organization
www.estrin.com

Advocate Legal Search
www.advocatelegalsearch.com

The Affiliates
www.affiliates.com

Alexander & Collins
www.alexander-collins.com

Bels.net
www.bels.com

Chosen Few Personnel Services, Inc.
www.chosenfew.com

Co-Counsel
www.co-counselinc.com

The Cushing Bicksler Group
www.clblawlink.com

Esquire Inc.
www.esquiresearch.com

ET Search, Inc.
www.etsearch.com

Fitzsimmons & Associates
www.fitzfirst.com

Gerard & Associates
www.preimnet.com/~dvnet gerard_associates

Ivy Associates
www.ivyassociates.com

The Jameson Group
www.thejamesongroup.com

Kearney Boyle & Associates, Inc.
www.hookednet/~kbajobs

Kerwin Associates
www.kerwin.com

Kristin Hebert Associates
www.khebert.com

Kelly Law Registry
www.thelawregistry.com

Legal Recruiter, Inc.
www.legalrecruiter.com

Legal Staff of San Diego
www.sdlegalstaff.com

McClure & Feuer
www.mcflegal.com

Miller Sabino & Lee
www.mslsearch.com

Special Counsel
www.specialcounsel.com

District of Columbia

The Kemp Group
www.kempgroup.com

Law Resources, Inc.
www.lawresources.com

LawCorps Legal Staffing Services
www.lawcorps.com

Mestel & Co.
www.mestel.com

Pat Taylor & Associates
www.pattaylor.com

Florida

Ankus & Ankus, Inc.
www.ankus.com

Bridgestone Legal Staffing
www.bridgestonelegal.com

Professional Placement Services, Inc.
www.ppsilaw.com

SouthSearch, Inc.
www.southsearch.com

Special Counsel
www.specialcounsel.com

Sterling Careers, Inc.
www.scilaw.com

Illinois

Chicago Legal Search, Ltd.
www.chicagolawjobs.com

Eary Cochran & Olson
www.ecollc.com

Kimball Legal Search, Inc.
www.kimballsearch.com

Salem Legal Staffing
www.salemservices.com

Massachusetts

Bickerton & Gordon Legal Placement Consultants
www.bickertongordon.com

Bostonian Personnel
www.bostonianpers.com

Kwatcher Legal Placement
www.kwatcherlegal.com

Management Recruiters International
www.mri-boston.com

Minnesota

The Affiliates
www.affiliates.com

HIRECounsel
www.hirecounsel.com

Lieberman-Nelson, Inc.
www.lieberman-nelson.com

Mississippi

Special Counsel
www.specialcounsel.com

Missouri

Kelly Law Registry
www.thelawregistry.com

New Hampshire

Emerald Legal Search
www.emeraldsearch.com

New Jersey

Assigned Counsel, Inc.
www.assignedcounsel.com

A.V. Search Consultants
www.avsearchconsultants.com

Law Pros Legal Placement
Services, Inc.
www.lawproslegal.com

Update Legal Staffing
www.updatelegal.com

New Mexico

Michael G. Jacobs & Associates
www.mgjacobs.com

New York

A-L Associates
www.alassoc.com

The Artemis Group Ltd.
www.artemissearch.net

Barrister Referrals, Inc.
www.barristerreferrals.com

Bridgestone Legal Staffing
www.bridgestonelegal.com

Career Directions
www.careerdirections.net

Fergus Legal Search & Consulting
www.feguslex.com

Howard Sloan Legal Research
www.howardsloan.com

Legal Options
www.legaloptions.com

The Legal Recruiters
www.thelegalrecruiters.com

Legal Support Personnel
www.legalsupportpersonnel.com

Major Hagen & Africa
www.mhasearch.com

Meridian Legal Search
www.meridianlegal.com

Metro Legal Search, Inc.
www.metrolegalsearch.com

Preferred Placements, Inc.
www.preferredplacement.com

Strategic Legal Resources
www.stratlegal.com

Update Legal Staffing
www.updatelegal.com

North Carolina

The Affiliates
www.affiliates.com

Special Counsel
www.specialcounsel.com

Legal Placement Specialists, Inc.
www.legalplacement.citysearch.com

Ohio

Assigned Counsel, Inc.
www.assignedcounsel.com

Major Legal Services, Inc.
www.lawplacement.com

Oregon

The Associates
www.theassociatesinc.com

Pennsylvania

Assigned Counsel, Inc.
www.assignedcounsel.com

Coleman Legal Search
www.colemanlegal.com

JuriStaff Legal Staffing
www.juristaff.com

Legal Network Ltd.
www.legalnetworkltd.com

Meridian Legal Staffing, Inc.
www.meridianlegal.com

AdHoc Legal Resources
www.adhoclegal.com

Carpenter Legal Search
www.carpenterlegalsearch.com

Hyde Danforth & Co.
www.hdco.net

IP Law Source
www.iplawsource.com

Quest Personnel Resources, Inc.
www.questpersonnel.com

Tennessee

Koerner & Associates, Inc.
www.koernerassociates.com

Special Counsel
www.specialcounsel.com

Texas

Cochran & Company
www.cochranco.com

Ad Hoc Legal Resources
www.adhoclegal.com

Gibson Arnold & Associates, Inc.
www.gibsonarnold.com

Kelly Law Registry
www.thelawregistry.com

Virginia

The Affiliates
www.affiliates.com

Washington

Houser Martin Morris
www.houser.com

Kamisar Legal Search, Inc.
www.seattlesearch.com

National Association of Legal
Assistants
www.

Australia

Garfield Robbins International
www.garfieldrobbins.com.au

Canada

The Affiliates
www.affiliates.com

China

Hughes-Castell (Hong Kong)
www.hughes-castell.com.hk

France

Michael Page
www.michaelpage.com

New Zealand

Michael Page
www.michaelpage.com

United Kingdom

Alexander & Collins/London
uklaw@alexander-collins.com

Badenoch & Clark
www.badenochandclark.com

Index